# CONTACT & CONTROL

## UFOs, DNA, and the Hidden War on Human Potential

JON MAJEROWSKI

ISBN: 979-8-9954352-0-4 (Paperback)

ISBN: 979-8-9954352-1-1 (Hardcover)

ISBN: 979-8-9954352-2-8 (eBook)

Library of Congress Control Number: 2026908392

Interior and Cover design by Jon Majerowski

Edited by John W. Warner IV

Published by MAJESTIC 13 Press, Maumee, Ohio

contactandcontrol.com

# DEDICATION

To my wife, Becca, who embraces our weirdness while keeping us grounded and encourages me to pursue the impossible. You are the light that always guides me.

To Stella, who inspired me to look up, who witnessed the impossible turn into reality, and who continues to do so every day.

To Addison, who has so many wonderful gifts, even more than she might realize.

To my Father, who set me on this path even before I was born, and to my Mother, whose saintly patience has guided me all along.

To Jessina, you survived growing up with me. I know that wasn't easy. Sorry for the hard parts I caused. I'm grateful you're still here.

To every experiencer who ever felt alone, crazy, or afraid to speak their truth.

And to The Phenomenon itself: whatever you are, wherever you're from, however long you've been here (thank you).

# CONTENTS

# FOREWORD

In 2020, three bizarre characters contacted me by email regarding my first book Little Anton, an historical novel about Ferdinand Porsche, Grand Prix racing in Nazi Germany and the super-duper-secret SS high technology programs. (Jean-Luc had stumbled upon a long-lost article I wrote on Axis Forum about my book). Jon, Jay and Jean-Luc, the "Dream Team" they called themselves. Really? Seriously? Honestly now. My eyes rolled. Chills of ill foreboding came forthwith. I thus yawned in excitement. Wait, hang on a tick…did my acumen in military history, passion for alternative history, madness for UFO, Star Trek, ET everything and lifetime proximity to iffy power structures actually bear some fellow esoteric, academic fruit? Well, mmm, sort of.

Jean-Luc had read my 1007-page juggernaut and was shocked, nay, gob smacked that an "middle-aged Mellon Illuminati banking & military family insider idiot" had some chops regarding UFO history, the occult, Freemasonry, secret societies, U.S. Government skullduggery, intel agency and military cover-ups, weird elite bloodlines, megalithic constructions, Nazi Thule Society occultism, non-linear physics torsion field energy, Prediluvian high civilizations, interdimensional portals, Norse Asatru pagan cults, janky religions and funky alternative esoteric ancient history? It was partly their main focus as well, seeing they were compatriot "experiencers and researchers." Hells-bells, I had even quoted Rudolph Steiner and Manly P. Hall in my book for chrissakes. This had deeply impressed them, the nefarious dimbulbs, even though I had barely, kinda-sorta finished, or even understood, Hall's famous, monstrous tome: The Secret Teachings Of All Ages.

Yet through time via chit-chats, interviews and bouts of sundry, esoteric UFO gossip rants, some ale, and wine swilling, it was crystal ball-clear we were all cut from the same hide of tough, smelly buffalo leather dyed "black-ops" black. They were kindred spirits, fellow travelers of the road not taken, tipsy romantic windmill tilters a la Don Quixote and certainly not the assumed dimbulbs by any megalithic yard measure. Thus, it was my turn to be shocked. Stunned. And all four of us today completely and irrevocably understand at least the gist of the gist of Hall's book…I think. Well, mostly. At least I surmise we do. Do we, chaps?

After getting to know Jon in person, a fellow vintage car buff, I took a greater interest in the history of Freemasonry and the Knights Templar. (Childhood story ALERT) You see, when I was a wee lad of four, I was attending St. Patrick's School in Washington, D.C. (a Freemasonic city state bar none), and in the chapel when we sang "Onward Christian Soldiers," I would constantly gaze up at a stained-glass window of a Templar Crusader Knight with his red Maltese Cross, sword, shield and shiny, squire-polished armor. Thus, I have always thought I may have been a foolhardy Templar Crusader in a former lifetime given that reincarnation ("resurrection" in the Bible) is probably standard operating procedure in our universe. Anyhoo, my mystic mother was proud of me for that.

Hallowed Mr. Majerowski has taught me many important things, Masonic, automotive, and otherwise, and I am truly grateful. When he interviews dummy me and clever Jean-Luc on his podcast, he informally calls the chat "the three Johns." Or…something worse.

For the last forty-odd years, I have harbored suspicions that my Father and Grandfather, both powerful military men with strong intelligence ties—strong, I say!—were clandestine Freemasons. It's been said that many powerful military, scientific and government people with high security clearances were given quick and dirty "I will keep secrets upon penalty of death!" oaths. These were super-fast Masonic initiations for the sake of National Security performed on the spot since at least WW2—and done in their own offices! Jon has clarified and confirmed this for me, so I have more confidence on the matter. Hey, why wasn't I asked to join? I'm an over-the-top smarty pants UFO-minded super-secret squirrel club occultist too, you know.

•••

Today, all four of us mercurial misfit mystics are bathed in Carl Jung's concept of Synchronicity to the point of drowning. It's become a routine metaphysical happening for us now. Sigh. Boring even. OK, I admit it's fun. It's how we came to know one another in this madcap universe of ours. All points of space and time are connected. Oh-h-h, yes they are! Don't know what ye olde Synchronicity entails? Look it up, lazybones.

Jon has taken a mighty stab at explaining "The UFO/ET/MIC, WW2 Foo-Fighter, religious, occulted weird history phenomenon issue" simply, personally and straightforwardly in this half-decent book, and I praise and admire his courage for doing it through the eyes of a devout, moral, family-man Freemason of positive Yin-Yang polarity. It's a much-needed perspective at this time in history. No joke, no drill.

—John William Warner IV

# ACKNOWLEDGMENTS

This book exists because of conversations, hundreds of hours across countless podcasts with researchers, experiencers, practitioners, and seekers who generously shared their knowledge, experiences, and wisdom.

To my Brothers and Fraters, thank you for preserving knowledge and creating space for genuine seeking.

To John W. Warner IV for classic car rides, believing in the power of friendship, insider perspective, common horse sense, and critical thinking that cuts through narratives without any bullshit. Also, for his help in editing this book, I could not have done it without you!

To Jean-Luc Infini for teaching me that the psi realm is real and that history reveals more than we imagine.

To Jay Anderson of Project Unity, our conversations and friendship have been amazing.

To everyone whose voice appears in these pages, named and unnamed, thank you for your contribution.

# PREFACE

There are things you are not supposed to know.

I am talking about the real machinery that shapes what the public is allowed to see. The systems that decide which concepts and technologies are allowed to move forward and which are buried in classified files, Vatican archives, or forgotten out of convenience. We will get to the agencies and institutions later. For now, you only need to understand that the filtering is deliberate.

I learned this the hard way. I had personal encounters with UFOs and what researchers call The Phenomena. Things I could not explain and were not expected to discuss because of a stigma engineered in the 1950s. I work in information security, and my CISSP certification, the Certified Information Systems Security Professional credential, means you have mastered the eight domains of protection. It teaches you that every system built to hide information has a flaw. I have spent my career finding those cracks, and the same discipline I use to break down a security architecture is what I brought to this subject. For seventy years, a masterfully engineered stigma kept the public from looking too closely. From my experience, no system is perfect. I am also a Freemason, and that path opened doors into older knowledge streams that still shape the present. Through my podcast, UFOs on the Level, I have spoken with experiencers, researchers, and whistleblowers who all describe the same walls of silence.

This book brings all of that together. It is part personal story, part investigation, and part exploration of consciousness. I wrote it the same way I would say it to a friend over a drink. Direct, open, and at times very raw. I am not claiming that I have every answer. What I do have are patterns, evidence, lived moments, and questions that deserve real attention. The UFO subject is not only about lights in the sky. It reveals how human potential has been shaped, limited, and guided.

I am not an academic, and I am not writing from a place of official authority. My point of view comes from personal experience, curiosity, and a refusal to ignore things just because they do not fit an accepted narrative. I am a father, husband, and an experiencer who followed my questions until they brought me here.

Everything in this book is accurate to the best of my ability. It is based on documents, interviews, research, and my own experiences. If I'm speculating, I'll say it. If I don't know, I'll say that too. If it comes from someone else, I'll cite it. I am a human being, and I make mistakes. I am learning, growing, and trying to understand this strange thing we call life.

Some readers will come to this book because they have had experiences and want to feel less alone. Some will be researchers who want specific details. Some will be skeptics searching for something solid. I wrote this with honesty and respect for all of you.

You do not have to believe every story or conclusion in these pages. I only ask that you look at the evidence, follow the patterns, and listen to your own sense of truth. I have included citations and documents you can check for yourself. Please do this; there is a wealth of information here that will serve you well. The glossary will help as well. My goal is not to hand you the final truth; it's to show that the official story falls apart when you take a real good look at it.

This book is not the end of anything. It is a snapshot of where I am today. By the time you read it, I will probably know things that would make me rewrite parts of it. That is fine. A book should start conversations, not finish them.

I am writing this for the experiencers who were told they imagined it. For the people who know something has been hidden, and anyone who has ever heard the official explanation and thought that cannot be the whole story.

You are right. It is not.

Read this with a critical mind. Question everything. Question me. Trust your own experience over any authority. If this book helps you feel less isolated and more empowered, then it has done its job.

Welcome to Contact and Control and a reality that is stranger, richer, and far more powerful than anything we have been taught to accept.

Jon Majerowski

January 1/27/2026

# CHAPTER 1

## "WELCOME TO YOUR LIFE, THERE'S NO TURNING BACK."

*"The greatest secrets are hidden not in vaults, but in what we're taught is impossible."-Jon Majerowski*

I never thought I would have written this book. I've been a lifelong student and researcher of esoteric subjects, fringe topics, UFOs, cryptids, ghosts, the afterlife, the occult, secret societies, and consciousness. Anything that didn't lend itself to being "mainstream" in the public consciousness interested me. So much so that I spent much of my youth in the library. I was a very quick learner, and I had a very good memory. I tired easily of school, or the American school system of learning, that is. Although my teachers said I could have gone to college while still in high school, I decided to spend my time studying the paranormal and anything exotic or esoteric that interested me. I decided to dive deep into all the literature I could get my hands on about UFOs and the paranormal, then see if I could find anything that lent itself to a rational explanation.

What started me on this journey was an encounter with the paranormal. When I was about five or six, I came face-to-face with the ghost of a deceased man standing in the doorway of the basement of our house. He looked at me and smiled. He was wearing a full suit and a dark brown hat. I ran into the other room to tell my Dad what I had seen and was scared out of my mind. After he calmed me down, I was able to describe the man to him. Based on my description, Dad knew exactly who it was: Jerry Brown, the dead neighbor. From that moment on, I decided to always be aware of my surroundings and the world in general. Plus, it scared the living shit out of me.

I don't think I slept in my own bed for another few years after that. Of course, there were also ghosts, spirits, or non-human intelligences that visited me at night. They would sit in the corner and sometimes try to converse. This also scared me to the point that I slept with all the lights on in my room, the doors open, and something covering my head. A lot of the time, I slept with a radio on as well. At one point, I slept in a tent I set up in my room because I could close the zipper and not see the things in the corners.

Now, you can chalk this all up to an overactive imagination, but I know what I saw. It wasn't until I was much older that, after we moved out of the house, my Dad told me he thought it was haunted. In retrospect, that's hilarious. These events even plagued my dreams, and I really don't know if they were dead or just not human. I look back and wonder now what that interaction meant to me at such a young age. This type of interaction continued at least into my teens.

I saw a woman all in white at the top of the stairs in the next house we lived in. I was at the bottom of the stairs looking up in the dark, and it was a glowing white gown, like a one-piece. I got the impression it was my mother, so I flipped the light switch, thinking it was odd for my mom to be standing at the top of the stairs in the dark. When I flipped the switch on, the woman vanished, and I got the feeling that this was what my mind told me was a ghost. At ten, I was more scared than I could create words to express.

I might as well give you the overview, and if you're already an experiencer and want to skip this part about all my experiences that led up to this moment for me to write this book and do this research, then I totally get it. For everyone else, or if you really would like to know what the hell happened to me, keep on reading.

What really started this journey for me was moving away from home. I was working at WTUE, which is still a rock radio station in Dayton, Ohio. When I was 18, I produced the Kerrigan and Christopher morning show, which was hugely popular and had many years of success in the pre-Bob and Tom show era. This was 1998, and I had the most amazing times; I was the overnight DJ. Yes, I know I was lucky, and I had the time of my life doing the job. I got to meet and hang out with some of the most amazing people, musicians, and bands in the world.

While I was in one of the studios, I saw a giant, dark figure, outlined like a man, walk in front of the glass partition facing the hallway. The radio station is on Fifth Street, in one of the city's oldest parts. In the 1800s, the building had been a slaughterhouse; it was gutted and turned into the home of five different radio stations. There were all kinds of people wandering downtown, and I was responsible for making sure the building was secure from about 11 p.m. until about 4 a.m.

When I saw this happen, I thought somebody had broken into the building. I ran out of the studio to chase the man around the corner of the hallway, but he had vanished. Poof, gone. There was nowhere to go. The studio at the end of the hall was empty, and there was no other exit. That really freaked me out, but not as much as when I came down from the third floor to the second to watch an office chair slowly start spinning by itself in a circle, increasing speed, and then suddenly stop.

Here I am, alone in a former slaughterhouse as an eighteen-year-old radio DJ, in what appears to be a haunted building full of ghosts. When I told my stories to the people I worked with, asking whether they had similar experiences or had heard of hauntings, most people laughed; a few didn't and thought I was being honest.

A couple of months later, in October, we had Chris Woodyard as a guest on the Kerrigan and Christopher morning show. She was there to talk about her Haunted Ohio book series. The books are a seven-volume series about true ghost sightings and hauntings in Ohio.1 She was a very nice middle-aged person, and we had her as a guest on the air to cover some of the obvious Halloween festivities.

It was off the air that I asked her about my lifelong sightings when we were alone. I told her about the incident that took place in the very room we were sitting in at the radio station. She looked at me in a way that no one had ever done before whenever I spoke about these experiences. It was a look of compassion and understanding, like she really understood the occulted world, without me trying to convince her, and that my experiences were indeed real. She was sitting in the same room and could see the same entities.

She could tell that I was bothered by all of this, and I probably had been my whole life. She looked at me with all sincerity and told me, "You can make this stop if you want to." I couldn't believe what I had just heard. I had the power to control this gift? I was under the impression that this shit just happened, and that I was either lucky or unlucky to be part of it.

She said that we all have this ability, and whether we choose to tune into it or not, and how we interact with it, determines the strength or weakness of the interaction. Basically, if you want the entity to go away, you tell it to leave. You say it out loud with emotion and tell it to go away because you are in control.

I thought this was great because all I really cared about was chasing girls around and having a great time, and I didn't really want to be bothered by this paranormal nonsense. Not that it was all the time, but apparently, it's always been around me. So it was at this moment that I decided to take my power back, but not before I did a few other things.

See, there was another guest that we had who was experimenting with (EVP)—electronic voice phenomenon. Basically, EVP entails leaving an audio recorder in a room alone or being in the room with it, then asking questions and hoping for a response. You won't hear anything audibly with your ears, but when you play it back, sometimes you'll get answers from a disincarnate voice. Other times, just static or nothing at all.

Yet because I was eighteen years old and had access to walls and walls of blank reel-to-reel tapes that fed into a computer where you could visually see the waveforms of the audio files, I thought this was fair game. This was 1998, and digital audio recording was in its infancy. I was young enough and quick enough to pick it up, so I was tasked with creating most of the spots, aka commercials, for the radio station. I could record them all digitally, copy them to a cart (basically a glorified eight-track tape), and have that ready faster than most experienced DJs who were used to working with old-fashioned tapes, cutting and splicing them with razor blades.

One night, in the very room that I had my experience, I set up a four-hour reel-to-reel tape, turned on the microphone all the way up, walked out of the room, and shut the door. No one entered that room for another four hours. The first thing I did once I entered the room was rewind that tape and get it into the computer. What happened next was terrible. Well, it was frightening to me anyway.

I saw there was a blank audio track for the first hour or more, and then it sounded like someone trying to scream through a hundred pillows from the depths of hell. It was as if an echo from a lost universe was trying to communicate with me from beyond space and time, and it wasn't happy. It was really frightening just listening to it with studio-quality headphones. It gave you the chills, and honestly, I didn't know what to make of it all. I looked for every explanation, but I had isolated the audio, and there was no other way this would make sense.

I tried the same experiment again in different studios throughout the building, and I did not get the same results. Looking back, I shouldn't have done this because it scared me so much that I erased the tape, and after that, I threw it in the dumpster out back. Whatever that sound pierced my soul, and I never want another human to have to experience what I did.

I wasn't completely sold on all this wild stuff up until about a month later, when this bizarre event happened to me. I voice-tracked my entire show. Listen to a DJ live on the air, which nobody does anymore, but listeners thought I was sitting there talking live between all the songs before the commercials. That used to be the case, but in 1998, we started recording all of that in advance and just playing it back. You see, I could record my show in about 30 minutes and then spend the rest of the night recording those commercials that paid the station's bills.

Well, one night I got all my work done very fast, and I had gone to a bar and had a couple too many beers the night before, so I lay down on the couch in the main studio to rest away a hangover, but this wasn't the studio that I had my experience in. Regardless, I was lying on the couch in full view of a giant clock. It was atomic, down to the second, accurate.

I must have been asleep for maybe thirty minutes when I was awoken by an incredibly bizarre feeling; it was as if somebody had smacked me in the head with a buzzer, and everything was electric and erratic. My eyes were the only bits that were working. I was experiencing sleep paralysis. Basically, I couldn't move anything but my eyes, and I watched that clock for about an hour and a half, slowly ticking away second by second. It was the most excruciating hour and a half of my life, along with this impossible feeling that I would never be able to move again.

I tried everything in my body to move myself, to fall off that couch. It didn't happen. I prayed. I did everything I could think of, and I couldn't move. Just watched that clock and panicked. Finally, then, at some point, I finally did fall off that couch. Much later, I learned via John Warner and trans-Arabian texts that (archons) or (jinn) cause and use sleep paralysis for taking over a human body.

This was the sign I was looking for, and at that moment, I realized that it was it. I was done with this nonsense. When I sat up, I screamed at the top of my lungs for it to "go the fuck away. I'm done with this and don't want to be part of it anymore. I don't want to interact with you, and you can go mess with somebody else." I meant it. I was very emotional, and I did not want to interact with the paranormal anymore.

For some reason, I knew all that stuff was connected. Here is where it gets weird, as if it wasn't already. It was from that moment on that almost twenty years went by before I had another paranormal experience. I've come to find out that it's easy to shut all of this down, push it out, get it away from you. Don't interact with it anymore. If you tell yourself, it's not real, then it's not real. However, it's very hard to turn that knob back in the other direction. After spending all that time trying not to see or interact with any of this, getting it back was almost impossible.

I think everybody who has any interest in this subject has some experience, whether it's personal or someone they know and love shares something strange that happened to them. I really did not give a crap about a ghost, a spirit, or whatever you wanted to call it, but at a very early age, my Dad told me he had seen not one but two UFOs during his life.

Growing up, I didn't think UFOs were anything but real. There's no reason my Dad would make this up, none. He had two amazing experiences: one in broad daylight with several people outside of a gas station in Toledo, Ohio, and another at home on the south side of Toledo with our neighbor also as a witness. So, my Dad was totally into UFOs in the '80s and '90s, still is today, so I grew up instinctively knowing that they were genuine.

However, the world had a different perspective because of the Robertson Panel2, which is basically what the government created as a vehicle to provide cover for their covert UFO research by making anyone who reported UFO activity look like a tinfoil-hat-wearing, crazy person, "conspiracy theorist." The CIA invented that phrase during the ongoing JFK murder investigations in 1967, and it's worked wonders for them ever since. This was the shadow government's way to be able to do UFO research in private and basically turn human against human through shame and ridicule, both very powerful mind control tools.3

I didn't give a hot damn. I knew my Dad wasn't lying to me. All the UFO magazines, VHS tapes of conferences, books about abductions, and, finally, in the '80s, Unsolved Mysteries and other TV programs started broadcasting episodes about UFOs, so the tide of consciousness started to turn. There have always been a few brave former government or military personnel who have come forward to share their experiences with something not of this world.

We can talk about the Bible, other religious texts, and everything else that you can consider lights in the sky or beings from somewhere else, but let's skip that topic for now. Let's focus on modern times here. One theory is that the government, or the Deep State powers that be, have been trying to do a slow-drip disclosure to the public in a way that would not incite panic or a revolution. Basically, Steven Spielberg was probably read into some of these classified projects and, through the magic of Hollywood, was tasked to help disclose some of this truth to the general public with his film Close Encounters. It wasn't just him. There are other directors in film and television, authors, and the like who have been used to disseminate this information or, more importantly, disinformation slowly.[364]

The intelligence community wants to have a handle on all this UFO information. Obviously, this is a massive national security issue. We wouldn't want our enemies to get any of this advanced technology or knowledge and use it against us. I understand the national security implications, and I'm sure others do as well. However, at some point, someone with the knowledge of this information decided that the public had a right to know or needed to know for some reason, so they started to drip it out throughout the years since the 1960s. Here we are in 2026, and that faucet has been turned up. We can speculate all we want on why. We might even do that in a later chapter, but for now, this is not the '80s or '90s anymore. What we are experiencing is a global awakening to non-human intelligences at the direction and discretion of clandestine intelligence agencies and the MIC.

You're probably asking yourself, "Why the hell did you tell me this giant backstory? I got this book because I want to know about UFOs and maybe something about Freemasonry and this giant government cover-up."

Well, here's something that I figured out for you: pretty much everyone on the planet has had an anomalous experience at some point in their life, and some people don't talk about it at all due to ridicule. Others do, and if you were open to the possibility that something that does not fit into the normal paradigm of waking reality could exist all around you at any moment, well, that's when some magical things happen.

You must be honest with yourself. I know some people who will see the most amazing thing that's paranormal, and they will explicitly tell themselves that they were imagining it, that it wasn't real, or that they didn't even see it. "The most effective cloaking device has always been the human mind."

In the book The Invisible Gorilla, the authors explain how our brains trick us into thinking we see and know far more than we actually do. The phrase "the invisible gorilla" comes from an experiment created to test selective attention. In it, study participants are asked to watch a video in which two teams, one in black shirts and one in white shirts, are passing a ball. Participants are told to count how many times players in white shirts pass the ball.

Midway through the video, a gorilla walks through the game, stands in the middle, pounds her chest, then exits. Then, study participants are asked, "But did you see the gorilla?" More than half the time, subjects miss the gorilla entirely. More than that, even after the participants are told about the gorilla, they're certain they couldn't have missed it.

"Our intuition is that we will notice something that's that visible, that's that distinctive," explains Simons, "and that intuition is consistently wrong."[4]

In my opinion, they are correct. Belief is stronger than we all realize, and what I think this current U.S. Government/MIC/IC "disclosure" effort might be is akin to a global awakening to the possibility of something more than humanity. Are they creating a new religion? Are they pushing for a new world order? Or is it that if most of the world believes that something could be real, that in essence, we as humanity birth it into existence, much like a tulpa?

A tulpa is a thought form. Basically, it is a thought or projection of a thought that, at some point, creates its own existence and exists outside of the original thought. I'm really paraphrasing that, but do some homework and check it out. It's Tibetan and very old, and I believe it's truthful.

I really believe you must forget all your preconceived notions about who we are and what we are as humans. We cannot listen to the authority figures, religions, the people who are supposed to be wiser and stronger than us, our spiritual or consciousness guardians. We must be open and forget everything we know to learn something new, and here's a spoiler: it's already right inside of you. So, forget everything that you know, or at least most of it.

Here we are. I've had a bunch of experiences. I pushed it all away, then wanted it back and had a hard time making it happen. It wasn't until through the eyes of someone I love next to me, seeing the same orange orbs flying overhead, that I believe my connection really came back.

My wife and I were driving through an ice storm when we saw several orange orbs in an erratic, shifting formation over the Maumee River. Here is where that belief structure comes into play. In that moment, and even for years afterwards, she would come up with every excuse she could for her own mind to tell herself that what she was seeing was anything but something that she could not identify. She did this with just me. When there is no one else around, you can force yourself to believe that what she was saying was real, these were UFOs, and she had seen them. Everything about that night was improbable. It was an ice storm. The wind was ten to fifteen miles an hour, and these things were going against the wind, brighter than anything around. We saw many orange orbs that day, at least a dozen in the sky.

I like to call the orange orbs the gateway drug to the paranormal because a lot of people start by seeing them, and afterward, a whole bunch of other paranormal experiences and sightings occur.

She finally will now admit that she saw something completely abnormal and, by definition, a UFO. They were possibly balls of intelligent plasma, and as some physicists have stated, plasma may be conscious. That is a topic for another book altogether.

This wasn't the only joint experience of seeing a UFO. Two years later, after we had our daughter Stella, we experienced two more UFOs in broad daylight with her, our other daughter, Addison, and the neighbors. It was July 5, 2020. It was almost 100 degrees, and we were all outside in the backyard, hanging out and playing with water balloons to cool down.

At the time, Stella was two years old. She lay down on the deck. This is something that she has never done and still hasn't. She lay down and looked at me and said, "Daddy, lie down with me right here," and insisted that I do so, head-to-head on the deck. I did, and as I looked up, there was a white orb directly over the back of my house. The funny thing is, she called them "yeah-yeahs" at the time. At two years old, I had not told her what a UFO was. She just knew, instinctively, to lie down, get me to do the same, and look up at this UFO. She, too, must have my gift of paranormal sight. My wife and stepdaughter saw an orb along with us, and we have videos and photos to prove it. I submitted it to MUFON (case number 109930, 7-6-2020), who told me it was probably a weather balloon, which is the funniest, most overused excuse in the world, next to it being the planet Venus or swamp gas. As my stepdaughter, Addison, stepped back outside to look, she noticed another one directly to the south of the current white orb. I brought out binoculars to look more closely, but could not make out anything beyond a throbbing white orb. The neighbors were seeing them, too, and no one could figure out what the hell this thing was. Now there were two of them!

As soon as they appeared, they disappeared, but it wasn't for about another hour or so. They hung out for so long that everybody became bored and just went about their business, which is often reported during strange paranormal experiences. People get the impression or the thought to go back to bed or just to go about their business and basically ignore what is happening, which is so profoundly obscure and paranormal that it's almost as if their brain can't process it properly. Well, whatever that paranormal thing was, it directly affected some people, leading them to think in that fashion.

However, once your paradigm opens, all kinds of new experiences can occur, and that's what happened to our family. I feel that unconditional love is truly a bridge to the paranormal as well.

Through this journey, I've met and interviewed some truly amazing people for my podcast. I've learned so much and have gotten to share with people from all over the globe. So, I said to myself, "To hell with it. I've always wanted to write all of this down and get it out of my head; all these ideas and research were just digital bookmarks, old out-of-print books, and newspaper clippings strewn throughout my headspace. I figured it was time to put some connections together for myself personally, and... why not share them with the world?"

# CHAPTER 2

## "THERE IS NO TRUTH."

*The Cigarette Man, X-Files*

I'm not going to spend countless black and white pages trying to convince you of the fact—yes, fact—that since time immemorial, there have been ongoing interactions with advanced anomalies on land, sea, air, space, and underground that we humans have not readily identified or understood. Since about 1947 in the USA, we've collectively called these anomalies "flying saucers," or more commonly "UFOs" (Unidentified Flying Objects), and since 2016, "UAPs."

During the writing of this book, there have been two congressional hearings with U.S. government and military whistleblowers under oath speaking about everything from crash retrievals to non-human intelligence to biological issues associated with the UFO phenomenon. As my friend John Warner IV points out, perjury is considered a felony in most U.S. states. However, prosecutions for perjury are rare, and people do it all the time.

A former DIA official, John (Jay) F. Stratton Jr., has publicly taken credit for "rebranding" the term UFO as UAP. "UAP" stands for "Unidentified Anomalous Phenomena," a catch-all term to describe unusual and unidentified objects detected in the air, sea, and space that defy easy explanation. Stratton retired from his role as a Defense Intelligence Senior Executive with the Office of Naval Intelligence (ONI) after 32 years of highly distinguished service within the National Intelligence Community. "Office of Naval Intelligence" is the key department here, and I'll address that organization a bit later. The U.S. Navy, not the U.S. Air Force, has been behind the latest public disclosure initiatives, and there's a lot to unpack here.

Traditionally, the U.S. Navy has always had the lion's share of cutting-edge technology and funding, going back to the successful ships the USS Constitution (1812) and the steam-driven Monitor ironclad (1864), so it's logical to conclude they were given exotic UFO technology to examine and understand since World War II. They had the technical expertise. We will discuss the hidden MIC tech advancements in detail in a coming chapter.

What Stratton is best known for, at least in UFO research circles, is being the first Director of the Unidentified Aerial Phenomenon Task Force (UAPTF), which was created in 2020. His government reports acknowledge that there are documented cases of airborne objects demonstrating flight characteristics and technological capabilities far beyond our current understanding, at least the overt general public's understanding.[5]

The UAPTF delivered an interagency "whole of government" approach to standardize the collection and reporting of sightings of Unidentified Aerial Phenomena. The UAPTF was mandated by Congress in 2020 and was included in the Senate Intelligence Committee's Report 116-233, accompanying the Intelligence Authorization Act for Fiscal Year 2021.[6] On June 24, 2020, the committee voted to require the United States Intelligence Community and the Department of Defense to publicly track and analyze data on unidentified aerial phenomena. The directive required a report to Congress within 180 days of the act's passage. The UAPTF was officially approved on August 4, 2020, by Deputy Secretary of Defense David Norquist and announced on August 14, 2020, formalizing its establishment within the Office of Naval Intelligence. This congressional action built on earlier efforts, such as the Advanced Aerospace Threat Identification Program (AATIP), and set the stage for subsequent developments, including the UAPTF's preliminary report released on June 25, 2021. As we see here, this was established within the U.S. Office of Naval Intelligence and not the U.S. Air Force.[7]

The approach has been pushed to address an aviation safety hazard to our USN and USAF aviators. Thus, the rationale for rebranding as UAP will hopefully remove some of the stigma artificially created by the 1952 Robertson Panel around the original military acronym "UFO." The Robertson Panel recommended that the National Security Council debunk UFO reports and institute a policy of public education to reassure the understandably ignorant populace of the lack of evidence behind UFOs. It suggested using the mass media, advertising, business clubs, schools, and even the Disney corporation to get the misleading message across. Reporting at the height of McCarthyism, the panel also recommended that such private UFO groups as the Civilian Flying Saucer Investigators in Los Angeles and the Aerial Phenomena Research Organization in Wisconsin be monitored for "subversive activities."

The panel was convened from January 14 to January 17, 1953, under the direction of the Central Intelligence Agency (CIA) and chaired by physicist H.P. Robertson. Its report was completed shortly thereafter, with the final memorandum dated January 17, 1953. However, this document remained classified and was not released to the public immediately. The Robertson Panel's findings were initially distributed internally within the CIA and select government agencies, such as the Air Force, to guide policy on UFO sightings. It was not intended for public dissemination at the time. Partial details of the Robertson Panel's conclusions emerged in the mid-1950s through leaks and secondary sources, and the full report was not widely available until it was declassified and released under the Freedom of Information Act (FOIA). The CIA declassified the Robertson Panel report in 1977, making it available to researchers and the public as part of a broader release of UFO-related documents following increased public pressure and FOIA requests.

The Army-McCarthy hearings of 1954, televised from April 22 to June 17, are often remembered as the public unraveling of Senator Joseph McCarthy, a Wisconsin Republican whose anti-Communist crusade had gripped the nation. However, in his 2019 book McCarthy, Monmouth, and the Deep State, historian Joseph P. Farrell offers a provocative reinterpretation, suggesting that McCarthy and his chief counsel, Roy Cohn, inadvertently stumbled upon a secret far greater than Communist infiltration: a hidden black budget within the U.S. Army's financial records, potentially funding the emerging National Security State and its covert projects. These hearings, centered on alleged subversion at the Army Signal Corps laboratory at Fort Monmouth, New Jersey, took an unexpected turn that Farrell argues threatened to expose a shadowy financial apparatus established after World War II.

Farrell contends that during their budget analysis, McCarthy and Cohn uncovered anomalies suggesting covert funding for classified projects, possibly linked to the 1947 Roswell incident and early UFO research. He writes, "McCarthy and Cohn, in their relentless pursuit of Communist phantoms, tripped over a far greater secret: a hidden financial pipeline, buried in the Army's budget analysis, which funded classified projects beyond congressional oversight." Farrell suggests this discovery was the embryonic black budget of the National Security State, designed to shield advanced technological and extraterrestrial research. He further asserts, "This was no mere accounting irregularity; it was the financial backbone of a secret state, one that McCarthy's probe at Monmouth threatened to lay bare."

The consequences were dire for McCarthy, already a controversial figure known for his heavy drinking and abrasive tactics. Farrell suggests his public ruin was orchestrated to silence this revelation, noting, "His public ruin was orchestrated not merely for his reckless anti-Communist zeal, but to silence him before he could unravel the deeper truth. McCarthy's alcoholism, well-documented by contemporaries, made him an easy target for discredit." The hearings concluded with no definitive evidence of McCarthy's wrongdoing, but his reputation was shattered; his Gallup approval rating dropped from 50% in January 1954 to 34% by June. He was censured by the Senate on December 2, 1954, and died in 1957, his legacy tarnished. Farrell argues, "The televised spectacle of the Army-McCarthy hearings was a convenient stage to dismantle McCarthy's credibility, ensuring the black budget remained in the shadows."[8]

So basically, the idea was to make citizens think that they were crazy if they saw UFOs, and more importantly, if they formally reported UFO activity to the authorities. At the same time, the Robertson Panel cleverly used the mass media to deliver this untrue message, covertly infiltrated public UFO organizations, and, in my opinion, spread disinformation en masse. This was a military intelligence-style "Psy-Op," or "Psychological Operation."

Stratton is also the man who told the Pentagon that a wide range of anomalous phenomena was occurring regularly at Skinwalker Ranch in Utah, including a possible interdimensional portal on the property, according to Native Americans. He has been instrumental in securing DIA (Defense Intelligence Agency) funding to research the ranch and associated phenomena using U.S. tax dollars. He asked his friend, Dr. Travis Taylor, to join him on the UAPTF board. Travis is also one of the stars of the hit reality TV show The Secret of Skinwalker Ranch. This program is on the History Channel, and it is somewhat entertaining to say the least. As of this writing, it is currently in its fifth season, and so far, zero secrets have been revealed. I know that's very subjective, but it's true. They are slowly revealing valid but vague data points that could be associated with The Phenomenon and are conducting experiments in a repeatable manner. We will see later how all these people run in the same connected circles.

To paraphrase George Carlin: "It's NOT that big of a club, and YOU ain't in it." But I digress.

What I want to get out of the way is this: You can call them whatever the hell you want, I still like the old-fashioned term "flying saucer." If you ask me, UFOs are REAL.

Some of them are human-made, and others are most likely not from this world or dimension. Most likely, we have successfully reverse-engineered hundreds of these antigravity and spacetime-fabric-warping crafts after we've picked them apart, as a starving cat does the bones of a juicy, fat rat. Many nations have probably done so throughout history. What might be more concerning today is that our global adversaries have most likely done the same. What highly advanced and dangerous weapons and technology could have been developed over the years since World War II?

Okay, so UFOs are real in my opinion, so what? There has been a concerted effort by the U.S. Government to conceal this fact from the American public and the world since at least 1947 and probably far before. The U.S. Government, the Pentagon's high ranks, and our multitude of alphabet agencies have lied and possibly even killed to keep the "UFO File" a secret from the public. I ask why?

There are entire divisions and branches of three-letter agencies assigned to keep this phenomenon an impenetrable secret. This toxic secrecy is the highest form of classification, far exceeding nuclear weapons secrecy. In fact, that's where most of the UFO-related information is held within the government to hide it from congressional and public prying eyes. Most of it is stored under the umbrella of the Department of Energy (DOE), which could be an entire exposé book, and in fact, I believe there are several.

The U.S. Government has taken a stance that there is "something" going on regarding UFOs, and now they are being studied seriously once again. Legislation has been passed to fund and staff programs in a classified setting to deliver reports to Congress. Oh, and all of this is now happening on the public stage as well.

I believe this new wave of disclosure started again at a higher rate around 2015, driven by a rock star named Tom DeLonge. Tom DeLonge is a member of one of the biggest punk bands in the world, Blink-182. In fact, he quit his very successful band, lost a great deal of money, and, like many other publicly oriented researchers before him, dedicated his life to being a responsible citizen, informing the world that UFOs, along with a host of other paranormal phenomena, were indeed real.

Tom isn't the first "UFO messiah," to quote author Grant Cameron, but stands on the shoulders of giants in the field of Ufology. Here are just a few men who, without their advocacy, we would not be talking publicly about UFOs. I know that these are all men, and that really does make me cringe a bit. I feel that women should play a stronger role in Ufology and in all aspects of society. This is just a very high-level overview of some of the most prominent researchers to have ever graced the field.

**Donald Keyhoe** was a former Marine Corps pilot who turned ufologist and authored influential books such as The Flying Saucers Are Real (1950) and Flying Saucers from Outer Space (1953). He argued that UFOs were extraterrestrial and accused the U.S. government of a cover-up, fostering public skepticism about official narratives and setting the stage for future disclosure advocacy.[9]

**J. Allen Hynek** was an astronomer whom the U.S. Air Force initially hired to debunk UFO sightings; later, he became a believer and developed the "close encounter" classification system. His work with Project Blue Book (1952–1969) and the Center for UFO Studies (CUFOS, founded 1973) brought scientific credibility to the field.[10]

**Jacques Vallée** is a computer scientist and ufologist who proposed that UFOs might be interdimensional rather than extraterrestrial and worked with Hynek on Project Blue Book. His book Passport to Magonia (1969) explored parallels between UFO encounters and folklore, offering alternative theories that influenced later researchers, including DeLonge, and he even wrote the foreword to his book.[11]

**Stanton Friedman** was a nuclear physicist turned ufologist who devoted over four decades to researching and lecturing on UFOs, beginning in the 1950s as a physicist for companies like General Electric and transitioning to full-time UFO research in 1970. Known for his work on the 1947 Roswell incident, Friedman authored key books such as Flying Saucers and Science (2008) and Captured! The Betty and Barney Hill UFO Experience (2007, co-authored by Kathleen Marden). He delivered lectures at over 600 colleges and universities across the U.S., Canada, and 19 other countries, advocating for the extraterrestrial hypothesis. Friedman's debates with skeptics, such as Michael Shermer, and his extensive public outreach made him a cornerstone of ufology until he died in 2019.[12]

**Dr. Steven Greer**, a retired physician and ufologist, organized a press conference at the National Press Club in Washington, D.C. on May 9, 2001, as part of his Disclosure Project, founded in 1993. Greer, who also established the Center for the Study of Extraterrestrial Intelligence (CSETI) in 1990, brought together 20 retired military, government, and intelligence officials to testify about their firsthand experiences with UFOs and alleged government cover-ups. The event aimed to pressure the U.S. government to release classified UFO information and was described by Greer as a moment of "historic, indeed planetary, significance." It garnered significant media attention, though it did not prompt immediate congressional action. Greer later expanded on these efforts in his 2013 documentary Sirius and in several other documentaries. This press conference remains a landmark in UFO advocacy due to its use of credible witnesses and large public exposure.[13] [14]

The contributions of Donald Keyhoe, J. Allen Hynek, Jacques Vallée, Stanton Friedman, Steven Greer, and countless others laid the foundation for modern ufology, shaping public perception and government responses to UFOs from the 1940s to the present day.

DeLonge's pre-To The Stars Academy of Arts and Sciences (TTSA) connections to Greer, rooted in a shared desire for disclosure, marked a transitional moment in this history. While Greer's work provided a model of public advocacy, DeLonge's TTSA introduced a new phase, blending insider access with mainstream outreach, further advancing the UFO disclosure movement. Currently, there is a rift between the two of them. If you listen to the internet chatter, Greer believes all non-human intelligences are love and light, while Tom paints them as a potential threat. Either way, the two spent a great deal of time together and helped Tom to launch his current endeavor with TTSA.

Tom was invited to an employee-only party at Lockheed's Skunk Works, a division responsible for the most advanced aircraft and projects of the 20th and 21st centuries. Tom said that he would introduce the Lockheed CEO if he got to spend ten minutes alone with him, and they remarkably granted his wish. All of this catapulted him into the world of the U.S. Intelligence Community, the vast U.S. Military-Industrial Complex, and the dark world of espionage, black projects, and rough-and-tumble U.S. politics. It's hard not to question whether this entire interaction was suspiciously CIA-approved.

This quote is directly from Tom DeLonge on the March 27, 2016, Coast to Coast AM interview with George Knapp. I felt that this conversation was valid and needed to be examined to understand not only the current state of "UFO disclosure," but also how we arrived at it publicly. We are here because of both

George Knapp and Tom DeLonge, and, like it or not, without them, we would not be having this no-stigma conversation about UFOs right now in 2026.

During this telling Coast to Coast AM interview, we learn that Tom DeLonge, a rock musician with a deep interest in UFOs, gained unprecedented access to high-level government and military officials to discuss the UFO phenomenon. Through a series of meetings initiated by an invitation to an event hosted by a secretive group of engineers and scientists within the military-industrial complex, DeLonge pitched a project aimed at reversing public cynicism about the government and disclosing the reality of UFOs in a controlled manner. He explained his approach, saying, "I think if it's done correctly, [it] will reverse the cynicism that people have about government and... the Military Industrial Complex."[15]

DeLonge met with top Lockheed Martin engineers, CIA representatives, NASA officials, and high-ranking military personnel, including a general who became a key advisor. He proposed the "Sekret Machines" project, combining fiction and non-fiction works to educate the public, particularly young adults, about UFOs and the government's efforts to understand and defend against them. In one pivotal meeting, he boldly said, "I understand the national security implications of what I'm about to say. I am not naive to the topic, and I think if you hear me out, you're gonna see that there's merit in what I'm about to propose." DeLonge emphasized his academic knowledge, respectful approach, and ability to reach a wide audience as reasons for his involvement.

A significant moment in DeLonge's discussions involved invoking Edgar Mitchell, the sixth man to walk on the Moon and a known advocate for UFO disclosure. Mitchell, a Freemason (Artesia Lodge #29, New Mexico) and Apollo 14 astronaut, had publicly claimed that extraterrestrial life was real and that the government had covered it up.[16] During a tense meeting with the head of the engineering group, after being challenged on the UFO topic, DeLonge recalled, "So, the only thing that I can think of at the moment, is I said, 'Well, Edgar Alan Mitchell, the sixth man to walk on the Moon, is out telling all the young people of the world that this is real. So, we have a credibility issue that we have to attack, but we don't have to attack it here or now, and we could talk this through." By citing Mitchell, DeLonge leveraged the astronaut's credibility to deflect skepticism and underscore the need for his project, suggesting that prominent figures like Mitchell had already begun to shift public perception, creating a "credibility issue" that his initiative could address.

After listening to this conversation and leveraging my own theory, I couldn't help but think Tom was speaking with another Mason. Did he say this to relate it back to the importance of the topic and the other Masons' direct connections to it? I think it makes sense.

The officials DeLonge was working with revealed that during the Cold War, the U.S. discovered an extraterrestrial life form and kept it secret due to the constant threat of nuclear war with Russia. One official told him, "It was the Cold War, and every single day we lived under the threat of nuclear war... and somewhere in those years, we found a life form, and everything that we did and every decision that we made with that life form was because of the consciousness at that time." UFOs were observed activating U.S. nuclear weapons, potentially to provoke a response from Russia, leading to a secretive defense program. DeLonge was told that various government agencies, such as the National Reconnaissance Office (NRO)[17], Air Material Command, and CIA, work on different aspects of The Phenomenon, with a small group possibly overseeing the big picture.

DeLonge assembled an advisory team of experts in space, intelligence, and biowarfare, facilitated by the general. He kept close relationships with these advisors, running his project materials by them for approval and releasing information gradually to avoid scaring the public. Reflecting on his role, he noted, "I'm not some kind of Hollywood prick. I'm treating the material the way it needs to be treated... once they gave me a little bit, I executed exactly the way I said I would." DeLonge believes this disclosure effort could unify people, change how governments operate, and inspire support for defense and space programs, revealing breakthroughs like anti-gravity technology. He asserted, "Yes, we have cracked gravity and yes, we are building machinery that have anti-gravity, yes, I was told that. It's a big deal."

This interview, detailing DeLonge's interactions with government insiders and his strategic use of Edgar Mitchell's public statements, laid the groundwork for the UFO disclosure movement over the past decade, encouraging a gradual public acknowledgment of The Phenomenon's reality.

During the interview, DeLonge refers to a key figure he calls "the General," a high-ranking military official who played a significant role in advising him on his UFO disclosure efforts and the Sekret Machines project. While DeLonge does not explicitly name this individual in the interview, he describes "the General" as someone with extensive authority and knowledge, saying, "There was nobody above him. There's nobody. Maybe a couple, but when you look at the divisions of how the Department of Defense works, in this specific division, it's just extraordinary that I have this contact." This indicates that "the General" held a top-tier position within a specific Department of Defense division related to UFO research or advanced technology.

The identity of "the General" was discovered from WikiLeaks documents, and all indications point to Major General William N. McCasland as the likely individual. In emails released by WikiLeaks in 2016 from John Podesta's email account (Hillary Clinton's campaign chairman), DeLonge specifically mentions McCasland. In an email dated January 25, 2016, with the subject line "General McCasland," DeLonge writes to Podesta: "He mentioned he's a 'skeptic', he's not. I've been working with him for four months. I just got done giving him a four-hour presentation on the entire project a few weeks ago. Trust me, the advice has already been happening on how to do all this. He just has to say that out loud, but he is very, very aware as he was in charge of all of the stuff. When Roswell crashed, they shipped it to the laboratory at Wright Patterson Air Force Base. General McCasland was in charge of that exact laboratory up to a couple years ago. He not only knows what I'm trying to achieve, he helped assemble my advisory team. He's a very important man."[18]

McCasland served as the Commander of the Air Force Research Laboratory (AFRL) at Wright-Patterson Air Force Base in Ohio until his retirement in 2013. Wright-Patterson is historically significant in UFO lore, often cited as the location where debris from the 1947 Roswell crash was allegedly taken for study. DeLonge's mention of McCasland's role in assembling his advisory team aligns with the interview's description of "the General" providing advisors from fields such as space, intelligence, and biowarfare.

Major General William N. McCasland was a highly decorated officer who oversaw the Air Force's $2.2 billion science and technology program at AFRL. His tenure at Wright-Patterson included managing advanced research and development, including classified projects related to aerospace and unidentified aerial phenomena (UAP). After retiring from the Air Force, McCasland's involvement with DeLonge suggests he continued to engage with sensitive topics, albeit in a private capacity, and possibly supporting DeLonge's disclosure initiative.

DeLonge uses the pseudonym "the General" throughout the interview without revealing a specific name. However, the WikiLeaks emails explicitly name Major General William N. McCasland as the individual DeLonge was working with, connecting him to the broader narrative described in the interview. This connection is further supported by DeLonge's public statements and writings, such as in his book Sekret Machines: Chasing Shadows, where he alludes to a "General" who helped assemble his team, consistent with the WikiLeaks reference to McCasland.[19]

The WikiLeaks disclosure set the stage for a pivotal Coast to Coast AM interview later that year on February 26, 2017, conducted by George Knapp with DeLonge and co-author Peter Levenda. The discussion centered on their nonfiction book Sekret Machines: Gods, Man, and War, released in 2016 with a foreword by Dr. Jacques Vallée, a prominent UFO researcher who had initially been skeptical but endorsed the work.

This interview, aired after the WikiLeaks disclosures, captured DeLonge at his most candid, offering specific claims about the UFO phenomenon that he later tempered in public statements. Knapp introduced the segment by noting Vallée's contribution, highlighting the book's bold re-examination of unexplained aerial phenomena.

DeLonge asserted the existence of multiple extraterrestrial races with conflicting agendas, stating, "Number one, there's multiple different races, it's not just one specific kind, and the different races don't get along with each other, and we don't really get along with them either." This claim suggested a complex cosmic dynamic, a perspective informed by his interactions with high-level insiders like McCasland.

When Knapp directly asked if he had been told about visitors from elsewhere, DeLonge confirmed, "Have you been told that there are visitors from elsewhere, either dimensional or other planets or both? ... Absolutely, yes." He elaborated, tying these entities to human history as "Gods intervening in human events at a time and at times where there's industrialized warfare and trying to help different sides ... it's taking sides, gods taking sides." This claim of extraterrestrial influence on human conflicts, particularly during industrialized warfare, was a rare and specific revelation not said since this interview.

DeLonge also shared a recurring directive from his advisors, pointing to Greek mythology as a historical clue. "I was told three different times from different people at those levels ... 'When I was a kid, I used to read a lot of Greek mythology,' and he just stares at me." He interpreted this as evidence of a specific alien race's visibility in ancient Greece, stating, "I think when it comes down to the Greek mythology ... that's really when they made themselves visibly known ... and that's why if you look at Washington, D.C., the architecture is very similar." This connection between Greek culture and modern Western civilization suggested a profound extraterrestrial influence on human development that persists to this day.

Peter Levenda provided a scholarly framework, introducing the "cargo cult" concept to explain how ancient societies interpreted these encounters. He described cargo cults as Stone Age Pacific Islanders mimicking World War II technology, noting, "They're mimicking something that they saw, and they're trying to get back to that state." Levenda extended this to argue that ancient texts, such as Genesis 6's "sons of God" and "daughters of men," documented real non-human interactions that shaped religious and cultural narratives.

DeLonge's disclosures in this interview were bolstered by his earlier efforts, detailed in his prior Knapp interview, in which he described meetings with officials at the Pentagon, NASA, and other agencies, presumably facilitated by McCasland.

Following the 2016 interview, DeLonge launched TTSA in October 2017, alongside former, and some say possibly current, clandestine government officials such as Luis Elizondo and Christopher Mellon. TTSA released declassified UFO videos, including the "Gimbal" and "Go Fast" footage, which the Pentagon later confirmed in April 2020. These developments marked a significant shift in public discourse on UFOs, now rebranded as Unidentified Aerial Phenomena (UAP).

Basically, DeLonge told them that the military industrial complex has painted itself in a horrible light over the years, and their image was completely garbage in the public. This was especially true for young "millennials." What he wanted to do was change the public's perception of the Military Industrial Complex (MIC); he wanted to help change the narrative, reach younger audiences, and make them want to work with the government on big historic issues like UFOs. He was assigned a group of advisors and told that he could release small bits of factual information piece by piece over time.

The U.S. Government authorities responsible for managing the UFO narrative chose to collaborate with DeLonge. They assisted him in gathering former government officials and respected figures to lend credibility to the UFO disclosure initiative and its connection to the military-industrial complex.

Who did the military general and all these other people give their precious time to work with? Well, there is an impressive group of men on the company board (and a woman from Lockheed). All these men would never be together under any other terms. I've seen this in only one other setting: a Masonic Lodge. Inside a Masonic Lodge, you get a wide group of men who normally would not be together. For example, you could have the local high school janitor sitting right next to a congressman, and in the lodge, we are all equal.

That's exactly what I saw when Tom DeLonge presented his new company, and everybody associated with it. You have Luis

Elizondo involved, who allegedly ran a UFO program for the government. I said "allegedly" because there has been no official documentation to prove this.[20]

The ringleader in all of this, in my opinion, is Christopher K. Mellon. He was the former Deputy Assistant Director of Defense for Intelligence under several presidents and a member of one of the richest old-money Eastern Establishment families on Earth, the Mellon banking dynasty of Pittsburgh, which has had many members in military intelligence since before World War II. Mellon has also publicly admitted to helping release the three famous videos that the New York Times blasted across the front page, which started this whole "new" disclosure initiative back in 2017, along with "Lou" Elizondo. Allegedly, they arranged for the three famous videos to be declassified and handed over to Ralph Blumenthal and Leslie Kean.[21] That article kickstarted this entire disclosure movement, and Mellon was the ringleader.

So, you have all these intelligence community men on stage saying they want to change the world by forcing the government to admit that UFOs are real, and they were going to try to build an antigravity craft of their own, too. That statement fell flat when they could not raise anywhere near enough money. To be fair, the COVID-19 outbreak also happened during this same time. The company sold stock as a "public benefit corporation," raised only $1 million of the $50 million offering, and, as of this writing, is reporting massive debt.

It's still a mystery why they chose to form this as a Public Benefit Corporation (PBC) rather than a standard corporation. Traditional corporations have a primary duty to maximize shareholder value; PBCs' directors have a broader fiduciary duty to balance the interests of all stakeholders, including the public benefit. So, UFOs should be revealed for the public's benefit?

Full disclosure here: I am a shareholder. You see, I do believe what they're trying to do, and I think that Tom DeLonge really did convince enough people in the military industrial complex that he was the guy to bring about all this information to the public through entertainment. He even said it himself that he wants TTSA to be the Disney Corp. of the paranormal.

Tom DeLonge is a Freemason. I am as well. We are brothers. I've had a brother personally verify that he was, in fact, made a Mason in a Prince Hall Lodge. He was raised to the sublime degree of Master Mason at Widow's Son Lodge, No.17, PHA, Kansas City. His side band/art project, entitled Angels & Airwaves, has a logo that is basically a square-and-compass. He uses the Masonic square and compass on his guitars, and he also admitted he was a Mason on Coast to Coast AM with George Knapp in the early 2000s. My theory here is that DeLonge is a Freemason, and that at least some of the other founding members of TTSA are as well.

Were all these initiatives possible because Tom found a group of U.S. government men, Freemasons, that he could trust? Did he find people who might help him bring about more disclosure of the UFO phenomenon? There might be many more Masons as well behind the scenes, and that makes perfect sense to me. Be advised, it only makes sense to me in this context because I am a Mason. Nothing else makes sense about the entire operation, but upon being told an insane story about another group of Masons, all this just clicked into place for me.

The story goes something like this. A brother of mine was traveling with three other brothers from Ohio to Canada to visit a lodge. Inside the car were a financial planner, a construction worker, a lawyer, and a plumber. That might not be correct, as it's just to illustrate that all four of these men came from very different asset classes and professions. They all drove to the U.S./Canada border in one car. The Canadian Royal Mountain Police could not understand why four men of different ages and different backgrounds were all traveling together into Canada. They explained that they were going to visit a Masonic Lodge and that they were all Freemasons. The border patrol, thinking that something was wrong and didn't believe their story, pulled them out of the line and detained all of them as the suspicious authorities thought they might be terrorists, etc. One of the border guards heard all this commotion on the radio and approached the Masons and his companion officer. The second border patrol guard was a member of the Canadian Masonic Lodge, a "fellow traveler," and knew these brothers were road-tripping from the U.S. to Canada for an important meeting. He explained to the other officer how they all were very unlikely companions, exactly because they were Masonic Brothers. The four U.S. Masons were all released and arrived at the Masonic meeting on time. Because of that story, I knew instinctively, when I saw those TTSA men, Steve Justice, Tom DeLonge, Jim Semivan, and the others on that stage, that's exactly what ran through my mind. I have not been able to officially confirm whether any of the other members of TTSA are Masons, but I have a strong suspicion they just might be. Did DeLonge pull this off using the bonds of "The Fraternity"? Was he able to meet with these men, on the level, so to say, and then assemble a team of men from all different walks of life with the goal to disclose to the human population that we are in fact not alone? These men have impressive backgrounds, but, in my opinion, never would have interacted with each other on a day-to-day basis.

Let's look at the founding members and their bios.

Jim Semivan, co-founder and VP of TTSA Operations, is a retired CIA officer with a 25-year career in the agency's National Clandestine Service (Directorate of Operations). He served in multiple overseas and domestic tours, held senior management positions at CIA headquarters, and retired in 2007 as a member of the CIA's Senior Intelligence Service, receiving the Career Intelligence Medal for his contributions. Semivan is also known for his personal experiences with UAP and nonhuman intelligences, including a profound 1990 encounter, and has been an outspoken advocate for greater transparency and serious study of the phenomenon in interviews, podcasts, and public discussions.

Dr. Harold Puthoff, co-founder and TTSA VP Science and Technology, is an experimental physicist advisor to the U.S. government, with extensive CIA and DIA research experience. Puthoff's work with the U.S. government and military as a contractor spans decades. It includes: NSA Service (early 1960s, focusing on advanced computing and optics), Stargate Project (1972–1985, directing CIA/DIA-funded remote viewing research at SRI), AATIP (2007–2012, advising the DoD on UAP investigations), and consulting (ongoing roles with NASA, DoD, and intelligence agencies on cutting-edge tech and "Psi Research"). There is enough of Puthoff and his direct ties to the MIC that it would take an entire book to add it all here. Trust me, it will be worth your time to do some homework and investigate Hal if you don't already have an idea of what this man has accomplished and been part of on the secret, highly classified side of the MIC over the last 60-plus years. I will say that he does hold some very interesting patents, and his journals are cookie crumbs themselves. He holds three patents related to scalar-vector potentials and their use in communications.[22]

Steve Justice directs the TTSA Aerospace Division, exploring new, cutting-edge technologies. He retired after 31 years at Lockheed Martin's Skunk Works, where he led advanced aircraft programs. Legend has it that Lockheed has long been rumored to possess crashed UFOs and has been actively reverse-engineering them since the late 1940s.

Luis Elizondo, a career U.S. Army G2 and DIA intelligence officer, formerly led some Pentagon investigations into Unidentified Aerial Threats (UAT), with career roles across the U.S. Defense and Intelligence Agencies. Christopher K. Mellon, a national security consultant, investor, and commentator, served as the Deputy Assistant Secretary of Defense for Security and Information Operations and later for Intelligence. Mellon is a prominent member of the Mellon family, one of America's most prominent banking dynasties.

The Mellon family's influence spans business, politics, military service, and philanthropy, with descendants like Paul Mellon continuing their legacy through CIA service, art, and charity, and others like Paul's son Timothy Mellon, a railroad tycoon, engaging in modern political funding. Known for their diversification and quiet power, the Mellons have maintained wealth and prominence across generations, though some critique their role in economic inequality. Today, they remain a symbol of enduring American industrial and cultural might.

Some say Chris Mellon is the Deep State's driving force behind this recent push for "official" disclosure. With his power, influence, and previous governmental access, he appears to be the frontrunner. Chris was responsible, along with Lue Elizondo, for releasing the now infamous U.S.S. Nimitz gun camera videos of UFOs in 2017. In my opinion, these coordinated articles in the New York Times, along with the formation of TTSA and its press conference, led to the History Channel series Unidentified: Inside America's UFO Investigation in 2019. All of which was intended to secure support from within the military and the U.S. government to disclose the existence of nonhuman intelligence to the world. Or at least that was the plan.

In 2022, TTSA rebranded from To The Stars Academy of Arts & Science to just To The Stars, and what is left is the forlorn "entertainment division." Mellon, Elizondo, and Justice have all left the company. Chris is still an active force, but more in writing op-eds and working behind the scenes in Washington, and Steve Justice landed another gig with Virgin Galactic as a Senior VP. He has since removed any mention of working at TTSA from his LinkedIn page. I wonder why?

The word is that President Trump's election win threw the entire TTSA disclosure project into a tailspin. Hillary Clinton and John Podesta were supposed to be part of the White House group that would disclose this to the public, but when Trump won the first election, everything went south. I also heard rumors that after this happened, the money that was supposed to flow into TTSA dried up, and the people who left did so to ensure they could make a living. Can you blame them?

You can't blame its demise solely on Trump. Pentagon black hats were furious at TTSA. Greer, Joseph P., Farrell, Warner, and Dark Journalist publicly slammed TTSA. Many others, too. It was hailed as a CIA "limited hangout." A farce by the same intel people who covered it all up by keeping quiet for decades. Justice went back to what he knew. As for Lue? Well, Lue is still doing what he was always good at: counterintelligence.

Elizondo has appeared on many podcasts and news shows, too many in my opinion. He also authored a book and currently has a tour where you can pay a hefty fee to hear him speak. He also testified under oath before the U.S. House of Representatives Oversight Committee at a hearing on Unidentified Aerial Phenomena (UAP) on November 13, 2024. When asked by Rep. Nancy Mace, "Has the government conducted secret crash retrieval programs, yes or no?"

Elizondo responded: "Yes." Followed by, "Were they designed to identify and reverse engineer alien craft, yes or no?" To which Elizondo replied again: "Yes."

Testimony without hard evidence only goes so far. Lue has said things that many other military personnel, such as Bob Dean, Philip Corso, U.S. Army pilot Alex Collier, and others, have already said. Lue gets media press today via NewsNation, etc.; the others don't. Why?

That's what he said in a 2022 interview clip that circulated widely online: "In 2008, I was asked to apply those same skill sets [counterintelligence and counterespionage] into the UFO community." Some people have interpreted this comment as an admission that part of his role involves monitoring and influencing the UFO research community, though the context and intent remain debated. The idea that he was explicitly directed to "use counterintelligence" against the UFO community stems partly from this 2022 statement and has fueled speculation and criticism. Some in the UFO community interpret it as evidence of a broader effort to manipulate and control the "official" narrative around UFOs. Elizondo himself is quoted as saying he wants to "Kill Ufology," thus shifting focus to a more "scientific approach." I ask: whose science, exactly? Others say these Elizondo comments reflect standard security measures for a classified program he was a part of during his tenure at the purported Advanced Aerospace Threat Identification Program (AATIP) rather than a targeted operation against researchers. His expertise in this field is well-documented from his time in various intelligence roles, including with the Department of Defense and the Office of the Under Secretary of Defense for Intelligence. No one is doubting his expertise, but some are questioning where that ability is being directed. Elizondo's claims have stirred intense debate, with supporters hailing them as historic and heroic, while skeptics question their specificity, truthfulness, and evidence.

There is a saying: "once counter intel, always counter intel." There is an unspoken understanding: "the training rewires how you see the world, and you don't just turn it off." That can also be said of people who have had anomalous experiences. So, how do we as observers judge this?

Are we in the middle of actual "Big D" Disclosure brought to you by some faction of ex-military and government representatives, or is this just another in the long line of pseudo-disclosure efforts in the vein of pretending to have an open and honest investigation only to arrive at the same conclusions the government people needed from the beginning: "nothing to see here, move along people"?

Discernment will serve you in all things, especially this.

## PATTERNS IN THE PHENOMENON: THE SULFUR CONNECTION

Before we move on, I want to point out something curious that appears across UFO and paranormal cases spanning centuries: the smell of sulfur. It repeatedly appears in encounters with the unexplained, creating a pattern that demands attention. Is the smell of sulfur a natural byproduct of propulsion systems, materials, or biology? Could this be an intentional "side effect" being produced? Could there be something more sinister at play?

Consider the bizarre "Devil's Footprints" case from 19th-century England. The strange event began after a heavy snowfall between February 8th and 9th, 1855. Villagers across a nearly 100-mile stretch of countryside in Devon, England, woke to discover a mysterious trail of hoof-like prints in the snow. The tracks appeared overnight and traveled through remote woodlands, rooftops, and enclosed barns, traversing seemingly impossible terrain.

Locals were baffled by the bizarre prints, which looked like cloven hooves from a large animal. Yet the strides were unnaturally long—when measured, they were spaced eight feet apart or more in some areas. There was no sign of churned-up snow between steps either, as if the creature had impossibly floating leaps.

Even odder, the prints seemed to "ascend" up walls, pass over haystacks, and appear suddenly out of nowhere or disappear just as abruptly. Adding to the unsettling nature of the sightings, a few witnesses reported smelling sulfur or burnt matches near the tracks. Fearing witchcraft or the Devil's presence, many townsfolk avoided going outside during this period.

Newspapers had a field day sensationalizing the story as "Devil's Hoofmarks." By the middle of February, the story had gone international. It hit the London papers and then ran in major publications like The Times. What is very compelling is that dozens of signed eyewitness testimonies and letters to the editor were printed in these papers. Debate raged trying to rationally explain the prints as exotic animal escapes, bizarre weather effects, or mass hysteria. Still, the accounts of nearly 100 miles of prints and strange phenomena led others to truly suspect the supernatural or paranormal.

To this day, the 1855 "Devil's Footprints" saga is still one of Britain's most famous and unsolved mysteries. Just what manner of phenomena could produce such an extensive trackway overnight in varied terrain and somehow emit an odor of sulfur in its wake?

Or consider an even earlier case from the Missouri Democrat on October 19th, 1865. The newspaper reported a remarkable tale from Mr. James Lumley, an old Rocky Mountain trapper. Lumley said that in mid-September, while trapping in the mountains above the Great Falls of the Upper Missouri, he beheld a bright luminous body in the heavens moving with great rapidity in an easterly direction. It was plainly visible for at least five seconds before suddenly separating into particles, resembling the bursting of a skyrocket in the air.

A few minutes later, he heard a heavy explosion which jarred the earth perceptibly, followed by a rushing sound akin to a tornado sweeping through the forest. A strong wind sprang up about the same time, then suddenly subsided. The air was also filled with a peculiar sulfurous odor.

The following day, Lumley discovered, about two miles from his camping place, that a path had been cut through the forest, several rods wide, with giant trees uprooted or broken off near the ground, the tops of hills shaved off, and the earth plowed up in many places. Following this track of desolation, he soon found an immense stone driven into the side of a mountain. An examination showed that it was divided into compartments and carved with curious hieroglyphics.

The description of a "bright luminous body" moving rapidly in the sky and then seemingly exploding is reminiscent of some other alleged UFO crashes. The "rushing sound, like a tornado" heard after the explosion could suggest that whatever it was in the sky was moving very rapidly through the air before impact. Strange winds, low pulses or hums, and smells, like the sulfurous odor described here, have been reported after other famous UFO incidents.

There are other notable modern cases where a sulfur-like smell has been reported in association with UFOs or anomalous phenomena. We could write an entire book about Skinwalker Ranch, but we don't need to. As of this writing, there have been multiple books written about this infamous ranch for over twenty years. This infamous paranormal hotspot in Utah has long been a source of UFO sightings, cattle mutilations, and other strange occurrences. Various investigators and witnesses have reported smelling sulfur, rotten eggs, or other noxious odors emanating from sites of anomalous activity on the ranch. Some have theorized the smell may be related to a phenomenon called "portal activity."[23]

The dry west has been described as "leaky" because it has many naturally occurring rips in the dimensional fabric, according to Native American traditions.

The 1980 Rendlesham Forest Incident is another famous UK UFO case, involving multiple witnesses who reported a craft that landed in the woods. Some described smelling something akin to sulfur as they approached the site. One witness said it was like being engulfed in the smell after an artillery shell blast.

The Cash-Landrum Incident in 1980 involved two women and a boy who encountered a glowing diamond-shaped UFO on a Texas road and later suffered radiation sickness. All witnesses reported smelling sulfur as the object hovered above their car.

During the wave of Mothman reports in 1960s Point Pleasant, West Virginia, witnesses sometimes reported a sulfuric odor emanating from the ominous flying creature or at locations where it was spotted.

A pattern does appear linking the smell of sulfur to many prominent UFO and paranormal cases. We'll explore the deeper mystical significance of sulfur in Chapter 6, where ancient alchemical wisdom might hold clues to why this element appears so often in encounters with the unexplained.

# CHAPTER 3

## FORGET ABOUT WHAT YOU KNOW

### THIS IS JUST THE START OF YOUR UNRAVELING

Around 2012, I reached a turning point in my journey. I did several weeks of EMDR sessions with a licensed therapist. Eye Movement Desensitization and Reprocessing (EMDR) therapy is a psychotherapy approach designed to help individuals process and recover from traumatic experiences by using bilateral stimulation, such as guided eye movements, to reduce the emotional distress associated with traumatic memories.[24] It is typically structured in eight phases, focusing on past memories, present triggers, and future coping strategies. It has been widely recognized as an effective treatment for post-traumatic stress disorder (PTSD).[25]

In addition to guided eye movements, EMDR therapy can also incorporate bilateral stimulation through auditory tones delivered via headphones, alternating between the left and right ears to facilitate the processing of traumatic memories. It was an audio I used, and it helped me process things I never would have known were bothering me from the past.

During these sessions, I found myself revisiting my childhood bedroom and seeing those dark figures once again, the ones that would linger in the corners when I was four or five years old. They were the size of a normal adult but would stand there in the shadows, watching and waiting. No interaction at all, just an odd sense of presence they left me with. I was rattled, to say the least. They would come and go leisurely, and I only felt fear because I knew they were real, and there wasn't anything I could do about it.

What appeared during the EMDR processing was unexpected. While working through this early childhood event, I somehow concluded that this entity might have been my future self, checking in on my younger self. I am not sure, as this was not a hypnotic regression, but during the EMDR session, it seemed that there was such a close connection between me and the dark entities that I could not see a separation. It's as if I were somehow able to time-travel into the bedroom of my own childhood and watch myself. Why would I be hanging out and scaring myself as a child? The entity may have been a version of me, or something altogether different. Growing up Catholic, I always associated it with a demon; today, I don't know if that would be correct.

This revelation opened up questions I hadn't expected. If consciousness can transcend linear time, if some part of us can reach back or forward across the years, what does that mean for our understanding of the paranormal? What does it mean for our understanding of ourselves?

The experience taught me something essential: we carry more within us than we realize. Our past experiences, especially the anomalous ones, don't just happen to us; they shape us by connecting us to something larger, and sometimes they wait patiently for us to be ready to understand them.

The Robertson Panel's psychological operations were designed to make people like my father, and by extension, people like me, feel crazy for talking about what they witnessed.[26] Here's what the shadow government didn't count on: you can suppress testimony, you can ridicule witnesses, you can control narratives in the press, but you cannot erase experience. My father knew what he saw. I know what I've seen, and across the world, millions of others know too.

Since the 1930s, there have always been ex-government, science, civilian, and military people who have had similar paranormal experiences. Many have come forward via channels like my YouTube show, UFOs On The Level, to share their encounters. I feel they are kindred spirits, people who have had out-of-this-world events thrust upon them and found the courage to speak.

My childhood bedroom taught me more in one EMDR session than years of researching and reading ever could. Whatever those figures were, wherever they exist in space and time, they pointed me toward questions I'm still answering. The fear has turned into a lifelong curiosity that I cannot quit, and that's where the real journey begins.

# CHAPTER 4

## TIME IS NOT LINEAR

We experience time as an arrow, with the past behind us, the present happening now, and our future ahead. Time is a simple straight line, right? That is what we were taught, but that is not reality. That is the illusion.

It's useful for navigating daily life, but fundamentally incorrect about the nature of reality. We've been sold the idea that time moves like an arrow with the past behind us, future ahead, and the present ticking by in neat little seconds, but that's not how it really works. Time is slippery. It stretches, it compresses, and sometimes it feels like it folds in on itself. Ever notice how childhood summers seemed endless, yet now entire years vanish in a blink? That is not nostalgia, it's a clue. A sign that the way we experience time is far stranger than the textbooks admit. I know it's hard to wrap your head around, but stick with me, this helps us understand UFOs and the nature of reality.

John Warner IV describes time as a flexible force, similar to gravity, and views gravity as the driving factor behind time. According to physicists Jack Sarfatti and Dr. Eric Davis, time occurs simultaneously and is always changing.

If we rationalize this concept, it changes everything we think we know about UFOs, consciousness, and what is possible. Because if time isn't linear, then precognition isn't paranormal; it's perception. Retrocausality isn't a paradox; it is physics, and the future influencing the past isn't science fiction; it's quantum mechanics.

The UFO phenomenon may understand this and operate within it. It may use time differently than we do. This is why UFO encounters often involve missing time, temporal anomalies, and experiences that don't fit the linear sequential narrative.

UFOs and their occupants, both ours and theirs, are not limited by time as understood in current scientific discourse. Period.

## QUANTUM TIME—THE PHYSICS

I did thorough research on all of this, and I will try to explain it as simply as I understand it. I am in no way an expert on any of this, but something has driven me to see this connection and to outline it as a plausible explanation for some aspects of The Phenomenon. Let's start with Einstein, who cracked the first layer of this mystery. Time is not absolute because gravity changes it, and so does speed. Your clock and mine do not tick at the same rate if we are moving at different speeds or standing in different places on Earth. That was shocking in 1905, and quantum physics takes it even further.[27]

This led theorists such as Cornelis Rietdijk and Hilary Putnam to argue that the past, present, and future coexist in a static "block universe."[28] We don't experience the flow of time. We have the illusion of movement along fixed spacetime world lines. They say that all moments exist simultaneously.

Quantum mechanics goes further. Way further. Into territory that sounds impossible but is experimentally verified. I had to look at all of this from the perspective of The Phenomenon and UFOs to make sense of it.

Here is where it gets wild. Experiments show that the future can influence the past. Decisions you make now can change what has already happened. Sounds impossible, right? It is not. The delayed choice experiments prove this. A photon goes through slits and acts like a wave or a particle, depending on what you decide after the fact. The past waits for the present to tell it what to be. It's also probable via the quantum eraser experiment, as it showed that the temporal order of events depends on the observer and the measurements made.[29]

Then you have quantum entanglement, which adds another layer of weirdness. Two particles separated by light-years act as if they were one. Einstein called it spooky action at a distance. It ignores space and time completely, and information moves without caring about sequence.

The act of measuring NOW determines what WAS. The past isn't fixed until it is observed.[30] Variants of Wheeler's delayed-choice experiment show that present observations can change how past events unfold. They observed quantum interference patterns even after "which path" information had been collected. From what I've seen in these experiments, it's clear that it's really the context, not just a simple sequence, that shapes both the order in which things happen and the reasons behind them.

Most fundamental equations work equally well forward or backward in time. The universe doesn't prefer one direction. We do because of entropy and consciousness. It's built into our structure.

This suggests that the past isn't a static collection of facts, but rather a cloud of possibilities that becomes defined when we observe it, much like the future. It implies that causation might move both forward and backward, and that time itself is simply an orientation within spacetime rather than an absolute limit. The sense of 'now' we have is actually created at the intersection of consciousness and reality, rather than being reality in its pure form. I know it's a lot to rationalize.

Mainstream physics also proposes multiple complex conceptions of time. If you think the leading minds in physics have this all figured out, you would be mistaken. Closed time-like curves from general relativity allow time travel and violate linear dynamics. Then you have multiverse theories and Everett's many-worlds interpretation, which all propose branching timelines[31]. Even the holographic models suggest time might be an emergent property from quantum fluctuations in space's microstructure.

Philosophy also challenges linear time. J. Ellis McTaggart argued that time is unreal because the past, present, and future all exist simultaneously. He saw the "flow" of time as an illusion.[32] Ancient philosophies like Hinduism and Buddhism describe cyclical time as a wheel that spins, always moving in a circle.

## THE NEUTRINO CONNECTION

Neutrinos are ghost particles that pass through everything, including the Earth, walls, and your body, without interacting. Trillions of them are passing through you right now. They are produced by stars, Earth's radioactive decay, cosmic rays, and nuclear reactions.

They're the second most abundant particle in the universe after photons, and we can barely detect them. They don't want to be measured like an antisocial particle avoiding interaction with normal matter at a party. They're weird in ways that suggest time isn't what we think it is at all.

Neutrino oscillation means that as neutrinos travel, they can transform from electron to muon to tau types, and back again. This transformation happens spontaneously rather than through interactions, implying that neutrinos shift between different states, possibilities, or even timelines as they move through spacetime. Nothing else we know of can do this at the moment.

Another theory says that neutrinos are massless. Experiments show they have mass, but it is almost immeasurable. This suggests that they exist partially outside the standard model and partially outside the constraints of normal physics.

Other experiments have detected neutrinos apparently arriving before they should. Seems like this would be faster than light travel, or are they accessing different temporal pathways we haven't yet understood? The results are controversial but persistent amongst the studies.

Tom DeLonge and others speculate that advanced civilizations might use neutrinos for communication. Why? Because they pass through everything. No shielding blocks them, and distance does not limit them. If they can carry information outside normal temporal constraints and if neutrino communication works retroactively or instantaneously, then you've got time-independent information transfer. If you want to send information forward or backward in time, for example, you could do it theoretically via neutrinos if you know how to encode and decode that information.

What if UFOs travel not only through space, but also across time? Maybe their seemingly impossible speeds and accelerations aren't about rapid movement through space, but rather about manipulating time itself. Instead of moving quickly in space, could they actually be shifting sideways through time?

This could explain instantaneous accelerations with no G-forces in their reference frame. Disappearing and reappearing by moving between temporal states. Multiple witness timelines in which different observers access different temporal slices, and missing time during encounters when consciousness desynchronizes from linear time. Precognitive sightings where craft are visible before "arriving" because time isn't linear for them.

Speculative? Absolutely, but consistent with quantum physics, neutrino research, and UFO phenomenology.

## RETROCAUSALITY AND THE PHENOMENON

If the future can influence the past, if causation flows in both directions, then the UFO phenomenon makes more sense.

Encounters often feel orchestrated. Like they were supposed to happen, people say that they were drawn to specific locations at specific times through seemingly random decisions that weren't random at all.

My family and I went outside to see the orbs, which was not planned, but it led to an orb experience that changed everything. Was that choice actually free will? Or was the future experience pulling us toward it, creating conditions for an encounter that needed to happen from a future perspective?

Experiencers report this again and again: "I was supposed to be there." "Something told me to look up." "I don't know why I went outside, but I felt compelled." Retrocausality explains this as the future encounter exerting backward influence, guiding participants into position and making "random" choices that ensure contact occurs.

This isn't determinism. It's probability manipulation. The future doesn't erase free will, but it influences the likelihood of choices leading to specific outcomes. You're still choosing, and your choices are being nudged from a temporal direction you don't or can't perceive.

The Phenomenon might operate this way naturally. Existing across time rather than in it. Seeing probabilities rather than a single timeline and interacting with the past and future simultaneously from their perspective. Making "first contact" is simultaneous contact across all points where connection is possible.

This explains prophecy, precognition, and remote viewing of future events. Maybe it's not magic or supernatural. Maybe it's just consciousness accessing information from a different temporal position than linear now.

It might explain why disclosure feels inevitable. Maybe it is, but from a future perspective. Maybe successful disclosure is already accomplished in the future, exerting backward influence on the present, making each step toward transparency feel necessary, guided, and orchestrated by forces we don't fully understand but are taking part in anyway.

## THE MANDELA EFFECT AND COLLECTIVE CONSCIOUSNESS

If these quantum theories are sound and there's no reason to believe they aren't, could quantum erasure, delayed choice, and retrocausality explain the Mandela Effect?

The Mandela Effect refers to large groups of people sharing "false memories" of past events. For example, many remember Nelson Mandela dying in prison, which contradicts historical records. Some theorists suggest parallel universes, simulated realities, or time travelers causing ripple effects, and quantum physics might offer clues without resorting to science fiction.

Quantum experiments show that linear time doesn't hold at microscopic scales. Quantum entanglement, delayed choice, and quantum erasing defy conventional cause-and-effect. Observations made now determine prior states of quantum systems. Researchers find evidence of nonlinear time in effects influencing their own causes.

Could these quantum properties scale up and explain the Mandela Effect? Maybe mental observation has enough power to ripple backward and reorder past timelines. People remembering alternate histories might not have "false" memories. Their minds could be introducing temporal discontinuities in the direction of subjective time.

Can the conscious mind act like a quantum measurement device? Individuals might experience altered timelines.

Collective consciousness entangled with surrounding matter might bend reality at subtle but detectable levels.

Could this be an example of a worldwide egregor, a tulpa, or both?

You are now trying to figure out what those two terms are, so let me explain both. A (Tulpa), from Tibetan Buddhism, is a thoughtform, an entity created entirely in the mind. Through focused meditation and visualization, people can bring these thoughtforms to life, giving them personalities, memories, and emotions.[33]

An (Egregor) is a non-physical entity created by the collective energy, emotions, and beliefs of a group. It's like a shared pool of energy that grows stronger with group focus. It can influence behavior and even manifest in the real world.[34]

One famous case involves the Berenstain Bears. Many remember it as "Berenstein" with an "e." Searches show hundreds of examples of the wrong spelling. It's hard to explain this widespread memory without temporal anomalies.

In quantum delayed choice, present measurements determine past outcomes. For example, whether a photon behaves like a wave or a particle. In quantum eraser experiments, erasing "which path" information in the present changes past behavior. Likewise, the spelling of "Berenstain" might have existed in multiple quantum possibilities until mass observation locked in the "stain" version.

One of my favorite examples is "Mirror, mirror on the wall." Many people remember this line from Snow White. If you watch the current versions, she actually says, "Magic mirror." Could mass observation have collapsed the timeline into the "magic" version? Could the egregor have formed and become stronger than individual consciousness? It might mean that each of us has a different interpretation of "time" and "space," separate from the "global consciousness."

## CONSCIOUSNESS OUTSIDE OF TIME

Here's where it gets strange. Consciousness might not be bound by time at all. Near-death experiences describe life reviews that happen in an instant yet contain entire lifetimes. Meditation can dissolve time completely. Awareness exists, but sequence disappears. Past and future become accessible as now.

Psychedelic experiences often destroy linear time. Users report millennia passing in minutes, or hours compressed into seconds, or complete dissolution of temporal structure where cause and effect become meaningless categories.

Remote-viewing experiments show that consciousness can access information regardless of temporal distance. Past, present, and future are equally accessible to trained viewers. Not perfectly or clearly, but consistently enough to prove consciousness isn't locked to "now."

What if consciousness is fundamentally atemporal? What if temporal experience is an interface, like a spatial interface constructed by the brain to navigate physical reality, but not reflecting consciousness's actual nature?

Then you, the consciousness that you are, exist outside of time. Your brain creates a linear experience. Your memories create a narrative self that exists in time, and underneath, awareness itself doesn't happen in time. It exists in something else, the eternal now that encompasses all moments simultaneously.

That's what mystics have said forever, and various mystery schools have taught. That is what psychedelic experiences reveal, and increasingly, it's what quantum physics and neuroscience data suggest.

**You don't exist within time. Time exists within you.**

In other words, our sense of time is shaped by consciousness, rather than consciousness taking place inside time. I know it's still hard to conceptualize, believe me.

## A NECESSARY ASIDE: EVENTS THAT SHAPE COLLECTIVE CONSCIOUSNESS

Massive world-changing events create powerful (egregors). The collective emotional energy, focused attention, and shared trauma of billions of people might generate thoughtforms powerful enough to influence reality itself.

One notable example is 9/11, an event that fundamentally altered global consciousness, justified unprecedented surveillance powers, and reshaped international relations. A growing body of research and eyewitness accounts suggests anomalies in the official narrative, like documented insider trading predicting airline stock crashes, alleged hijackers later found alive, and a hijacker's passport found on the street. At the same time, aircraft black boxes were vaporized, warnings from intelligence agencies were ignored, and Ground Zero recovery was halted with debris disposed of without forensic analysis.[35]

These contradictions make people question official stories. For many, 9/11 is their first "conspiracy theory," a term, incidentally, coined by the CIA to discredit people questioning JFK's assassination.[36]

Whether inside job or not, 9/11 demonstrates how the U.S. Intelligence Community can operate without oversight, how official narratives can override evidence, and how collective trauma creates lasting reality distortions. It shows the power of egregors formed by shared belief and the malleability of consensus reality when enough energy focuses on a single narrative.

This connects to UFO disclosure because it reveals the same control mechanisms, classification systems hiding truth, ridicule preventing inquiry, official stories contradicting evidence, and institutional power determining what gets called "real."

## LIVING WITH NON-LINEAR TIME

So, what do you do with this? How does understanding time's non-linearity change how you live? Here are some ways to surf the timeline.

Time isn't what we've been told it is. Once you embrace that, your experience of reality shifts.

Those precognitive flashes you get, the ones where you *know* something before it happens? Pay attention to them. Test and track them. You might be accessing information from possible futures. I've learned to trust these intuitive hits, even when they don't make sense in the moment.

Synchronicities matter too. Those meaningful coincidences that make you stop and think, they're not just random. Future events might be reaching back, subtly shaping your present choices. Retrocausality. It sounds like science fiction, but quantum eraser experiments suggest your present actions can influence what's already happened. The changes might be subtle, visible only at the quantum level, but they're real.

And the past? It's not as fixed as we think.

If you've experienced missing time, especially after an unusual encounter, the first thing to do is not to panic. Your consciousness may have slipped out of step with linear time. I know how unsettling that feels and how insane that sounds when you say it out loud, but try not to force it into a tidy narrative. Just document what you remember, as it comes, because even the fragments matter.

Meditation helps. It gives you direct access to states beyond temporal thinking, where you experience firsthand that awareness isn't confined by time. This isn't a belief. It's knowing, developed through practice. Sometimes it's challenging. It's so hard for me to do this personally, but at times it's profound.

Consider the block universe, which is the idea that every moment, past, present, and future, exists simultaneously. You're just moving through slices of this timeless whole. All of your choices matter, and nothing is truly lost. No one is truly lost. There's comfort in that.

Then there's the Mandela Effect. Collective memories of alternate histories. Does the past change through observation, or does conscious awareness shift between timelines? There's no definitive proof, but it invites us to appreciate something essential: time is fluid, our choices are powerful, and the interplay between awareness and reality is far more mysterious than we've been taught.

Time flows in one direction because entropy increases and because we remember the past, not the future. Experimentation shows that causation appears unidirectional. This is because our brains construct experience this way.

Underneath time is a dimension in spacetime and a direction you can move or a perspective you can shift. It is not a destiny you're imprisoned in.

The Phenomenon knows this and operates with it, using time as a tool rather than a constraint. Increasingly, we're learning the same through quantum physics and, separately, through consciousness research. Most of all, through direct personal experiences that show time isn't what we think.

While the arrow of time helps us navigate everyday life, it does not represent an absolute "truth." It's a lens through which our biology interprets a reality that is far more complex. It helps to remember that you are not confined by time; you are only experiencing it. As your awareness, understanding, and abilities grow, you gain greater freedom in time. It's not a guarantee but a way to conceptualize day-to-day reality.

This is not time travel as science fiction imagines. Still, more like time awareness, time navigation, or time consciousness that lets you access information outside the linear now and influence probability in ways that seem magical but are just an advanced understanding of physics we're still discovering.

That's part of human awakening, evolution, and ultimately a large part of disclosure.

Time is not your prison. It's your playground, and once we know the rules can change, we should all learn to play.

You are way more powerful than you know.

# CHAPTER 5

## YOU ARE MORE POWERFUL THAN YOU KNOW

The biggest lie is not that UFOs do not exist, or that we are alone in the universe, or that consciousness is nothing more than brain activity. The largest lie is simpler, quieter, and far more consequential. You are powerless.

You are described as limited, mundane, and ordinary. A biological accident stumbling through meaningless existence. Consciousness emerged from matter through random processes. You are told consciousness is an emergent quirk of matter, and when the brain stops, you stop with it. No connection to anything greater. No capacity for direct knowing, healing, manifesting, or influencing reality through intention.

That is the deception, and it is not a single claim floating on its own. It underwrites the materialist worldview, validates institutional authority, and feeds systems that operate best when humans see themselves as small, dependent, and manageable. It worked for generations because it was absorbed and repeated until it sounded like common sense. Entire civilizations were built on the assumption that humans are weak by nature and therefore require external authority for meaning, order, and truth.

That assumption is no longer holding. It is cracking under the weight of accumulated evidence, lived experience, and the slow rediscovery of capacities that were never lost, only dismissed, ridiculed, and suppressed.

You are more powerful than you know. Recognizing that, developing it, and learning to hold it responsibly is the real disclosure. Personal reclamation of capacities you always had but were told didn't exist. Not a formal announcement, not an admission from authority, but a personal reclamation of abilities that were always present and consistently denied.

What you are about to read is not theory, and it isn't meant to be passively consumed. It's a reframing, one that challenges the assumptions most of us were given about who we are, where consciousness comes from, and what is possible within this reality. We are taught from early childhood to see ourselves as isolated, limited, and dependent, and that worldview did not arise by accident.

This chapter is about reclamation. About stripping away the inherited narratives that deny human potential and reconnecting with what has always been present beneath them. It is about understanding what you are beyond social roles, credentials, or biology, not as an accident, but as a localized expression of something far more capable than we were encouraged to believe.

For centuries, we have been told that imagination is fantasy, intuition is coincidence, and meaning is projection. History does not support that claim, and neither do the experiences of countless individuals who have encountered something that behaves less like randomness and more like interaction. Once the assumption of powerlessness begins to fail, the structures built upon it rapidly lose stability.

What follows is a framework for understanding reality not from the outside looking in, but from the inside remembering itself. It begins with the source from which all things arise and the simple yet disruptive truth that changes what it means to be human and to be connected to Cosmic Source.

When I refer to Cosmic Source, I am not describing a god in the traditional religious sense, nor a vague spiritual abstraction. I am pointing to the underlying intelligence from which all reality emerges. It is a source of consciousness that generates matter, energy, time, and the laws that govern them. Every system we observe, from quantum behavior to biological life to human awareness itself, appears to arise from the same foundational substrate. Whether described in scientific terms as a unified field or in philosophical language as infinite intelligence, the implication is the same: consciousness is not a byproduct of the universe; it is fundamental to it.

The Law of One is the simplest and most disruptive implication of this idea. It is the idea that all things, at their most fundamental level, are expressions of the same source consciousness. Separation is not an objective feature of reality but a functional illusion, one that allows for experience, contrast, learning, and growth. Individual identity exists, but it exists within unity, not apart from it. The universe is not a collection of isolated objects interacting randomly; it is a single system of awareness temporarily experiencing itself as many.

According to the Law of One framework, consciousness evolves through experience. Individual beings move through expanded states of perception by making choices under conditions of uncertainty. Free will is not a narrative convenience. Without it, growth would be impossible. The tension between control and cooperation, between service to self and service to others, is not moral theater. It is the engine of development itself, and each choice reinforces either the illusion of separation or the remembrance of unity.

This model reframes humanity's role in the universe in an uncomfortable way. We are not insignificant observers in the cold, mechanistic cosmos, nor are we powerless victims of forces beyond our comprehension. Instead, we are participants in a larger evolutionary process of consciousness, capable of shaping both individual reality and collective outcomes through intention, perception, and action. This has profound implications, especially when examined alongside historical power structures, technological suppression, and the recurring theme of controlled access to knowledge.

If consciousness is foundational, then controlling perception becomes a form of dominance more effective than controlling territory or resources. Limiting what people believe about reality limits what they believe they are capable of. From that perspective, the Law of One is not merely a philosophical framework; it is a threat. A population that understands itself as fragmented, separate, and powerless is easier to manage than one that recognizes its shared origin and latent creative potential.

Cosmic Source and the Law of One do not demand belief. They invite examination. If examined seriously, they raise an unavoidable question: if unity is the base state of reality, then who benefits from convincing us that we are alone, divided, and small?

## ABILITIES YOU MAY HAVE

What does mystical "power" look like? These are not Hollywood magic or superhero fantasies, but real abilities documented across cultures, practiced in mystery schools, and emerging spontaneously in experiencers.

Intuition isn't magic; it's knowing without the usual steps, the gut feeling that turns out to be right. Healing? That's not fantasy either. People have influenced their own bodies and others' for centuries, whether through prayer, energy work, or sheer intention, and telepathy. It's not about reading minds like a comic book villain; it's about connection, sensing emotions, and sharing impressions without a single word spoken.

None of this is supernatural. It's natural and a normal part of human capacity that gets suppressed by cultural conditioning, educational systems, and religious frameworks that deny these abilities exist. The ancient Mystery Schools knew, and they preserved the practices for developing these capacities. That's what initiation cultivated, not belief systems, but actual abilities through progressive training, and now those abilities are spontaneously emerging. Experiencers develop them without formal training. I believe that contact accelerates this development. UFO encounters often trigger latent capacities.

Why? Because The Phenomenon interacts at a consciousness level. It stimulates development, tests capability, and responds to awareness, expanding beyond normal parameters.

These abilities aren't fantasy. They're your birthright, and developing them is crucial not just for personal growth but for humanity's evolution and response to what's coming.

## THE SUPPRESSION OF POWER

If these capacities are real and documented, their absence from mainstream understanding requires an explanation. The explanation is suppression, layered and persistent, enforced through ridicule, fear, and institutional certainty.

Religious institutions historically labeled these abilities heretical or demonic, and that continues even now. Scientific frameworks dismissed them as impossible while educational systems excluded them entirely. Media portrayed them as absurd, fraudulent, or sinister, and medicine often pathologized those who reported them, training them to distrust their own perceptions.

The message stayed consistent across channels.

These abilities are not real. If you believe you have them, something is wrong with you.

The result was an internal shutdown. People learned not to trust intuition, ignore synchronicities, and not to acknowledge non-ordinary perception. That disconnection creates vulnerability. When intuition is ignored, deception becomes easier. When embodied awareness is dismissed, dependency on external authority increases.

Suppression does not protect humanity from danger. It protects power structures from empowered individuals. Once you develop direct knowing and trust inner authority, governance becomes more difficult, and control becomes less reliable. That is why reclamation has always been disruptive.

## CONSCIOUSNESS AS TECHNOLOGY

Imagine consciousness not as a byproduct of matter but as a fundamental force or a technology in itself. Not metaphorically, but an actual mechanism for interfacing with reality at levels mainstream science doesn't acknowledge.

Ancient mystery schools understood this. Their practices weren't superstition. They were engineering manuals for consciousness, precise techniques producing repeatable results, passed from teacher to student because they worked. Meditation isn't just a relaxation exercise. It's consciousness technology that allows for altering brainwave states and accessing non-ordinary awareness. Creating conditions for abilities that seem impossible from normal waking consciousness.

Ritual functions as operational protocol, using gesture, symbol, and focused intention to direct consciousness toward specific outcomes. This works whether you believe in supernatural forces or understand it as applied psychotechnology. Consider prayer not as begging a supernatural entity for favors, but as a focused intention broadcast at the level of consciousness, with documented effects on healing, manifestation, and synchronicity, regardless of the theological framework explaining why it works. Visualization operates the same way. Far from daydreaming, it programs probability. Consciousness creates templates that reality tends toward. Athletes and other successful people use it, and this also works whether you call it manifestation, mental rehearsal, or the law of attraction. Energy work isn't pseudoscience either. It's consciousness interacting with biological fields. Reiki, healing touch, and therapeutic touch all have documented effects, even when practitioners can't explain the mechanism, and the effects defy explanation.

These aren't beliefs but technologies, techniques producing measurable results. Suppressed not because they don't work but because they work too well. Widespread access would shift power away from institutions and toward individuals.

Mystery schools preserved them through centuries of persecution, and now they're appearing again, available to anyone willing to practice. No special gifts are needed. However, some people have a natural aptitude, just like any skill. We can all play basketball, but there are some of us, like Michael Jordan or LeBron James, who excel at it with natural talent. The same is true of consciousness abilities; we all can do it, but the more we practice, the better we become.

## SOUND AS A CONSCIOUSNESS TOOL

Sonic technology can influence human experience through specific frequencies. Binaural beats, created by playing different tones in each ear, generate a perceived third frequency that entrains brainwaves to desired states such as Theta for meditation, Delta for deep rest, and Gamma for heightened awareness.

Ancient traditions knew this. For example, Tibetan singing bowls, Shamanic drumming, Gregorian chants, and Aboriginal didgeridoo. Each of these uses sound to shift consciousness, open perception, facilitate healing, and induce spiritual experience.

This is not superstition, it's physics. Sound is vibration. Bodies are matter vibrating at specific frequencies. If you introduce sound at resonant frequencies, matter responds: cells reorganize, neural patterns shift, and consciousness expands.

Many composers create music specifically for CE5/HIC (Human-Initiated Contact), meditation, consciousness exploration, and healing.

Listeners describe powerful experiences like visions, contact, healing, and synchronicities that are not due to magic, but because sound is a rediscovered, refined, and systematically applied technology.

You can develop abilities faster with proper sonic support. Meditation deepens, intuition strengthens, and perception expands by just using tools designed for this purpose.

RECLAIMING YOUR POWER—PRACTICAL STEPS.

Understanding that you're powerful means nothing without development, practice, and the cultivation of these capacities. Here are some steps you can take now that, at the very least, make you more aware of yourself and your place within the greater cosmos.

Start with daily meditation, even just 10 minutes. Quiet your mind, access stillness. Everything else is built from this foundation. I know this is hard for almost everyone, but if you force yourself to try this daily, it will get easier. From there, trust your intuition and pay attention to those gut feelings, test them, and track their accuracy. If the first thought you get at a crossroads is left, GO LEFT. Trust the Gestalt instincts and thoughts. Listen to them and follow wherever they lead you. Learn to distinguish intuition from fear and wishful thinking from ego. They're not the same thing, and with practice, you'll know the difference.

Then practice energy awareness. Notice your own energy and sense others' energy. Walk into different spaces and feel how some feel heavy, others light. These feelings are real, even if mainstream science doesn't yet measure them. Work with synchronicities, too. Observe meaningful coincidences, follow their guidance. Reality is far more responsive than you've been taught.

Next, set clear, focused intentions, then let go. Release attachment to specific outcomes. Allow reality to organize itself around your purpose. This paradox is essential. Develop a daily practice such as yoga, tai chi, qigong, ritual magic, Christian mysticism, or anything that resonates with you. The tradition matters less than the consistency, and abilities grow through regular use.

It is also important to connect with others who are developing similar capacities. Share experiences and learn from those ahead of you. Support those just beginning the journey. This work isn't meant to be done alone. Study mystery school teachings, not as belief systems but as methods. These are techniques preserved across centuries for understanding how consciousness works.

Most of all, stay grounded. This is crucial. Spiritual growth without practical grounding leads to instability. Maintain your physical health, your relationships, and your career. Balance the mystical with the pragmatic. I've seen too many people lose themselves by going too far, too fast, without a proper foundation.

Finally, use your abilities in service, for healing, truth, and the evolution of humanity, not for ego or power. That's what this is all about.

Power without wisdom is dangerous, and abilities without ethics become vulnerable to manipulation. Consciousness development that lacks grounding produces instability.

If these skills are developed responsibly, wielded ethically, and grounded in service, it transforms not just you but everyone you encounter. That's how paradigm shifts. Change happens individually as each person grows, each awakening unfolds, and each ability is restored, one step at a time.

## MANIFESTATION IS REAL—BUT NOT WHAT YOU THINK.

Let's explore this controversial idea: manifestation. Creating reality through consciousness. Thoughts becoming actual things.

New Age corrupted this concept and made it simplistic. "Think positive, and you'll be rich!" "Visualize, and it manifests!" "The universe is your wish-granting genie!" This reductive nonsense set up millions of people for failure and disappointment.

That's not how it works, and it is exactly why so many people try manifestation, fail spectacularly, then dismiss the entire concept as nonsense without understanding what they were actually attempting.

However, manifestation is real. Just more nuanced than the Law of Attraction marketing suggests, requiring understanding of actual mechanics rather than magical thinking.

What gets missed is that manifestation isn't about desire; it's about alignment. Alignment isn't emotional excitement or positive thinking layered on top of doubt. It's coherence between consciousness, belief, intention, and action, all moving in the same direction without internal contradiction. This idea isn't new; it's ancient. Long before modern self-help repackaged it into marketable content, the Hermetic principles laid out the mechanics of how consciousness interacts with reality in precise detail.

Hermetic teaching begins with a direct premise: all is mind. Not metaphorically but functionally, as an operational principle. Reality is structured consciousness, expressed through matter according to laws we're only beginning to understand. Thought alone doesn't create outcomes in a simple cause-and-effect relationship, but mental states shape perception, perception shapes behavior, and behavior alters probability fields. Manifestation, in this model, is not magic or supernatural intervention. Its leverage is applied to reality's underlying structure.

Another core principle is correspondence, the idea that patterns repeat across layers of reality from quantum to cosmic. Internal order reflects and influences external order. Internal chaos produces external friction and resistance. This is exactly why manifestation fails when someone tries to "think" their way into change while staying internally fragmented, conflicted, or chaotic. The outer world mirrors the true internal state, not the affirmations layered on top, like paint over rust.

Vibration explains why intention without clarity goes nowhere productive. Emotional state, belief structure, and focus all carry momentum, an actual energetic signature that reality responds to. Indecision, fear, or contradiction dilute force, scattering energy across multiple incompatible outcomes. You don't need constant positivity or relentless optimism; you need consistency in what you're broadcasting. Reality responds less to what you say you want and more to what you repeatedly reinforce through thought, feeling, and action.

Hermeticism also acknowledges polarity and rhythm; movement between extremes is natural in any system. Mastery isn't avoiding lows or maintaining an artificial high; it's learning to stabilize awareness within fluctuation. This is where discipline replaces fantasy, where real work begins. Conscious creation requires understanding when to act, when to wait, and when internal conditions are misaligned for forward motion.

Then there's the principle most New Age teaching avoids because it requires responsibility, Cause and Effect. Nothing manifests randomly or by cosmic accident. If you're living reactively, you are experiencing effects generated elsewhere by systems, beliefs, or decisions you didn't consciously choose. Reclamation begins when awareness allows you to move back into the role of cause rather than remaining in the perpetual role of effect. Finally, Gender, not biological sex, but the creative dynamic itself, requires both receptive and projective forces. All creation requires interaction between these polarities. Vision without execution is a fantasy that never touches ground. Action without insight is blind momentum, producing random results. Reality forms where the two meet and integrate.

This is why manifestation isn't magic or wish fulfillment. It's disciplined participation in a structured system with rules and mechanics. The Hermetic principles don't promise instant results or guarantee specific outcomes, but they explain clearly why reclaiming power requires self-knowledge, internal order, and sustained intent aligned with action. When those conditions are met, reality doesn't resist your efforts. It responds and reorganizes.

Consciousness does not bring objects into existence from nothing by sheer will, but consciousness can interact with probability fields and has a subtle but measurable influence on outcomes. It's not magic in a supernatural sense; it's quantum mechanics meeting intention in ways we're only beginning to measure scientifically.

The observer effect in physics demonstrates that measurement changes the system being observed in fundamental ways. Consciousness collapses the wave function, selecting one outcome from multiple possibilities. Not woo or mystical thinking; it's a documented scientific phenomenon with implications that extend far beyond the laboratory.

If observation affects quantum events, if consciousness shapes measurement outcomes at the smallest scales, then intention might influence probability at the macro scale through accumulated effect. Not deterministically guaranteeing specific results, but probabilistically, shifting the likelihood of outcomes without controlling every variable and creating conditions where the desired outcome becomes more probable than it was before the intention was applied.

That's real manifestation. Not a cosmic door dash or the universe bending to your will, but probability engineering through focused awareness applied consistently over time.

Group consciousness has demonstrated the ability to manifest physical phenomena observable by multiple witnesses. Multiple people are seeing the same impossible things at the same time. Not individual hallucination or mass delusion, but collective creation or perception of something responding to collective focus and intention.

Ancient traditions understood this, and maybe that's the real reason rituals produce tangible results and group meditation creates measurable effects, or timing your intentions with astrologically significant moments seems to amplify what manifests. These people weren't superstitious; they were working with consciousness-reality interaction in practical ways, they just didn't have our modern vocabulary to explain the mechanics.

Mystery schools taught practical techniques developed through centuries of experimentation. Clear intention setting, not vague wishes, but a directed will toward a specific outcome. Along with emotional alignment, feeling as if already achieved, saturating awareness with the reality of the desired state. Release of attachment, letting go of a specific path while maintaining clarity of destination and keeping a consistent focus through regular practice, not occasionally hoping when it is convenient. All while holding an ethical framework, ensuring manifestation serves the highest good rather than ego gratification.

This isn't "think positive and get a Porsche" nonsense sold by self-help gurus. This is understanding that you participate in reality creation, whether you're conscious of it or not. Your consciousness matters because your focus affects outcomes and your expectations shape experiences in measurable ways.

Not because the universe bends to your desires like a cosmic servant, but because you're part of the probability field and not a separate observer. Your awareness, intention, and emotional state all influence which possibilities actualize from the quantum foam of potential.

So how does this work in actual practice? Let's say you want something specific. Get absolutely clear on what that is, write it down in detail, make it concrete and specific. Feel it as if it's already real, let that feeling saturate your awareness completely. Then comes the hard part: let go of your expectations about how it's supposed to arrive or what form it should take. Let reality organize itself around your intention rather than micromanaging the process from a limited perspective. Watch for synchronicities that point the way, follow the doors that open naturally, but don't force paths that resist you or require constant struggle.

Your latent abilities develop the same way through intention and practice. You want intuition? Set a clear intention to develop it. Practice noticing subtle signals. Notice small hits, validate them, and build confidence through accumulated success. Trust develops through validation, and validation comes through practice. Practice requires maintaining the intention consistently.

It's not magic in a supernatural sense. It's an applied consciousness technology working through natural law, and it works whether you understand the mechanism or not, just like electricity works without understanding the physics of electron flow.

## THE COLLECTIVE AWAKENING

Individual power matters enormously, but something larger is happening simultaneously, and some are calling it a collective awakening. Millions of humans are developing these capacities at the same time across the planet. It feels coordinated because, in some sense, it is, not through centralized planning but through resonance and mutual reinforcement.

The Consortium, described as a loose group of beings from other star systems and dimensions assisting humanity's awakening, says it is helping, supporting, and guiding this process. They are not doing it for us because that would defeat the purpose. We must do the work ourselves and develop these capacities through our own effort. They are helping by creating conditions for awakening, removing certain blocks, amplifying certain frequencies, and making development easier than it's been in previous eras.

Why now? There could be a multitude of factors operating simultaneously.

One theory connects to cosmic timing. Our solar system is moving through regions of the galaxy with varying energetic properties, electromagnetic fields, and cosmic radiation patterns. Ancient calendars from the Mayan, Vedic, and other traditions predicted this transition thousands of years in advance. Astronomy meets consciousness in ways that sound mystical but might be measurable physics.

Why now may also have less to do with belief and more to do with pattern recognition through history. Civilizations across history treated celestial cycles as meaningful markers of transition, not superstition. From Mayan and Vedic calendars to long-term astronomical tracking that linked cosmic movement to societal change, the pattern holds. Even in the modern era, astrology never disappeared; it simply went underground, out of academic scrutiny. Astrologer Jeane Dixon famously advised multiple U.S. presidents, and administrations from Franklin D. Roosevelt through Richard Nixon quietly consulted astrologers and timing advisors when making decisions of consequence.[37] Whatever one thinks of the practice itself, the behavior reveals something important. Those closest to power have long understood that timing matters, belief shapes outcome, and cycles influence events. The public was taught to dismiss these ideas as irrational and pseudoscience, while private rooms operated entirely under different assumptions. That contrast alone raises uncomfortable questions. If celestial timing is meaningless, why has it so consistently been taken seriously behind closed doors by people with access to the best information?

We may have reached a technological threshold where we're now powerful enough to destroy ourselves completely, requiring consciousness evolution to match our current technological capability or face extinction. Evolution or annihilation might be our only options, forcing development whether we're ready or not.

There may be enough humans awakening simultaneously that collective consciousness shifts, like the Hundredth Monkey Effect. At this theoretical tipping point, knowledge spreads rapidly throughout the species, reaching a critical mass that makes further suppression impossible.

Could non-human intelligence be helping us? Not saving us, but providing tools, information, and energetic support. Contact experiences as well as near-death experiences often trigger the development of abilities instantly, like a consciousness firmware upgrade through direct transmission.

Call it God, Source, Universal Intelligence, The Great Architect of the Universe, but maybe something is orchestrating this moment in human development. Not controlling outcomes or forcing compliance, but guiding gently, offering assistance, creating conditions while respecting free will.

You are not developing these capacities alone, isolated in your own journey. You're part of a massive wave, with millions of people awakening simultaneously across the planet. Each person who develops their abilities makes it easier for the next person to do the same, like a path being worn through a dense forest by years of walking near the water's edge. Each breakthrough weakens the suppression structure for everyone else, and that builds hope. That's powerful, and it's exactly why disclosure is accelerating, control systems are weakening despite their efforts, and why we're actually witnessing a paradigm shift in real time.

You're not just an individual developing capacities for personal benefit. You are part of species evolution, humanity remembering what it forgot, reclaiming power that has been purposefully and systematically suppressed. Stepping into a potential that is always present but deliberately hidden by those who stand to benefit from human limitation. The paradigm shifts when enough people refuse to pretend they're powerless, when enough people reclaim abilities and trust inner knowing over external authority, when enough people demonstrate what's possible, and others can no longer deny it.

Be one of those people. Develop your capacities through consistent practice. Trust your experiences even when others dismiss them. Share your journey to help others find their way. You are more powerful than you know. It is time to start knowing it and owning it.

## THE BENGSTON METHOD: DOCUMENTED HEALING

Exceptional individuals can reportedly induce measurable changes in timepiece function simply by entering heightened emotional states while gazing at the watch or clock face, suggesting that our energies directly interface with material reality. My Uncle Frank, who had no blood relation, could not wear a watch after WW2. The battery would die within a day or two at most. The only watch I believe he could wear was a wind-up watch, which was odd. I chalked it up to random strangeness until I started researching quantum mechanics and the human mind. Maybe he influenced the watch's behavior with strong beliefs or emotions when he looked at the watch face, or maybe he just bought cheap watches and batteries.

The empirical evidence keeps accruing that we harbor profound innate abilities that exceed the presently accepted scientific limits.

By better understanding the reach of our minds, we open pathways to vastly develop our human potential. When I started learning about energy healing, I came across the work of William Bengston and found it important to share it here.

William Bengston is a professor of sociology who has conducted extensive research on energy healing. As a young man, he befriended a psychic healer named Bennett Mayrick and tested his abilities, finding positive results. He later learned hands-on healing techniques from Mayrick.

In his book The Energy Cure, Bengston outlined the method and conducted controlled experiments showing high cure rates of induced cancers in mice using psychic healing, including having skeptical volunteers successfully heal the mice. He formulated a theory of resonant bonding to explain the efficacy of healing through a shared energetic bond between living things that can influence health.[38]

Further experiments supported his theories, but he faced resistance and disbelief from the mainstream scientific community. He speculated that psi phenomena contradict dominant scientific paradigms and explored the recording and storage of healing energy in materials such as cotton and water, finding positive effects on cell cultures.

His current research investigates the transmission of healing intention through audio recordings. Recent experiments show reduced tumor growth in mice. Other laboratories have directly replicated his original cancer-curing experiments twice, with different personnel each time, achieving similar high cure rates.[39]

An additional informal replication of the mouse experiments was carried out by David Krinsley at Arizona State University, reportedly yielding the same positive results, but the details have not been published. A 2007 study coauthored by Bengston replicated the mouse experiments and explored the effects of distance healing. His original method of hands-on healing of cancers in mice appears to have been officially replicated twice in published studies, with an additional, unpublished, informal replication. His more recent work on transmitting intentions via audio recordings is still in the piloting phase.

Independent, direct replications of his studies by other research teams are still lacking. Bengston has indicated the scientific community has shown little interest in replicating or following up on his experiments so far.

The most amazing thing about this is that he injects these mice with cancer, which, no matter what, will kill them within 28 to 30 days. They perform this hands-on healing technique, which is essentially rapid mental-image cycling by the healer. The mouse looks like it's going to die, and then suddenly these tumors completely vanish.

It gets wilder than that. If you inject the same mouse that has been healed again with the cancer, it cannot get that same cancer again. Furthermore, if you take the blood from the healed mouse and inject it into another mouse that has been injected with the same cancer, it will cure that mouse.[40] I know this sounds wild and improbable, but it's a very fascinating area of study.

Bengston currently sells water through a third-party company that has been treated with its energy cure. You can charge certain items with this healing, like cotton, audio files, and it has the same effect. A large group of people has undergone this hands-on healing, with remarkable results. Check out his book, his many podcast appearances, his website, and all his research information and data. It would be well worth your time, in my opinion.

The results of his peer-reviewed research paper show that reproducible biological changes have been induced by healing energy, whether through direct hands-on healing or through a recording of healing activity. Healing intention can be captured and released, thereby potentially allowing the phenomenon to be more widely disseminated.

Hands-on delivery of the healing intention is stronger than with the recording used in this study, suggesting that the recording may not have fully captured the healing potential.

I found out about Bengston by listening to Tom DeLonge's interviews and following his social media posts.

Did DeLonge have a hand in the healing of his bandmate Mark Hoppus of terminal pancreatic cancer by connecting him with practitioners of the Bengston Method?

This has never been confirmed publicly, but the timing of Hoppus beating stage 4 cancer and DeLonge talking about Bengston is uncanny. Bengston was asked about this in a podcast and declined to comment due to HIPAA and doctor-patient confidentiality. Personally, I believe that Tom helped his longtime friend and bandmate beat cancer with the help of energy healing. Either way, I am thankful that Mark is cancer-free and that Blink-182 is back together, touring the world.

## THE HOPPUS FAMILY AND CHINA LAKE

Mark Hoppus's dad is George "Tex" Hoppus. He has a B.S. in aerospace engineering and an M.S. in electronics engineering. He has worked for thirty-five years as an aerospace engineer, electrical engineer, project manager, and Division Head for the Navy at China Lake. Then he worked for another 10 years as a project manager and Deputy Director of Operations for Jacobs Engineering.[41]

Tex spent over 34 years working as a civilian engineer for the U.S. Naval Air Warfare Center Weapons Division at China Lake, California. His wife, Marti, was a Navy system analyst. Their daughter, Anne, is a project manager for wind energy development. Their son, Steve, is a certified miller at a historic Virginia mill, and their "auxiliary son," Brian, is a Navy software engineer in Seattle.[42]

The entire Hoppus family is deeply entrenched in the military-industrial complex. Also, Mark is a famous rock star in Blink-182 with Tom DeLonge.

Imagine that. What are the odds that DeLonge would go on to lead the current disclosure movement in the United States?

If you look at the correlations, it appears DeLonge was privy to, or at least adjacent to, this weird black special access program world his entire life through his connection to Mark. At the very least, he knew the right people to ask or had enough knowledge to point him in the right direction. Mark's dad spent 34 years at China Lake. Let's look at what is happening there.

# CHINA LAKE: THE NAVY'S SECRET WEAPONS LAB

China Lake is a massive Naval Air Weapons Station in the Mojave Desert covering over 1.1 million acres. It's the Navy's largest single landholding and its biggest weapons research, development, testing, and evaluation facility. I find it very interesting that the Navy has a giant base in the middle of the desert.

Established in 1943, it has been developing advanced weapons and technology for the Navy and other military branches ever since. Most of it is classified. What we do know is that China Lake created the Sidewinder missile and other guided weapons that revolutionized air-to-air combat, including laser weapons systems, unmanned aerial vehicles, and autonomous systems.

The Division has been awarded over 1,600 patents and achieved 50+ world-firsts,[43] including breakthroughs that have shaped the modern world. They pioneered digital computer search 43 years before Google existed. They developed a vast array of technologies, including body-scanning that led to the MRI, automatic airbag sensors, stop-action video, and chemiluminescent light sticks. They also developed non-nuclear components for the first atomic bomb, plastic-bonded explosives, and the Sidewinder air-to-air guided missile. The first sea-based ballistic missile intercept happened there as well. They launched NOTSNIK, the first U.S. satellite, and they built subsystems for the first lunar and Mars landers.

Think about that list. China Lake wasn't just making missiles. They were pioneering technologies that would shape the entire modern world, decades before the public knew they existed.

There are plenty of theories that China Lake has been involved in advanced propulsion and anti-gravity research to develop exotic aircraft and spacecraft. Some speculate that this research led to back-engineering crashed extraterrestrial craft.

In the late 1980s, China Lake began using cloud seeding generators to produce massive artificial clouds over the base to block imaging satellites and spy planes from monitoring secret weapons tests. Lt. Col. Thomas Loh, commander of the program, confirmed they were actively "opaque-ing the overhead sensors" to conceal what was happening on the ground during weapons trials.[44]

There are also claims that China Lake has underground facilities associated with secret, advanced-technology programs. In his book Underground Bases and Tunnels, Richard Sauder details China Lake as one of the most extensive tunneling sites in the U.S., with contractors confirming the existence of multi-level underground projects.[45]

Several patents for underground excavation machines filed by Navy researchers demonstrate that they had significant underground construction capability. A government report from the 1970s mentioned a protective underground structure built for ordnance assembly. They also let a patent slip for a nuclear-powered tunneling machine that melts rock to bore tunnels.[46][47]

I have heard several rumors of subterranean aqua channels that run from the Pacific Ocean to the Naval Undersea Warfare Center in Hawthorne, Nevada. There could be a 200-mile underwater tunnel that connects Walker Lake in Nevada to the Pacific Ocean, used to transfer submarines back and forth from the coast and whatever else you can imagine. Could these massive atomic-powered tunneling machines have created these passages in the 60s or 70s?

To put this all together, Tom DeLonge's longtime bandmate and friend, Mark Hoppus, comes from a family deeply embedded in the military-industrial complex. His father spent 34 years at one of the Navy's most classified weapons research facilities. His mother was a Navy system analyst. All his siblings work in defense-adjacent fields.

DeLonge discovers Bengston's energy healing research. Around the same time, Mark Hoppus beat stage 4 pancreatic cancer. Before all this, DeLonge somehow gains unprecedented access to the highest levels of the intelligence community, gets invited to Lockheed's Skunkworks, meets with CIA officials, and launches To The Stars Academy with former intelligence operatives.

Was it through Mark's family connections that DeLonge got his foot in the door? Did Tex Hoppus or his Navy colleagues see potential in using a rock star as a disclosure frontman and make introductions?

The timing is suspicious. The connections are there, and DeLonge went from punk rock musician to leading the current UFO disclosure movement faster than anyone expected.

Either he's incredibly lucky, incredibly talented at networking, or someone with deep connections to China Lake and the classified world decided he was the perfect person to manage public perception of UFO reality. I know which option seems most likely to me.

The pattern keeps repeating itself. Classified programs research advanced capabilities, test them in controlled settings, and then decide whether to suppress or selectively release the findings.

Bengston's healing research proves consciousness can influence biological systems in measurable ways. China Lake develops technologies decades ahead of public knowledge. DeLonge bridges the gap between the classified world and public disclosure through entertainment and carefully orchestrated revelation.

This control of knowledge, this gatekeeping of human capabilities and advanced technologies, isn't new. It's ancient. The same power structures that suppress breakthrough healing methods and revolutionary propulsion systems have been controlling access to transformative knowledge for millennia.

To understand how deep this goes, we need to go back further than China Lake, further than the modern military-industrial complex, all the way back to the cradle of civilization itself and examine what was stolen when American forces made their rush to Baghdad in 2003.

# CHAPTER 6

## ANCIENT FOUNDATIONS

What was stolen during the Baghdad heist?

In April 2003, American forces made a beeline for Baghdad. Not the typical military strategy of taking an objective, consolidating your position, securing the surrounding territory, then moving to the next target. No, they went straight to the capital with an urgency and focus that suggested they knew exactly what they were after and had no intention of deviating from that mission.

Then the Iraqi National Museum was looted,[48] but this wasn't the first time someone had their eyes on its treasures. Warner reminded me that the Germans and Ahnenerbe raided the same museum in 1940[49] and that they remained in Iraq for a while until the British kicked them out.[50]

More than 700,000 pieces disappeared overnight.[51] Gone. An entire repository of human history vanished, Sumerian tablets, Babylonian artifacts, objects dating back to the very dawn of civilization, all ransacked. At the same time, American troops stood down and watched it happen. The Pentagon had pledged to protect the museum. Historians around the world had begged them to safeguard it. This wasn't just valuable cultural property; this was irreplaceable material, our collective heritage stretching back to the origins of written language itself.

Yet when the mob showed up, US servicemen were ordered to withdraw.[52]

Jim Marrs figured this out decades ago and called it what it was, an inside job orchestrated at the highest levels. For years, people dismissed him as a conspiracy theorist, always finding connections that supposedly weren't there. Except now we know he was right all along. We have the evidence sitting in front of us, admissions from officials involved, and just recently, the returned artifacts sitting in museums today with little plaques that don't quite explain where they've been for the past twenty years or why it took so long to give them back.

Colonel Matthew Bogdanos, deputy director of the Joint Interagency Coordination Group, investigated the looting extensively, and his conclusion leaves no room for misinterpretation.

---

**"The basement is what we've been calling an inside job. I'll say it forever like a mantra. It is inconceivable to me that the basement was breached and the items stolen without an intimate knowledge of the museum."**[53][54]

---

Let that sink in. Not "might have been." Not "possibly." He's saying it's inconceivable that this happened without insider knowledge, detailed planning, and people who knew exactly what they were doing and where to find it.

Investigators found glass cutters that were not commercially available in Iraq at the scene. Guards were suspiciously absent, called in sick, or didn't show up that day when the museum needed them most. Whoever did this had keys, actual physical keys to specific exhibits and the basement storage areas. They walked past expensive, museum-quality fakes (the kind that would fool most people, which were displayed prominently for tourists to see) and went straight for the real artifacts locked away in storage, where only staff with proper access should have been able to reach[55]

A professional operation that was planned and executed with military precision.

The mob out front was just cover, chaos to hide the real mission happening in the basement while the world's cameras focused on the looting above.

Fast forward to March 2025. Iraqi News reports that 27,000 artifacts have been returned to the Iraqi National Museum.[56] 7000 of them were recovered from abroad through various channels, and here's the kicker that nobody wants to talk about: 17,300 were held in the United States for two full decades. That's 17,300 pieces of Iraqi cultural heritage (Sumerian, Babylonian, Assyrian material) sitting in America for 20 years while officials claimed they were working to return them.[57]

Among them was the Epic of Gilgamesh tablet. The first clay tablet recorded the epic poem about the historical King Gilgamesh, who ruled the Sumerian Ur around 2700 BC. One of humanity's oldest written stories. A text that predates the Bible by over a thousand years. It is a narrative that contains flood myths, divine encounters, the search for immortality, and themes that echo through every major religion that followed.

The British Museum held 6,000 artifacts for a hundred years before returning them. Just sitting in their archives. "Safekeeping," they called it, sure, they were keeping them "safe."[58]

So, here's my question: What did they learn? What were they looking for?

What did American intelligence agencies (and, let's be honest, this wasn't some random art theft ring operating independently) extract from those artifacts before returning them? You don't hold 17,300 pieces of ancient Sumerian material for twenty years without studying every single one. Scanning them with every technology available publicly, and all of the black project tech that is 30 years more advanced than that. Without translating every cuneiform tablet, analyzing every fragment, cataloging every symbol, and running everything through the most advanced quantum AI systems money can buy.

In 1999-2000, right before the invasion, German and French archaeological teams were making extraordinary discoveries in Iraq. They believed they'd found the tomb of Gilgamesh himself, a figure previously thought to be mythical, just a legend passed down through stories, now understood as a real historical king who lived nearly 5,000 years ago. Where would these discoveries and excavated materials go? Straight to the Iraqi National Museum for preservation and study.

The same museum that would be systematically looted three years later.

Jim Marrs once traced the lineage of hidden knowledge through history, showing how information passes through centuries and how power structures preserve and weaponize ancient wisdom for their own purposes. Here is a hard-and-fast flow of the lineage that Marrs outlines in his many books and lectures.

Ancient Sumer → Egyptian mystery schools → Greek philosophical traditions → Solomon's Temple → Knights Templars → Stone masons → Freemasonry → Rosicrucian orders → Bavarian Illuminati infiltration → Nazi occult programs → Operation Paperclip → US military-industrial complex → Council on Foreign Relations → Trilateral Commission → Bilderberger Group → Today's banking elite.

It's all the same thread running through different eras. The same families control the flow of information, the same power structures preserve what matters. Just wearing different masks across millennia while maintaining continuity behind the scenes.

A 2011 study by the Swiss Federal Institute of Technology examined 43,000 multinational corporations worldwide. They found these corporations are actually controlled by only 1,318 companies, most with interlocking directorships and ownership structures designed to concentrate power. These 1,318 companies are themselves controlled by 147 firms at the top of the pyramid, and these 147 firms control more than 60% of global revenues across every industry you can imagine.

Let me say that again for emphasis: 147 companies control 60% of everything that happens economically on this planet. The majority of those 147 are controlled by about 20 major banking institutions that set policy and direct global capital flows.

When people say, "the banks run the world," there's actual data backing that statement up. This isn't conspiracy theory based on speculation. This is published research from a respected Swiss technical institute analyzing hard economic data.[59]

The same power structure that looted Baghdad in 2003 is the same structure that suppresses UFO disclosure today. It controls technology release through the 30-year rule we'll discuss later in this book, harvests DNA from experiencers without consent, infiltrates Freemasonry, corrupts Rosicrucianism, funds Nazi occultism, and brings those same

Nazi scientists and occultists to America through Operation Paperclip after World War II.

These networks went to Baghdad for a reason, and it wasn't for oil or weapons of mass destruction.

What is in the Epic of Gilgamesh tablets that matters so much to them? What did ancient Sumer know that modern power structures are desperate to understand and control?

Well, here is a bit of history about the Sumerians that might provide some context. Even if you are not a history fan, this story will be worth your time. They appeared suddenly in Mesopotamia around 4500 BC with a fully formed civilization already in place. Writing systems, mathematics, astronomy, legal codes, architecture, and agricultural techniques all appeared at once. They didn't evolve these capabilities over thousands of years, as other cultures did; they arrived with them fully developed. Their own texts say the Anunnaki (gods who came from the sky) taught them everything they knew and gave them knowledge directly. These beings changed them from primitive humans into civilized people capable of building cities and reading the stars. According to their records, genetic construction, too, humans were created in a laboratory. These are all translations from their own writings.

Most modern scholars dismiss this as mythology, primitive people trying to explain their own cultural development through colorful stories about gods and heroes, but what if it's not mythology at all? What if its history were recorded in the only language they had to describe what they witnessed?

The Anunnaki. The Watchers. The Shining Ones. The gods who descended from above. Every ancient culture has the same story with different names attached. Beings from the sky who taught humanity forbidden knowledge. Who interbred with humans, producing the Nephilim, the Titans, the heroes of old who were bigger and stronger than normal humans. They were eventually punished for sharing too much knowledge, for elevating humanity too quickly before we were ready.

Every ancient culture also has the Flood myth. The Great Deluge. The divine reset button. A catastrophe that wiped out most of what came before, leaving only fragments preserved by those who saw it coming and prepared by building boats and preserving knowledge.

Gilgamesh's story includes the Flood narrative. His quest for immortality takes him to meet Utnapishtim (the Sumerian Noah), who survived the deluge by building a boat and preserving the knowledge of the pre-flood world inside it. This story predates the biblical Noah by at least 1,500 years. Which means either the Bible copied from Gilgamesh, or both are recording the same actual event that happened in human history. I have no idea which could be true, but dates are dates.

What else is in those tablets beyond flood stories? Technologies, cosmologies, an understanding of consciousness, of genetics, of the relationship between humanity and non-human intelligence that could still be relevant today?

The artifacts sat in America for twenty years, being studied. If you had unlimited resources, unlimited access to the world's top linguists, archaeologists, geneticists, physicists, if you had DARPA, the CIA, the NSA backing you with billions in black budget funding, and the most advanced quantum AI on Earth available to analyze everything, what could you learn from 17,300 pieces of Sumerian material?

Everything. You could learn everything they knew and probably reverse-engineer technologies we're not supposed to have yet.

Then you could return the artifacts with great fanfare. Mission accomplished: banner flying overhead for everyone during the press conference, with all knowledge extracted and cataloged. Now you take the evidence back where it belongs, complete with certificates of authenticity and museum plaques celebrating international cooperation. No one would ever know what you found, learned, or are using now.

History repeats itself, Marrs said, or more accurately, history echoes. The same patterns appear again and again, the same players wearing different masks using perfected methods refined across centuries.

The Templars found something in Solomon's Temple during their occupation of Jerusalem. Something that changed them fundamentally. It made them wealthy beyond measure, powerful enough to negotiate with kings as equals, dangerous enough that the Pope and the King of France conspired to destroy them on Friday the 13th, 1307. What did they find buried under that temple? No one knows for certain. Whatever it was, they scattered when the order fell. They fled to Scotland, Switzerland, Germany, and eventually to the United States, taking their knowledge with them wherever they went.

That knowledge became Freemasonry over time. It branches into Rosicrucianism. It became the foundation of Western esoteric traditions that influenced everything that came after. It influenced the Enlightenment, the Scientific Revolution, and the founding of America itself. It's woven into the architecture of Washington D.C., into the symbols on the dollar bill, into the structure of our government by men who knew exactly what they were encoding.

Someone connected to modern power structures wanted the original source material. So you go back to Sumer, Babylon, and to the texts that came before Solomon, before the Templars, before everything we think we know about where Western civilization and Western esotericism actually began.

So, they invaded Iraq.

Oh, they sold it to the public as weapons of mass destruction, as Saddam Hussein being an imminent threat to world peace, as liberation for the Iraqi people, and bringing democracy to the Middle East. Still, we know now (and some of us knew then if we were paying attention), there were no WMDs. There was no imminent threat to anyone. Iraq's oil production actually decreased after the invasion, so it wasn't about oil either, despite what critics claimed.

Could it have been partially about artifacts? The massive amounts of knowledge that could be obtained, and the library of human origins sitting in a museum in Baghdad, waiting to be studied.

Now they have it, studied it, and extracted whatever they needed. Then they've quietly returned most of it, laundering the theft through "recovery operations," international cooperation agreements, and feel-good stories about cultural heritage being restored to its rightful owners.

Mission accomplished.

So, what did they learn from two decades of classified study?

That's the question I can't answer, the classified part locked away in underground facilities and need-to-know compartments. It connects to the UFO phenomenon, to DNA harvesting, to consciousness research, to technologies we don't officially have but somehow keep seeing in operation.

I can tell you this much: the fact that they went to such extraordinary lengths (invading an entire country in the Gulf War, destabilizing an entire region for decades, spending trillions of dollars, killing hundreds of thousands of people) means what they found was worth it to them. Worth the cost, the risk, the blood, the international condemnation. At least to the people making those decisions.

It means the knowledge preserved in those Sumerian tablets connects to everything else we'll explore in this chapter. The mystery schools that preserved fragments of this wisdom through persecution. The Templars, who found more of it in Jerusalem. The Freemasons who inherited it and encoded it into their rituals. The occultists who corrupted it for their own purposes. The Nazis who weaponized it for genocide. The intelligence agencies that control it today.

It's all the same knowledge flowing through different hands across millennia. The same thread being woven through history, the same secret that's been guarded, suppressed, fought over, and killed for since the beginning of recorded time.

Welcome to the hidden history of esoteric knowledge.

This is where it starts. In ancient Sumer. In Baghdad. In the looted basement of a museum that held humanity's oldest stories and our earliest attempts to record what the gods taught us.

This is where we begin to understand exactly why certain people, groups, networks, and power structures don't want you to know what those stories actually say when carefully translated.

Because once you know, you can't unknow it.

Once you see the thread, you see it everywhere you look.

You understand that The Phenomenon (UFOs, consciousness, non-human intelligence, genetic manipulation, ancient mysteries) isn't separate from history but is woven into it from the very beginning, from the moment humans started writing things down. And then everything changes.

Everything.

So, let's pull that thread and see where it goes.

Let's start with what came before the Flood, before the reset, when knowledge was supposedly different, when civilizations were supposedly more advanced, and the "gods" still walked among us, teaching humans forbidden things.

Now we dive into. Atlantis. See what I did there?

## GIANTS AND FORBIDDEN ARCHAEOLOGY— WHAT DON'T THEY WANT US FINDING?

In 2008, a video surfaced on YouTube showing what appeared to be giant humanoid bodies in stasis. Not dead but suspended in some containment system, medical or otherwise. One had flowing reddish hair and a beard cascading down massive shoulders. Beautiful in an otherworldly way, almost ethereal, but definitely not human scale. Maybe nine, ten, possibly twelve feet tall based on the proportions visible in the footage, though it's hard to gauge precisely from the angles shown.

The video is said to have originated from an Iranian military or government facility and was reportedly leaked. In the video, multiple beings are visible in different states; some appear deceased, while others look like they might be alive but frozen, preserved, or in some form of suspended animation.

I saw it in 2010. At first, I thought it was an elaborate hoax, but the more you watch, the more it feels like a fake. The setting looks genuine. The beings look biological, not props. The footage has the authentic, low-quality feel of actual leaked material rather than a polished production.

So, what was it? Who were those beings? Why Iran, and where's the video now?

Scrubbed and deleted, gone from most platforms. A few copies survive in deep archives if you know where to look, but mainstream availability? Gone. Memory-holed. Like it never existed.

Which raises the question, why suppress video of giants if giants never existed?

Because they did exist, the evidence is everywhere if you know where to look and can access materials before they're confiscated or "lost."

Newspaper accounts from the 1800s and early 1900s regularly reported the discovery of giant skeletons. Not tabloid nonsense, but local newspapers reporting archaeological finds. Skeletons measuring 7 to 9 feet tall have been observed, displaying features such as double rows of teeth, elongated skulls, and six fingers. Although anatomically human, their proportions and scale differ from typical human standards. [60]

The Smithsonian was consistently mentioned in these reports. They'd hear about discovery, send representatives, collect the bones, and promise further study. Then nothing. No published research. No skeletons on display. No follow-up. Just… gone.

This happened repeatedly. Different locations. Different decades. Same pattern, discovery, Smithsonian collection, disappearance.

Why? What's the Smithsonian protecting?[61]

Official answer: The reports were exaggerated. Amateur excavators misidentify normal human skeletons without anatomical training. Hoaxes and mistakes, nothing more.

Several reports were prepared by trained archaeologists and included measurements, photographs, and accounts from multiple witnesses. In certain cases, doctors analyzed the bones and confirmed that they were authentic but unusual. The pattern of suppression observed appears to go beyond simply correcting amateur errors. You don't consistently confiscate and hide evidence unless that evidence threatens something.

What does the giant skeleton evidence threaten? The narrative of human evolution or the timeline of human history. The story we tell ourselves about who we are and where we come from.

Because if giants existed, if a race of large humanoids lived alongside or before modern humans, then biblical and mythological accounts aren't entirely metaphorical. The Nephilim and the Titans were real. The "mighty men of old, men of renown" were actual beings, not legend.

If that's true, then the rest might be true as well. The gods who interbred with humans. The genetic manipulation and fall of pre-flood civilizations, along with the intervention by non-human intelligence in human development.

All of it stops being mythology and becomes suppressed history.

That's dangerous. Dangerous to religious institutions that claim unique revelation, to scientific establishments that claim materialist evolution explains everything, and to every power structure built on controlling the narrative about human origins.

So, the Smithsonian makes bones disappear, and when they can't, they reinterpret the evidence. The elongated Paracas skulls in Peru? [62]Cranial deformation, they say. Cultural practice of binding children's heads to create an elongated shape. However, DNA testing revealed unexpected results. The DNA did not match any known human population, indicating that these were not simply deformed humans but potentially a different species with a distinct origin and lineage.

That research? Marginalized. Researchers? Attacked. Conclusions? Dismissed without proper refutation.

Same pattern with other anomalies:

**<u>Göbekli Tepe in Turkey</u>:** Massive stone structures built 11,600 years ago by hunter-gatherers who supposedly didn't have organizational capacity, specialized labor, or architectural knowledge. Mainstream archaeology struggles to explain it.[63] Alternative researchers say it's pre-flood. It's what survived from the advanced civilization that got destroyed.[64]

**<u>The Pyramids:</u>** The official timeline says they were built in 2500 BC by the Egyptians, using copper tools and wooden ramps. Water erosion on the Sphinx suggests it's far older, possibly 10,000 BC or earlier.[65] That would predate Egyptian civilization and require reconsidering who built it and how.

**<u>Puma Punku in Bolivia:</u>** Stone blocks weighing hundreds of tons, precision-cut to tolerances that modern machinery struggles to achieve, assembled in ways we can't fully explain. Either ancient humans had technologies we didn't know about, or someone else did.[66]

**<u>The Osireion in Egypt</u>**: An underground temple that conventional archaeology dates to the 13th century BC. The megalithic blocks, the water erosion, and the architectural style all suggest it's much older, possibly contemporary with Göbekli Tepe.[67][68]

**<u>Underwater structures</u>** off Japan[69], India[70], the Caribbean: Ruins that submerged when sea levels rose at the end of the last Ice Age. Which means they were built before 10,000 BC, and advanced maritime civilizations existed in periods we're told humans were primitive.

Each piece of anomalous archaeology is dismissed individually. Different excuses for each. Like, there is not enough evidence, or people have misinterpreted the data. Or that they are natural formations misidentified as ruins. They claim that all alternative researchers are driven by pseudoscience, but taken together, a pattern emerges. Evidence consistently suggests human history is longer, stranger, and more advanced than official narratives claim.

Consistently, institutions suppress this evidence. Not through conspiracy meetings where they decide what to hide, but through institutional inertia, funding decisions, career pressures, and paradigm enforcement.

The archaeologists who propose controversial dates get denied funding. Peer reviewers reject papers that challenge consensus. Universities don't grant tenure to researchers pursuing "fringe" questions. The media doesn't cover discoveries that complicate the accepted timeline.

It is not a conspiracy, but an incentive structure. If you stay within the paradigm, you get rewarded. Challenge paradigm, get marginalized.

Occasionally, when evidence is too strong to ignore, institutions actively intervene. The Smithsonian is collecting giant bones. The Vatican has been locking away ancient texts and relics for centuries. Governments classify archaeological findings in sensitive areas.

Why? Because paradigm shift threatens power. Consider the possibilities that humanity has risen and fallen before, that we've been more advanced, that non-human intelligence has been involved in our development. Consciousness is more than brain activity, and it survives death. All of it threatens institutions built on materialist, reductionist, human-centered narratives.

Religious authority collapses if direct experience trumps doctrine. Scientific credibility dissolves if materialism can't explain consciousness. Political legitimacy evaporates if people recognize they've been systematically lied to.

So, the bones disappear, and the texts get locked away. The research gets defunded. The evidence gets classified, videos of giants in stasis are scrubbed from the internet, and one begins to wonder: what else are they hiding?

The Iranian video specifically raises questions beyond just giants. Why would a modern military or government facility have giant beings in preservation? Were they found recently? Have they been held for decades? Are they alive or dead, or something in between, and are they connected to the UFO phenomenon? Because experiencers report seeing beings of various sizes, some small (Greys), some human-sized (Nordics), some large (various tall species). If giants are part of non-human intelligence, interacted with ancient humans, and still exist, then mythology turns into present-day reality.

The connections are there for anyone wanting to see them. Sumerian texts describe Anunnaki as tall, powerful, god-like. Biblical Nephilim were "mighty men," giants born from angels and humans. Greek Titans were enormous, pre-human intelligences. Norse mythology is full of giants, Jotun, who predate the gods. Native American traditions speak of "tall ones" who taught and sometimes destroyed. Pacific Islander legends describe gods who arrived from the sky, much larger than humans. African tribes preserve stories of giant ancestors.

Same story. Every culture. Different names but with consistent details, tall beings, advanced knowledge, interaction with humans, sometimes helpful, sometimes destructive, ultimately receding or being destroyed.

Either every culture independently invented similar myths for no reason, or they're recording actual events using mythological language because that's the only framework they had.

If ancient cultures were not merely inventing stories, but instead recording actual events, then the existence of giants is just the beginning. If giants truly existed and are still being discovered and concealed by governments, it compels us to ask, what else might be real?

Throughout history, accounts of gods could very well describe real entities equipped with advanced technology. To early humans, these beings would have appeared divine, their abilities and knowledge far surpassing anything known at the time.

The possibility of genetic intervention in human development emerges in legends of the Nephilim, demigods, and heroes. These stories suggest that external forces may have played a direct role in producing extraordinary individuals, blending human traits with those of powerful outsiders.

References to an advanced civilization that existed before a catastrophic flood can be interpreted as memories of a sophisticated society, wiped out almost entirely, but leaving behind fragments of its achievements and knowledge.

In recent times, the deliberate suppression of evidence has become a critical issue. Information that could radically alter our understanding of history is hidden because its revelation would require rewriting the established narrative.

When viewed together, these elements transition from being dismissed offhand as conspiracy theories or fringe pseudoscience to forming a narrative of hidden history and suppressed facts waiting to be uncovered.

This pattern is persistent, stretching from ancient eras to the present day. Those who wield control over the narrative effectively shape reality, while those who suppress or withhold evidence keep their hold on power.

Evidence keeps surfacing, and videos leak. Researchers publish despite the pressure, and people compare notes online. The cover-up becomes harder to maintain, and some of those investigating forbidden archaeology realize the suppression itself is proof. You don't hide what does not exist. You do not confiscate what isn't threatening.

The giants were real. The evidence exists, and the Smithsonian has it or had it. There are rumors that the bones were ground up and destroyed years ago. You best believe that various governments have it, and they're not releasing it because it's too destabilizing.

Which means everything connected to it, the gods, the genetic manipulation, the non-human intelligence, the advanced pre-flood civilizations, all of that is real too.

We're living in the moment when that knowledge is emerging despite suppression. When enough people have seen enough evidence that official denials stop working, the paradigm is shifting, whether institutions like it or not.

Giants existed.

Then what else existed that we're being told didn't? What other evidence has been hidden, what other truths systematically suppressed, and most importantly, why is this happening? That's what this entire chapter has been about. Tracing the thread of hidden knowledge from ancient Sumer to the Templars, the Freemasons, the Nazis, and into modern intelligence agencies. Showing that esoteric knowledge isn't fantasy but real or at least real enough to fight over, weaponize, and suppress for centuries. Today, that suppression is fading, knowledge is surfacing, evidence is growing, and the paradigm is shifting.

# BEFORE THE DELUGE - WHAT WAS ATLANTIS?

Atlantis. Say the word in most circles and watch eyes roll. Ancient astronaut theorists. New Age mystics. People who believe crystals heal cancer and dolphins speak telepathically. The word has been so thoroughly associated with pseudoscience and wishful thinking that serious researchers won't touch it.

Which is exactly how you suppress inquiry into something real.

Plato wrote about Atlantis in Timaeus and Critias around 360 BC. He described it as an advanced naval power that existed 9,000 years before his time, which would put it around 9600 BC, with three concentric rings of water separated by land, a sophisticated harbor system, advanced architecture, and extensive trade networks. The civilization conquered much of Europe and Africa before being defeated by Athens, and then, in a single day and night, it sank beneath the sea due to earthquakes and floods.

For centuries, people assumed Plato made it up. A philosophical allegory. A cautionary tale about hubris and divine punishment. Nobody actually believed there was a real Atlantis.

What I find interesting is that Plato didn't present it as an allegory. He presented it as a history passed down by Egyptian priests to Solon, the Athenian lawgiver, who heard it from them at Sais during his travels. Plato's great-grandfather was supposedly Solon's cousin. The story came through his family. He framed it as a historical fact, not a philosophical fiction.

The Egyptian priests? They had written records stating that their civilization was already ancient when Atlantis fell, dating back more than 11,000 years.

They kept meticulous records because they understood something we've forgotten: history is long, civilizations rise and fall, and if you don't preserve the knowledge, it dies with you.

Eirik Sinclair spent years researching what he calls "Templar Science," a methodology that seeks to uncover facts intentionally woven into historical accounts that later cultures tried to hide or suppress. His work on Atlantis, detailed in "Voyage of the Thundergods," suggests something radical:

Atlantis wasn't one place. It was a civilization that existed across multiple locations, connected by advanced seafaring technology, which survived in fragments after a cataclysm that destroyed most of it.[71]

What are the three concentric rings Plato described? It was not just architecture but a pattern that repeated almost like a signature. Sinclair argues that survivors of the Atlantean catastrophe, whatever it was, flood or crustal displacement or comet impact, fled to different locations and tried to preserve what they could.

They became the mysterious "Sea Peoples" mentioned in Egyptian records, the builders of Göbekli Tepe in Turkey (dated to 9600 BC, the exact time Plato said Atlantis fell), and the source of sudden agricultural and architectural knowledge that appeared in multiple locations around the Mediterranean and beyond within a relatively narrow timeframe.[72]

They became "the gods."

Think about it. You're a primitive hunter-gatherer living in the Stone Age. Then strangers arrive in ships. They have metals you've never seen. Tools that cut stone like butter. Knowledge of astronomy, agriculture, mathematics, and medicine. They can predict eclipses, navigate by the stars, and build structures aligned to celestial events that won't happen for thousands of years.

What do you call them?

Gods. Obviously. What else would you call beings with knowledge so far beyond yours that it seems like magic?

If some of them interbreed with your people, as the texts consistently say happened, you get the Nephilim. The Titans. The heroes of old. The demigod offspring of gods and humans, possessing unusual size, strength, longevity, and abilities.

This isn't separate from the Sumerian story of the Anunnaki or the Watchers in the Book of Enoch. The same thread runs through Prometheus, giving fire to humanity; Quetzalcoatl teaching the Maya; and Viracocha teaching the Inca. It's the same story, just with different names, because the same thing is happening in different places.

Advanced knowledge-bearers, whether they were literally non-human, human survivors of a more advanced pre-flood civilization, or some combination interacting with post-catastrophe humanity and jump-starting civilizations.

Here's where it connects to what we're discussing: knowledge didn't disappear. It was preserved. Passed down through priesthoods, through mystery schools, through initiatic orders that understood its value and guarded it carefully.

The Egyptians somehow had access to this knowledge. That's why their civilization appeared suddenly, fully formed, with monumental architecture and sophisticated astronomical knowledge around 3100 BC. That is why their own texts say the knowledge came from before, from the "First Time," when the gods walked the earth.

The Babylonians had it as well, and that's why the Sumerian civilization appeared fully formed with writing, mathematics, and legal codes.

The Maya had calendars more accurate than anything Europe would produce for another thousand years. That's why they built pyramids aligned to stellar configurations.

The builders of Göbekli Tepe were hunter-gatherers, then suddenly started carving massive stone pillars with sophisticated astronomical alignments 11,600 years ago, a construction that required organizational capacity, organized farming, specialized labor, and engineering knowledge that supposedly didn't exist yet.

Somebody in the modern world knows about this because they went to extraordinary lengths to get the source material from Iraq. They've been suppressing archaeological discoveries that don't fit the accepted timeline, and they've built their power structures around controlling access to this knowledge.

Author Eirik Sinclair argues that Viking sagas preserve echoes of Atlantis. The Norse myths aren't purely inventions but distorted memories of real events, places, and advanced maritime civilizations that existed in the North Atlantic before the climate changed and the seas rose. The Templar connection to Scotland is not random. The Norse myths aren't purely inventions but distorted memories of real events, places, and advanced maritime civilizations that existed in the North Atlantic before the climate changed. The seas rose, and the Templar connection to Scotland is not random; the Templars went there because that's where fragments of the pre-flood knowledge were preserved. It is said that the Phoenicians may have sailed to America, too. Possibly an Atlantis colony like Greece and the Minoans.

Is he right? I don't know, but what I do know is this: there's too much that doesn't fit. There are too many advanced structures built by people who supposedly couldn't build them with stone-age tools, flood myths across too many cultures with specific details that match among them, and genetic anomalies in human DNA that suggest something unusual happened in our past.

There has been widespread suppression in archaeology, with lost texts, missing researchers, and serious inquiry often dismissed as pseudoscience. Those who pursue these topics are marginalized, denied funding, and excluded from academic circles.

Why? If Atlantis was just a myth, who cares? Let researchers waste their time, but if there was something real, and if there was advanced pre-flood knowledge that survived in fragments that may explain some of the anomalies in human history, that connects to the UFO phenomenon and consciousness research, as well as genetic manipulation. If any of this is true, then suddenly the gatekeeping makes sense.

One framework that attempts to unify these fragments is outlined by Michael Tsarion, who argues that anomalies in human history, lost civilizations, sudden advances in cognitive capability, persistent mythological contact narratives, and enduring elite gatekeeping are not separate mysteries but symptoms of the same suppressed story.

His analysis suggests that advanced prehistorical knowledge, possibly originating from a technologically capable civilization or external non-human intelligence, survived global cataclysms only in fragments encoded in myth, esoteric systems, and controlled institutions. Within this model, human genetics are not purely the product of natural selection but were altered in ways that expanded cognition while constraining other perceptual or energetic capacities, making consciousness both powerful and manageable. When viewed alongside modern UFO encounters, in which technology, consciousness, and biological effects consistently intersect, and contemporary research indicating that consciousness is not confined to the brain, patterns emerge that challenge the official narrative. From that vantage point, long-term information compartmentalization and ridicule are no longer random; they serve an intelligible function. If knowledge of humanity's true origin and latent capability were universally accessible, established power structures built on dependence and limitation would become difficult, if not impossible, to maintain.

Suddenly, the Baghdad Museum heist, the Smithsonian's suppression of giant skeletons, and the classification of ancient texts and artifacts all make sense.

The pattern appears, control the past and the narrative about human origins, and in doing so, you control what people believe is possible.

Because if people knew we've been more advanced before, if they knew civilizations rose and fell long before recorded history, if they knew we're not the first technological species on this planet, might not even be the first version of humanity on this planet, then all the control structures based on limiting what people think is possible would collapse.

The Church's authority collapses if direct gnosis is real and accessible. The State's authority falls apart the moment people realize they've been lied to about fundamental history. Scientific establishment credibility dissolves if materialist reductionism can't explain consciousness or UFOs or ancient advanced knowledge, and the banking elite lose their grip the moment people see the debt-based monetary system for what it is, a control mechanism rather than a natural feature of civilization.

Everything collapses if the foundation, the story we tell ourselves about who we are, where we come from, and what we're capable of, turns out to be wrong.

So, these institutions guard the knowledge against any investigation. They classify the artifacts, suppress the research, discredit the investigators, and preserve fragments of the real knowledge within secret societies and mystery schools, initiatic order groups that understand its value but also the danger of releasing it to unprepared masses.

Which brings us to those mystery schools. The Egyptian priesthoods. The Greek philosophical traditions. The organizations that preserved pre-flood wisdom through the dark ages of ignorance that followed whatever catastrophe ended the advanced civilizations.

They were not making this up or inventing mythology. They were preserving history, history that would be systematically erased and replaced with a sanitized version that made the current power structures seem inevitable, natural, the only way things have ever been, but the evidence remains. The evidence can be found in structural designs, genetic research, and recurring myths that appear across numerous cultures. Additionally, artifacts are frequently reclassified or become inaccessible to the public, and certain texts remain secured in repositories such as the Vatican archives, Smithsonian basements, and CIA vaults.

The evidence stays because you can't completely erase the past. You can only bury it and hope people stop digging.

We're still digging, and what we're finding, what researchers like Jay Anderson, Graham Hancock, Randall Carlson, and Robert Schoch have been finding, is that human history is far longer, far stranger, and far more advanced than we've been told.

Whether Atlantis existed is not the point; what matters is why it's important.

What did they know, where did that knowledge go, and who controls it now?

Those are the questions that get people killed, get funding pulled, careers destroyed, and researchers marginalized. Still, those are also the questions we need to answer if we want to understand why certain groups went to such lengths to loot a museum in Baghdad, why they're harvesting DNA from experiencers, why they're suppressing UFO disclosure, and why they're afraid of what people might learn about consciousness and human potential.

Because it's all connected. Ancient mysteries. The modern cover-up. The Phenomenon. The control systems.

It's all the same thread.

That thread runs through the mystery schools into the organizations that understood what was lost and worked to preserve it through centuries of persecution, suppression, and systematic destruction.

## MYSTERY SCHOOLS–THE SECRET SUPERHEROES OR VILLAINS?

When knowledge becomes dangerous, it goes underground.

When the church declares your studies heretical, when kings outlaw your practices, when mobs burn your libraries and hang your teachers, you don't announce your beliefs, publish your findings, or wear identifying symbols in public.

You become a what Kevin Fuller calls a "secret superhero."

Kevin Fuller is a modern practitioner of multiple mystery school traditions: Rosicrucianism, Martinism, Freemasonry, Kabbalah, and Hermeticism. He's not just reading about these systems; he's doing the work, practicing the rituals, and developing the consciousness capabilities. He understands that these traditions aren't separate, but they are branches of the same tree, preserving different aspects of the same fundamental knowledge.[73]

As a "secret superhero", you practice in private, pass knowledge person to person, teacher to student, and initiate. You encode wisdom in symbols, rituals, and architecture that only the initiated can read. You build networks of people who understand what you've experienced these mysteries and know what can be safely spoken aloud.

These are the people who create mystery schools.

The lineage of mystery schools is ancient. There were Egyptian priesthoods teaching initiation rites in the temples of Memphis and Thebes, and Greek mystery cults at Eleusis, where initiates experienced direct contact with the divine through sacred rituals that were never written down or fully explained to outsiders. The Romans had their own mystery religions, like Mithraism and the cult of Isis, as well as the Orphic mysteries. These were all competing philosophies and practices for achieving gnosis, the direct experiential knowledge of spiritual truth.

These weren't social clubs or primitive superstitions. They were sophisticated systems for consciousness development, accessing non-ordinary states of awareness, and connecting with what they experienced as divine or cosmic intelligence.

These mystery schools were dangerous to the institutions because people who experience the divine directly don't need priests to interpret for them. People who develop their consciousness don't need kings to think for them, and people who understand their own power don't need control systems to manage them.

The religious, political, and economic control systems worked to eliminate the mystery schools. Sometimes through outright violence, sometimes through infiltration and corruption, and also through simply waiting for the practitioners to die and the knowledge to fade, but fragments survived. The wisdom was preserved by people who understood what would be lost if they didn't pass it on to future generations.

Kevin explained the historical context that made mystery schools necessary. In the 1500s and 1600s, when Rosicrucianism appeared as a distinct tradition, Europe was a dangerous place for anyone studying what we now call the occult. The Catholic Church had the Inquisition. Practicing alchemy could get you arrested. Studying astrology could get you burned. Even owning certain books was a death sentence.

So, practitioners went underground. They met in secret, used coded language, and claimed to be studying "legitimate" subjects like medicine or natural philosophy while actually working on consciousness technologies, alchemical transformation, and communication with non-human intelligence.

The Rosicrucian manifestos were published anonymously in the early 1600s and announced the existence of a secret brotherhood possessing advanced knowledge and seeking to reform the world. Were they real? Partially. The manifestos themselves inspired people to form organizations based on the ideas presented. The knowledge they claimed to possess? That was real, passed down through initiatic chains from earlier mystery schools.

The key principles Kevin emphasized:

**First: Reintegration, not escape.** Eastern traditions focused on removing yourself from the world, meditating in isolation, and transcending material existence. Mystery school traditions, particularly Rosicrucianism and Martinism, taught something different. You're supposed to develop your consciousness and then bring that back into the world. Essentially, transform yourself to transform society and become a force for healing and evolution while living an ordinary life.

Become a secret superhero. You don't go around in robes or announce your spiritual achievements. Instead, you're a carpenter, a teacher, or a business owner quietly doing the inner work and cultivating compassion, practicing meditation, and opening yourself to greater consciousness. This subtle transformation has a profound effect on everything around you.

**Second: Direct experience over belief.** The mystery schools weren't about adopting a set of dogmas. They were about having experiences: mystical states, altered consciousness, direct contact with what they called the Divine, and then learning to interpret and integrate those experiences. You weren't saved by faith. You were transformed by gnosis.

This is why the Church hated the mystery schools, because once people have direct spiritual experiences, they don't need intermediaries. No one needs a priest telling them what God wants. You know. You've experienced it.

Or as my friend Warner points out, "they might realize (male) God or Source is not what religions describe using fear and threats, they may find that gnostic 'Sophia' is a feminine creational consciousness in the cosmos."

**Third: Initiation as consciousness technology.** The rituals weren't arbitrary, and the degrees weren't just ranks. Each initiation was designed to trigger specific psychological and spiritual experiences. To break down ego structures, open awareness to larger realities, and to develop capacities that most people never access.

Kevin explained how initiatory systems use psychological pressure, symbolic death and rebirth, sensory manipulation, oath-taking, and community bonding to create genuine transformation. It's not play-acting. When done correctly, these initiations produce real changes in consciousness.

Here's where it connects to everything else we're exploring. What if the UFO phenomenon, the experiences with non-human intelligence, and the consciousness abilities that experiencers develop are the same things mystery schools have been cultivating for millennia?

Kevin and I have done CE5/HIC (Human Initiated Contact) together. We've meditated with groups and brought orbs down. Two nights in a row! We filmed them with multiple witnesses and have clear color night vision footage. We witnessed objects responding to consciousness, intention, and collective focus.

What is that technology, consciousness, or both?

The mystery schools would say, it's natural, something humans can do when they develop the capacities that most people never develop. Accessing non-ordinary states of consciousness and discovering that consciousness itself is the interface between physical and non-physical reality.

The Rosicrucians called it the "secret fire." The Martinists called it "reintegration with the Divine." The Freemasons call it "the light." These are all different terms that describe the same experience of consciousness expansion, connecting you to something vast, intelligent, and responsive.

Religious, scientific, and political gatekeepers have long prevented people from discovering these abilities, discouraging both their development and challenges to the materialist view that consciousness is merely brain activity with no existence beyond the physical.

The reason is that humans who cultivate these skills become difficult to control. They can recognize propaganda, resist manipulation through fear, and understand that consciousness persists beyond death. Additionally, they realize that there is a far deeper, different reality than the one official narratives preach to us. Human potential far surpasses the limitations we're told exist.

Kevin emphasized something critical, that these traditions preserve real technologies of consciousness through the dark ages of ignorance. When Christian Europe was burning books and killing scholars, mystery schools kept the knowledge alive. As the Enlightenment sought to reduce everything to "mechanistic materialism," esoteric orders maintained that consciousness is primary, not secondary. And even after modern science claimed to have explained everything while explaining almost nothing about the hard problems, consciousness, the observer effect, non-locality, and the nature of reality itself, the mystery schools kept teaching what direct experience reveals.

These traditions maintained that consciousness can exist apart from the body, intention influences reality on all levels, non-human intelligence is real and contactable, humans possess hidden abilities, death is a transition, and we are all connected to a greater consciousness often referred to as God, Source, or the great Architect of the Universe.

For practitioners who do the work and undergo initiations, these are not beliefs but repeatable experiences that others in the community can verify.

This can't be discussed publicly in any era because control systems continue to keep it hidden.

So, you become a secret superhero. Do the work quietly, help where you can, and hold space for others who are awakening. Preserve the knowledge for those who come after.

That's what Rosicrucianism taught, Martinism teaches, and, at its ethical core, what Freemasonry embodies: making good men better, not through indoctrination but through experiences that expand consciousness and cultivate virtue.

Kevin helped me understand that the same forces that persecuted mystery schools in the 1600s are the forces that burned heretics, banned books, and suppressed knowledge that are still operating today.

Now, instead of burning you at the stake, they destroy your academic career. Instead of banning books, they control funding and publication. Rather than physical torture, they use ridicule, marginalization, and social pressure, but the pattern is the same: suppress direct experience, consciousness development, and anything that threatens the control paradigm.

That's why Freemasonry and UFOs face parallel stigmas. They both involve knowledge that threatens power structures, offer paths to understanding reality beyond official narratives, and have been systematically ridiculed, infiltrated, and misrepresented.

The mystery schools understood something critical: knowledge must be guarded not because it's false but because it's true and dangerous. Dangerous to those who want humanity limited, controlled, and domesticated. Mystery schools empower those who use them responsibly, with the understanding that with great power comes great responsibility.

Candidates had to pass tests proving they were ready and able to handle the teachings responsibly. The screening was not elitist as it served to protect knowledge, students, and society.

Once you've experienced consciousness beyond the body, encountered non-human intelligence, or witnessed reality reshape itself through intention, you can't forget it. Without psychological stability and an ethical framework, integrating these experiences can be overwhelming or harmful.

It is preferable to maintain knowledge within traditions that demand years of dedication, commitment, and constant practice. Sharing wisdom directly from one person to another, through mentorship and guided experience, ensures its preservation.

That's not gatekeeping in the negative sense; it's more like stewardship.

The mystery schools were (and are) repositories of human knowledge that mainstream institutions either lost or never had. They preserved what the Church tried to erase, what universities refuse to study, what governments classify when they discover it, and they did it by going underground, by becoming secret superheroes, practicing without broadcasting, helping without credit, and preserving knowledge for future generations.

That's not a conspiracy; it is a historical fact.

What does this really mean, and what did they preserve? The knowledge, practices, and understanding of reality that these traditions maintained through centuries of suppression deserve a closer look.

How does that ancient knowledge connect to modern phenomena like UFOs, consciousness abilities, genetic anomalies, and the systematic cover-up of anything that doesn't fit the approved narrative?

## THE MYSTICAL SIGNIFICANCE OF SULFUR

Before we examine the Emerald Tablet, I want to explore something that connects ancient mystical traditions to modern UFO encounters- sulfur. As we saw in Chapter 2, sulfur appears repeatedly in paranormal and UFO cases, and sulfur has long been associated with mystical and occult significance in various esoteric traditions over the centuries.

Paracelsus, the famous Renaissance physician and alchemist, wrote: "He who does not know the sulfur knows nothing, and can accomplish nothing, neither of medicine, nor of philosophy, nor of the secrets of nature."

Alchemists believed sulfur represented the soul, spirit, or inner radiance because it combusts into a pure flame, and they used it as a key symbolic ingredient. In alchemy, the three principles of sulfur, mercury, and salt form the basis of the alchemical perspective on nature, people, plants, and, ultimately, life as a whole.

For old alchemists, sulfur was a mystical material. With its bright yellow color and ability to burn with a pure flame, they saw it as representing the human soul itself. The fiery sulfur was thought to give off an immortal, spiritual energy tied to our consciousness. UFOs are intrinsically connected to consciousness in various ways, as we've explored throughout this book.

The Greeks believed sulfur was associated with the concept of Logos, a divine force behind human reason and speech. There were theories linking sulfur to "psyche," which could mean mind, spirit, or soul.

Similar ideas emerged in Hebrew culture, where the word for soul, "nephesh," literally means "living being." It was almost like sulfur had this vibrant life-force of its own. Over time, cultures noticed sulfur turning up everywhere, in our bodies, in plants and animals, and throughout different minerals. Alchemists began to believe that gaining control over sulfur could be the key to unlocking the secrets of spirituality, soul transformation, and maybe even immortality.

That's why the fiery yellow powder became such a big symbol in alchemy and occultism. It seemed like tangible proof that matter and spirit are connected. By tapping into sulfur's energetic power, spiritual seekers could light the way to elevated states of consciousness, almost as if striking a match to reveal hidden dimensions of reality.

In demonology and ancient rituals, sulfur is sometimes invoked or used to summon, contain, or repel demonic forces. In European witchcraft and folk magic, powdered sulfur, or "brimstone," is used in various rituals and spells for spiritual cleansing, breaking hexes, or driving away evil spirits. Many occultists believe sulfur reacts to and marks places of high psychical energy or paranormal phenomena through its smells or visual cues. Its alchemical symbol even resembles the trident associated with Satanic and demonic icons.

The symbolic and literal role of sulfur is prominent across demonic, spiritual, and paranormal matters. The hellish, otherworldly smell and its combustible nature seem to give it an innate occult power or resonance. These associations help explain why reports of sulfur persist around phenomena such as UFOs, ghosts, demons, or magic that span centuries, even to the present day. It remains a deeply evocative element for the unexplained.

The connections here are remarkably interesting and deserve far more in-depth research. What if sulfur's appearance in UFO encounters isn't just a chemical byproduct but a marker, and the ancients understood something about this element we've forgotten, that it appears at the intersection of physical and non-physical reality?

Let's start with the Emerald Tablet, one of the most famous mystery school texts, foundational to Western esotericism, and according to proper translation, completely misunderstood for centuries.

## THE EMERALD TABLET - HOW WE GOT IT WRONG

"As above, so below."

Four words. Probably the most famous phrase in Western esotericism. The foundation of Hermetic philosophy. The "Law of Correspondence" between macrocosm and microcosm. Every occultist knows it, and every New Age teacher quotes it. It's printed on t-shirts, tattooed on bodies, repeated in countless books as the core wisdom of the Emerald Tablet.

According to the proper translation of the original Arabic source material, it's wrong.

Not close. Not "well, technically..." Not "depends on how you interpret it." Just wrong. We've been misreading one of the foundational texts of Western esoteric thought for centuries because we didn't have proper Arabic dictionaries, didn't understand medieval translation methods, and didn't question the received wisdom passed down through occult traditions.

John Gilbert changed that.

Gilbert's an interesting guy. An M1 tank crewman turned Arabic cryptologic linguist. He served 21 years in the military, including in cyber security and intelligence. Not your typical academic or the typical occultist, but exactly the person needed to tackle a translation problem that required both linguistic expertise in medieval Arabic and a willingness to challenge centuries of established interpretation.

His book "Not as Above, Not as Below: How We Got the Emerald Tablet Wrong"[74] does something remarkable: it goes back to the oldest extant manuscripts, 8th or 9th century Arabic texts preserved in Paris and other collections, and translates them properly. He brings an actual understanding of Arabic morphology, knowledge of medieval translation errors, and a structured analytical technique rather than wishful mystical interpretation. What he found destroys the standard interpretation.

The Emerald Tablet, as we know it, comes to us through multiple layers of translation. The source is unknown, possibly Egyptian or even earlier. It was transmitted through Greek philosophical schools and translated into Arabic by scholars in Baghdad (yes, Baghdad again). Are you noticing the pattern? Then it was translated from Arabic into Latin by medieval European scholars who didn't have proper Arabic dictionaries because those didn't exist until the 1800s. It was once again translated from Latin into modern European languages by people already embedded in occult traditions, whose knowledge swayed them into believing they knew what it was supposed to mean.

Each layer introduced errors. Assumptions. Interpretations passed off as translations. By the time we get to the modern occult version, we're reading something that preserves the general vibe but misses crucial specifics.

Gilbert shows this systematically. He translates the Arabic text accurately using current dictionaries, and "as above, so below" does not appear in it.

The proper translation uses "the above" and "the below" in the context of something completely different: the transmigration of souls. The cycle of incarnation, spiritual ascent, and the process by which souls descend into material existence and afterwards work their way back to the divine source.

This is standard Hermetic cosmology. You find it throughout the Corpus Hermeticum, in texts like the "Virgin of the World." God creates a system in which souls descend from divine unity into material separation, which is "the below." Then, through experience, learning, and spiritual development, they ascend back, that's "the above." It's not about macrocosm and microcosm. It's about the soul's journey through creation.

What I found fascinating was that Gilbert shows that "Hermes Thrice-Wise," the supposed author, is also a mistranslation. The Arabic morphologically reads exactly the same as "Hermes the Triangle of Wisdom." The word for "thrice" and the word for "triangle" are identical in structure. Medieval translators chose "thrice" because it sounded more mystical, but "triangle" makes more sense contextually and connects to geometric symbolism throughout Hermetic traditions. Here is the new translation in full via Gilbert.

This is the Art of Nature

Without a doubt it is correct

That the above is from the below, and the below is from the above.

He worked the wonders from One, as all things were from One by a single move.

His father is the Sun, his mother is the Moon.

The Wind carried him in her belly, the Earth nourished him.

Father of Talismans, treasurer of wonders, full of powers.

Fire yielded some earth, isolating the earth from the fire.

The ethereal is more noble than the dense.

Gently and wisely, he ascends from the Earth to the Sky and descends to the Earth from the Sky,

And in him is the power of the above and the below

Because with him is the light of lights, therefore darkness flees from him.

Power of powers,

He surmounts everything ethereal, he penetrates everything dense.

Toward the formation of the macrocosm and microcosm, he brings forth the work.

This is my glory, and that is why I am called Hermes Thrice Wise.

This version is John Gilbert's own translation, arrived at by examining three Arabic language sources. One of those is considered by many scholars to be the authoritative Arabic version, which appears in Dr. Ursula Weisser's 1979 academic work Buch Über Das Geheimnis Der Schöpfung und Die Darstellung der Natur (Buch der Ursachen). Sirr Al-Khalīqa Wa-á¹¢inʿat Al-á¹¬abīʿa. Kitāl al-ʿIlal, an impressive and intimidating title. It states in German, then in transliterated Arabic: "Book of the Secret of Creation and the Art of Nature (Book of Causes)." This is the original title of an ancient book that purports, within its pages, to have been written by the Greek philosopher Apollonius of Tyana.

As Gilbert notes, modern scholars consider this a false attribution, so we often see the author listed as "pseudo-Apollonius of Tyana" in articles and bibliographies. They also think the handful of Arabic versions that have come down to us through the ages were originally composed in the late 700s or early 800s A.D. Dr. Weisser and others think these Arabic texts came from yet an earlier translator, Sagiyus, a priest at Nablus, who translated them from a Greek source in the sixth century A.D. The Book of Causes contains the oldest known versions of the Emerald Tablet. Dr. Weisser analyzed four original manuscripts of this work to synthesize her detailed version.

In addition to Dr. Weisser's work, Gilbert examined two of these handwritten Arabic manuscripts in their original form. The first is held at the Bibliothèque nationale de France in their Department of Manuscripts. The second is found at the British Library, Oriental Manuscripts Department, but is viewable at the Qatar National Library's Digital Library. This last one, from the British and Qatar Libraries, is known to have been one actually used by Dr. Weisser in her study of the text. A look at these original documents immediately gives one an idea of how difficult the translation can be.

Why is this important? Building philosophical frameworks on misinterpreted ancient texts turns esotericism into speculation. Creative interpretation may have merit, and modern magical systems might function regardless of their historical basis, but misunderstanding original sources poses risks.

Danger because the people who control access to original source material, the Vatican archives, museum collections, and the classified archaeological findings, know what these texts really say. They have the resources to translate them properly; we don't have the context, and they're making decisions about what to reveal and what to suppress based on knowledge we don't have access to.

That's an information asymmetry problem. They know, and we guess at it, and our guesses are well-intentioned, even beautiful, but functionally are not the same as knowledge.

Gilbert's work matters because it shows that we can return to source materials when they're available. We can correct centuries of error, discover that what we thought we knew isn't what the text actually says, and that should make us humble about how much else we might have wrong.

The Law of Correspondence between macrocosm and microcosm? Beautiful idea. Useful framework. Might be completely true as a philosophical principle, but it's not what the Emerald Tablet teaches according to the Arabic source material. The Emerald Tablet teaches something else: there's a cycle, a system, a divine mechanism by which souls descend into matter and ascend back to spirit. That's still profound and important.

Here's what really bothers me about all of this. The mistake wasn't innocent. Medieval Christian scholars translating Arabic texts had theological axes to grind. They were working in a framework where certain ideas were heretical, certain concepts were forbidden, certain interpretations could get you killed. When they encountered texts about soul transmigration, about reincarnation cycles, about consciousness existing independent of body, concepts fundamental to Hermetic and Neoplatonic philosophy, they had every incentive to mistranslate, to obscure, to make the text say something less threatening to Church doctrine.

"As above, so below" sounds mystical but vague. It can be interpreted in ways that don't challenge Christian cosmology, but "souls descend from divine unity into material separation and then ascend back through purification and gnosis" is reincarnation. That's heresy. That gets you burned.

So maybe the mistranslation wasn't accidental. It could have been protective, a case in which earlier scholars knew what it said and deliberately obscured it to preserve the text, all while making it acceptable to Church authorities.

We see this pattern everywhere in esoteric transmission. Encode the real knowledge in symbols and allegories. Make it sound like philosophy or mythology. Hide the technical instructions behind poetic language. That way, if it's discovered, if it's read by hostile authorities, they see mystical nonsense instead of practical consciousness technologies.

The Emerald Tablet, properly understood, isn't mystical nonsense. It's a description of a cosmological system, a map of consciousness evolution, instructions for spiritual ascent encoded in terse, compressed language that assumes the reader has context.

We lost that context and the proper translation, along with the understanding that this isn't poetry, it's engineering. Consciousness engineering. The blueprint for how souls interface with material reality.

Gilbert's work restores some context, though we lack the full picture and all relevant texts to fully understand previous misreadings. Those with better translations had more knowledge, highlighting how control over translation influences access to information.

That matters for everything else we're exploring in this chapter. Because if they can mistranslate the Emerald Tablet for centuries and have everyone accept the wrong version, what else are they mistranslating? What else are they deliberately obscuring?

The Dead Sea Scrolls? The Nag Hammadi texts? The Vatican's secret archives are full of documents that never get released. The Sumerian tablets that spent twenty years in America before being returned to Iraq?

Who's translating those? What are they really saying, and what are we being told they say instead?

This is why the mystery schools insisted on direct experience over received wisdom. They knew texts could be corrupted, translations could be wrong, and the only way to verify spiritual truth was to have the experience yourself. To undergo initiation, make contact, develop capacity, and then see what reality reveals.

You can't mistranslate gnosis or corrupt direct experience. You can obscure it, make people doubt it, shame them for talking about it, but you can't change what they experienced. This is the safeguard, the reason consciousness development matters more than textual scholarship. Texts can be destroyed, mistranslated, or suppressed. Still, the practices and actual techniques for expanding consciousness, for making contact, for developing capacities can be passed person to person, teacher to student, through direct demonstration and supervised experience. The mystery schools understood this, which is why they had initiations rather than just books, and why you couldn't just read your way to enlightenment. You had to do the work, undergo the experiences, and develop the capacities. The control systems fear mystery school knowledge becoming widespread for exactly this reason. Once people start having direct experiences that contradict official narratives, develop consciousness abilities that materialist science says shouldn't be possible, and make contact with non-human intelligence that official disclosure says doesn't exist, the control collapses. No one can gaslight you about your own direct experience. They can make you doubt it, question your sanity, feel afraid to talk about it, but they can't make you unsee what you saw, unfeel what you felt, or unknow what you directly experienced. This is the power of gnosis, the reason it threatens control systems, and the reason proper translation of texts matters. When we get the texts right and understand what the ancients were teaching, we can better replicate the practices that produce the experiences.

Gilbert's work on the Emerald Tablet isn't just academic correction. It's opening a door to a better understanding of Hermetic cosmology, which means a better understanding of consciousness technologies, which means potentially recovering capacities humanity has lost, forgotten, or had systematically suppressed.

The ancients knew things we don't, had experiences we can't explain, and developed capacities we dismiss as impossible, and the proof is in the texts. When we translate them correctly and read what they say, not what later interpreters wanted them to say.

"As above, so below" is beautiful. Use it if it resonates, just know that it's not what the Emerald Tablet teaches according to the best available translation of the earliest source material, and know that this mistranslation, whether accidental or protective, is just one example of how knowledge gets corrupted, obscured, and controlled across centuries.

The pattern continues. From ancient Sumer through medieval Baghdad through modern cover-ups. Those who control the translations control the narrative, and those who control the narrative control what people believe is possible.

However, direct experience breaks that control, and so do the practices themselves, because developing actual capacities renders the whole suppression apparatus irrelevant.

The mystery schools preserved more than texts and symbols. They preserved actual practices, techniques, and initiations that produce real experiences.[75]

Those practices and that knowledge found their way into organizations that survived the persecutions. Organizations that made it through the centuries of suppression and arrived in modern times with fragments of ancient wisdom still intact.

Organizations like the Knights Templar and, after their destruction, their successors, the Freemasons.

Now we dive into how that knowledge transferred. How it survived Friday the 13th, 1307, influenced the founding of America and the structure of Western civilization, and why the same forces that destroyed the Templars are still trying to control access to what they knew.

These mystery school teachings didn't disappear when civilizations fell or when empires suppressed them. The knowledge survived, passed from teacher to student, encoded in architecture and symbol, hidden in plain sight for those with eyes to see. Organizations emerged to carry this wisdom forward through centuries of persecution, organizations that would face their own destruction precisely because of what they knew and what they refused to surrender to institutional control. The most famous of these were warrior monks who found something beneath Jerusalem's Temple Mount, something that would change the course of Western civilization and cost them everything. This is the story of the Knights Templar and the forces that destroyed them, and the deeper story of how their knowledge survived that destruction to influence the very foundations of the modern world.

# CHAPTER 7

## TEMPLAR SECRETS

The story we've been handed about the Knights Templar is a fairy tale crafted for textbooks, a comfortable myth about warrior monks protecting pilgrims and inventing early banking. Still, the real story lies elsewhere entirely, buried beneath centuries of fear, suppression, and deliberate misdirection. The Templars were not simply a military order. They were the inheritors of something older and far more subversive, a current of initiatic knowledge that was fundamentally incompatible with the power structures of medieval Europe.[76]

Tim Wallace Murphy argued that the Templars were never Christian in the way modern churches would define it. According to his research, the founders of the Order traced their lineage to the Mammodai, the twenty-four high priestly families of Jerusalem who fled after Rome destroyed the city in 70 CE. These were hereditary initiates whose spiritual technologies predated Rabbinic Judaism, predated Christianity, and reached back into the First Temple itself.[77]

When the first nine knights arrived in Jerusalem in the early 1100s and established their base on the Temple Mount, they were not merely guarding ruins. They were returning to the center of their ancestral inheritance, and somewhere beneath those stones, they found something powerful enough that the Church rushed to bury the record and disruptive enough to reshape the inner theology of the Order.[78]

Whatever they uncovered was almost certainly tied to Gnostic priestly wisdom, the kind of experiential teachings designed to transform consciousness. Wallace Murphy believed these doctrines were closer to the original message of Jesus than anything endorsed by the institutional Church. That alone could have condemned them, but they went further. They practiced these teachings privately, initiated others, built rituals around them, and spread them quietly outside the Church's chain of command.[79]

Rome could tolerate armed monks, wealth, and rival institutions. They would not tolerate an order of spiritually autonomous warrior initiates who bypassed priestly authority and accessed the divine directly.[80]

This set the stage for the accusation that never disappeared: Baphomet. Mentions of Baphomet appear as early as the 11th century. A Crusader's letter from 1090 references the term, and medieval chroniclers even described mosques as "Bafumarias," suggesting the name may originally have been associated with Islamic worship rather than demons.[81]

Historians have interpreted "Baphomet" as an Old French corruption of "Mahomet," the Latinized form of Muhammad's name. During the Crusades, the Templars lived for extended periods in the Middle East, where they became well-versed in Arabian mysticism. They studied with local teachers, absorbed new forms of spiritual psychology, and brought these teachings back to Europe, contributing to what would later become Western occultism. Their affinity for these traditions, combined with their secrecy, led the Church to claim they were worshiping a Muslim idol.[82]

Arkon Daraul offered another view, that Baphomet derives from the Arabic phrase *Abu fihama(t)*, meaning "Father of Understanding," a title that points toward a symbolic embodiment of divine intelligence rather than an idol.[83]

The most compelling explanation came from Dr. Hugh J. Schonfield, a scholar of the Dead Sea Scrolls and expert in the Hebrew Atbash cipher. When Schonfield applied the cipher to the Hebrew spelling of "Baphomet"-בפומת-the transformed letters spelled שופיא (ShVPIA), read as *Sophia* in Greek, meaning divine wisdom.[84]

This suggests that Baphomet was not a demon, nor an Islamic figure, but a cipher, a secret name for the sacred feminine wisdom revered across esoteric traditions.[85]

This decoding aligns with broader scribal practices. Jewish sages known as the Tannaim wrote in alternating directions, which is a pattern called "plowing the field," or boustrophedon writing. Codes, reversals, and mirrored texts were common in esoteric manuscripts, layered structures intended to conceal sacred meaning from the uninitiated.[86]

If Baphomet encoded Sophia, then the Templars were not worshiping an idol. They were venerating divine wisdom, the feminine intelligence found in Gnosticism, Kabbalah, Hermeticism, Sufism, and the esoteric currents they encountered in the East.[87]

This interpretation aligns with their architecture, symbols, and rituals. The Black Madonna, the geometric arrangements, the roses, and the doves are all signs of Sophia's presence embedded in Templar tradition. The Church saw heresy, but the Templars saw a lineage.[88]

Their time in the Holy Land only deepened this integration. They did not merely fight Muslims; they also learned from them. Historical analyses suggest they had substantial contact with Sufi mystics, Ismaili initiates, and the Ikhwan al-Safa, the Brethren of Purity, whose encyclopedic writings blended Hermeticism, Neoplatonism, mathematics, and esoteric psychology.[89 90 91]

Here is where your original insight fits perfectly. I feel the Templars had more than casual interactions with the Sufis, Ismailis, and possibly the Ikhwan al-Safa, and that a large amount of secret esoteric knowledge and practices was shared among them. This goes back to my theory that syncretism is always occurring amongst these orders, and often not publicly, for fear of reprisals. This could have been done only with a few of the higher-ranking members to stem the fear of persecution, and then filtered down to the rank and file.

This insight is supported by scholars of comparative esotericism, who note that medieval initiatic groups often quietly exchanged techniques, transmitting practices at higher levels while shielding outer members.[92]

When the Templars were persecuted, this knowledge was passed down further to what we recognize as modern-day Freemasonry. Some of it has been lost, and other parts have been hidden even deeper, but the symbology remains, and syncretism is apparent. Studies of early Freemasonry suggest that strands of Templar ritual symbolism, sacred geometry, and initiation structures flowed into proto-Masonic societies, particularly in Scotland.[93] [94]

You're probably asking yourself now, what does this have to do with UFOs? Stay with me. As I mentioned before, I think that modern occultism and Western esoteric traditions lend themselves to unraveling hidden knowledge and using it in practice. All sorts of groups were created based on the foundational knowledge of these pre-Freemasonic organizations. This connection resonates strongly with modern esoteric historians who trace contemporary occult frameworks back to the synthesis of Hermetic, Kabbalistic, Islamic, and Templar-influenced knowledge streams.[95]

If all of this sounds familiar, the hidden wisdom, the encoded pathways, the spiritual transformation disguised as myth. That's because the theme shows up everywhere these mystery traditions left their fingerprints. Even Joseph Campbell, the American professor whose work unlocked the meaning of myth for the modern world, pointed directly at this. When asked about the Grail, he didn't treat it as a relic hunt. He said something that almost everyone overlooks.

> **"Why should any medieval knight go searching for a relic, however holy, when all he had to do was go to church and take communion?"96**

Then Campbell dropped the real key. The Grail wasn't an object. It was a coded allegory for the path to enlightenment. To support this, he pointed to a line from the Gospel of Thomas.

> **"He who drinks from my mouth will become as I am, and I shall become he."97**

That's not about a chalice; it is initiation and transformation. Exactly what the Templars were practicing in private and the kind of knowledge the Church feared.

Campbell explained that alchemy worked the same way. It was never about turning lead into literal gold but about transmuting yourself, turning base, unrefined humanity into the gold of awakened consciousness.[98]

The people who understood this couldn't teach it openly. If they had, the Church would've come down on them with the full weight of the Inquisition. So, they encoded their teachings in architecture, in church art, in allegories, in symbols carved into stone, the same way esoteric schools have always done under oppression.

These teachings filtered into early Freemasonry as well, not through a direct organizational line we can definitively trace with evidence at this time, but through families and initiatic traditions that carried the same inner knowledge forward.[99]

Campbell later referenced one of the great Sufi teachers, Jalal al'Din Rumi, who said that beneath all religions there is a single path, a single river feeding every stream. A path of love, of awakening, found in Jesus, in the Kabbalah, in Sufi mysticism, and in Buddhism.[100]

Everything points to the same conclusion.

The Templars weren't just out of step with the Church.

They were following a path that transcended the Church, and that is exactly why the crackdown that followed was so violent, so total, and so catastrophic.

Today, people joke about Friday the 13th being unlucky, but almost nobody remembers why. The superstition didn't come from folklore, paganism, or cheap horror movies. It came from a single moment in history—a state-sanctioned act of spiritual terrorism conducted with precision. **Friday, October 13th, 1307,** was the day King Philip IV of France launched a coordinated purge of the Knights Templar across the entire kingdom. Before sunrise, hundreds of knights were dragged from their beds, chained, tortured, and accused of impossible crimes. The date stuck. It became a cultural wound so deep that its echo survived for centuries. People could feel something "bad" in the number without remembering what happened. The unlucky superstition wasn't mystical; it was historical trauma.[101]

That history converges into one man, Jacques de Molay, the last Grand Master of the Knights Templar. According to eyewitnesses, de Molay showed no fear as they tied him to the stake. No panic or pleading. He did everything in his power not to cry out during the slow burn, and as the flames climbed his body, he unleashed a curse—and yes, that's the right word, calling out Pope Clement and King Philip directly. He declared that within a year, they would stand before God for judgment and that Philip's bloodline would soon be erased from the earth.[102]

It takes a special kind of spiritual confidence to do that while your skin is melting off your bones. The man had steel in his soul.

The universe responded. Clement was dead within a year, taken by illness. Philip followed soon after, felled by a stroke, and by 1328, every son and grandson of Philip IV was dead, wiping out the Capetian line exactly as de Molay had prophesied.[103]

Was it a curse? Was de Molay plugged so deeply into some primal collective consciousness that he pulled a cosmic lever on his way out? Did he call on a power older than Christianity, or was it simply the universe righting a wrong? We don't know, but the timing feels uncanny, so much so that even the most skeptical historians hesitate to dismiss it outright. And what makes all of this more infuriating in retrospect is the document the Vatican tried to hide: the Chinon Parchment. Discovered in 2001 by Italian paleographer Barbara Frale inside the Vatican Secret Archives, this parchment was written in 1308, one year after the Templars were arrested, and it absolves Jacques de Molay and the Templar leadership of heresy. Yes, **absolves**. The Church knew the charges were false. The Pope had this information while the Templars were being tortured, imprisoned, and burned alive.[104]

The Chinon Parchment records the testimony of de Molay himself, saying clearly that he had not confessed under torture. It documents the cardinals granting him absolution and restoring him to communion with the Church while Philip continued to pressure Clement politically and financially.

The commission itself is almost comedic. Guillaume de Mandagot, Bishop of Pamiers, was the legal mind. Guillaume

Arnaud, Grand Inquisitor of Toulouse, was notorious for his brutality. Jean de Castres, Bishop of Clermont, was the quieter member and notably not named Guillaume.

Yes, everyone was apparently named Guillaume, which sounds less like an inquisitorial panel and more like the lineup of a French punk band. Funny enough, Guillaume translates to 'Goodman' in English. The irony is thick here.

Despite the stacked deck, the findings were surprisingly lenient. The accusations lacked proof. The Templar leaders were absolved. The Vatican then sat on this document for seven centuries. When they finally published it in 2007, they printed only 800 copies, as if hoping nobody would notice. It took until 2011 for Pope Benedict XVI to publicly acknowledge the injustice, with the kind of apology you give when you want the conversation to end, not because you feel remorse.[105]

Remember the timing, the Church in 1314 knew the Templars were innocent. They had the document in 1308. They buried it. Meanwhile, the wealth of the Templars flowed straight into the hands of Philip and the Church, conveniently wiping out massive debts. It costs a lot of money to run a global religious empire, and wherever there is money, there is motivation.

In 2020, I was shocked by a headline about a major financial event involving the Catholic Church. The same motives that led kings and popes to seize the Templars' wealth in the 14th century resurfaced in modern times, this time under a new name: the COVID-19 Paycheck Protection Program. Once again, fate seemed to have a sense of irony. We'll explore that soon, but first, let's look at what they're doing with all that old wealth.

## CONSCIOUSNESS AS TECHNOLOGY: REMOTE VIEWING

The CIA's research into psychic abilities is legendary.[106]

Now we dive into remote viewing. The government's interest in consciousness abilities isn't a conspiracy theory. It's a documented fact.

The CIA and military intelligence agencies spent decades researching and operationalizing psychic abilities like remote viewing, telepathy, and precognition. They didn't do this because they believed in woo-woo mysticism; they did it because it worked.

Programs like Project Star Gate, Project Grill Flame, and Project Sun Streak weren't fringe experiments. They were serious intelligence-gathering operations using consciousness as technology.

Here is what declassified CIA documents say (all available in the CIA Reading Room at cia.gov/readingroom).

---

**"With the scientific community in general agreement on the physical possibility of such disciplines as psychokinesis, remote viewing, and remote communications. What can only be described as astounding successes in remote viewing research by two laser physicists at SRI International."**

---

These two laser physicists were Dr. Russell Targ and Dr. Harold Puthoff from SRI (Stanford Research Institute), who pioneered remote viewing research for the U.S. intelligence community (Russell Targ and Harold Puthoff, "Information Transmission Under Conditions of Sensory Shielding," Nature, 1974).[107]

Targ and Puthoff had amazing success with earlier intelligence-gathering activities involving RV and wanted to keep the ball rolling. They have done more research throughout the years since these releases, but nothing has been officially released since these projects were discovered via FOIA.

There were other projects like Project Sun Streak, which operationalized RV and apparently had success. They even created other branches of remote viewing, including CRV (Controlled Remote Viewing) and ERV (Extended Remote Viewing).

You can find all these documents online in the CIA Reading Room (https://www.cia.gov/readingroom/search/site) or the National Archives (https://catalog.archives.gov/).

Countless websites are dedicated to RVs, and you can even take online training to learn more about them. Several workshops and in-person courses let you spend a week and learn how to be a remote viewer.

I want to point out that most of the documents are still classified, so this is only a glimpse into the past of what had occurred, what was being taught by defense and intelligence agencies, the CIA, the U.S. Army, and others, and what was operationalized. What we have learned is that they had the basics figured out and created them into a training regimen. They distilled it down so they could basically turn any Army grunt into a remote viewer through repeatable steps.[108]

The military RV trainers created forms to make it easy, step-by-step, and that is the program I went through on my own by watching the videos and using the forms. Unbelievably, it worked for me.

Now that we've established what remote viewing is, let me tell you about a fascinating experiment conducted by researcher Linda Mount.

What Linda wanted to do was create a report to affirm what she was given and highlight how remote viewing can be used in research. It was interesting that she wanted to see what remote viewers at various levels of training could come up with. Some people had no prior training or experience in reporting. She told us to report anything we got and not to filter anything out.

The target? The Vatican Observatory on Mount Graham in Arizona.

Of the five people involved, one offered leads to previously unknown factual information that could help her research. What people received was, for the most part, in consensus: "Trees, steep mountain, river below, cement, etc., were all described in several viewers' comments."

Here are some quotes from individuals about the results after she told us the basic information.

"I've never heard of this place. Didn't know Vatican was involved in this sort of research." "Yeah, definitely saw all the trees." "The area looked unusual to me. Interesting."

What I personally discovered in my remote viewing session was a "time machine volcano." The impression I got was that it was a way or portal to traverse space and time vertically. I didn't get a picture of the telescope as others did, but the volcano aspect really stood out to me.

None of the other viewers got that, but they nailed the mountain and telescope. After we got the feedback, I had to look up whether the mountain was indeed an old volcano, and in fact it is! It has been inactive for millions of years, but geologists classify Mount Graham as a "dormant volcano," meaning it retains the potential to erupt in the future. However, volcanologists say that this is highly unlikely in the foreseeable future.

The Time Machine Metaphor.

While I wasn't seeing an actual time machine, I think my subconscious picked up that when we look at a star through a telescope, we're seeing it as it was when it emitted that light, which could be minutes, hours, years, or even millions of years ago. By peering deeper into the cosmos, we're essentially looking further back in time, observing galaxies from billions of years ago when the universe was much younger.

Looking at objects at varying distances is like examining snapshots of the universe at different points in its history. This allows astronomers to study the evolution of galaxies, stars, and planets and to reconstruct the timeline of cosmic events.

Telescopes aren't literal time machines, but they unlock a window to the past, letting us witness the universe unfold and unravel its mysteries one photon at a time, and that is what I saw the Vatican doing in my RV session. I think they are looking to the past to reveal the future in a way that benefits them and their religion. That was the impression I got, and I haven't been able to confirm it as fact; it's just my educated guess based on my subconscious RV session.

The following is a quote from Linda's report on Mount Graham.

"Mount Graham is in the Superstition Mountains in Arizona, and it is said to be dangerous, haunted, and has different paranormal activity. ET, giants in the past, etc. This mountain is the highest point, over 10,000 ft., where the observatory is located. It was the High Place, the only part of the mountain chain not considered a volcano. You cannot go up there at all without a permit because a particular rare squirrel is found only on that mountain.[109]

"The Jesuits were there even way back before a lot of others. It was rumored they had gold from the mines nearby and could still have it. Interesting comments on the remote viewers being pushed away, blocked, etc. An eternity symbol drawn by a couple of people.

"I believe the observatory structure probably has underground facilities. The Vatican group does not give public tours, from information I read, but I would totally expect to have some type of meeting room or viewing room as drawn out. The Observatory doesn't function year-round, from what I have seen.

"This area is known for a lot of UFO and black triangle sightings. Many missing people and bodies are recovered near there, and if you realize how steep the mountain is, it wouldn't be unlikely for people to attempt climbing it.

The tip I received from a retired law enforcement officer last year was that when the Observatory reopened after annual maintenance (I believe in October, based on research I could do), the law enforcement officers were told to stay away. Special Ops-type soldiers would be there in full battle-type clothing, weapons, and equipment. When the big lights show, it would attract beings. The officers would watch the activity with curiosity, seeing what was happening.

"Beings were mentioned in the remote viewing. Jesuits in the US seem to be extremely interested in the phenomena, extraterrestrials, and related topics. I cannot rule out such activity."

## THE VATICAN'S SACRED LAND SEIZURE

We have the Vatican kicking out an indigenous tribe of Native Americans from their sacred land and then building a multi-million-dollar telescope named LUCIFER on top of that mountain to look for habitable worlds and other mysteries of the universe.

Sure, all of that makes sense, right?

That entire mountain has a long history of strange, anomalous phenomena, including UFO sightings, cryptids, Bigfoot sightings, human disappearances, and much more. The Apache say it's the home of one of their deities. Well, maybe deity is in the eye of the mountain beholder?

The Vatican Advanced Technology Telescope (VATT) was built on Mount Graham despite protests from the San Carlos Apache Tribe, who consider the mountain sacred. The telescope's LUCIFER acronym (Large Binocular Telescope Near-infrared Utility with Camera and Integral Field Unit for Extragalactic Research) stoked conspiracy theories, though it has since been renamed LUCI.[110]

## WHAT THE VATICAN WAS REALLY SEARCHING FOR.

The Vatican has been involved in astronomical research for centuries, operating sophisticated observatories worldwide. They monitor the skies with technology, rivaling any government agency.[111] What are they looking for? What data do they have that we don't get to see publicly?

In 2008, the Vatican's chief astronomer, Father José Gabriel Funes, published an article titled "The Extraterrestrial Is My Brother," stating that belief in extraterrestrial life doesn't contradict Catholic faith. God could have created life elsewhere, and meeting aliens wouldn't challenge the church's teaching.[112]

If the Church is preparing theologically for contact, what do they know that we don't? What have they seen through their telescopes that prompted this theological pivot?

## THE CHURCH'S MODERN FINANCIAL HYPOCRISY

Now, let's take a closer look at the Catholic Church's priorities and what happened during COVID-19.

**While the Vatican reported losing $100 million[113] in revenue during the pandemic, Catholic dioceses and affiliated organizations in the United States received between $1.4 billion and $3.5 billion in taxpayer-funded PPP (Paycheck Protection Program) loans.[114][115]**

Think about that for a moment. The Catholic Church is tax-exempt. They pay zero taxes.

Yet during a global crisis when ordinary people were losing everything, the Church successfully lobbied for and received billions in taxpayer money.

Even more disturbing, some dioceses that had filed for bankruptcy, claiming inability to pay sexual abuse settlements, simultaneously received millions in federal aid.

The Church lobbied successfully for exemptions from PPP restrictions that applied to other organizations. Several dioceses that had laid off employees still received millions.[116]

The Church received taxpayer funds while sitting on vast unreported wealth.

The Vatican Bank (officially the Institute for the Works of Religion) has faced decades of scandal about its holdings and lack of transparency.

During COVID, while the Vatican claimed financial hardship, they took billions from American taxpayers who had no say in the matter because the Church doesn't contribute to the tax system.

Tax-exempt institution taking taxpayer money during crisis while sitting on unreported wealth and protecting itself from abuse settlements.

The pattern that started with the Templars continues: accumulation of wealth and power, suppression of truth, and protection of institutional interests over people's needs.

Honestly, I could author an entire book about the Vatican and its history of unexplained phenomena, cover-ups, scandals, and more, but I really don't want to. I'm fairly sure you don't want to read that either, or if you do, there are probably literally hundreds of books about this already.

That is, unless, of course, they have not already been suppressed by the Vatican itself.

The connection between consciousness abilities (remote viewing), ancient esoteric knowledge (Templars, Gnostics, mystery schools), the Vatican's astronomical research, and their modern financial maneuvering points to something larger.

Something the Church has known about for centuries. Something they've been preparing for while ensuring they maintain wealth and control, regardless of what ordinary people suffer.

## FROM TEMPLE TO LODGE, THE TEMPLAR TRANSMISSION

The official story is that the Knights Templar were destroyed, wealth seized, the order disbanded, and their heresy was punished. The Church and Crown were victorious over a corrupt brotherhood that had strayed from righteousness.

The actual story is different. The Templars saw it coming and prepared for it.

Scott Wolter and Hayley Ramsey have spent years researching Templar movements in the months and years leading up to the arrests. New documentary evidence, records from Scotland, carvings at Rosslyn Chapel, land grants, and ship manifests show that the Templars were quietly relocating assets, knowledge, and personnel to safe locations well before Philip made his move.

Scotland was the primary destination. The Pope had excommunicated King Robert the Bruce for various political reasons. An excommunicated king in an excommunicated country meant papal authority didn't reach there. It was a safe haven.[117] [118] and archaeological evidence at Rosslyn Chapel and other locations shows unmistakable Templar influence arriving precisely during this period.

What did they bring with them? They brought both knowledge and wealth. Enough wealth to create banks that would eventually become the modern financial system. Political influence, certainly, but most importantly, occult (hidden) knowledge. Everything they had found in Solomon's Temple during their two centuries controlling the Temple Mount in Jerusalem. The secrets they had acquired from interacting with Eastern mystics, Sufi masters, Kabbalists, and mystery school initiates across the Mediterranean. The understanding that had made them wealthy beyond measure and powerful enough to negotiate with kings as equals.

That knowledge didn't disappear when the order was officially destroyed. Instead, it went underground, spreading to places like Scotland and Switzerland, where the country's banking laws are known for shielding secret accounts. In Portugal, the Templars adopted a new name, the Order of Christ, and continued their activities. The legacy also survived through various European noble families connected to the Templars, who protected former knights. Many people believe that this knowledge eventually found its way into Freemasonry, and I do as well.

The timeline is suspiciously perfect. Templars destroyed in France: 1307-1314. First recorded Masonic lodge in Scotland: 1598 (though almost certainly older, just not documented earlier). The Grand Lodge system was formalized in Scotland in the early 1600s. Freemasonry spreading rapidly across Europe: 1600s-1700s.

Rosslyn Chapel (built by the St. Clair family between 1446 and 1484) is absolutely loaded with Masonic symbolism that shouldn't exist, yet according to official histories. Green Men carved into the stone. Corn (maize) was depicted decades before Columbus "discovered" America. Architectural features that match Masonic lodge layouts exactly. Symbols and carvings that only make sense if you understand both Templar traditions and Masonic degrees.

Hayley Ramsey's research into newly discovered Templar documents in Scotland confirms what many have suspected: the Templars didn't vanish. They transformed. They took their knowledge, their structure, and their rituals. They embedded them into a new organization that could operate openly, claiming to be focused on building and architecture rather than on military religious orders.

Stonemasons. Builders. Craftsmen. What better cover for preserving sacred geometry, architectural secrets, and initiatic rituals based on the building of Solomon's Temple?

These massive, complex cathedrals appeared out of nowhere in 1350. Where was that tech from? Atlantis? The French called the shocking style "Gothic," but it wasn't.

"The first cathedral is often identified as Etchmiadzin Cathedral in Armenia, founded between 301, 303 CE following Armenia's adoption of Christianity, although the core of its present structure dates to the fifth century; in the Western Roman world, the Archbasilica of St. John Lateran in Rome, commissioned by Emperor Constantine and dedicated in 324 CE, is recognized as the earliest imperial Christian cathedral."[119]

Operative masons, who were skilled stoneworkers responsible for building cathedrals, established their own lodge networks and guarded construction methods closely. The Templars became part of this established structure. Eventually, these lodges shifted to "speculative" membership, welcoming people who were not stonemasons but were drawn to the craft's philosophical and spiritual dimensions. Templar knowledge was preserved through degrees, rituals, and symbols, which only those initiated could truly understand.

This isn't conspiracy theory. This is a documented history that mainstream academia tries to downplay because it suggests continuity of esoteric knowledge from ancient times through medieval orders to modern fraternal organizations. That continuity threatens the narrative that Western civilization is purely Judeo-Christian, that the Enlightenment happened independent of mystery school influence, that modern science and modern democracy emerged spontaneously from rational thought rather than from esoteric traditions that understood consciousness, natural law, and human potential in ways that materialist frameworks don't acknowledge.

What did the Templars find in Solomon's Temple?

We don't know with certainty, but we do know they went there poor and left wealthy. They ran under their own charter, answering to no king or pope and developed banking systems centuries ahead of their time. They had diplomatic relations across religious and political boundaries and were feared by the most powerful institutions of their era. When they were destroyed, something of enormous value was hidden. Scott Wolter's research shows that Templars traveled to America, yes, America, in the 1300s, over a century before Columbus, and they left markings, runestones, symbols at various locations. Why? What were they hiding that required traveling across the Atlantic to unpopulated continents?

One theory is that they were preserving knowledge that couldn't safely remain in Europe. Libraries, artifacts, texts, and physical proof of whatever they'd discovered made them so dangerous to Church and Crown.

Another theory is that they were following older maps. Charts showing continents that hadn't been officially discovered. Maps from ancient sources, possibly from the same library that survived from pre-flood civilizations, contain the same knowledge as the artifacts from the Baghdad Museum.

Or maybe both. Maybe they had ancient maps and texts, and used the maps to hide the texts in places where European authorities couldn't reach them.

Whatever the truth, the knowledge survived through Freemasonry, Rosicrucianism, and various mystery school lineages that claimed Templar descent. That knowledge influenced the founding of America, a nation whose symbolism, architecture, and founding documents reflect Masonic and Rosicrucian philosophy far more than most people realize.

The Great Seal of the United States, featuring an eye in a pyramid and the inscription "Novus Ordo Seclorum" (New Order of the Ages), has been associated with Masonic symbolism.

Washington D.C.'s layout, designed by Pierre Charles L'Enfant, a Freemason, with streets aligned to create Masonic symbols visible from above.

The Declaration of Independence and Constitution were written primarily by Freemasons, who believed in natural law, individual sovereignty, and limited government, concepts that come directly from mystery school philosophy, not from mainstream Christianity or European monarchism.

The American experiment was a Templar/Masonic/Rosicrucian project from the start. Creating a nation where religious freedom allowed mystery school traditions to operate openly. Constitutional protections prevented the kind of persecution that destroyed the Templars. Where Enlightenment ideals, rooted in Hermetic and Neoplatonic thought, could be implemented in government structure.

This isn't to say America is perfect or that Masonic influence made it perfect. Just that the philosophical foundation isn't what most people think it is. It's not purely Christian or secular rational thought. The foundation is esoteric knowledge, ancient wisdom, mystery school philosophy encoded into the structure of a modern nation-state, and that knowledge still exists in Freemasonry today. Corrupted in some lodges, diluted in others, barely understood by many members, but present, preserved, and available to those who seek it seriously and undergo the initiations with proper attention.

I know because I'm a Freemason and a Knight Templar. I have multiple degrees from multiple bodies, including the York Rite (which has explicit Templar degrees) and the Scottish Rite. I've undergone these initiations. I've experienced what they're designed to trigger, and I can tell you there's real knowledge here. Real consciousness technologies are hidden in ritual and symbol. Real initiatic experiences that change how you perceive reality.

There's also a problem; most Freemasons today don't understand what they've inherited. They go through degrees, treating them as theater, as tradition, as social bonding. Members memorize lines without understanding the psychological engineering behind the initiations, and wear regalia without understanding the symbolic language they convey.

The knowledge is there. The structure is there. The rituals are preserved, but the experiential context that makes them meaningful is often lost to the individual.

That's the danger of transmission through institutions. The forms survive, but the essence fades. The degrees continue, but the transformative power weakens. People go through initiations without being initiated, and meanwhile, some lodges were infiltrated and corrupted. The Bavarian Illuminati infiltrated Freemasonry in the 1700s. Nazi occultists infiltrated lodges in Germany in the 1920s-1930s and confiscated everything for the SS-incorporated Thule Society.

Intelligence agencies have been using Masonic networks for recruitment and communication since at least World War II.

You have this duality with legitimate Masonic lineages preserving real knowledge alongside corrupted lodges serving as fronts for intelligence operations or worse. How do you tell the difference? From outside, you can't. From inside, it requires discernment, experience, and knowing what you're looking for. I give a lecture to (Rubicon Lodge #237) about UFOs, consciousness, and the connections to Masonic philosophy. Some brothers got it. They see the parallels between "the light" we talk about in Masonry and the lights in the sky that don't behave according to known physics. These brothers understand that the degrees teach consciousness development, not just moral lessons, and recognize that the Templar connection isn't just historical, it's active, present, and ongoing.

Other brothers think I'm nuts. That's fine. Freemasonry allows that diversity. As long as you believe in a higher power (which keeps atheistic materialism from corrupting the initiatic system), as long as you act with honor, as long as you support your brothers, you can interpret the degrees however you want.

There's a deeper layer. A layer that certain brothers have access to, one that connects to the original Templar knowledge, the mystery school wisdom, the consciousness technologies that have been preserved through persecution and suppression for millennia.

That layer is still there. Still functional. Still dangerous to those who want humanity controlled.

The parallel stigmas are unmistakable. Freemasonry and UFOs both face ridicule, infiltration, and systematic efforts to discredit them for the same reason; both offer paths to understanding that threaten control systems. Freemasonry teaches that consciousness can be developed, that reality operates according to principles most people don't understand, and that humans have capacities beyond the material. UFOs demonstrate something complementary: consciousness interacts with technology in ways defying physicalist assumptions, that non-human intelligence exists and contacts humans, and that reality is far stranger than official narratives admit. The response is identical (ridicule, infiltration, suppression), yet neither is destroyed. Freemasonry endures. UFOs keep appearing. The knowledge continues to be transmitted, and The Phenomenon manifests regardless, transforming people through genuine Masonic initiations that expand consciousness, UFO encounters that break materialist paradigms, and mystery school practices that produce gnosis.

The Templars knew that experiential knowledge couldn't be fully suppressed. Rituals preserve wisdom even when the meaning is temporarily lost, and if you embed consciousness technologies into institutional structures with sufficient redundancy and protection, they survive even centuries of persecution.

As a result, this was incorporated into Freemasonry, Rosicrucianism, and several other esoteric groups that assert their lineage. That knowledge remains present, active, and available to anyone who earnestly seeks it.

The chain runs from ancient mysteries to Egyptian priesthoods to Greek mystery schools to Gnostic traditions to Templars in Jerusalem and Scotland to Freemasonry to Modern esoteric organizations.

Unbroken, preserved, and always waiting.

For what? For humanity to be ready and the control systems to weaken enough that people can access this knowledge without being burned at the stake. Mystery schools have been preparing for the Great Awakening for many centuries.

And maybe, just maybe, that time is now. With 21st-century UFO disclosure happening, with consciousness research advancing, with mystery school knowledge spreading through books, lectures, and podcasts instead of just through secret initiation.

Maybe the Templars preserved this knowledge for exactly this moment, when it would be needed, when humanity would be ready, and the gatekeepers could no longer fully suppress what was always meant to be shared.

That's the hope, anyway.

There's a darker side, too: while some lineages preserved knowledge for enlightenment, others perverted it for power and advanced physics-based weapons. While some occultists sought to expand consciousness, others looked to exploit it.

What happens when mystery school knowledge falls into the wrong hands and illumination becomes manipulation?

## DARK INVERSIONS—WHEN KNOWLEDGE CORRUPTS.

Aleister Crowley was not a Freemason.

Let's start there because the myth needs to die. There is no record (none) of Aleister Crowley in any legitimate Masonic lodge. The story about him being made a 33rd degree Mason in Mexico by some random Mexican gentleman? Fiction. Were the claims initiated on-site during a mountain climb? No documentation exists. The supposed Masonic connections? He hung around people who were Masons. Theodore Reuss of the OTO was a Mason. Samuel Liddell MacGregor Mathers was a Mason. But Crowley himself never went through legitimate Masonic initiation.

This matters for one reason: it changes everything. Crowley's entire career was built on stolen legitimacy. He took initiatic systems developed by others, corrupted them for his purposes, and sold them as his own revelations. He was a charlatan. A talented charlatan with genuine magnetism and probably some real occult experiences, but a charlatan, nonetheless, and he's important to understand because he represents what happens when mystery school knowledge falls into the wrong hands. When consciousness technologies designed for elevation are perverted for exploitation. When the power dynamics of initiatic systems are weaponized rather than liberated.

Edward Alexander Crowley, who later adopted the name Aleister, was born into wealth in 1875. His family made their money from Crowley's Ale. They were Plymouth Brethren, a strict Christian sect that made Puritans look relaxed. No holidays. No celebrations. No joy. Everything pleasurable was sin. His father preached constantly. Young Aleister went with him, absorbing fundamentalist fire-and-brimstone theology.

Then his father died, and Crowley rebelled against everything. He threw himself into the opposite extreme, hedonism, occultism, sexual experimentation, and drug use. He joined the Hermetic Order of the Golden Dawn in 1898, bringing money and enthusiasm but immediately annoying everyone with his arrogance and lack of genuine humility.

The Golden Dawn was serious. Founded by Freemasons and Rosicrucians who sought to revive Hermetic magical practices, it had legitimate lineages, serious scholarship, and members such as W.B. Yeats and Arthur Conan Doyle. It required work, discipline, and progressive initiation through carefully structured degrees.

Crowley wanted shortcuts. He showed up at one meeting wearing a fake mustache and a bad Russian accent, trying to pass himself off as a Russian aristocrat. People saw through it immediately. He had money and charisma, but he was fundamentally unserious about the work. He wanted power without earning it, knowledge without transformation, the status without virtue.

So, he manipulated his way up. Crowley hooked up with Elaine Simpson, wife of one of the Golden Dawn members, and used sexual magnetism, which he had in abundance by all accounts, to create leverage. He threw money around and bought an estate in Scotland at Loch Ness called Boleskine, specifically to perform the Abramelin operation, a six-month ritual designed to contact one's Holy Guardian Angel.

However, he didn't complete the ritual. Samuel Liddell MacGregor Mathers called him away to Paris for some political issue in the Golden Dawn, and Crowley abandoned the ritual mid-process. You don't do that. These aren't games. These are consciousness technologies with specific protocols for specific reasons. Abandoning a major work halfway through is like starting surgery and walking away, dangerous, potentially catastrophic.

Crowley didn't care. He had what he wanted from the ritual: weird experiences, psychological destabilization, contact with something (whether external entities or his own fractured psyche, depending on interpretation), and that was enough for him.

Then came the breakthrough moment that defined his career, Cairo, 1904. His wife, Rose, in a trance state, told him, "They are waiting for you." She led him to a museum and pointed at a stele, exhibit number 666, which Crowley took as cosmic confirmation. Rose, still in trance, said an entity named Aiwass wanted to communicate with him.

For three days, April 8-10, 1904, Crowley sat in his hotel room and received dictation. The result was "The Book of the Law," the foundational text of Thelema, Crowley's religious philosophy. The core teaching was "Do what thou wilt shall be the whole of the Law."

Was it real? Did a non-human entity actually dictate this text? Or was it Crowley's fractured psyche, destabilized by the incomplete Abramelin operation and years of drug use, producing coherent content through dissociative states?

Both are possible. The text has qualities that suggest something beyond Crowley's conscious authorship, linguistic patterns that don't match his other writing, prophetic statements that proved accurate, and symbolic density that has kept occultists analyzing it for over a century.

Whether Aiwass was real or not, Crowley used the text to justify everything he wanted to do anyway. "Do what thou wilt" became license for hedonism, exploitation, and cruelty. The philosophy had depth, true Will isn't whim, it's alignment with cosmic purpose (but Crowley implemented it as "do whatever I want and claim cosmic authority."

The Abbey of Thelema in Sicily became his base. Followers arrived, many wealthy, funding his lifestyle. He performed sex magic rituals, sometimes consensual, sometimes coercive, and had followers cut themselves if they said "I," breaking ego attachment or sadistic control? Both, probably.

Victor Neuberg became his devoted follower. Crowley took him into the Algerian desert for the Enochian Working, a ritual designed to contact angelic intelligences. For days, they walked, dehydrated, disoriented. Crowley put Neuberg in a protective salt circle. At the same time, he performed the ritual outside it, deliberately inverting the usual practice in which the magician protects himself and summons entities outside the circle.

Then, as Crowley later reported, he sodomized Neuberg at the moment of ritual climax, claiming this released power that completed the working. Neuberg was never the same, mentally broken, psychologically shattered. Crowley had used him, exploited him sexually and spiritually, and discarded him.

Later, when Neuberg's family wanted him back, Crowley allegedly ransomed him for 500 pounds. Using a human being he'd destroyed as leverage for money.

That's not mystery school practice. That's predation wearing an occult costume, and the pattern repeats. Crowley attracted people, used them financially and sexually, broke them psychologically, and discarded them. His first wife, Rose, descended into alcoholism and mental illness. His children died, some from illness, some from neglect. Multiple followers ended up institutionalized or dead.

The Abbey of Thelema in Sicily was eventually shut down when Raoul Loveday died there, possibly from drinking cat blood during a ritual, possibly from contaminated water. His widow fled to England and told newspapers about the conditions, drug use, sexual abuse, psychological manipulation, and dangerous practices.

Crowley was expelled from Italy and spent his later years impoverished, addicted to heroin, writing prolifically but living in squalor. He died in 1947, broke and largely forgotten except by a small circle of devoted followers.

So why does he matter?

Because his influence didn't die with him, Jack Parsons, brilliant rocket scientist and co-founder of JPL (Jet Propulsion

Laboratory), became a devoted Thelemite. Parsons was doing groundbreaking work in solid rocket fuel while simultaneously practicing Crowley's rituals, performing sex magic, and trying to incarnate the "Moonchild," a divine being that would usher in Crowley's New Aeon.

Parsons worked with L. Ron Hubbard, who later founded Scientology. They performed the Babylon Working together, trying to manifest the Scarlet Woman, the feminine lunar power that Thelemic philosophy said was necessary for cosmic transformation.

Did it work? Parsons thought so. He met Marjorie Cameron shortly after, believed she was the incarnate Scarlet Woman, and married her, but the rituals may also have destabilized him further. He died in 1952 in a laboratory explosion, officially an accident, but some researchers suggest he was eliminated because he'd become a liability. He was being watched by the FBI, suspected of passing rocket technology secrets to foreign governments, and known for associating with communists and occultists.

Here's what's interesting: the government kept using his rocket science while monitoring his occult practices. They didn't dismiss it as nonsense. Instead, they watched, documented, and kept files. Why? Because intelligence agencies understood something the public didn't, that consciousness technologies work. Ritual practice affects reality in ways that can't be easily explained but can be observed and potentially weaponized.

Crowley's influence spread through counterculture. The Beatles put him on the Sgt Pepper's album cover. Led Zeppelin's Jimmy Page bought Boleskine House. David Bowie studied Thelema. The 1960s "do your own thing" ethos came partly from misunderstood Crowleyan philosophy filtered through drugs and rebellion, and intelligence agencies paid close attention to it all. MKUltra research into LSD and consciousness manipulation borrowed from occult traditions. Remote viewing programs used meditation and trance techniques developed in mystery schools. The CIA's interest in Jack Parsons wasn't just about rocket technology. It was about whether his occult practices were accessing real phenomena.

So, we have this weird situation, Crowley was a charlatan who exploited people, but he was also accessing something real. The rituals work. Sex magic has effects. Consciousness can be manipulated through specific techniques—entities, whether external or psychological complexes, can be contacted and interacted with.

The ethical framework matters enormously in this regard. The mystery schools developed ethical training alongside occult practice for a variety of reasons. You don't give loaded weapons to children or teach consciousness manipulation to people who lack compassion, discipline, and humility.

Crowley had a couple of accidental brilliances but no ethics. He had courage but no compassion, knowledge but used it for exploitation rather than elevation.

That's the dark inversion. Mystery school technologies serving ego instead of transcending it, power serving domination instead of liberation, knowledge serving control instead of enlightenment. And here's the scary part: Crowley's methods are more accessible now than mystery school practices ever were. You can buy his books on Amazon. Watch YouTube videos explaining his rituals and find online communities teaching Thelemic magic.

There's no initiation, vetting, or ethical training. No experienced teacher supervising your practice and ensuring you don't destabilize yourself or hurt others.

Just techniques. Powerful techniques. Available to anyone.

What could go wrong?

The mystery schools understood this well. They established specific requirements, used a step-by-step initiation process, and closely supervised each stage. Instead of merely reading about the practices, students had to experience them directly with proper guidance, demonstrate their worth at every level, and cultivate their ethical abilities alongside their magical skills.

Without that structure, you get chaos. You get people doing Crowley's rituals without understanding the psychological dangers, exploitation dressed as enlightenment, and charlatans claiming to be enlightened masters while abusing students.

You get, in other words, exactly what we see in modern occult communities. Knowledge is abundant, but a lack of wisdom, an emphasis on technique but little regard for ethics, and a drive for power that rarely leads to meaningful change.

The Catholic Church understood this, too. They suppressed occult knowledge not just because it threatened their authority but because they'd seen what happened when it spread without proper safeguards. The Inquisition wasn't only about maintaining power; it was about preventing precisely the kind of chaos and exploitation that Crowley represented.

Were they right to suppress it? No. Suppression never works in the long term and creates the problem it tries to solve. Knowledge goes underground, becomes corrupted, and appears in dangerous forms.

Neither is unrestricted access to the answer. Not everyone should have access to nuclear weapons, and not everyone should have access to consciousness manipulation techniques either.

There needs to be a middle way, and the mystery schools had it: progressive initiation, ethical development, supervised practice, and community accountability.

Modern attempts to recreate these legitimate Thelemic orders, serious Golden Dawn reconstructions, and genuine Rosicrucian groups try to implement these safeguards. Still, they're fighting against a culture that wants instant gratification, rejects gatekeeping as elitism, and demands immediate access to everything, and meanwhile, the intelligence agencies know what Crowley tapped into. They've been researching it since at least the 1950s. MKUltra wasn't just about LSD; it was about consciousness manipulation, about what Crowley called "magick," about techniques that work regardless of whether you believe in spirits or interpret everything psychologically.

The intelligence agencies know that rituals affect consciousness in measurable ways, that sex magic has neurological effects, that meditation and trance states can produce remote viewing, precognition, and telepathy, phenomena that shouldn't exist according to materialist science but consistently appear in controlled studies when the right protocols are used.

These agencies classify the research, study it in secret, use it operationally, remote viewing programs, psychic espionage, consciousness manipulation techniques deployed in interrogation and propaganda, and publicly, they maintain that it's all nonsense. That Crowley was just a drug addict. That occultism is superstition. That consciousness is just brain activity.

Same pattern we've seen repeatedly. Study it secretly, suppress it publicly, use it operationally, deny it exists.

Crowley's legacy is complicated. He was a charlatan and an abuser, but also a genuine magician who may have accessed real phenomena.

He democratized occult knowledge in ways that were both liberating and dangerous, and he influenced both genuine seekers and intelligence agencies studying consciousness as a weapon.

Crowley's just one of those puzzle pieces you can never really fit. All my friend Warner's Churchill research from the war years points to this, Churchill saw Crowley as the living definition of paradox, he was never fully saint, never fully sinner, and get this, some say that Crowley was a bona fide MI-6 operative. He did legit work for the Allies. Does that make him a villain or a hero?

His warning is still relevant because these techniques work, but without an ethical foundation, without progressive development, without wise guidance, they corrupt and destroy, turning seekers into predators and students into victims.

The mystery schools knew this. The Templars knew this. Freemasonry knows this.

That is why the knowledge was guarded. Not to hoard power but to protect both knowledge and those who seek it.

Crowley proved what happens when that protection fails, when someone with brilliance but no ethics gets access to consciousness technologies, when knowledge spreads faster than wisdom.

His example should terrify us as we move into an age of widespread access to these techniques, with neurotechnology advancing, psychedelics becoming mainstream, and meditation and consciousness exploration moving from fringe to commonplace. These technologies will spread further into society. Will the ethical frameworks spread with them, or will we produce thousands of little Crowleys, manipulating consciousness for ego and exploitation?

That is why mystery school wisdom matters. Not just the techniques, but the complete system. Ethical development, progressive initiation, supervised practice, and community accountability. Without that, we get chaos. With it, we get transformation. Choose wisely.

## THE VATICAN'S LOCKED ARCHIVES—WHAT ARE THEY HIDING?

The Vatican Secret Archives hold 53 linear miles of shelving that the public is aware of. Twelve centuries of documents, papal correspondence, state papers, account books, and trial records. All public access is restricted. You need special credentials, must request specific documents in advance, and even then, most of the collection remains off-limits to researchers.[120]

The official name changed in 2019 to the Vatican Apostolic Archives. "Secret" had bad optics, but changing the name doesn't change what's there or who controls access.

What are they hiding?

The Church's official position is that there's nothing to hide. The archives hold administrative records, historical documents, and materials that are restricted to protect privacy and maintain order. Any conspiracy theories about hidden gospels, alien contact records, or suppressed knowledge are fantasy; history suggests otherwise.

The Library of Alexandria and the Apollo library in Rome, too, held hundreds of thousands of scrolls before they were burned or systematically looted across multiple incidents. Knowledge from across the ancient world. Texts that predate Christianity. Philosophical works. Scientific treatises. Mathematical discoveries. Astronomical charts. Mystery school teachings.

Some texts were burned, others lost or taken, and a few were preserved in secret. During the destruction of pagan temples and libraries by Christian mobs, materials considered valuable or threatening were often selectively kept rather than destroyed.

The Nag Hammadi library, discovered in Egypt in 1945, contained Gnostic gospels that had been buried around 400 AD, precisely when Christian orthodoxy was consolidating power and eliminating competing interpretations of Jesus's teachings. Someone preserved those texts, buried them to protect them from destruction.[121]

If Gnostic Christians were burying texts to protect them from the Church, what was the Church doing? Taking texts, studying them, and locking them away in archives where they could control who had access.

The pattern continues through history. When the Templars were destroyed, the Church confiscated their libraries. As the Cathar strongholds fell, their texts were seized. Rosicrucian and Hermetic practitioners arrested during the Inquisition had their books taken. And when Mesoamerican civilizations were conquered, their codices were burned, but copies were sent to Spain and the Vatican for study.[122]

The Church wasn't destroying knowledge indiscriminately; it was centralizing control, taking originals, studying them, and deciding what could be released and what must remain hidden.

Why? What are they protecting?

One theory is that they're protecting Church authority. If people knew that Jesus studied in India, that Christian teachings borrowed heavily from Egyptian mystery schools and Gnostic philosophy, that the resurrection narrative has parallels in dozens of earlier traditions, faith would be shaken. The Church's claim to unique divine revelation would collapse.

Another theory is that they're protecting humanity from dangerous knowledge. This includes consciousness technologies that could destabilize unprepared minds, scalar weaponry, and protocols for A.I. contact with non-human intelligence. It also references ancient warnings about cycles of destruction and technologies that could be weaponized.

A stronger case can be made with the third theory, which is that they're protecting themselves.

The Church worked with power structures for centuries, entered into agreements with various entities, and engaged in activities that would shock believers if revealed.

I am assuming that probably all three could be true. Different documents are hidden for different reasons.

The Dead Sea Scrolls provide a model. Discovered in 1947, they contained Hebrew and Aramaic texts that predated previously known biblical manuscripts by a thousand years. They showed that biblical texts were far more diverse, far more contested, far more edited than Church tradition acknowledged. Multiple versions of books. Texts that didn't make it into the canon. Evidence of theological debates that had been erased from official history.

Who controlled initial access to the Dead Sea Scrolls? A small team, primarily Catholic, that took decades to release full translations. Why so slow? What were they checking, editing?

Or consider the Gospel of Judas, discovered in the 1970s but not published until 2006. It presents Judas not as a betrayer but as Jesus's most trusted disciple, the only one who understood his true mission. Jesus asked Judas to turn him in. Judas was doing what Jesus needed him to do.

If that's true, the entire foundation of Christian anti-Semitism collapses. Two thousand years of "the Jews killed Christ" rhetoric becomes an obscene misunderstanding. Pogroms, persecution, and the Holocaust were all built on a lie that early Church fathers perpetuated for political reasons.

Would the Vatican want that known? Or would they prefer the Gospel of Judas stay hidden?

The Vatican didn't burn it or destroy it, and didn't rush to publish it either. It surfaced through the black market, got passed through dealers and collectors, and eventually reached scholars who recognized its significance. The Vatican could have bought it and locked it away, as they have with numerous other documents throughout history. They didn't, but only because they lost control of it before they knew what it was.

How many other texts did they successfully lock away? How about the alternative gospels, Gnostic teachings, mystery school texts that never surfaced because the Vatican secured them first?

Then there's the UFO question.

The Church has been involved in UFO investigations since at least the 1950s. Vatican astronomers run sophisticated observatories. They monitor the skies. They have data we don't see. In 2008, the Vatican's chief astronomer, Father José Gabriel Funes, published an article saying that belief in extraterrestrial life doesn't contradict Catholic faith. God could have created life elsewhere. Meeting aliens wouldn't challenge Church teaching.[123]

Interesting timing. Why did they make that statement in 2008, and what are they preparing for? Do they already have foreknowledge of a future event, and what about historical UFO encounters? The "Miracle of the Sun"[124] at Fatima in 1917, witnessed by 70,000 people[125], described a spinning disc[126] that descended from the sky, changed colors, and performed aerial maneuvers. Sounds like a UFO sighting. The Church calls it a miracle, a sign from the Virgin Mary; what if it were both? What if non-human intelligence uses religious iconography as an interface and the Marian apparitions are contact events filtered through Catholic cultural expectations?[127] [128]

The Church would have records, witness testimonies, and investigations. And reports from clergy who experienced these events directly. Are those in the Vatican Archives? Are they classified alongside other phenomena the Church can't explain but won't deny?

What really bothers me is the Church's relationship with indigenous knowledge. When Spanish conquistadors destroyed Mayan codices, when missionaries burned Native American sacred texts[129], when colonial powers suppressed African tribal wisdom[130], the Church was there.[131] Sometimes it leads to destruction. Sometimes quietly preserving copies "for study."

Those copies went to the Vatican archives, where Church scholars could examine them away from public scrutiny.

What did those texts contain? Astronomical knowledge that rivaled or exceeded European understanding; agricultural techniques; medical practices; and something else: contact histories. Stories of sky people or gods who descended from the sky. Stories of beings who taught, transformed, and promised to return.[132]

These are the same stories that Sumerian texts tell, which Egyptian and Greek mystery schools preserved, carved into temples, and encoded in myths across every continent.[133]

The Church knew this, saw the patterns, understood these weren't separate myths but something consistent, evidence of something real that pre-dated all civilizations, all religions, all recorded history.

What did they do with that knowledge? Did they destroy it to protect their narrative about human origins and salvation history? Or did they preserve it because they knew it was true and dangerous?

I guess that they preserved it because you don't destroy evidence. You classify it. You lock it away and control who has access. You study it carefully in secret, extract what's useful, and suppress public knowledge.

That's what intelligence agencies do with UFO evidence, what governments do with technologies that threaten existing power structures, what the Baghdad Museum looters did with Sumerian artifacts. It's what the Vatican has been doing for centuries.[134] [135]

The difference is duration. Intelligence agencies are decades old, and most modern nation-states are centuries old. The banking system is centuries old, but the Catholic Church is two thousand years old, and it's been centralizing knowledge, suppressing alternatives, and controlling narratives longer than any other existing institution.

The Vatican is good at it, having two thousand years of practice.

So, when researchers request access to the Vatican Archives and are denied, when documents remain restricted, and when only approved scholars with proper credentials can examine specific materials under supervision, this isn't about privacy protection. This is about information control.[136]

What are they hiding? Alternative gospels that undermine Church authority, mystery school texts that show Christianity borrowed from earlier traditions. Contact histories that prove non-human intelligence has interacted with humanity for millennia. Technologies and knowledge that would shift power away from institutional control. Evidence of Church collaboration with forces they now publicly condemn. Astronomical data and calendars predating accepted chronologies. Proof that consciousness survives death in ways Church doctrine doesn't adequately explain.

All of the above. Locked in 53 miles of shelving (and perhaps a sub- archive down deep, as some say?). Available to researchers who already agree with Church positions. Hidden from those who might use the knowledge to challenge institutional authority.

This is the same pattern we've been tracking: Baghdad Museum artifacts, Sumerian tablets, Templar discoveries, mystery school teachings, and Masonic knowledge. Power structures controlling access to information that would transform human understanding of our origins, our capabilities, and our relationship to non-human intelligence.

The Church isn't unique in this. They're just the oldest, most experienced, most thorough, and they're protecting something. Now ask yourself this: are they protecting us from dangerous knowledge? Or protecting themselves from dangerous truth?

Probably both.

Here's what's changing: information wants to be free. Digital technology makes perfect copies. Whistleblowers leak documents. Researchers share findings before authorities can suppress them. The control systems that have been working for centuries are breaking down.

The Vatican can lock its archives, but it can't lock human consciousness. Direct encounters, the presence of UFOs, ongoing contact experiences, and manifestations of consciousness-related abilities cannot be suppressed.

The Church tried to suppress gnosis and burned Gnostics as heretics. They labeled direct spiritual experience as demonic and insisted that only through Church intermediaries could access the divine.[137]

Throughout all this, people kept having direct experiences anyway. Mystics and saints throughout Church history experienced phenomena that technically contradicted official theology, including union with God, communication with divine intelligence, and cosmic consciousness that transcended doctrinal boundaries.[138]

The Church canonized some of them and condemned others. The difference boils down to politics. Saints who supported Church authority got canonized. Mystics who challenged it got burned.[139]

Same experiences but different political and life-altering or ending outcomes.

What does that tell you about what the Church believes versus what they publicly teach?

The Church knows gnosis is real, that direct contact with divine/cosmic intelligence occurs, and that consciousness extends beyond the physical. Church leadership knows non-human intelligence exists. They just don't want you to know it directly.

That's what 53 miles of locked archives protect, not the faithful from dangerous knowledge, but the institution from dangerous truth, and as disclosure accelerates, as more UFO evidence becomes public, as more consciousness research validates mystical experiences, as more people have direct contact that contradicts materialist paradigms, the Church's locked archives become less relevant.

When individuals gain direct understanding, institutional gatekeeping becomes ineffective. Personal experience makes theological debates less significant. As people cultivate their own consciousness capacities, the need for priests to connect to the divine diminishes.

That's the threat, and what they have been trying to prevent for 2,000 years.

That's why the Vatican Archives matter, not because of what's in them, but because of what their existence represents: an institutional control of knowledge, gatekeeping of human potential, suppression of direct experience in favor of mediated interpretation.

The mystery schools understood this. They taught practices, not doctrines. Experience, not belief. Development, not submission, and that's why the Church suppressed the mystery schools. Burned their temple, killed their practitioners, and confiscated their texts.

Because the Church couldn't compete with direct experience, they could only suppress it and claim exclusive authority.

History proves that suppression is temporary. When truth is locked away in one vault, it inevitably escapes through another door, wanting to be seen.

The same wisdom the Church locked away in Vatican Archives survived in Hermetic texts, in Masonic ritual, in Rosicrucian practice, in oral traditions passed master to student, and now, in the digital age, it spreads faster than any institution can control.

The Vatican's locked archives are a symbol of a dying paradigm. The age of institutional gatekeeping is ending, and direct access is beginning.

Whether that's progress or danger depends on whether wisdom spreads as fast as knowledge.

Which brings us to the darkest application of mystery school knowledge in modern history, Nazi occultism, and the systematic attempt to weaponize consciousness for genocidal purposes.

## NAZI OCCULTISM, THE DARKEST APPLICATION.

The Thule Society. The Vril Society. The Ahnenerbe. Names that sound like bad fiction but represent actual Nazi organizations dedicated to occult research, racial mysticism, and attempting to weaponize esoteric knowledge for genocidal purposes.[140]

This isn't conspiracy theory. This is documented history that mainstream narratives downplay because it complicates the clean story of good versus evil, rational democracy versus irrational fascism. The Nazis weren't just evil; they were evil, empowered by corrupted mystery school knowledge, ancient symbolism inverted for domination, consciousness technologies weaponized for horror.

When World War II ended, those same Nazi occultists didn't disappear. Through Operation Paperclip, they came to America. Brought their knowledge and integrated it into intelligence agencies, military research, and consciousness studies. Their methods, understanding, and approaches continue to influence Western power structures today.

Let's trace how this happened.

The Thule Society was formed in Munich in 1918, named after the northern mythical homeland of the Aryan peoples. Their core beliefs held that Germans descended from a superior race that originated in Hyperborea or Atlantis. This master race possessed advanced knowledge, abilities, and consciousness. Modern Germans needed to recover this heritage, purify their bloodline, and eliminate inferior races that diluted Aryan genetic potential.

This wasn't fringe belief. The Thule Society included judges, police chiefs, lawyers, university professors, and industrialists. These were educated elites who genuinely believed in racial esotericism, who thought ancient mystery school knowledge confirmed their supremacy, who interpreted Hermetic and Norse mythology as the literal history of Aryan origins.[141]

Key members: Rudolf von Sebottendorf (founder), Dietrich Eckart (early Hitler mentor), Rudolf Hess (Deputy Führer), Alfred Rosenberg (chief Nazi ideologue). These weren't random occultists (these were people who shaped Nazi ideology at its foundation.

The Vril Society (*Vril-Gesellschaft*) developed alongside Thule, focused on more esoteric aspects. They believed in Vril, a mysterious energy force described [142]in Edward Bulwer-Lytton's 1871 novel "The Coming Race." The novel was fiction, but the Vril Society treated it as revealed knowledge, as disclosure disguised as a story.[143]

Vril, they believed, was the fundamental life force, the power source that superior races could learn to manipulate. Control Vril, and you control reality, achieve superpowers, build technologies that would dwarf anything materialist science could produce.

Were they crazy? Partially. Accessing something real? Possibly.

Because what they called Vril sounds remarkably similar to what other traditions call chi, prana, orgone energy, the Force, consciousness-as-energy that can be cultivated and directed.

If that's real and mystery schools have been teaching techniques to manipulate it for millennia, then Nazi occultists were attempting to weaponize consciousness technologies that weren't inherently evil but became evil through application.

The Ahnenerbe (Ancestral Heritage Research Society) was the official Nazi organization for archaeological and anthropological research. Heinrich Himmler founded it in 1935 with official sanction.[144] Their mission was to prove Aryan racial superiority through archaeology, anthropology, and historical research. (Baghdad looting for Anunnaki goods? Author JP Farrell says yes.

They mounted expeditions to Tibet in search of ancient Aryan origins, researched runes and Norse mythology, and examined skulls to prove racial hierarchies. The organization confiscated archaeological artifacts from occupied territories and conducted medical experiments on concentration camp prisoners, trying to prove genetic theories.[145]

The Ahnenerbe had university professors, legitimate archaeologists, and trained researchers. This wasn't amateur hour. This was a systematic application of academic methodology in the service of genocidal ideology.

What's terrifying is that they found things. Real things. The expeditions to Tibet made contact with Buddhist monasteries that possessed ancient texts. Archaeological digs in Europe have uncovered genuine pre-Christian sites. The research into runes and symbols revealed patterns in ancient mystery school teachings.[146]

They just interpreted everything through the lens of racial supremacy. They took real knowledge and consciousness technologies, ancient wisdom, mystery school practices, and corrupted them. Inverted it. Turned practices designed for elevation into practices designed for domination.

The swastika, an ancient symbol in Hindu, Buddhist, Native American, and Greek cultures, originally represented solar energy and cosmic motion. The Nazis altered their orientation and meaning, transforming it from a sign of creation to one associated with genocide and conquest.

The Vatican thought it had buried the Templar knowledge forever when the last Grand Master was burned at the stake in 1314, but suppression never works permanently. Knowledge finds a way, and this particular knowledge found its way into underground networks, secret societies, and initiatic orders that preserved fragments of what the Templars had discovered. Centuries later, these same esoteric teachings would resurface in the most unexpected and horrifying context in 1930s Germany, where a cocktail of racial mythology, occult research, and authentic mystery school practices would be inverted into the darkest political movement in modern history. What the Templars had used for spiritual elevation, the Nazis would weaponize for genocide and conquest. This wasn't just historical curiosity or academic interest in ancient symbols. This was systematic corruption of real power, and the consequences of that corruption echo into our present moment through channels most people never suspect.

# CHAPTER 8

## NAZI OCCULTISM & MODERN POWER

The Germans were responsible for developing significant technological advancements during the Nazi era. These included the chemical laser, improved jet aircraft, advanced rockets, enhanced blood plasma techniques, the Bell plasma accelerator, transistors, and radar. Many of these innovations, especially those considered neutral technologies, have likely found peaceful applications over time.[147] The distinction between good and evil in the context of technology, as noted by Crowley, is simplistic. It is more accurate to view these developments in terms of positive and negative impacts.

Hitler's goal was to strengthen and advance the German people through conquest and genocide, an approach that nearly succeeded from their point of view. From the Nazi perspective, these actions were not considered evil but were seen as necessary for the survival of the Aryan race, a group they believed had been targeted for extermination since Roman times by various peoples, such as the Visigoths and others. This approach exemplifies how the Nazis took genuine knowledge and systematically inverted its meaning and purpose.

The Nazis appropriated and distorted ancient symbols to serve their ideology. Runes, the ancient Germanic alphabet used by Norse peoples, originally carried deep symbolic meanings. The Nazi regime transformed these runes into emblems of racial identity, combat insignia for the SS, and symbols of Aryan supremacy. For example, the lightning bolt SS runes were derived from Sowilo, a rune representing the sun and victory. This legitimate ancient symbol was corrupted into an insignia for SS units responsible for mass murder.

Mystery school initiation practices? Himmler created SS initiation rituals based on Teutonic Knight ceremonies mixed with occult practices. New SS officers underwent ceremonies at Wewelsburg Castle, designed as the "center of the new world" after the final Nazi victory. The castle's North Tower was arranged like Arthurian round-table mythology: 12 SS *Obergruppenführers* sitting in a circle, Himmler as the mystic leader, performing rituals meant to channel Vril energy for Nazi purposes. [148]

## OCCULT RITUALS, CONSCIOUSNESS MANIPULATION, AND TECHNOLOGICAL PURSUITS IN THE NAZI ERA

Heinrich Himmler, leader of the SS, was convinced that the initiation rituals he designed were effective. He envisioned the SS transforming into a mystical brotherhood, an order of warrior-mystics entrusted with guiding the Aryan race toward cosmic supremacy. These rituals were not mere theatrics. For Himmler, they were instrumental in building an elite cadre dedicated to the Nazi cause.

Officially, no high-ranking Nazi signed the surrender at the end of World War II. Many fled to Argentina and the United States, fueling speculation among researchers like Marrs[149] and Joseph P. Farrell[150] about the emergence of a "Fourth Reich" which they theorize is a covert continuation of the Nazi agenda outside Germany. [151]

Initiation rituals, as employed by the Nazis, were powerful psychological tools. These ceremonies produced tangible effects, strengthening group cohesion, expanding consciousness, and forging a sense of fanaticism. The Nazis harnessed these practices to override personal morality, transforming SS officers and soldiers into individuals willing to commit atrocities without hesitation.

The Nazi regime weaponized consciousness technologies, using ancient knowledge and ritual practices to manipulate minds and ensure loyalty to their ideology.

The Nazis also carried out research into unidentified flying objects (UFOs) and advanced aerial technologies. Historical documentation confirms their investigation of unusual aerial phenomena and their attempts to develop flying disc technology.[152] Researchers frequently cite SS General Hans Kammler and the Riese Project in Silesia as central to these efforts. After World War II, Operation Paperclip facilitated the transfer of Nazi scientists to the United States, where similar research into UFOs, antigravity, and consciousness manipulation began to take place.

This raises important questions. Is there a connection between Nazi pursuits and postwar American programs, or is it simply a coincidence? The continuity of certain research areas suggests the possibility of ongoing influence and legacy.

Werner von Braun came to America through the Paperclip program, became the father of American rocketry, and put humans on the moon. He was also a Nazi SS officer who used concentration camp slave labor at Peenemünde. Did he come alone? No. He brought his entire team of SS Scientists who worked on V-2 rockets while prisoners died building them.[153]

Researcher Tino Struckmann, along with historians such as Joseph P. Farrell, claimed that Kammler did go to America. During the Cold War, many American underground DUMBS bases were constructed using advanced German technologies[154] in electrical systems, ventilation, concrete, and rebar. During World War II, Kammler had utilized a vast amount of slave labor, and he introduced the concept of "renting" prisoners to other German companies to finance the SS.[155]

According to author Joseph P. Farrell, General Kurt Debus was the second-in-command at NASA. As a high-voltage plasma scientist, Debus wasn't involved in chemical rockets. Plasma plays a role in free-energy and antigravity research. Could this be significant?

Paperclip member Viktor Schauberger, a torsion-field and spin-antigravity scientist who incorporated scientific principles from nature, was just one of the publicly acknowledged Paperclip scientists. How many others came quietly, occultists, consciousness researchers? Ahnenerbe and Thule Society archaeologists found new positions in CIA programs, military research, and intelligence operations.

We know MKUltra began in 1953, less than a decade after Paperclip, and that it involved consciousness manipulation, mind control research, experiments with drugs, torture, and psychological programming. Nazi doctors had been conducting similar experiments in concentration camps.

In WW1, German and British doctors and scientists found that "shell-shocked" (PTSD) soldiers created several alternate personalities to contain their severe trauma. These "alters" could be programmed with suggestions and tasks. It could also be sadly created artificially as a technique for spies using trauma therapy.

The Church Committee investigations in 1975 confirmed that the CIA had recruited Nazi scientists, that MKUltra existed, and that illegal experiments on unwitting subjects had occurred. What they didn't fully expose was how much of MKUltra methodology came directly from Nazi occult research.

Because that would require acknowledging something uncomfortable, the Nazis weren't just evil; they were effective. The occult research produced results. Nazi consciousness manipulation techniques worked, and American intelligence agencies wanted that knowledge.

US intelligence brought the Nazis over, gave them new identities, positions, access to funding, and facilities. Then let them continue their research with one change; instead of serving Aryan racial supremacy, they were serving the American National Security State.

Same methods and the same research, different flag, and some of that exotic research is connected to the UFO phenomenon. Nazi Bell projects, Die Glocke, allegedly anti-gravity experiments. (See physicist Walter Gerlach and Heisenberg). The Bell was said to be a nonlinear physics, red mercury, free-energy torsion-field plasma accelerator that magnified energy from the very fabric of space-time. Some researchers say that the Bell, or an American copy, crashed during the Kecksburg UFO incident on December 9, 1965, because its description closely matched the German Haunebu flying disc designs and Vril-powered craft. Some think it was ejected from a flying disc.

These might be exaggerated legends, or they might be partially true, partially successful attempts to reverse-engineer technologies the Nazis had encountered or been given access to. It's a thought, given today's multiple worldwide sightings of black triangle and saucer craft that are supposedly man-made.

Because here's another uncomfortable truth: if non-human intelligence exists and monitors human development, they would have noticed Nazi occult research. They would have seen humans trying to weaponize consciousness, to develop racial genetics programs, and create "master race" super soldiers.

What would non-human intelligence do? Intervene? Give regressive aid to conquerors? Observe? Provide limited technology to see what humans would do with it? All the above?

UFO sightings increased dramatically during World War II. The U.S. Military named them "Foo fighters." They were mysterious, glowing orbs that followed aircraft and were possibly sentient plasma drones (the same as the orbs I saw?). Both Allied and Axis pilots reported them across all theaters of war. Some Foos flew rings around B-29 bombers in the Pacific, and their gunners shot at them to no effect. Neither side knew what they were, and both sides thought they might be enemy technology.

Some researchers have said that in 1941 or 1942, a UFO crashed at Cape Girardeau, Missouri. Apparently, the FBI was on the scene first, then the U.S. Army G2 intelligence unit. Was the debris brought to Wright Field in Ohio possibly the Foreign Technology Division?

Post-war, UFO sightings exploded. Roswell happened in 1947, two years after Paperclip began. More crashes were reported near Corona, New Mexico, and another at Pelona Mountain. Kenneth Arnold's 1947 sighting launched the modern UFO era. The Washington, D.C., flyovers in 1952 showed objects appearing on radar over the Capitol and the White House. (Some researchers like Farrell have posited that these discs may have been of German origin from Base 211, Neuschwabenland, Antarctica. The base was indeed genuine. A show of force, perhaps?

Quietly, Nazi scientists and occultists were settling into American facilities, continuing research, bringing their understanding of consciousness and technology, and contact with non-human intelligence.

Jim Marrs proposed that Paperclip was the beginning of a Nazi Fourth Reich, one in America, not Germany. The NASA Nazis all drove expensive Mercedes cars and bought big houses on a U.S. Military standard salary. American personnel were furious. Was Martin Bormann their secret financier, as some have said?

Did the Germans know something we didn't? Had they made contact and received information that explained how to interface consciousness with technology? Did they know how to use specific symbols and rituals to attract or communicate with non-human intelligence?

I don't know, however, the timing is suspicious. The connections are documented, research continuity is clear, and the philosophical inversion continues. The Nazis took mystery school knowledge designed for spiritual evolution and used it for war and genocide. American intelligence agencies took Nazi research and used it for mind control and social manipulation. Modern defense contractors use consciousness research for weapons development (See: Anduril, Raytheon, Grumman, Boeing, Lockheed Martin, Clark Engineering, Tesla, SpaceX, and Palantir).

Same thread, knowledge, but different applications, and all inverted from the original purpose.

Mystery schools taught that consciousness expansion should serve enlightenment, compassion, and connection to the divine. Increase your awareness to recognize unity with all beings and develop your capacities to serve humanity's evolution.

The inversions use consciousness manipulation to create division, enforce hierarchy, and control populations. Increase awareness, but channel it toward serving power structures. Develop capacities but weaponize them against perceived enemies.

Light magic versus dark magic is not as Hollywood drama but as actual practices with actual ethical dimensions. Same techniques, opposite intentions, and the Nazis proved what happens when these techniques serve regressive evil, when initiation rituals create fanatics instead of mystics, consciousness expansion produces supremacy instead of compassion, and ancient symbols channel domination instead of wisdom.

Hey, ours is a duality universe, Yin-Yang.

The Holocaust wasn't just industrial murder; it was occult inversion, a possible Vril energy harvest for interdimensional ETs, the systematic destruction of humans viewed as impure, the attempted creation of a master race through genetic selection, and the belief that eliminating "inferior" peoples would unlock superior Aryan potential.

Six million Jews, Russians, Poles, and undesirables. Millions of others, Romani, Slavs, disabled people, homosexuals, political dissidents. Not just killed but murdered according to systematic plans developed by educated people who believed esoteric knowledge justified genocide.

That's the clear and present danger.

Mystery schools insisted on ethics because esoteric knowledge, without virtue, can be dangerous. Progressive, supervised initiation aimed at ensuring wisdom and power would only be used responsibly.

Knowledge without wisdom becomes perilous, and power without compassion leads to destruction. Expanding consciousness without ethics risks creating monsters, not enlightenment.

History shows the consequences; Nazi misuse of esoteric teachings led to tragedy, and Operation Paperclip transferred these hard lessons to American intelligence. The need for ethical vigilance remains wherever power and knowledge intersect.

The Nazis and Operation Paperclip cemented these harsh lessons; their scientists observed what worked and what didn't, and the Germans transferred all their knowledge to the American National Security State in exchange for high positions in our government, military, corporations, and banking system.

When we talk about hidden esoteric knowledge, mystery school teachings, and consciousness technologies, we can't ignore what happens when that knowledge gets weaponized.

We can't pretend it's all benign wisdom waiting to enlighten humanity.

Some lineages preserved light, and others inverted it into darkness.

Both exist, have power, and produce effects that are embedded in modern power structures. The mystery schools are trying to preserve and protect knowledge; the corrupted inversions are trying to weaponize and control it.

The existence of esoteric knowledge is not in question. It is a recognized reality.

The question we should be asking is who has it, what they are doing with it, and in which direction they are taking humanity. Is it toward enlightenment or toward control?

That question brings us to modern power structures. The networks that inherited both traditions, the light and the dark. The families, corporations, and organizations that run the world today use knowledge that most people don't believe exists.

Time to unpack this.

## MODERN POWER STRUCTURES. WHO RUNS THE WORLD?

Remember the Swiss Study? Those 147 firms that control 60% of global revenues and the twenty major banking institutions running the show.

This isn't conspiracy theory. This is published research from the Swiss Federal Institute of Technology. Network analysis. Hard data. Proof that global economic power is concentrated in fewer hands than most people imagine, but economics is just one network. Others overlap and are interconnected. Sometimes competing, often cooperating. All preserving and wielding knowledge that most people don't have access to.

Let's lay each one out clearly.

**The Council on Foreign Relations (CFR):** Founded in 1921, it is officially a think tank promoting American foreign policy dialogue. A recruiting ground and coordination center for intelligence assets, policymakers, and corporate leaders.

Membership includes former presidents, CIA directors, major media executives, and banking CEOs. Warner happily told me that his grandfather, Paul Mellon, was a member of the CFR along with the Dulles brothers.[156]

You can't apply to join CFR. You must be invited, nominated by existing members, then vetted and approved. It's an exclusive club that decides American foreign policy behind closed doors, then implements those policies through members placed in government, the media, and industry.

This is not a conspiracy; their membership roster is public. Their influence is well documented. Presidents consult the CFR, media frame issues according to CFR position papers, and wars start after a CFR consensus forms.

Henry Kissinger? CFR. Zbigniew Brzeziński? CFR. Madeleine Albright? CFR. Dick Cheney? CFR. Dozens of CIA directors and National Security Advisors are all members of the CFR.

When different administrations, Democrat and Republican, pursue identical foreign policies, CFR explains it because the people making decisions are the same network, regardless of which party wins elections.

**<u>The Trilateral Commission:</u>** Founded in 1973 by David Rockefeller (yes, that Rockefeller: banking dynasty, oil empire, multiple generations of influence). Membership spans North America, Europe, and Asia-Pacific. Their goal is to coordinate policy among these regions, manage global economics, and prepare for the "new world order."[157]

The Trilateral Commission doesn't hide this. Zbigniew Brzezinski, co-founder, authored books that explained their vision: global governance, technocratic management, and reducing national sovereignty in favor of international cooperation.

Is that pure evil? I would say that it depends on your own perspective. Technocrats argue that global problems require global solutions. Skeptics argue that unelected elites making decisions for entire populations is tyranny regardless of intentions.

Trilateral Commission members occupy positions of enormous power. Elections are unnecessary when you have wealth, connections, and institutional access. Policy gets implemented through networks most people never see.

**The Bilderberg Group:** Started in 1954 at Hotel de Bilderberg in the Netherlands. Annual meeting of about 150 political leaders, financial executives, media magnates, and academics. Completely closed. No press. No minutes published. No accountability.

Officially, it's an informal discussion forum where European and North American elites exchange ideas. Unofficially, it's a coordination meeting where major policy decisions get made before they're implemented publicly.

The attendee list is partially public, but participation is invitation-only. What gets discussed remains confidential. The decisions that are made aren't announced. However, policies discussed at Bilderberg meetings are consistently implemented months or years later.

Brexit was a Bilderberg topic years before the referendum. The Euro was a Bilderberg topic before the European Union was established. Wars, economic policies, technological rollouts, and these patterns suggest that Bilderberg isn't just discussing these topics but coordinating them.

Is this a conspiracy? No. It's an oligarchy. It's how power actually works. Elites coordinate privately, then implement publicly through democratic/bureaucratic processes that give the appearance of bottom-up decision-making.

**Banking Dynasties:** The Rothschilds. The Rockefellers. The Morgans. The Warburgs. The Mellons. Families that accumulated wealth over centuries and converted that wealth into institutional power.

Rothschilds financed both sides of the Napoleonic Wars and the American Civil War, and perhaps more. The Rockefellers built Standard Oil into a monopoly[158] that controlled the American economy. Morgans created the US Federal Reserve, a private banking cartel that controls American currency despite the word "Federal" in its name.[159] [160]

**Mellons:** Standard Oil, Mellon Bank (BNYM), U.S. Steel, ALCOA.

These aren't ancient history dynasties. These families still exist, control enormous wealth and influence policy through foundations, think tanks, political donations, strategic investments, and they're connected to everything we've been discussing. The Rockefeller Foundation funded eugenics research that influenced Nazi ideology.[161] Rothschild banking interests were involved in establishing modern Israel. Morgan and Mellon interests are tied to the military-industrial complex and intelligence agencies.[162]

Not simple good-versus-evil; it is complex networks pursuing agendas that sometimes align with public interest, sometimes don't, and always benefit those inside the network.

**Secret Societies at Elite Levels:** Skull and Bones (Yale). Bohemian Grove (San Francisco). Le Cercle (European intelligence network). These aren't mystery schools; they're power coordination mechanisms that do include some occultists.

**Skull and Bones:** George H.W. Bush was a member. George W. Bush was a member. John Kerry was a member. When both presidential candidates in 2004 were Bonesmen, questions about whether elections matter became legitimate.

Initiation involves rituals in a windowless tomb, psychological pressure, and bonding through shared secrets. Sound familiar? Corrupted mystery school techniques are evident in the elite recruitment process.[163]

**Bohemian Grove:** Annual gathering in California redwood forest where America's power elite: presidents, CEOs, military leaders perform rituals, make deals, and coordinate policy. The "Cremation of Care"[164] ceremony involves burning an effigy before a giant owl statue. Is this symbolic of Anunnaki god worship of the deity Molech, with occult symbolism on display?[165]

Alex Jones infiltrated in 2000, filmed the ceremony, and got labeled a conspiracy theorist for reporting what he saw. Grove membership is semipublic, and attendance is documented (Christopher K. Mellon is a member, John Warner IV says). The rituals do happen. Whether they're meaningful beyond theater or actually invoke something…that's the question.

**Le Cercle:** European intelligence coordination group, CIA connections, involved in various Cold War operations. Functions as a shadow network coordinating policy above democratic oversight.[166]

These organizations aren't separate from the government. They are the government, or rather, they're the network that controls government through strategic placement of members.

**The Intelligence Community:** CIA. NSA. NRO. MI6. Mossad. BND. Networks that operate in classified spaces answer to no electorate and conduct operations that the public never learns about.

Intelligence agencies are where all threads converge. They research consciousness and UFOs (remote viewing programs, MKUltra, current UAP programs). They recruit from secret societies (documented CIA-Skull and Bones pipeline. Warner tells me that UVA's august and secret Seven Society is also a possibility. They interface with banking elites (CIA operations often fronted through banks and corporations) and coordinate with foreign agencies through groups like Le Cercle. Then they implement policies developed at the CFR, Trilateral Commission, and Bilderberg meetings, and they preserve knowledge. Classified knowledge about UFOs, consciousness technologies, ancient mysteries, and advanced technologies that could transform civilization but remain locked in special access programs.

Why? National security is the official answer, but the real answer is more complex because information asymmetry is power. Those who know more control those who know less. These power structures keep revolutionary technologies classified to maintain current power, releasing them only to enable a new power center that they control and govern.

These agencies sit at the interfaces for zero-point energy, anti-gravity, and consciousness. On everything that could make current economic models obsolete. Not because the technology doesn't work, but because it works too well. It would disrupt everything and upset existing hierarchies, enabling decentralized power, causing economic turmoil and religious upheaval.

Can't have that, not if you're invested in centralized control.

**<u>Corporate Monopolies:</u>** The Swiss Study revealed a corporate network structure, and there's another layer: technologies that could threaten these monopolies, which are suppressed.

Here is an example: Nikola Tesla's wireless power transmission would have provided free energy globally. J.P. Morgan was funding Tesla's research until he understood the implications. You can't meter free energy, can't charge for it, or control the distribution. Morgan withdrew funding, and Tesla supposedly died poor. Until today, the technology has remained undeveloped.

Consider cancer treatments that work too well? Big Pharma profits from management, not the cure. Treatments that actually cure are suppressed, researchers are threatened, patents are bought and buried.

Oil companies buy renewable patents, fund climate denial, bribe politicians to maintain fossil fuel subsidies, anything to preserve a trillion-dollar industry.

This has been documented and proven; it demonstrates how power defends itself and how esoteric knowledge operates in a similar way. Mystery school teachings about consciousness, human potential, and direct access to cosmic intelligence threaten every single control system. If they can't be dismissed, they face ridicule, marginalization, or classification.

Author Jim Marrs traced the thread from Ancient Sumer to modern banking cartels. Let's specify how some of that knowledge is shared.

Sumerian texts described the Anunnaki, sky gods who created humans as enslaved people for gold mining, etc., through genetic manipulation; taught civilization; gave us law and caste systems; and ruled as priest-kings. Those texts went to the Baghdad Museum, got looted, then spent 20 years in US custody!

Egyptian mystery schools preserve Sumerian knowledge and encode it in initiatory systems. Those systems influenced Greek philosophy, which influenced Christianity.

Solomon's Temple becomes a repository for ancient wisdom. The Templars spent 200 years excavating Temple Mount and found something, then they became wealthy and powerful.

The Templars fled to Scotland after 1307 and introduced esoteric knowledge into Freemasonry. Freemasonry spreads across Europe, influences the Enlightenment, and shapes the founding of America.

Simultaneously, the Rosicrucians preserved Hermetic and alchemical traditions; both streams (Masonic and Rosicrucian) contain fragments of this original knowledge.

In the 1700s, the Bavarian Illuminati infiltrated Freemasonry and tried to weaponize it for political purposes. Some lodges were corrupted. Others resisted.

In the 1800s, banking families consolidated power through the Industrial Revolution. Used their networks for coordination while also funding competing ideologies like capitalism, communism, and fascism to create dialectical conflicts they can manage and profit from.

In the 1900s, Nazi occultists attempted to weaponize esoteric knowledge for genocide and conquest. After WWII, Operation Paperclip brought them to American intelligence agencies, which absorbed both Nazi research and earlier mystery school knowledge.

In the 2000s, UFO disclosure accelerates, consciousness research advances, and ancient mystery school knowledge starts entering mainstream through books, lectures, and personal experiences.

The global control systems are trying to manage this recent acceleration. Hence, the ridicule of experiencers, suppression of research, classification of evidence, infiltration of disclosure movement, limited hangouts, and disinformation.

All information wants to be free. Digital technology enables perfect copying and instant distribution, making gatekeeping harder. People compare notes globally, patterns emerge that can't be hidden, and entities, human and non-human, that prefer humanity to stay controlled and limited are losing their grip.

That's the battle. It's not good versus evil in simple terms, but those who want humanity empowered versus those who profit from humanity staying controlled.

Both sides have resources, knowledge, and networks spanning centuries.

We're living through the climax of this conflict. Disclosure of UFOs. Awakening of consciousness, rediscovery of ancient knowledge, and a breakdown of institutional authority.

Groups like the Bilderbergs, banking families, and intelligence agencies all seek narrative control because they recognize a shift of power from centralized institutions to distributed networks of individuals. They are trying to manage and retain dominance during this transition. Will they succeed? That depends on how many people wake up, develop their own capacities, reclaim agency, and refuse to be controlled.

The knowledge is available, practices exist, and consciousness technologies, real technologies, can be learned and applied.

Mystery schools preserved them through the dark ages, and they're emerging into the light now.

Will enough people recognize and use them before control systems adapt?

That's the race, and it's happening now in real time.

While most people watch Netflix and their favorite football, soccer, or baseball team on TV.

## THE THREAD THROUGH TIME.

So let me tie all this information together, since this chapter covered a lot of ground and might feel scattered. Baghdad Museum heists, Atlantis, Lemuria, impossible ancient megaliths, pyramids, mystery schools, Emerald Tablets, Templars, Freemasons, Crowley, Vatican archives, Nazi occultism, modern elite networks, giant skeletons. It's all the same thread running through human history, and once you see how it connects, everything else in this book makes more sense.

The story starts with ancient knowledge that existed long before recorded history, whether it came from Atlantis, the

Anunnaki, earlier human civilizations we don't remember, or from non-human intelligence teaching primitive humans. There was advanced knowledge in the ancient world, possibly going back millions of years, considering Earth was probably Grand Central Station for visitation, geology, science, genetic experimentation, cosmic commerce, all of it. The Sumerians knew about consciousness, genetics, and technologies we're still trying to rediscover. So did the Egyptians and the ancient Chinese, with their pyramids, have it too. Cultures worldwide preserved fragments of what was once a complete understanding.

When civilizations fell through catastrophe, conquest, or cultural transformation, certain groups understood what would be lost and worked desperately to preserve it. Egyptian priesthoods encoded it, Greek mystery schools protected it, Gnostic Christians hid it, Persian, Sufi, and Arabian mystics safeguarded it. They encoded wisdom in symbols, rituals, and initiatory systems designed to transmit not just information but experiential understanding, because you can't just read this knowledge in a book and understand it. You must experience it.

Then Christianity consolidated power and faced a problem. These competing systems offered direct spiritual experience rather than mediated salvation through Church authority, which threatened institutional control. Gnostics were declared heretics. Mystery schools were persecuted. Texts were burned or confiscated. The knowledge went underground or into Vatican archives, where access could be controlled and weaponized by those who understood what they were sitting on.

The Templars spent two centuries on the Temple Mount with access to whatever Solomon's Temple contained, possibly texts predating the Bible, energetic gems for frequency science, possibly technologies, or an understanding of how consciousness interfaces with reality. Whatever they found made them wealthy, powerful, and dangerous enough that Church and Crown conspired to destroy them, but they saw it coming. They fled, scattered, and preserved what they'd learned through networks that would eventually resurface as Freemasonry.

The knowledge found its way into Masonic ritual, Rosicrucian practice, and various esoteric orders claiming Templar lineage. This wasn't just historical curiosity or fraternal tradition. It's functional wisdom, practices that produced real effects, and initiations that genuinely expanded consciousness. Some lodges preserved it faithfully, staying true to the original intent of human elevation and brotherhood. Others were infiltrated and corrupted, turning the same practices toward domination and control, but both streams continued to flow for centuries.

That's when the dark inversions emerged: when consciousness technologies serve ego rather than transcending it, you get figures like Crowley wielding real power for personal aggrandizement. Apply mystery school knowledge to racial supremacy and military conquest instead of universal brotherhood, and you get the Nazis systematically corrupting ancient wisdom into genocidal ideology. Turn esoteric understanding toward domination instead of liberation, and you get intelligence agencies using consciousness manipulation for control. Knowledge itself isn't good or evil. It's neutral. What matters is how it's applied and who's applying it.

Modern power structures continue to control access through the same banking families, intelligence networks, and elite institutions that have managed information for centuries. The CFR, Trilateral Commission, and Bilderberg aren't secret cabals in the sense of conspiracy theory with robes and rituals. They're actual networks coordinating policy above democratic oversight with real documentation, membership lists, and meeting minutes. These networks know things most people don't, have technologies most people can't access, and make decisions affecting billions without accountability.

Meanwhile, the evidence keeps surfacing despite their efforts. Giant skeletons that the Smithsonian makes disappear. Ancient ruins that shouldn't exist according to accepted timelines. Artifacts that get looted and immediately classified. Technologies that get suppressed because they threaten existing industries and power structures. Consciousness research that gets publicly ridiculed while being studied in classified programs. The pattern is consistent across every domain: evidence emerges, authorities intervene, the narrative gets managed, and the truth gets buried.

But now it's all coming apart because digital technology makes it harder to suppress information completely. Enough people have had direct experiences with UFO encounters, consciousness expansion, and mystical states that ridicule doesn't work anymore. The control systems that have functioned for centuries are breaking down under the weight of accumulated evidence and human awakening, and there's nothing they can do to stop it short of completely shutting down the internet and memory-wiping billions of people.

That's the thread running through this entire chapter. From Sumerian tablets in the Baghdad Museum to elite networks meeting at Bilderberg. Atlantean survivors teaching primitive humans to NASA scientists recruited from Nazi occult programs. Egyptian initiation rites to Freemasons influenced the founding of the United States. Mystery school wisdom to intelligence agency classified research. It's all connected, the same knowledge circulating through different hands across millennia, sometimes preserved for enlightenment or weaponized for control. It is always threatening existing paradigms and suppressed by those who benefit from keeping humanity limited. This is why it connects directly to the other topics we are examining throughout this book. The people who suppressed mystery school knowledge are suppressing UFO disclosure. The networks that looted the Baghdad Museum control what is revealed about non-human intelligence. Institutions that made giant skeletons disappear now classify technologies that could transform civilization. Power structures that infiltrated Freemasonry manage the CIA's "limited hangout" of gradual disclosure, a purpose-built dead-end street using cherry-picked disclosure, Congressional hearings, and CIA-linked documentaries like "Age of Disclosure." It's not separate conspiracies; it's one giant conspiracy, if you want to call it that. It is better to call it the systematic effort by those with access to hidden knowledge to maintain information asymmetry and thereby maintain power.

These power structures know things we don't about ancient history, human origins, consciousness, and non-human intelligence. About technologies that could make current economic models obsolete, and they're not telling us. They're controlling the release, managing the narrative, and ensuring the power structure survives even as paradigms shift.

Here's what they can't control: direct experience. Individuals having UFO encounters without permission. Others are developing consciousness abilities through practice, rediscovering mystery school techniques, and realizing they work. Communities are comparing notes globally and recognizing patterns.

Gatekeeping is failing, and suppression is breaking down. Knowledge is spreading despite institutional resistance, which brings us to the next chapter, because one of the primary mechanisms of technological suppression is the 30-year rule. The systematic delay between when technologies are developed in classified programs and when they're released to the public.

We've just covered the hidden history of esoteric knowledge and how consciousness technologies and mystery school wisdom have been preserved, corrupted, and controlled across millennia.

Now we need to examine how material technologies get controlled, how the military-industrial complex operates, how classified programs work, and how the same families and networks that control esoteric knowledge also control technological development and deployment. The hidden history of consciousness technologies and the classified reality of material technologies both serve the same function: maintaining information asymmetry and, therefore, keeping power.

Those who possess hidden knowledge control those who don't, and those with access to advanced technologies (material and consciousness-based) control those who remain limited by conventional capabilities and old, rigid paradigms.

That's why disclosure and awakening matter, as does reclaiming our agency and developing our own capacities.

Because once we know what they know, have access to what they've been hiding, and we develop abilities they claim we don't have, the power imbalance shifts, and they're afraid of that. Very afraid.

Which is why they fight so hard to control the narrative, managing disclosure, ridiculing experiencers, and suppressing research, classifying evidence, and maintaining the lie that we're alone, powerless, dependent on government, military, and corporate institutions for truth. We're not alone or powerless, and we're waking up to that reality despite their best efforts.

Ancient mystery schools knew the truth of our world and universe. Consciousness can be expanded, reality can be navigated, and a connection with cosmic intelligence can be established. Knowledge survived through persecution because it's real and it works.

Modern experiencers know UFOs are real, contact happens, consciousness extends beyond the physical, non-human intelligence exists, and ancient Prediluvian high civilizations thrived. The phenomenon continues despite suppression because it's real and happening right before our eyes every day.

Are the world's religions incomplete, artificial, or even corrupt? There is a recurring theme that connects everything from ancient mysteries to today's revelations and hidden knowledge to personal experiences. This thread weaves through institutional control, leading toward individual awakening at a key turning point where suppression fails, knowledge spreads, and worldviews begin to shift.

Let's take a closer look at how technology is suppressed in the modern era, including the "30-year rule," innovations developed in secret programs, and how, or if, they ever become known to the public.

The gap between what humanity could have and what we're allowed to have, and the difference between where we should be and where they're keeping us. The conspiracy is revealed in concrete terms, along with the mechanisms of technological control. The proof that they're not telling us everything.

Not even close.

# CHAPTER 9

## THE 30-YEAR RULE: TECHNOLOGY SUPPRESSION

We've established that hidden history exists and explored consciousness abilities that have been suppressed systematically. Now we examine material technologies, physical innovations that could transform civilization but remain locked behind classification, corporate patents, and institutional gatekeeping.

This is the 30-year rule: technologies developed in classified programs don't reach the public for at least 30 years. Often longer. Sometimes never, and when they do emerge, they're presented as recent breakthroughs rather than decades-old capabilities finally considered safe for release, and most are watered-down versions of the classified ones.

This isn't conspiracy theory. This is a documented pattern across aerospace, energy, computing, materials science, and biotechnology. Look at any transformative technology and trace it backward. You'll find military or intelligence agency development preceding public disclosure by decades.

The Pattern:

**Stealth technology.** Public unveiling: 1988 with F-117 Nighthawk[167]. Actual development began in the 1970s.[168] Nearly 20 years of classified work before official acknowledgment, and only acknowledged because aircraft couldn't be hidden once deployed. [169]

**GPS. Public availability:** 2000. Full constellation operational for military: 1995.[170] Initial satellites launched: 1978—system functional for the Department of Defense: 1980s. Civilians got a degraded version[171] two decades after the military had a precise capability.[172]

**Internet. Public adoption:** mid-1990s. ARPANET (precursor by DARPA): 1969.[173] Military and academic use throughout the 1970s and 1980s. TCP/IP protocols: 1983.[174] World Wide Web: 1989.[175] The internet as a tool for civilian communication was not available until commercial interests saw profit potential 25 years after its initial development.[176]

**<u>Night vision technology.</u>** Widely available: 1990s.[177] Military deployment: 1960s (Vietnam War).[178] Development: 1940s and 1950s.[179] Forty years from development to civilian availability.

**<u>Apple Siri.</u>** What people met as "Siri" in 2011 wasn't some shiny Silicon Valley miracle; it was the public-friendly mask of an intelligence that had already lived an entire secret lifetime before Apple ever touched it. The real origin story began in 2003, inside DARPA's CALO project, a massive, $150-million government AI initiative where 300 researchers quietly spent years teaching machines to learn, reason, interpret, and adapt. By the time Apple bought the spinoff in 2010, the technology was already old, battle-hardened, refined, and proven inside a Pentagon-funded ecosystem the public never saw. Apple didn't "invent" the future; they inherited a diluted, sanitized fragment of a far older intelligence that had been maturing behind classified doors while consumers were still playing with flip phones. Siri entered the world as a breakthrough, but in reality, she was the late-stage release of a system that had already served its purpose in the shadows for years and was deemed safe enough only then to trickle down into the civilian world, because it was old tech and no longer needed. What they have now is still classified, but use your imagination.[180]

The pattern holds across domains such as drones, composite materials, advanced cryptography, biotechnology, and energy technologies. Military use precedes civilian access by decades. The list includes technology the Defense Advanced Research Projects Agency (DARPA)[181] developed and later transferred to civilian use: A.I., GPS, the internet, radar, sonar, microwave communication and ovens, fiber optics, touchscreens, massive advances in computers and electronics, night vision, and medical treatments for trauma victims and antibiotics. All this technology was in operational use for years, potentially decades, before release to the public.

People often ask why they are suppressed, and various reasons come together to explain this.

**National security:** genuine concern about adversaries accessing capabilities, and "national security" covers everything. Often, technologies with no military application get classified simply because they're paradigm-shifting. Ex: antigravity propulsion and cold fusion would upset the oil, natural gas, and coal energy paradigms.

**Economic control:** releasing technologies that make existing industries obsolete, crash markets, destroy corporations, and eliminate jobs. It is better to introduce changes gradually, allowing economic systems to adapt while maintaining power structures.

**The deeper reason:** power structures depend on scarcity, limitation, and dependency. Current elites (banking families, energy corporations, powerful royal dynasties, the military-industrial complex, corporate tech monopolies) maintain dominance by controlling access to essential technologies.

Remember the Swiss study showed that 1,318 companies controlled 43,000 multinationals, with a core group of 147 firms holding sway over 40% of the network's wealth. Most were financial institutions: Barclays, JPMorgan Chase, Goldman Sachs, the Fed, and approximately 20 other major banks dominated this core group.

This concentration of economic power means that releasing transformative technologies threatens the entire structure. Release the classified torsion field, over-unity free-energy tech? Oil and gas companies collapse. Banking systems built on energy debt become obsolete. Geopolitical power is shifting away from oil states. Trillions in assets become worthless overnight.

Release advanced propulsion, and military advantages disappear. Transportation industries are becoming obsolete. Space suddenly becomes accessible to most everyone, and off-world resources are no longer locked behind massive launch costs.

This isn't theoretical; in 2015, the United States quietly passed legislation explicitly granting private companies the right to extract, own, and sell resources obtained from asteroids and other celestial bodies without claiming sovereign ownership of space itself. The law effectively acknowledges a future where access to space and off-world materials is economically viable, legally protected, and commercially motivated. [182]

If launch costs collapse through advanced propulsion or energy breakthroughs, the implications become immediate. Orbital infrastructure, asteroid mining, and resource extraction move from speculative industries to strategic realities overnight. At that point, control over space is no longer determined by nation-states or fossil-fuel-dependent logistics, but by whoever controls the enabling technology and the legal frameworks already in place for it. In all scenarios, we discover that you can't mine the solar system with rockets. The Deep State, or whatever you would like to call them, has probably been mining asteroids, the Moon, Mars, and Saturn's Rings for decades in secret.

Introducing life extension technology could escalate population challenges, strain social security networks, disrupt the transfer of generational wealth, and prevent powerful individuals from stepping aside to allow younger generations to assume control.

Technologies that expand consciousness, such as telepathy, might render covert surveillance as obsolete. Remote viewing would make it impossible to keep secrets, and with direct knowing, propaganda loses its power. Ultimately, control systems that depend on unequal access to information will fall apart.

These technologies are classified not because they are inefficient or lack value, but because their effectiveness threatens existing power structures.

## DARPA AND THE MILITARY-INDUSTRIAL PIPELINE.

DARPA is historically known for this controlled-release pattern. Their mission statement is "to prevent and to create technological surprise and to make key investments that create or prevent strategic surprise for U.S. national security". [183] The department started in 1958 as ARPA after the USSR launched Sputnik. The U.S. no longer wanted to be surprised by another country's innovation. [184]

The prevailing military incentive is to maintain an asymmetric technological and capability edge over adversaries. Sputnik was a massive wake-up call. The public outcry was enormous, and the political pressure to prevent the United States from lagging any longer led to massive funding increases.

However, be advised that there is a rumor amongst researchers that the U.S. Air Force launched a modified V-2 rocket with a crude orbital satellite in the late 1940s or early fifties. They wanted that secret, the beginning of the "U.S. Secret Space Program," so they let the Russians have the glory.

If you look at trends in classification review processes, you see that new technology tends to lose secrecy restrictions only after confirmation that competing foreign capabilities have already caught up or overtaken it. Only then is classification stripped, clearing the way for controlled public access, and make no mistake, it's still controlled. We don't want a non-ally partner to gain an advantage through these releases either. The secrecy lifespan extends well beyond incremental technological innovations.

Hundreds of military labs, contractors, and acronym-heavy government programs/divisions (DARPA, DISA, DITA, and more) hint at the expansiveness of black-budget projects and unacknowledged special-access programs exploring cutting-edge innovations under extreme classification and security. A much bigger unseen iceberg totally exists beneath the visible technology presence that enters declassification.

THE SPY TELESCOPE GIFT.

Did you know the NSA and NRO gave NASA two high-powered decommissioned spy telescopes originally made for classified missions?[185] In 2011, the National Reconnaissance Office (NRO), which oversees the U.S. intelligence satellite network, gave NASA two surplus optical spy telescopes. Just pulled them out of storage and contacted NASA to see if they were interested.

The telescopes were originally built for classified use by the NRO and National Security Agency (NSA). One telescope has a 2.4-meter (7.9-foot) mirror, making it the same size as the Hubble Space Telescope's main mirror. The other has a 3.67-

meter (12-foot) mirror. The telescopes were valued at over $1 billion when built, but were given to NASA at no cost other than transportation expenses.[186]

I just want to level-set here; the NRO is not looking into space. They are looking down at you and me. At us.

We know that the military-industrial complex will not just hand over its top-of-the-line tech unless it's obsolete, and they already possess something far more advanced. The stealth Black Hawk helicopters at the Osama bin Laden raid were a perfect example.[187] A stealth helicopter crashed during an operation in 2011, revealing technology the public had no idea existed.[188] If those were deployed in 2011, they must have been operational for years beforehand. Military analysts estimate the stealth Black Hawk program probably began development in the 1980s or 1990s.[189] That's 20 to 30 years of classified operations before accidental disclosure, and we only found out because one crashed. How many other aircraft programs exist that haven't crashed yet? How many capabilities remain completely hidden?

The bin Laden raid also revealed that stealth technology had progressed far beyond what was publicly acknowledged. The F-117 was retired in 2008, suggesting the military already had better stealth capabilities. The stealth Black Hawk proved it, and what about the next generation? What's operational now that won't be acknowledged for another twenty years?

## THE DECEPTICON MOMENT

Robert O'Neil, one of the Navy SEALs who participated in Operation Neptune Spear, described his first reaction to seeing the stealth Black Hawks before the raid. When the team arrived in Nevada for training at a full-scale mockup of bin Laden's compound, O'Neil recalled: "We turned the corner, saw the helos we'd actually use, and I started laughing. I told the guys, "The odds just changed. There's a 90 percent chance we'll survive. They asked why. I said,

---

### "I didn't know they were sending us to war on a fucking Decepticon."[190]

---

That quote captures everything about the 30-year rule in one moment.

Elite special operations forces, people who routinely use cutting-edge military technology, were stunned by what they saw. These weren't modified standard helicopters but platforms radically different from anything they'd encountered, even for operators with top-level security clearances, who had no idea they existed.

At the time of the 2011 raid, stealth Black Hawks were a well-kept secret that likely would have remained with the military if the crash hadn't occurred. Even after the crash exposed the program, definitive data on its design and capabilities remain scarce. Based on the success of the operation and its capabilities, the stealth Black Hawk remains a highly regarded military aircraft, with newer variants reportedly used in subsequent operations in Syria.[191]

But here's the thing that should blow your mind. The stealth Black Hawk wasn't the first stealth helicopter. Not even close.

## QUIET ONE: THE 1972 STEALTH HELICOPTER

An extremely interesting article published in 2008 by Air & Space magazine recalls the story of two OH-6A helicopters modified to fly with Air America. These aircraft were designed "to drop off and pick up agents in enemy territory quietly." Dubbed "Quiet One," these stealth helicopters conducted their secret mission on December 5 and 6, 1972, carrying commandos into North Vietnam to place a wiretap and a solar-powered relay station that enabled Americans to eavesdrop on communications used by enemy commanders.[192]

Let that sink in for a second. This technology wasn't publicly revealed until a 2008 magazine article, and it was operationally deployed in 1972. That's 36 years of classification for technology that actively worked in combat conditions.

The Quiet One grew out of ARPA research (later DARPA) that began in 1968. The Advanced Research Projects Agency wanted helicopters quiet enough for covert insertion missions. Engineers at Hughes Tool Company modified their OH-6A "Loach" helicopter with a revolutionary five-bladed main rotor instead of the standard four-bladed rotor, a new four-bladed tail rotor design, and extensive sound-dampening modifications, including a large exhaust muffler.[193]

The CIA took an interest in the program and acquired two of these experimental helicopters through Air America, their proprietary airline front company. Training began in Taiwan in 1972. The helicopters were so classified that photographing them was strictly forbidden, even at the secret base in Laos designated PS-44, where they operated.[194]

The mission into North Vietnam on December 6–7, 1972, was a complete success. The Quiet One flew deep into enemy territory, covered 48 kilometers at an altitude of 200 feet, passed directly over North Vietnamese anti-aircraft positions without being detected, and successfully placed both the wiretap and relay station. The wiretap provided "excellent intelligence" to Henry Kissinger throughout the Paris Peace Talks, operating continuously from December 1972 through May 1973.[195]

Once again, technology that was not publicly revealed until 2008 was in operational use by 1972 at the latest, and 1968 if you count the development phase. That's 40 years from development to public acknowledgment, and we only found out because the CIA finally declassified documents about it decades later.

# THE ELECTRONIC BATTLEFIELD: OPERATION IGLOO WHITE

The Vietnam War saw the development and deployment of some fantastic future weaponry and technology that the public wasn't supposed to know about. One of the most significant was Operation Igloo White, also known as the Electronic Battlefield.

The U.S. military faced significant challenges in disrupting the Ho Chi Minh Trail, a crucial supply route for North Vietnamese forces. Operation Igloo White was conceived as an innovative solution to this problem, combining cutting-edge technology with military strategy. This operation was initiated in the late 1960s. It used a variety of sophisticated sensors, including acoustic, seismic, and magnetic devices, which were air-dropped along the trail to detect enemy movements.[196]

These sensors would detect sounds, vibrations, or changes in the magnetic field caused by troops or vehicles, and transmit this data to overhead aircraft such as the EC-121R "Batcat" or to reconnaissance drones. Yes, you read that correctly. Reconnaissance UAVs (unmanned aerial vehicles) were first deployed on a large scale during the Vietnam War, starting in the early 1960s.[197]

The Ryan Model 147 Lightning Bug reconnaissance drones, derived from the Firebee target drone series, flew over 3,435 missions during the Vietnam War. Over 1,016 Lightning Bugs were deployed, with 578 lost to enemy action or accidents. These weren't simple remote-controlled aircraft. They had autonomous navigation systems, could fly programmed routes, and conducted reconnaissance missions deep into North Vietnam and China.[198] Drones began being used in a range of new roles, including decoy operations in combat, launching strikes against fixed targets, and dropping leaflets for psychological operations. Most people think that unmanned combat drones were a 21st-century innovation.

The heart of Operation Igloo White was the Infiltration Surveillance Center (ISC) at Nakhon Phanom Royal Thai Air Force Base in Thailand. Here, the relayed sensor data was processed by some of the era's most advanced computers, which analyzed the signals to guide immediate military responses. When a sensor was triggered, airstrikes were swiftly ordered, aiming to destroy the detected targets, whether they were supply trucks or troop formations.[199]

The sensors themselves were remarkably sophisticated for the 1960s. Different types included acoustic sensors that could detect engine sounds and human speech, seismic sensors that detected ground vibrations from trucks and troops, and even exotic "sniffer" sensors that could detect human urine by sensing sudden increases in airborne ammonia particles.[200]

However, Igloo White was not without its challenges. Technical issues such as sensor malfunctions and environmental interference often led to false positives. The North Vietnamese quickly adapted by using decoy movements, altering their operations to minimize detection. Once they figured out the ammonia sensors, they would leave buckets of urine near the sensors to trigger false alarms and waste American bombs on empty jungle.[201]

Despite these setbacks, the operation had a significant psychological impact, instilling constant fear of unseen surveillance among North Vietnamese forces. More importantly, Operation Igloo White represented a pioneering use of electronic warfare and surveillance, marking a shift toward technology-driven combat strategies that set the precedent for modern warfare.[202]

## A PERSONAL ENCOUNTER WITH CLASSIFIED HISTORY

My life sometimes seems so unbelievable that even writing this makes me wonder how and why all these synchronicities have happened to me my entire life. In my twenties, I bartended at a bar close to the 180th Air Force National Guard Base in Swanton, Ohio, my hometown. An older guy would come to the bar maybe once a month, sometimes more. Very quiet and would order three margaritas and stare out the window.

Some days it was slow, and I struck up a conversation with him. I could tell from the way he dressed and carried himself that he was a pilot. I was always into the secret world of classified military projects. On this particular day, this guy had two extra drinks, and I asked him to tell me something he worked on that was no longer classified.

He thought about it for a few minutes, then told me about Operation Igloo White. He didn't name the project outright; he only said it had been over 25 years and that he was sure it was no longer classified. This was maybe 2001 or 2002. I had no real way to research this at the time, so I took him at his word.

The guy told me about the sensors being so sophisticated that they even had ammonia sensors that could tell when the Vietcong were pissing. Through my research for this book, I found that this was completely true. Once the Viet Cong figured it out, they would leave buckets of piss near the sensors to thwart the reconnaissance and get the U.S. to waste bombs blowing up areas that the Viet Cong did not inhabit.

Here I was, hearing classified operational details from someone who had actually flown the missions decades before most of this information became public. The 30-year rule in action, directly confirmed by someone who lived it.

## BEYOND VIETNAM: THE PATTERN CONTINUES

There comes a point where the 30-year rule stops being an abstract idea and becomes something you can feel in your bones. A pilot in a quiet bar shares details he shouldn't, and decades later, you discover he wasn't exaggerating. Veterans from different generations recall using systems that didn't officially exist at the time, each describing tools far beyond the era in which they fought. After hearing enough of these stories, you realize the timeline is deliberate. The public is always handed the past while the present stays sealed away. The real breakthroughs live their entire lifespan in classified hangars and underground labs, waiting for the clock to hit whatever date someone in the shadows decides is safe. And when they finally surface, they don't arrive at random. They land in the hands of people chosen long before any of us hear their names. That's the part most people will never see. The technology isn't just hidden from the public; its release is orchestrated as well, which brings us to the men who carry it into the world and the machine behind them.

# CHAPTER 10

## FRONTMEN FOR THE MACHINE

### ELON MUSK IS THE NEW HOWARD HUGHES

We've established that the 30-year rule governs the release of technology and that classified capabilities remain hidden for decades before controlled disclosure to the public. Now we need to examine exactly how this controlled release happens in practice. The military-industrial complex doesn't just declassify patents and release blueprints to manufacturers. The classified programs don't publish technical papers and let the free market sort it out. Instead, they use charismatic front men, brilliant entrepreneurs with the right connections, the right background, and the willingness (whether conscious or not) to serve as conduits for controlled technology release into the commercial sphere.

Howard Hughes was that man throughout the 1940s, 1950s, and into the 1960s, and in my opinion, he has been replaced in that exact role by none other than Elon Musk.

### HOWARD HUGHES: THE ORIGINAL MIC FRONTMAN

Howard Hughes was an eccentric billionaire, aviator, movie producer, and industrialist known for his secretive, reclusive behavior in later life, much like Elon Musk in our current era, but, in my opinion, much cooler, smarter, and arguably better-looking. He was a multifaceted American icon who left his mark on aviation, film, and business, and his influence continues to shape us today.

Let's do some homework first. Elon Musk is the founder of SpaceX, Tesla, and several other extraordinarily successful companies known for ambitious projects and an unconventional approach. His somewhat suspicious, quick rise to fame and wealth is a story of calculated risks, technological innovation, and a relentless pursuit of ambitious goals. Or was he set up to be the next Howard Hughes?

This is an old story that continues to play out generation after generation. If you've been following along with the 30-year rule we established in the previous chapter, all the technology we currently have in public possession is at least 20 to 30 years old, developed in classified programs. Look at how Elon rose to the success he enjoys today. Apparently, he found early success in the tech industry through startups. Back in 1995, he founded Zip2 with his brother, an early software platform that provided city guides and map data for newspapers transitioning online.[203] He sold that company for $307 million in 1999 at the height of the dot-com bubble. Then he moved on to founding X.com and later PayPal, one of the first online financial services companies, which later merged with Confinity to form PayPal. It became a leader in online payment solutions, processing billions in transactions, and eBay bought PayPal for $1.5 billion in 2002.[204] These early deals helped bankroll the more famous companies we know today.

Starting with SpaceX, he expressed a vision for Earth's future focused on lowering the cost of space travel and enabling life on multiple planets. These are ambitious goals, especially considering he was not originally trained as an aerospace engineer. After founding SpaceX, Elon and the company have achieved some very impressive milestones over the years, including the first private rocket launches to the International Space Station, the development of reusable rockets that land vertically, and the successful launch of one of the largest rockets ever built despite initially using risky Russian engines. He also launched a global network of CubeSat internet service satellites called Starlink, which provides internet connectivity anywhere on the planet through low Earth orbit coverage. Through all of this, he has held major government and military contracts worth billions of dollars. Most of these contracts are completely classified and off the books, hidden from public scrutiny through national security exemptions. He has received millions of dollars in federal subsidies and tax breaks, along with grants funded by U.S. taxpayers, without most people realizing the extent of government support. Let's not forget Tesla Motors, which has the stated goal of getting everyone in the world driving an electric car to save the environment from fossil-fuel emissions. As of 2026, Elon Musk was one of the richest men on Earth with a net worth exceeding that of most small countries. He's done this in a big way by disrupting the current status quo in these industries and pushing for new, supposedly innovative technologies. Musk is very outspoken on social and political issues. He bought Twitter ostensibly to save it from censorship and is a very vocal voice on that platform, now rebranded as X. Always in the public eye, drawing attention and controversy, people are always paying attention to him and what he has to say, even when he sets outrageous goals that he often doesn't meet on the timeline promised. It's exceptionally good for the stock price and for the companies he owns and represents when he makes these grand announcements that capture imagination. Everybody thinks Elon was just an overnight success, the result of pure genius. That he was minted during the startup boom, sold his companies at perfect timing, and now is a household name through sheer brilliance and relentless hard work, but where did he really come from? What about his family background, and why does he have such tight connections with the U.S. government and intelligence agencies from the very beginning?

## THE HALDEMAN CONNECTION: SPIRITUALISM, TECHNOCRACY, AND THE LOST CITY.

There have been theories suggesting that Musk's family, particularly his father, Errol Musk, had ties to the CIA or other intelligence agencies operating in Africa. Errol's background as an engineer and his alleged emerald mine in Zambia during a period of heavy CIA activity in the region is seen by some researchers as a potential link to intelligence agencies operating across the continent. However, I think that his mother, Maye Musk (née Haldeman), is a far better place to look for these interesting connections to power structures, esoteric knowledge, and non-human intelligence.

Maye is a Canadian-born model, dietitian, and author. She has been modeling since she was fifteen. She has appeared on the covers of many magazines, including Time, Women's Day, Vogue, and Sports Illustrated Swimsuit Issue No. 25. Maye holds Canadian, South African, and American citizenship across three countries and, interestingly, is also a twin. The sisters started working for their father when they were eight years old, doing secretarial work. Serving as his secretaries at the age of twelve, they were introduced to his work and research very early in life. According to Wikipedia (2026), "Her parents, Winnifred Josephine 'Wyn' (Fletcher) and Dr. Joshua Norman Haldeman[205], a former director of Technocracy Incorporated, a former Regina chiropractor and amateur archaeologist, were adventurous and flew the family around the world in a prop plane in 1952. For over ten years, the family roamed the Kalahari Desert in search of its fabled Lost City of the Kalahari.[206] Their parents gave slide shows and talks about their journeys to audiences. 'My parents were very famous, but they were never snobs,' she said."

Well, to start this journey, let's look at Elon's great-grandmother and his maternal grandfather, Dr. Joshua Norman Haldeman.

Joshua Norman Haldeman, Elon's grandfather, was born in 1902 in a Minnesota log cabin, according to family records. The family moved north to Saskatchewan a few years later, seeking better opportunities. His mother, Almeda Haldeman, was the first chiropractor known to practice in Canada. At the time, chiropractic was less than a decade old and still tightly bound to its origins in pseudoscience and spiritualism according to the medical establishment's views. Its creator D.D. Palmer claimed he had received the knowledge from "the other world" through communication with a dead doctor and considered chiropractic practice akin to a religion rather than just medical treatment. Chiropractors at that time believed that the vertebral misalignments they treated were the cause of all disease, a claim that conflicted sharply with mainstream medicine.[207]

Warner recounts Joseph P. Farrell's statement that Elon Musk's father, an Afrikaner of German descent, is believed to have royal bloodlines that may trace back to Frederick the Great, according to genealogical research. Both researchers agree that such royal lineages often receive support from secret societies operating behind the scenes, suggesting a network of influences that goes far beyond mere family heritage and accidental success stories. Royals, even those from antiquity, continue to possess remarkable wealth and secret power that defy conventional economic explanations. This enduring affluence and influence suggest that their status and connections grant them access to resources and privileges that persist across generations without public accountability or democratic oversight.

There is speculation among researchers about whether royals are, in a sense, trustees or even enslaved people for extraterrestrial entities due to more potent Anunnaki genetics preserved through careful selective breeding over millennia. This idea implies that their unique genetic heritage could be a source of their persistent power and influence, perhaps linking them to ancient non-human intelligences that still maintain contact with certain bloodlines.

The involvement of royals extends deeply into all these areas we've been discussing throughout this book, whether it's secret societies like Freemasonry, concentrated wealth in banking dynasties, genetics research and eugenics programs, or connections to possible extraterrestrial legacies preserved through oral traditions. Their influence appears woven through multiple historical and contemporary threads, connecting power structures across centuries. There is a recurring observation that German ancestry is frequently present in these royal lineages and power connections, hinting at a pattern that continues to surface throughout history when you examine the backgrounds of influential figures who shape world events.

## D.D. PALMER AND NON-HUMAN INTELLIGENCE.

D.D. Palmer was a bit of an eccentric, to say the very least.

Palmer married Abba Lord, a self-declared "Dr." who described herself as a clairvoyant physician, business medium, psychometrist (fortune teller), and psychic healer. It looks like she introduced him to spiritualism, as no reports suggest that Palmer practiced spiritualism before this relationship. Palmer discovered that he could place Lord into a magnetic trance, claiming he could send her spirit to "distant places," places that were "in direct relation to another world." These experiences appear to have led Palmer further into the world of spiritualism.[208]

Palmer was communicating with what we now call non-human intelligence (NHI). Previously categorized as ghosts or aliens, what exactly was this entity that Palmer was conversing with? Was Lord doing what we call astral projecting and messaging back with information from other realms?

Well, it looks like Palmer was speaking with a dead doctor named Jim, who was giving him all the information and advice on how to start a practice that would later become chiropractic medicine. According to a study in the Chiropractic History journal, "Palmer claimed Dr. Jim Atkinson was a 'doctor' who disseminated principles analogous to chiropractic to the residents of Davenport, Iowa, some fifty years prior to Palmer beginning his chiropractic practice there in 1895. Palmer claimed Atkinson was an 'intelligent spirit being' from the "other world" who frequently conversed with him on a range of matters, including chiropractic philosophy and technique. However, no consensus has been reached on how Palmer and Atkinson "communicated." Palmer claimed that he "conversed" with Atkinson through 'inspiration' or 'spiritual promptings,' a method referred to by other 19th-century spiritualists and medico-religious writers. Others claim the communication occurred in spiritualist séances, but these claims are based on secondary sources and should not be relied on as being accurate."[209]

The National Post (2018) reports that "Palmer also considered chiropractic a kind of religion, saying in 1911 that the practice 'must have a religious head, one who is the founder, as did Christ, Mohamed, and others who have founded religions. I am the fountain head.'"

Palmer was communicating with non-human intelligence, and his wife was a fortune teller and clairvoyant. These people were all part of the "spiritualist movement" of the late 1800s and early 1900s, focused on communication with the dead and other entities, possibly inter-dimensional ones. Elon Musk's great-great-grandmother and great-great-grandfather were part of exactly this world. John Warner's thoughts on royal bloodlines: "They were desperate, and still are, to maintain their bloodlines by marriage despite genetic diseases. Why? One theory I hold is that they are trying to keep those ancient genes active, genes that gave them psychic and telekinetic powers as super-hybrids. The halos in paintings of clergy and aristocrats long ago were probably a secret code. "Holy," eh? My ass! Spiritualism? Only true psychics could communicate with higher intelligences, still true today."

I found this very interesting, especially since Elon's great-grandmother was the first licensed chiropractor in Canada. We must remember that in the late 1800s and early 1900s, spiritualism was a big movement in the Western world, so most of this seemed benign. Interesting to see that, nowadays, it's once again in fashion to believe in such things. Hell, you're reading this book right now, aren't you?

## JOSHUA HALDEMAN: RADICAL POLITICS AND THE MOVE TO APARTHEID SOUTH AFRICA.

Dr. Joshua Norman Haldeman, Elon's grandfather, is another interesting fellow. I found an article in The Atlantic titled "Elon Musk's Anti-Semitic, Apartheid-Loving Grandfather. The billionaire has described his grandfather as a risk-taking adventurer. A closer read of history reveals something much darker." The article delves into the background and radical beliefs of Dr. Haldeman, who moved his family from Canada to apartheid South Africa in 1950.[210]

Haldeman was a second-generation chiropractor who embraced fringe political movements like Technocracy

Incorporated and Social Credit in Canada, which espoused anti-democratic, racist, and anti-Semitic ideologies. He was arrested and convicted for his involvement with the Technocracy group, which the Canadian government banned as a threat during WWII. Members wore gray uniforms at one point and seemed really close to the Nazi movement in some of their rhetoric. The good doctor was also a leader of the Social Credit Party in Canada, defended publishing the fraudulent anti-Semitic text "The Protocols of the Elders of Zion," and made several documented anti-Jewish comments himself. Then Haldeman packed up his entire family and, instead of moving to Beverly Hills, moved to South Africa just as the apartheid system of racial segregation was being implemented, claiming it would lead to "White Christian Civilization." Those were his actual words.

He wrote a 1960 book praising apartheid South Africa as a "bulwark" against "anti-Christian, anti-White forces" and the "International Conspiracy" of Jewish bankers he believed controlled the world. This book is so rare that the only known copy of it and its existence are at Michigan State University for some reason. Maybe because it was self-published, or maybe because who knows what, but the title of this book is "The International Conspiracy to Establish a World Dictatorship and the Menace to South Africa," which just about sums it up, right? It also recommended far-right, anti-Semitic publications and defended the Sharpeville massacre of anti-apartheid protesters.

Haldeman amplified racist conspiracy theories and expressed strong support for the apartheid regime's subjugation of Black South Africans.

This article suggests that Haldeman's extreme, racist beliefs were an influential force that shaped Musk's worldview from a young age, despite Haldeman's death when Musk was two years old. That might be hard to swallow, but there is that old saying about not being blamed for the sins of your father and the apple not falling far from the tree. I mean, it's a stretch, but still, it seems very interesting.

# THE KALAHARI QUEST: A DECADE-LONG OBSESSION.

One thing his grandfather did while he was in Africa was spend an abnormally long time looking for the Lost City of Kalahari. He literally flew across the continent multiple times with his entire family, and this was all documented. He even considered himself an amateur archaeologist, for God's sake.

Haldeman was obsessed with finding this supposed "Lost City of the Kalahari." Every July for a decade straight, he'd pack up the whole family into their ride and head out on these epic treks across the desert on the hunt.

The whole Lost City thing started way back in the late 1800s, when this Canadian explorer named Guillermo Farini wrote a book about his travels through the Kalahari Desert, in places like Botswana, Namibia, and South Africa. In his book, Farini claimed to have found an ancient lost city out there, "a relic of a glorious past, a city once grand" that was destroyed by natural disasters.

That was enough to hook old Haldeman. Every year, Maye's mom would stock up on supplies (water, food, gas), and the five kids would pile into the car with just a map and a compass. Haldeman was convinced this Lost City was real and out there somewhere in the desert, waiting to be discovered on their yearly family adventure.

Did they find the Lost City of Kalahari, also known as the "Atlantis of the desert"?

Historian Bill Rehm documented that Dr. Haldeman "perhaps became best known in South Africa for his expertise in the 'Lost City of the Kalahari Desert.' [211]His first expedition into the Kalahari Desert was in 1953 to look for the lost city described by Farini in 1885. The second was an 8,400-mile aerial search at 200 feet off the ground in an uncharted desert. In all, he made 12 expeditions to search for the lost city. On every occasion, he was accompanied by Mrs. Haldeman and those of his children who were home.[212] Two books on the lost city (by F. Goldie[213] and A.J. Clement[214]) devoted large sections to his travels. Though he found no evidence, Dr. Haldeman remained convinced there was indeed a lost city in the Kalahari Desert." [215]

According to Geni.com (n.d.), "Haldeman led nine expeditions between 1953 and 1965, counting an initial exploratory trip to gather information, and several more afterwards. His search began in earnest in 1957 with an 8,400-mile air-ground search in the area around the Nossob River, followed by ground searches along Farini's suspected route each year from 1959 to 1965. The last was in 1969. These expeditions were into remote areas of what is now Botswana (at the time the Bechuanaland Protectorate)." [216] [217]

So, this guy spends a ridiculous amount of his life all over Africa (by air and by car), taking his entire family with him in search of this lost city. Just on a whim? No way. He had to have some advanced knowledge, or somebody had to have given him some information and verified everything in Farini's book, except for finding the actual city. Haldeman said that "Farini's story simply felt right." The man based much of his belief on first-hand knowledge; many expeditions into the Kalahari convinced him that Farini had actually been in the places he wrote about. He found Farini's descriptions accurate and his comments about his surroundings convincing, and continued to find locals who recognized depictions of the ruins. In an account of his aerial search in the South African Archaeological Bulletin, he stated unequivocally that 'someday the lost city of the Kalahari will be found' and, in a letter to one of Farini's descendants, 'we do not feel he made the "lost city" up as we have confirmed everything else in the book.'"[218]

Why did he stop searching in 1969? Had he discovered something valuable or hidden there, found the Atlantis of the desert with advanced technology and knowledge? Was any of this information passed down to Elon, who has set his sights on leaving Earth and colonizing Mars?

## THE TECHNOCRACY CONNECTION: FROM GRANDFATHER TO GRANDSON.

On June 23, 2019, Elon Musk tweeted, "accelerating Starship development to build the Martian Technocracy."[219]

You read that, and you're thinking, what the hell is he talking about? What is Technocracy? Well, Elon's grandfather was arrested in Canada for being a member of Technocracy during World War II.[220]

The Technocracy movement was an ideological movement that emerged in the early 20th century, gaining particular traction in the 1930s. It advocated for a system of governance and organization based on technical expertise and scientific principles, rather than traditional political or economic systems. Led by figures like Howard Scott and M. King Hubbert, the movement proposed a society governed by technical experts, engineers, and scientists instead of politicians or businesspeople.

Their vision was a system called the "Technate." It was a resource-based economy in which goods and services were distributed according to scientific principles and energy accounting, replacing conventional economic and political frameworks. I don't know if it's communist-like or what, but it seems very odd except for the politician part. I mean, nobody really likes politicians, do they?

During the Great Depression, the Technocracy movement gained some popularity as an alternative to capitalism. However, it faced criticism for its authoritarian tendencies, lack of democratic principles, and the proposed idea of a continental control board of technical experts making key decisions.

After World War II, the influence of the Technocracy movement declined, although some of its ideas around environmental management and resource efficiency later inspired related movements. At its core, the Technocracy movement advocated putting technical specialists and scientific management principles at the helm of societal organization and economic production. Seems like a global board of directors made up of all nerds, but in a good way. Not too sure, but Elon seems to think it was a great idea, and he wants to do the same thing on Mars. Is he doing that already by himself, buying companies, launching industries, forging ahead with the smartest and brightest, and in some ways influencing the politicians through monetary power or influence?

It seems like Elon's family comes from a line of people who had conversations with non-human intelligences and were very radical thinkers and adventurers. They were convinced of the existence of the so-called Atlantis of the desert, the Kalahari, and spent a large amount of time and resources searching for it. In the end, they dropped all of these efforts in 1969.

It is possible that discoveries were made, guided or influenced by external factors, and as a result, Elon Musk may now be benefiting from these outcomes. Did they find alien technology in the desert and are now reverse-engineering it for use in Elon's companies? Elon has been asked several times about aliens, and he says he has never seen evidence suggesting they exist. Seems like something you would say if you wanted to keep the Atlantis of the desert, Kalahari, ancient alien base top secret, right? Kind of along the lines of building denatured nuclear batteries for classified military contracts. At least that's what I was told, and I have no way to back that up. Do those nuclear batteries power the infamous Lockheed-Martin TR-3B flying black triangle? The one that supposedly makes it to the Moon in ten minutes and Mars in forty-five. Believe me, I hear all kinds of wild things, but perhaps it's not far from the truth?

Warner says, "batteries? They probably do not power it, but may be used for systems onboard. A torsion-field plasma generator is in the center, with the plasma ring around it. Three ballistic glass torsion field maneuvering nodes are on the underside. Sacred geometry construction is used throughout—hexagons, octagons, etc. TR3G is the latest model. Lockheed built."

## HOWARD HUGHES: THE ORIGINAL MIC FRONT MAN.

So, how is Elon the new Howard Hughes? First, who was Hughes? Most people know less about history now than ever before, so let's break down who he was and his impact on modern society. Howard Hughes was an eccentric billionaire, aviator, movie producer, and industrialist known for his secretive, reclusive behavior in later life, much like Elon Musk in our current era, but, in my opinion, cooler, smarter, and cut from a very different cloth. Hughes founded the Hughes Aircraft Company in 1932, showcasing his ambition to push technological boundaries beyond what anyone thought possible. He shattered numerous airspeed records during the 1930s, becoming a national hero and capturing the public imagination with daring flights and engineering innovations. His innovative designs, like the H-1 Racer, demonstrated capabilities that seemed almost impossible for the era and established him as America's premier aviation genius.[221]

With the outbreak of World War II, Hughes turned his attention to developing military aircraft. He secured massive government contracts for projects like the XF-11 reconnaissance plane and the gargantuan H-4 Hercules flying boat, famously known as the "Spruce Goose." These projects, however, were plagued by delays and cost overruns that drew intense government scrutiny. The Hercules, designed to carry 750 passengers across oceans, was ultimately deemed impractical for its intended purpose, though it demonstrated engineering capabilities far ahead of its time.[222]

The late delivery of these aircraft drew intense scrutiny, culminating in a highly publicized Senate investigation in 1947, where Hughes defended his work before Congress in dramatic fashion. While Hughes was officially cleared of wrongdoing, the controversy publicly tarnished his reputation with the government. At least that's what they wanted everyone to believe.[223] This led Hughes Aircraft to shift its focus to electronics and guided missiles, becoming a major defense contractor in the post-war era.

Hughes' empire extended far beyond aviation. He became a major Hollywood producer, financing films and launching the careers of stars like Katharine Hepburn. Additionally, his shrewd business acumen led him to acquire controlling interests in airlines and Las Vegas casinos, shaping both industries significantly and accumulating enormous wealth in the process.[224]

Howard Hughes' life was a whirlwind of ambition, innovation, and eccentricity. His accomplishments in aviation and business are undeniable. However, his dealings with the government were often contentious on the surface while deeply collaborative behind the scenes. Reminds me of the rise and fall of the 2025 bromance between Musk and President Trump over DOGE. I am sure that it will all come to light eventually, and it will most likely be in the next book.

## PROJECT AZORIAN: THE GLOMAR EXPLORER.

Project Azorian was a secret CIA operation in the 1970s to recover a sunken Soviet submarine from the Pacific Ocean floor. Hughes' company, Summa Corporation, was contracted by the CIA to build the Glomar Explorer, a massive ship, under the guise of deep-sea mining. Only a few individuals knew its true purpose.

Often cited as one of the most audacious engineering feats of the 20th century, the vessel was built from 1971 to 1972 by Sun Shipbuilding and Drydock Co. in Chester, Pennsylvania, under the direction of Howard Hughes and his company, Global Marine Development Inc. It cost over $350 million at the time (roughly $1.7 billion in 2023 dollars), making it one of the most expensive ships of its era. Officially, Hughes claimed the ship was designed for deep-sea mining, specifically to extract manganese nodules from the ocean floor. This cover story gained surprising traction and influenced marine geology research, but it was a front for its true purpose, orchestrated by the CIA.[225]

SECNAV John Warner III was involved with the Glomar Explorer. He told his son, John IV, that it was also used to recover USOs.

Project Azorian's real mission (sometimes referred to as "Project Jennifer" in early press reports) was to recover the sunken Soviet Golf-II class submarine K-129, which sank in the Pacific Ocean in March 1968, approximately 1,560 miles northwest of Hawaii, at a depth of about 16,500 feet. The diesel-electric submarine carrying ballistic missiles was of immense interest to U.S. intelligence due to its potential to yield Soviet technological secrets, nuclear weapons, codebooks, and other classified materials. It was amazing that the USSR could not find it. Every other country was scouring the ocean looking for the sub at the time.

The CIA enlisted Howard Hughes, known for his eccentricity and reclusiveness, to lend credibility to the cover story.

Hughes' reputation as a billionaire innovator made the deep-sea mining narrative plausible, masking the ship's true intent.

Built with cutting-edge technology, the ship featured a massive mechanical claw nicknamed "Clementine" (officially the "Capture Vehicle"), a dynamic positioning system to hold steady over the recovery site, and a large "moon pool" in the hull, a submerged opening through which the claw could operate and retrieve the submarine in secrecy. Think of the world's largest claw game, you play to pick up a stuffed animal, except this has never been accomplished before at such depths.

Construction began in November 1971, and the ship was launched in 1973, with its maiden voyage occurring on June 20, 1974. Too large to pass through the Panama Canal, it navigated around South America to reach its operational area in the Pacific.

On July 4, 1974, the Glomar Explorer arrived at the K-129 wreck site. Using its sophisticated systems, the ship lowered the claw to the ocean floor, where it grappled the submarine. The operation was fraught with challenges, including Soviet surveillance. Soviet ships and a helicopter monitored the Glomar Explorer, adding tension to the covert mission. As I said, everyone was desperately searching, and they were not shy about it.

On August 8, 1974, the ship successfully raised a part of the K-129. Still, a mechanical failure caused part of the submarine to break off and fall back to the ocean floor, losing two-thirds of the recovered section, including the missile control room and nuclear warheads. Despite this, the CIA recovered the forward section, which held Soviet communications equipment, codebooks, and the remains of six crew members. These sailors were given a ceremonial burial at sea with full honors, conducted in Russian, as a gesture of respect. Here is the kicker: it was not until the late 2000s that Russia was aware of the operation and the burials. It was kept secret for that long.

The mission's secrecy collapsed in March 1975, first through Jack Anderson's nationally syndicated broadcast. Then Seymour Hersh in the *New York Times*[226] prompted the CIA's now-famous "Glomar response" (neither confirm nor deny), later upheld in Phillippi v. CIA (1976), and ended all plans for the follow-up Operation Matador[227] to retrieve the remaining parts of the K-129. [228]The "Glomar response" is a tactic in which the CIA "neither confirms nor denies" inquiries about a project, a practice still used today for sensitive operations.

After the mission, the Glomar Explorer was mothballed due to its high cost and specialized design, which limited commercial interest. In 1976, it was transferred to the U.S. Navy and stored in the Suisun Bay Reserve Fleet. From 1996 to 1998, it was converted into a deepwater drillship for oil and gas exploration, leased to Global Marine Drilling (later Transocean) for $1 million per year. Renamed GSF Explorer, it operated in regions like the Gulf of Mexico, Nigeria, and the Black Sea until 2015, when Transocean announced its scrapping in China, marking the end of its 40-year career. What did it do all that time? Was it used to recover downed UFOs from the bottom of the ocean floor?

> Howard Hughes' involvement cemented his reputation as a
> figure capable of bridging private enterprise and covert
> government operations, just like Musk, in my opinion.

## THE MORMON CONNECTION: HUGHES, MUSK, AND INSTITUTIONAL POWER.

Here's what most people don't know about Howard Hughes in his later years: the detail that reveals the true pattern of how these operations work. Howard Hughes found an unexpected anchor in Bill Gay, a devout Mormon. Gay, with his unwavering loyalty, sobriety, and a moral compass shaped by his faith, became the fulcrum of Hughes' sprawling empire. There was an irony in this choice. Hughes, a man often depicted as a loner and recluse, found solace and perhaps a semblance of control through the very structure and discipline that Mormonism offered through Gay's management style. Gay managed Hughes' sprawling assets from the gambling dens of Las Vegas to the tech-driven behemoths like Hughes Aircraft, with a stewardship that was almost priestly in its dedication. This wasn't just business management or financial oversight but total financial control over one of America's wealthiest and most powerful men, exercised by a Mormon with absolute loyalty to principles larger than personal gain.

Fast forward to the present, and Elon Musk, another visionary with an attraction to the stars and Mars colonization, mirrors the Hughes pattern exactly through Jared Birchall. Birchall, while not as publicly known as Bill Gay was in his time, has been Musk's right-hand man for years, managing his wealth through Excession, LLC, and influencing decisions that span from the mundane financial operations to the cosmic ambitions of space colonization. Like Gay before him, Birchall's Mormon background has been speculated to infuse Musk's ventures with a sense of purpose and perhaps even a spiritual undercurrent beyond simple profit motives.[229]

The connection between these men isn't merely about personal management or financial oversight. It's about the pursuit of something greater, something almost divine in scope. Hughes's obsession with aviation, culminating in the Spruce Goose, and Musk's ambition with SpaceX to colonize Mars both echo the Mormon doctrine of eternal progression, a belief in the limitless potential of human achievement extending even beyond Earth into the cosmos.

For Mormons, being part of ventures that push the boundaries of human capability into the cosmos isn't just about technological advancement or making money. It's a validation of their faith's teachings about the universe and mankind's role within it, according to Mormon theology. The idea of colonizing Mars could be seen as a modern-day equivalent to the gathering of the early Saints in Utah, an exodus not to Zion on Earth but to the stars, where humanity might continue its journey of spiritual and physical ascension toward godhood.

Both Hughes and Musk, through their Mormon advisors who managed their empires, managed their fortunes in ways that went beyond mere financial strategies aimed at maximizing returns.[230] Hughes' estate planning, which eventually led to the creation of the Howard Hughes Medical Institute, was a testament to a legacy that transcended personal wealth. Similarly, Musk's ventures, while profit-driven, often carry an undercurrent of a mission to better humanity, possibly influenced by Birchall's values. The philanthropy of both men, whether intentionally or not, aligns with Mormon principles of stewardship and service to causes greater than oneself. Their religion teaches that there is no end to celestial glory or to the progression toward godhood. Or maybe they would like to "prove" that the Mormon religion is valid by finding evidence of people populating other "worlds" as Mormon doctrine suggests God has created?

## WHY MORMONS? UNDERSTANDING INSTITUTIONAL POWER

Now let's step back and understand WHY Mormons specifically keep appearing in these positions of absolute financial control over America's most powerful tech moguls and classified operations. This isn't a coincidence or random hiring, but systematic selection based on documented patterns spanning decades.

The connection between Mormons and U.S. intelligence agencies isn't speculation or conspiracy theory cooked up by paranoid researchers. It's a well-documented pattern that intelligence insiders and academic researchers have acknowledged openly for over half a century.

In 1971, Ramparts magazine reported that Latter-day Saints "provided both the CIA and FBI with some of their best men," according to their investigation into recruitment patterns.[231] By the 1980s, a Brigham Young University professor told the authors of *The Mormon Corporate Empire*, a 1985 social science study on the church and its power, that "we've never had any trouble placing anyone who has applied to the CIA." He added matter-of-factly, "Every year, they take almost anybody who applies."[232]

The 2017 book *The FBI and Religion* dedicates an entire chapter to this connection, calling church members "a natural recruiting ground for agents" due to their unique characteristics.[233] Tracy Walder, a former CIA officer and FBI special agent and author of *The Unexpected Spy*, stated that by the time she worked for the government in the 2000s, "it was a running joke that Mormons are what the agency wanted in their recruitment."[234]

While intelligence agencies don't officially track religious affiliation (doing so would violate employment law and constitutional protections), the Mormon recruitment pattern is "common knowledge" in Washington among those who work with or report on intelligence and law enforcement, according to multiple sources.[235] In his 2009 memoir *Agent Bishop*, Mike McPheters describes his years in which he doubled as an FBI agent and a Mormon bishop, a community leadership position he inherited from another FBI agent who was also Mormon.[236]

Intelligence agencies actively target Mormons for recruitment because they possess a unique combination of characteristics that make security clearances easier to obtain and operational success more likely compared to the general population.

The Mormon practice of sending young members on two-year missions (18 months for women) around the world creates a massive pool of candidates with critical foreign language fluency in exactly the languages intelligence agencies need most. Missionaries learn languages such as Arabic, Mandarin, Russian, Korean, Farsi, and many others while living abroad and communicating daily with native speakers in real operational environments. These aren't classroom skills learned from textbooks, but operational language abilities developed through real-world immersion in foreign cultures under challenging conditions.[237]

As Stanford professor Amy Zegart noted in her research on intelligence recruitment, this overseas exposure helps recruits "gain access" to intelligence operations by understanding cultural nuances, social dynamics, and communication patterns that can't be taught in training programs or simulated in classrooms.[238]

CIA applicants undergo rigorous background checks looking for any vulnerabilities or risk factors, and up to 60% of applicants fail these checks due to issues like drug use, criminal history, financial problems, or unstable relationships.[239] Mormons, who adhere strictly to the Church's Word of Wisdom (which prohibits alcohol, tobacco, coffee, tea, and all illicit drugs), are seen as significantly lower-risk candidates, making security clearances "cheaper and easier" to obtain, according to multiple intelligence officials who spoke about recruitment.

This clean lifestyle extends to strong family stability and low divorce rates. Mormons have significantly higher marriage rates (66% married vs. 48% in the general population, according to

Pew Research data), and those who marry tend to stay married at much higher rates than the general population.[240] Intelligence agencies view stable family life as a marker of reliability and reduced vulnerability to blackmail or compromise by foreign intelligence services.

Mormon culture emphasizes absolute obedience to authority figures, unwavering loyalty to institutions, and a strong sense of duty to serve causes greater than oneself without questioning leadership decisions. The Church teaches members to "sustain" their leaders without question and to view service as a sacred obligation directly tied to salvation. This cultural programming creates individuals who are extremely comfortable with hierarchy, secrecy, and following orders without demanding explanations or transparency, all highly desirable traits for classified intelligence work.[241]

A current Mormon intelligence agent explained this to me directly with a perfect real-world example that demonstrates exactly how deep this obedience programming goes. There's a viral trend called "Beer or Puppy" where students at Brigham Young University are asked a simple hypothetical question: would you rather take a single sip of alcohol or kill a puppy?[242]

The responses are absolutely chilling when you understand what they reveal. Many BYU students in these street interviews choose to "unalive the puppy" rather than break their religious covenants by consuming alcohol.[243] [244] While the videos are often framed humorously, these responses reflect something much darker and more useful to intelligence agencies. The BYU Honor Code and religious law dictate that consuming alcohol can lead to severe disciplinary actions, including expulsion, and more importantly, these responses demonstrate that following the rules takes absolute precedence over independent ethical reasoning.[245] [246]

Think about what this means for intelligence work. You have individuals so thoroughly programmed to follow institutional rules that they would choose to harm an innocent creature rather than violate a religious dietary code. This isn't about the specific choice of puppy versus beer; it's about demonstrating that the rule itself is more important than the ethical consequences of following it. This is exactly what intelligence agencies need. Operatives who will follow orders without applying independent moral judgment, who won't question whether what they're being asked to do is right or wrong, only whether it violates the explicit rules they've been given.

Critics call this "scrupulosity" or extreme rule-following that lacks ethical nuance, but intelligence agencies call it the perfect psychological profile. When you need someone to carry out classified operations without asking uncomfortable questions, without leaking to journalists because they're morally troubled, without refusing orders on ethical grounds, you want someone who's been trained since childhood that obeying institutional authority is more important than personal conscience.

This is why Mormons make perfect intelligence operatives. The same psychological conditioning that makes a BYU student choose puppy death over beer makes an intelligence analyst follow classification rules even when they witness potential crimes, makes an operative carry out questionable missions without moral hesitation, and makes an administrator like Bill Gay or Jared Birchall manage billions in potentially questionable operations without asking where the money really goes or what it's really funding.

Former FBI recruiter Rhonda Glover Reese explained in interviews that "the bureau is looking for people interested in serving communities, country, and the world," and that "many religious believers and Mormons in particular are instilled with a strong desire to serve a cause greater than themselves, including a patriotic duty and love of country," which makes them ideal candidates.[247] But what she didn't say explicitly is that this "service" means following orders without the ethical complications that conscience creates.

Intelligence work requires accepting significantly lower salaries than private-sector alternatives, especially for candidates with technical skills or foreign-language abilities that could command premium compensation in the private sector. Mormons, with their cultural emphasis on public service over personal enrichment and their community norms around duty and sacrifice, are more willing to make this substantial financial sacrifice than candidates from other backgrounds focused on wealth accumulation.[248]

Brigham Young University (BYU) serves as the primary recruitment pipeline connecting Mormon culture to intelligence agencies. The university has one of the highest concentrations of national security language students in the United States and actively markets its graduates to federal intelligence agencies.[249]

A 1975 CIA report declassified years later noted that one Mormon-owned PR firm made some of its "overseas offices available as cover for Agency employees operating abroad," showing how deep the institutional connections run between the Church and intelligence operations.[250] BYU itself has stated publicly that "we've tried to track down employment and recruitment numbers, and it's really hard to pin this down" because so many graduates enter highly classified positions where their employment can't be acknowledged.[251]

In 2013, the NSA completed construction of its largest domestic data storage facility in Bluffdale, Utah, located just south of Salt Lake City in the heart of Mormon country. The $1.5 billion Utah Data Center houses massive server farms capable of storing exabytes of intercepted communications data from around the world.[252]

While NSA officials publicly cited practical factors like cheap electricity, available land, and low risk of natural disasters as primary reasons for choosing Utah over 37 other potential locations[253], a former U.S. intelligence official speaking anonymously to Fox News told a very different story that reveals the real reason. "The Salt Lake City area is ideal because of a high concentration of Mormons who have served overseas missions and learned foreign languages. The NSA relies heavily on non-English speakers to translate communications from around the world, and Utah provides a deep pool of employees that meets this critical need."[254]

NPR reported in their coverage of the facility that "the NSA has another top-secret intelligence center in Utah where analysts, including former Mormon missionaries with extensive foreign language skills, translate communications intercepted by the agency" using the exact linguistic abilities developed during their mission service.[255]

The NSA and the University of Utah have even developed a specialized certificate program specifically to train data farm technicians to staff the facility with locally sourced Mormon talent.[256]

Senator Orrin Hatch, who served on the Senate Intelligence Committee for 14 years and had deep connections to the intelligence community, worked extremely hard to bring the massive data center to Utah, publicly crediting "the citizens of Utah" and "the good people that we have out here in Utah" for the NSA's decision to locate there.[257] Former Senator Bob Bennett similarly lauded Utah as having citizens who would be "politically more supportive of a data center than some states," a clear reference to the Mormon population's cultural tendency not to question authority or raise concerns about government surveillance programs that might trouble citizens in other locations.[258]

This brings us full circle to understanding why Bill Gay ran Howard Hughes' empire with total financial control and why Jared Birchall runs Elon Musk's finances with the same level of authority today.

The same exact qualities that make Mormons ideal intelligence recruits make them perfect administrators for classified operations disguised as private enterprise. They demonstrate absolute loyalty without question and don't leak secrets or question orders, following the program faithfully with clean backgrounds that pass any security scrutiny and effortlessly clear the hurdles that eliminate 60% of other candidates.

Their financial discipline and conservative management allow them to oversee enormous sums without being tempted by excess or corruption. Secrecy is ingrained in their culture through private temple rituals, sacred garments worn as continual reminders, and exclusive ceremonies where certain knowledge remains inaccessible to outsiders. Mormons are accustomed to keeping secrets that are never disclosed beyond their community. Their mission experience operating abroad means they've spent years in foreign environments, following strict protocols and rules, representing an institution larger than themselves without deviation. Perhaps most importantly, they view patriotic duty as equivalent to divine service, making their work sacred rather than just employment. Serving America becomes serving God directly.

When Howard Hughes needed someone to run his empire while maintaining deep CIA connections through classified projects like the Glomar Explorer submarine recovery operation, Bill Gay was the absolutely perfect choice. When Elon Musk needs someone to manage his immense wealth while maintaining classified contracts with the military-industrial complex through SpaceX, Tesla, and other ventures, Jared Birchall fits the same pattern and has the same qualifications.

It's no coincidence or random chance, but systematic selection based on proven patterns.

The Mormon Church, with its $236 billion in accumulated assets, its entrenched culture of absolute obedience to authority, its sophisticated global missionary network creating linguistically skilled young adults, and its deep decades-long integration with U.S. intelligence agencies at every level, has become the perfect institution for producing administrators who can operate seamlessly at the intersection of private enterprise and classified government operations without raising questions or concerns.

Hughes and Musk aren't outliers or exceptions to some rule. They're the most visible examples of a pattern that's been operating systematically for at least 80 years since World War II.

## JOSEPH SMITH: FREEMASONRY, FRAUD, AND THE FOUNDATION OF MORMONISM.

I'm not trying to upset members of the Mormon faith, but I want to highlight for those who may be unfamiliar with the notable similarities between Mormonism and Freemasonry.

The notion that Joseph Smith, the founder of the Church of Jesus Christ of Latter-day Saints (LDS Church), "stole" the first three degrees of Freemasonry (Entered Apprentice, Fellow Craft, and Master Mason) to create Mormonism is a theory rooted in historical overlap and observed similarities.[259]

Joseph Smith became a Freemason in 1842 in Nauvoo, Illinois, when he was initiated into the Nauvoo Masonic Lodge. [260] [261]

This was roughly 12 years after he founded the LDS Church in 1830 and published the Book of Mormon. Notably, just weeks after his initiation, Smith introduced the temple endowment ceremony[262], a key ritual in Mormonism. The timing has led some to speculate that Masonic rituals influenced this ceremony.[263]

## HISTORICAL CONTEXT: THE 1820S BURNED-OVER DISTRICT

Smith's rise occurred during a perfect storm of American history. The 1820s were chaotic. The nation was split over slavery, with the Missouri Compromise of 1820 splitting new states into "slave" and "free" zones. The Erie Canal's 1825 debut turned upstate New York, which was Smith's backyard, into a major trade hub. James Monroe was busy telling Europe to back off with the Monroe Doctrine, and the "Corrupt Bargain" election of 1824 [264]had folks pissed that John Quincy Adams pretty much stole the presidency from Andrew Jackson.[265]

Meanwhile, the Second Great Awakening[266] was underway in the Burned-Over District, an upstate New York region during the early 19th century, where religious fervor swept the area. The term refers to the intense religious revivals and the formation of new religious movements that took place there. Yet another coincidence, right? It's a perfect storm with restless, rowdy, and overzealous people searching for meaning in their existence.[267]

Eighty percent or so of the population at the time were farmers, clawing at the earth with primitive farming tools and praying the bank didn't foreclose on their patch of dirt. Frontier families like Smith's chased cheap land from Vermont to New York, dodging bears and shitting in outhouses. They took a monthly bath if they were lucky. Food was salt pork and cornbread, medicine was a leech-and-prayer crapshoot, and entertainment meant fiddles or gossip about the neighbor's cow. Women slogged through butter-churning and baby-making as their sole "occupations." Popping out ten kids was nothing. The more they could have meant, the more hands they had to work on the farms. Sundays brought church, which was half sermon, half social hour. In Smith's neck of the woods, revival fever had folks fainting in the pews, primed for his "God hates your church" pitch.[268]

This whole 1820s mess of religious frenzy, frontier scramble, and a DIY ethos was Smith's canvas. The Burned-Over District was a pressure cooker of lost souls. The Erie Canal[269] brought an audience to his Palmyra doorstep, and that gritty "make it big" spirit made his prophet act click.[270] I say he sniffed the chaos, saw a gap, and stuffed it with bullshit that was close enough to the Bible but still had a mystic flavor to make it stand out from the other religions of the time. No one else had golden plates, angel chats, and later, a Freemason crib sheet of handshakes and aprons. Who doesn't love a treasure-hunting kid turned God's newest prophet out there spinning revival vibes into a religion that'd make modern Americans choke on their lattes. Brilliant? Maybe. Full of it? Most would say yes.

## THE SEER STONE: JOHN DEE'S PLAYBOOK REVISITED.

Let's set the scene: we have Joseph Smith, our enterprising upstate New York farm boy turned self-proclaimed prophet, who is balls-deep in treasure-digging schemes with a magic rock in his hat. Yeah, you heard that right. This wasn't just a regular old magic rock; it was a "seer stone," he claimed, that let him gaze into the divine.

Elizabethan England's John Dee and his sketchy sidekick Edward Kelly were all about peering into the mystical with a slick obsidian seer stone, too. [271]If you are having trouble picturing this, think of it as their 16th-century Magic 8-Ball, or a shiny black stone that you can see your reflection in, the original black mirror.[272] From 1582 to 1587, these two huddled over this polished rock, claiming it let them speak with angels like Uriel and Raphael, who allegedly revealed cosmic secrets in a brand-new tongue called Enochian.[273] Kelly, the shady ex-con with a knack for scamming, "scryed" the stone while Dee scribbled notes.[274] All of this sounds suspiciously like Smith's hat-and-rock[275] routine, huh? Point is, Smith's seer stone shtick in the 1820s was just another page ripped from the grifter's playbook. What is old is new again, but if you have never heard of Dee and Kelly, then it's all magical.

Fast-forward a few centuries, and the same playbook reappears in the strangest of places, the modern UFO disclosure movement. In early 2025, a former Pentagon analyst named Matthew Brown appeared as a whistleblower, claiming insider knowledge of a classified program called "Immaculate Constellation". A shadowy repository allegedly hoarding high-resolution videos, images, and sensor data of unidentified anomalous phenomena UAP. [276] Brown described stumbling upon mislabeled files during routine work, accessing evidence of disc-shaped craft and massive black triangles, and feeling ethically compelled to go public because withholding knowledge of non-human intelligence (NHI) deprives humanity of its "birthright." Here's where the story takes a Dee-and-Kelley turn, shortly after his interviews on the Weaponized podcast, Brown posting under the handle (SunOfAbramelin), (which is a nod to the grimoire The Book of Abramelin, focused on contacting guardian angels) shared a cryptic image on X. It was a modified version of the Sigillum Dei Aemeth, the famous wax seal from John Dee's Enochian system, a circular diagram layered with symbols, numbers, and what appear to be altered angelic names, including annotations like "LOAGAETH" (the "Book of Speech from God" in Enochian) and a highlighted "ABORYMON" (a purported hidden eighth angelic name decoded from Dee's cipher in recent occult analyses).[277] [278]Community discussions quickly interpreted it as a "spell-wheel cipher" or symbolic framework possibly embedding program acronyms, hinting that UAP phenomena might intersect with ancient occult practices for contacting NHI, angels, demons, or something else entirely. Brown never explained the post directly, leaving it dangling like one of Dee's unresolved angelic riddles. Skeptics dismissed it as eccentricity or a LARP gone too far, especially given the Pentagon's denials of the program and the speculative frenzy in UFO circles online. Yet the parallel is striking, just as Dee and Kelley huddled over a black obsidian mirror to channel "angels" in a new language. Joseph Smith peered into a seer stone (often placed in a hat to block light) to translate sacred text. Brown seems to invoke Enochian symbolism to frame his revelations about hidden cosmic truths. What is old is new again, indeed. While the mediums have evolved from polished stones and obsidian mirrors to digital sigils, the motivation persists in using an intermediary object or cipher to access forbidden esoteric knowledge, whether from angels, God, or other non-human entities. If Dee and Kelley's angelic conversations sound suspiciously like scrying sessions, and Smith's hat-and-rock routine echoes folk magic traditions, then Brown's cryptic Enochian nod suggests the pattern persists even in the age of classified servers and congressional reports. The mystical and the modern collide, reminding us that claims of extraordinary revelation often rely on the same old human hunger for hidden meaning and the same old risks of deception, self-delusion, or outright grift.

## THE GOLDEN PLATES: MORONI AND MISSING EVIDENCE.

By 1830, Smith had churned out the Book of Mormon, a sprawling tale he said an angel named "Moroni" handed him on golden plates (conveniently whisked back to heaven once the translation was done). This kicks off the Church of Jesus Christ of Latter-day Saints, or as I like to call it, Smith's DIY religion kit. Here's where I raise an eyebrow, if you fast-forward to 1842, and Joey-boy joins the Freemasons in Nauvoo, Illinois. Weeks later, he unveils the temple endowment ceremony, and surprise! It's got handshakes, aprons, and secret signs that scream "Masonic Lite."[279] Coincidence? I think not. The guy clearly raided the Freemason playbook like a kid swiping cookies from the lodge jar.

According to Smith's own account in "Joseph Smith, History in the Pearl of Great Price,"[280] it all started in 1823, when he was a scrappy 17-year-old in Palmyra, New York. He claims an angel named "Moroni," who happens to be a dead warrior-prophet from ancient America, appears in his bedroom one night. Remind you of the current alien abduction lore of grey aliens removing people from their beds while they are asleep, much?

So "Moroni" tells him that there's a stash of golden plates buried in a hill nearby (later called the Hill Cumorah), etched with the history of some lost Israelite tribes who sailed to the Americas. Smith's told he's the chosen one to go and dig them up, but not right away. For four years, he's had to visit the hill annually for angelic pep talks, dodging temptation (and probably his Dad's chores). Finally, on September 22, 1827, Moroni greenlights the grab. Smith hikes up, pries open a stone box, and ta-da! There they are, the golden plates, bound like a fancy notebook, with weird text he calls "reformed Egyptian." Oh, and they come with bonus bling as well! A breastplate and two seer stones, the Urim and Thummim. They were described as looking like spectacles, with stones set in silver bows that connected over the top of his head, basically modern-day night vision goggles, right? I'm speculating as I have no idea; I am literally just regurgitating what is written, so stay with me.

After digging this up, he hauls it all home, and guess what, nobody else gets a good look at this stuff, **ever**. The plates conveniently vanish back to angel-land once he's "translated" them into the Book of Mormon by 1830, by squinting through his trusty hat-rock combo. This all makes perfect sense, right? If you are still following along, it's 1830, and he's got the Book of Mormon printed, courtesy of that angel Moroni and some golden plates nobody else ever saw aside from him.

## THE KING JAMES BIBLE CONNECTION: TYPOS AND ALL.

So, here's a fun little nugget to chew on: the Book of Mormon is cribbing not just ideas but the nitty-gritty typos and comma quirks from Bibles of his day.

Take the King James Version (KJV), the go-to holy book for 1820s American Protestants, including the Smith clan. The 1819 edition from H. & E. Phinney, printed right in Cooperstown, New York, which is just a hop, skip, and a seer stone's throw from Palmyra, had its own flavor of punctuation and occasional slip-ups, like odd spellings or dropped letters. Scholars like Royal Skousen, who've dissected the Book of Mormon's original manuscript, note that its first draft (dictated by Smith to scribes like Oliver Cowdery) leans hard into KJV, with the same erratic commas, odd semicolons, and even some archaic word forms.[281] This all happens to be a massive coincidence, right? [282]Or did Smith, with his farm-boy education, parrot the Bible he knew, mistakes and all, while "translating" his angelic tales?[283]

The Book of Mormon has verses like 1 Nephi 7:1 and Alma 7:10 that echo the KJV's cadence and phrasing, down to the "and it came to pass" that litters both texts. It's the typos and misspellings that are indicators. Early KJV printings weren't flawless by any means. Printers in the 1820s weren't exactly running spellcheck, and regional editions had quirks like "shew" for "show," and the word "saith" galore, or a comma where a period should've been. The Book of Mormon's printer's manuscript mirrors this chaos with minimal punctuation at first, then a punctuation overhaul by John Gilbert, the guy who typeset it for the 1830 edition, to match KJV norms. Critics like Dan Vogel argue Smith dictated it fast, leaning on his memory of Bible readings, so those hiccups (like "baptism" spelled weird or a misplaced dash) could've slipped in from whatever dog-eared KJV he'd thumbed through. If he's channeling divine gold plates, why does it look like a rushed copy of a Phinney Bible[284], typos and all?[285]

Here's my two cents, and it's dripping with, "Smith's full of shit."

As I said before, I am not trying to get hate mail from all the Mormons in the world here, and my goal is not to diminish someone's "faith." Still, just by examining all of these facts, anyone with an atheist bent or reviewing this from an impartial non-religious mindset would look at all of this data and say that the guy wasn't translating squat. He was riffing off the Bible he grew up with, warts and misspellings and all. The 1820s were awash in KJV reprints, and Palmyra had bookstores and revivals peddling them like hotcakes. Smith was no scholar, and he likely had a copy or at least its rhythms burned into his brain from all that Second Great Awakening preaching he was part of. The Book of Mormon's punctuation and spelling glitches match those of the Bible; it's no miracle, it's mimicry. Apologists claim divine style or ancient scribes, but how can you objectively posit that? He stole the Mason ritual handbook for his endowment; why not swipe the KJV's quirks too, even when he did so unknowingly? Some say it's another nail in the coffin of his prophet act, but that didn't stop his followers. Why would you question this when you can have 30 wives?

## MASONIC RITUAL THEFT: THE ENDOWMENT CEREMONY.

Freemasonry's first three degrees (Entered Apprentice, Fellow Craft, and Master Mason) are all about climbing a symbolic ladder with grips, oaths, and aprons, tied to Solomon's Temple. Smith, fresh off his Masonic initiation, trots out his endowment with eerily similar moves that include special handclasps, penalty gestures, and a green apron that'd make Adam and Eve blush. He even throws in an "all-seeing eye" nod, straight out of the Masonic lodge decor catalog. Smith saw those rituals, thought, "Ooh, shiny," and slapped a Moroni sticker on 'em, calling it divine revelation. Plagiarism with a prophet twist with dollar signs in his eyes.

Let's not kid ourselves. Mormonism wasn't just a Masonic knockoff. Smith had been cooking his stew since the 1820s, blending frontier revivalism, a pinch of Old Testament flair, and a hefty dose of "I'm God's VIP." The Book of Mormon, a tale of ancient American Israelites and Jesus popping by post-resurrection, came first, pre-Masonry. So yeah, he didn't steal the whole religion from the lodge, just the dress-up parts. Still, the timing's too perfect. I'm calling it as I see it; Smith was a Freemason fanboy who saw a good gig and ran with it.

How did this circus tent get set up? According to Smith, he had a vision as a teenager in 1820, in which God and Jesus supposedly appeared, declaring that all existing churches were flawed and appointing Him as the chosen one to restore things. In this account, the plates conveniently disappear back to an angelic realm, leaving only a published book, a hat, a stone, and a story that no independent party ever confirmed. The evidence tends to vanish just after serving its purpose, a pattern that repeats itself several times.

## POLYGAMY: THE WIVES CLUB THAT FREAKED EVERYONE OUT.

Now let's talk polygamy, Smith's spicier contribution to the Mormon brand. He didn't just dip a toe; he cannonballed into it, claiming God told him to marry multiple women (convenient, huh?). I love my wife more than anything, but I could not imagine having multiple wives telling me what to do daily. I have a hard enough time with one!

By the 1840s, Smith racked up 30 or more wives, some as young as 14, others already married to other men. The

Doctrine and Covenants (Section 132) lays it all out, plural marriage is the ticket to godhood. Brigham Young took it to eleven, with 55 wives and a brood that'd fill a school bus. Most Americans then (and now) gagged at the idea. Polygamy was so taboo that the U.S. government forced the church to stop it in 1890. Even today, the mainstream LDS Church swears its monogamy only, but splinter groups like the FLDS keep the old flame alive, creeping out the rest of us with their prairie dresses and underage brides. It is one of the things that really pisses off the left and the right.

## EXTRATERRESTRIALS AND GOD'S REAL ESTATE EMPIRE.

Mormonism's theology is a sci-fi fever-dream that'd make Spielberg jealous and possibly provided a foundation for Hubbard's Scientology, because Smith didn't stop at Earth. He went, full cosmic landlord. Here are some of the more "interesting" ideas within this religion.

The Mormon Book of Moses says God has "worlds without number,"[286] all packed with his spirit children. Yep, extraterrestrials are just cosmic cousins, living their own soap operas on planets we'll never RSVP to.[287]

God's an ex-human? Smith's King Follett sermon drops the bomb that God was once a human like us, worked his way up, and now runs the universe. The bonus here is that humans can level up, too, and become gods, and we can also get our own planets. An entire planet to call your own.

Heaven's a three-tier timeshare. Forget harps, flowing white robes, and fluffy clouds. Mormons get a three-level afterlife (Celestial, Terrestrial, Telestial), with the top tier for the VIPs who nailed the temple game. Everyone else gets a consolation prize or worse.

Magic underwear, also known as temple garments. They are not just an amazing fashion statement. They're holy armor, supposedly shielding wearers from evil.[288]

There are more interesting things to unpack, but let's get back to the timeline. In the 1830s, Smith gathered a crew of believers and set up shop in New York. Then he bounces around to other states (Ohio, Missouri, Illinois), all the while chased by pissed-off neighbors who didn't buy his prophet schtick. By 1844, he is running Nauvoo like a theocratic kingpin, complete with a Mormon militia, until a mob shoots him[289] dead in jail[290]. Some people speculate that the murders were, in fact, Freemasons acting out the penalty of the obligation that Smith took when he became a Freemason; however, there has never been any solid proof of this, just more rumor and speculation.[291]

Enter Brigham Young, stage left, who hauls the flock to Utah in 1847, turning Salt Lake into Mormon HQ.[292] That's the gist of it, but I am positive I didn't cover everything. Utah also plays a pivotal role in today's research on phenomena. Skinwalker Ranch in southern Utah has an ongoing History Channel series and a spin-off. Notably, everyone on that show who is part of the research into the UFO sightings, cryptids, and many more anomalous activities on this ranch is also a Mormon. The owner, Brandon Fugal[293], is a multimillionaire Mormon real estate titan. That adds an entire ball of red string to add to the paranoid connection board, but patterns tell stories.[294]

This stuff clashes hard with 2026 America. Polygamy's a relic most recoil from legally and morally. The extraterrestrial bit sounds like a Star Trek pitch, not a Sunday sermon, and the idea of God as a cosmic CEO with a wife (or wives) rubs monotheists raw. Baptists and Methodists might clutch pearls, and atheists roll their eyes. We know what the Catholics will say, and the only ones that might be on their team are the Scientologists, but I am not going there in this book, or ever, actually. I saw what they did to some members of the hacker group Anonymous in 2008, and I do not want to go down that rabbit hole.

Was Joseph Smith a treasure-hunting huckster who cribbed Freemasonry's rituals to spice up his endowment, built a religion that's equal parts audacious and absurd? From polygamy to planet-populating gods, Mormonism's a wild ride that'd make most Americans today spit out their craft beer. Some say he's full of it and just a slick salesman who turned lodge ritual into a divine grift, but it paid off. If you follow the money, it might be more than eye-opening.

THE MORMON MONEY MACHINE.

Mormonism has about 17.2 million members as of 2024[295], according to its latest reports. Christianity's at 2.4 billion worldwide, Islam's at 1.9 billion, and Hinduism's got 1.2 billion in its corner. Even Buddhism has 520 million followers. Mormonism is barely 0.2% of the world's 8 billion souls. Compared to the 1.4 billion Catholics alone, who dwarf Mormons by 80 times. Jehovah's Witnesses clock in at 8 million, half the size but still scrappy. Growth-wise, Mormonism's slowing down, 0.85% in 2021, barely keeping up with world population ticks, while Islam's at 1.8% annually.

Mormonism's got boots on the ground in 160+ countries, with 60% of its members outside the U.S. They're in Brazil, Mexico, and even the Philippines, thanks to a missionary machine that pumps out 54,539 full-time missionaries (as of 2023).[296] Let's be real, they're a rounding error compared to Catholicism's 1.36 billion or Islam's sprawl. Influence? In Utah, they dominate politics, with 88% of the state legislature being LDS members (as of 2021).[297] Outside Utah, they're influential but niche. Think Mitt Romney and Harry Reid as Mormon political heavyweights, but they're outliers, not trendsetters.[298]

Talk about wealth, the Mormon Church is filthy rich.[299] According to 2024 estimates, they're sitting on a $236 billion pile, per The Washington Post's analysis. That's $13,700 per member, a cash cushion that'd make Jeff Bezos whistle. Where's it from? Tithing. Members cough up 10% of their "income" (more on that vague term below), no receipt required, just the honor system and some guilt. In 2022 alone, the church raked in about $8.7 billion in tithing, per leaked estimates. The SEC then fined them for hiding $32 Billion in assets in 2023.[300]

Now, what counts as "income" for that 10%? The church leaves it maddeningly vague. Your paycheck? Yeah, that's income. You're expected to tithe 10% before taxes, not after, gross, not net. So, if you make $50,000 a year, you're dropping $5,000 into the collection plate. No audit, no receipt, just the bishop nodding and the congregation silently judging. It's honor-based, but with eternal consequences dangled overhead. If you skip tithing, you can't enter the temple, which means no celestial kingdom, no godhood, no planet. That's impressive religious leverage. The church isn't sending auditors to your house, but they are asking, and the culture's set up so saying "no" feels like spitting on the Savior. Guilt's the enforcer here, not the IRS. Ironically, the church doesn't owe the IRS a dime because it's tax-exempt.

All your wages are fixed at 10% sent directly to Salt Lake City.

What about selling your junk, say, a rusty bike or Grandma's creepy doll collection? Here's where it gets fuzzy. The church's official line, per the General Handbook (Section 34.4.1)[301], says tithing applies to "income," but it dodges defining what that means, like a politician sidestepping a scandal. Most bishops push the "10% of all increase" vibe, old-school Malachi 3:10 stuff, and hardcore Mormons take it to mean any cash coming in, including profits from flipping your garage-sale haul. So, sell a couch for $100? Some say you owe $10, no questions, but it's not policed like wages. Nobody's auditing your eBay receipts (yet). Plenty of members shrug it off as small potatoes, sticking to payroll only, while the zealots tithe every nickel. The church loves the ambiguity; it keeps the guilt flowing and the coffers fat. Either way, it's less "required" than "heavily suggested with a side of eternal guilt." Classic hustle, turning a vague revelation into a cash grab.

The Catholic Church, with its $30 to $500 billion spread (depending on who's counting Vatican art and land, and as we saw previously, billion-dollar handouts from the U.S. government as well), still laps them in raw totals, but per member? Catholics scrape by on $20 to $350 each. Islam's decentralized, no central pot, but Mecca's tourism rakes in billions. Hindus and Buddhists lean on temples and donations, nowhere near Mormon Inc.'s cash hoard. Scientology's got $3 billion from 20,000 devotees ($150,000 per head), but Mormonism's per-capita liquid wealth might edge out everyone.

Smith's treasure-digging roots sure paid off, huh? A true racket?

So, where does Mormonism stack up? Membership's a tiny club next to the titans; reach is wide but shallow; influence is loud in Utah, muted elsewhere; there are strong connections to the MIC as well as to military and government agencies, especially their wealth. They're filthy rich per head, outpacing even the Vatican's per-capita stash.

I have nothing against anyone practicing their own religion. However, I fully believe that knowing the truth and history is vital to making an informed decision about how you spend your time, money, and spiritual acumen in the world we live in today. I never bothered to understand Mormonism until I became a Freemason and learned everything I wrote here. Maybe I am biased because Freemasonry is not and never will be a religion, and to see someone turn its tenets into a money-making global enterprise, well, the least I can do is tell everyone else. So now you know, do with this knowledge what you will.

# CHAPTER 11

## THE DARPA PIPELINE

The official narrative paints a picture of a scrappy entrepreneur who, in 1994, launched an online bookstore from a garage in Bellevue, Washington, armed with little more than a vision and a knack for problem-solving.[302] Beneath this well-worn tale lies a tantalizing mystery, one that connects Bezos to the shadowy corridors of the Pentagon and a figure from his past whose influence may have been far greater than the public ever realized, his grandfather, Lawrence Preston Gise.

Gise was no ordinary man. In 1958, he played a pivotal role in the formation of the Advanced Research Projects Agency (ARPA), a secretive arm of the Department of Defense that would later evolve into DARPA, the birthplace of the internet and countless technological marvels that define our modern world. Gise's fingerprints are on the foundational years of an agency that would go on to pioneer high-speed networking, voice recognition, and the very infrastructure of the digital age.[303] Yet, when researcher John Greenewald Jr., a tenacious Freedom of Information Act (FOIA) sleuth, sought to uncover more about Gise's life through his FBI file, he hit a brick wall. The response was short and to the point. If such a file ever existed, it would have been destroyed.[304]

The destruction of Gise's FBI file raises more questions than it answers. Why would the records of a man so deeply entwined with one of the most powerful and secretive agencies in U.S. history be erased? Was it routine bureaucratic housekeeping, or does it hint at something more deliberate, a sanitization of history to obscure connections that might rewrite the story of one of the world's richest men? When we consider the possibility that Jeff Bezos, through his grandfather, may have had a head start on technologies that wouldn't reach the public for decades.

Bezos himself has often spoken fondly of Gise, whom he called "Pop." In interviews, he's credited his grandfather with instilling in him a sense of resourcefulness, a trait he claims was honed during summers spent on Gise's rural Texas ranch, fixing machinery and tackling problems with ingenuity. "He would take on major projects that he didn't know how to do and then figure out how to do them," Bezos once told an audience at a Summit LA panel. He paints a picture of a practical, hands-on mentor, but his words also leave us wondering, what else might Gise have shared with his grandson during those formative years?

Gise wasn't just a rancher with a knack for tinkering. By the time Bezos was born in 1964, Gise had already left ARPA and taken on a high-ranking role at the Atomic Energy Commission (AEC), [305] overseeing a sprawling operation across seven states with 26,000 employees. His career placed him at the nexus of cutting-edge science and national security, rubbing shoulders with the architects of America's technological dominance. DARPA, under his early influence, was already laying the groundwork for innovations that would transform society, innovations like ARPANET[306], the precursor to the internet, which went live in 1969. Could Gise, a man steeped in this world of classified projects and forward-thinking research, have passed along insights, ideas, or even privileged knowledge to his grandson?

The timeline pans out. Bezos founded Amazon in 1994, just one year before Gise died in 1995. By then, DARPA had already spent decades refining technologies that would later become the backbone of the digital economy, like scalable networks, data processing, and early artificial intelligence. While the public only began to grasp the internet's potential in the mid-1990s, DARPA insiders had been living in that future for years. If Gise maintained any ties to his old colleagues or even kept a mental repository of DARPA's visionary goals, it's not hard to imagine him imparting a sense of what was coming to a curious and ambitious young Jeff Bezos.

The revelation that Gise's FBI file (if it existed) has been destroyed adds fuel to this speculative fire. John Greenewald Jr., who runs The Black Vault, a treasure trove of declassified documents, uncovered this detail in 2024, sparking a flurry of discussion online. "I went after his FBI file, but found out if there was one, it has been destroyed," he posted on X, accompanied by a stark image of the FOIA response. The news website Leading Report's Patrick Webb chimed in, noting, "There has long been speculation that DARPA has been involved in the creation of many popular big tech companies, using 'frontmen' for the illusion of a startup led by outsiders." [307] The implication is clear. Amazon's origin story might not be as grassroots as it seems.

File destruction isn't unheard of in government archives. The FBI routinely purges records deemed obsolete or irrelevant, often after a set period or upon an individual's death. Gise, who passed away nearly three decades ago, might fall into this category. Yet, for a figure of his stature, someone instrumental in launching an agency like DARPA, the absence of any preserved record feels suspicious. Was there something in that file deemed too sensitive to remain, even decades later? Could it have documented meetings, correspondences, or projects that linked Gise's DARPA tenure to the technological empire his grandson would build?

Some speculate that Gise's file contained evidence of informal mentorship, perhaps notes on conversations with Bezos that hinted at DARPA's roadmap for the future. Others go further, suggesting that Amazon itself might have been seeded with DARPA's tacit blessing, a way to commercialize technologies the agency had incubated. After all, Amazon Web Services (AWS)[308], the cloud-computing juggernaut that now accounts for a massive share of the company's profits, hosts "secret" cloud services for the CIA, NSA, and other intelligence agencies, a relationship that echoes DARPA's own mission of advancing national security through tech.

To be clear, there's no smoking gun proving that Bezos received DARPA tech before its public release. Amazon's early days as an online bookstore relied on relatively rudimentary systems, and its growth into a tech titan can be traced through well-documented business decisions and market trends. The DARPA connection invites us to reconsider the narrative through a more skeptical lens. The agency's history is riddled with examples of indirect influence on private industry. Google, for instance, received early funding from DARPA grants[309], while Facebook's launch suspiciously coincided with the cancellation of DARPA's LifeLog project in 2004[310]. Could Amazon be another piece in this puzzle?

If Bezos did benefit from Gise's insider perspective, the advantage might not have been explicit blueprints or stolen code. It could have been subtler, a mindset attuned to the possibilities of networked systems, an understanding of scalability, or a hunch about where computing was headed. In the 1990s, while most entrepreneurs were still grappling with dial-up modems, Bezos was betting big on a future of seamless online commerce. This vision aligned uncannily with DARPA's decades-long push for interconnected digital infrastructure.

The destroyed FBI file only deepens the enigma. If it once held evidence of Gise's influence on Bezos (whether through casual chats or something more orchestrated), its absence ensures we may never know the full story. What remains is a tantalizing "what if." What if Jeff Bezos, knowingly or not, carried forward a DARPA legacy, leveraging his grandfather's proximity to the cutting edge to build an empire that now shapes our lives in ways Gise could only have dreamed of?

The mystery of the vanished file isn't just a historical footnote; it carries implications for how we view Amazon today. If Bezos did have an early glimpse of DARPA's playbook, it might explain Amazon's relentless innovation, its ability to pivot from books to cloud computing to artificial intelligence with a prescience that often outpaces competitors. It might also shed light on the company's cozy ties with the U.S. government, from AWS contracts to Bezos' ownership of The Washington Post, a publication with deep roots in the national security establishment.

For the broader public, this raises uncomfortable questions about the origins of our tech giants. Are they truly the products of individual genius, or are they, in some cases, extensions of a military-industrial complex that has long sought to harness technology for control and profit? The destruction of Gise's file leaves us only to speculate, but that speculation itself is a call to look more closely, to question the stories we're told about the architects of our digital world.

THE TECH TITAN PATTERN: PAGE, BRIN, ZUCKERBERG, ELLISON.

Musk and Bezos aren't the only tech titans with curious ties to the shadowy corners of the military-industrial complex. The threads of influence, once pulled, reveal a tapestry far more complex and far more unsettling than the Silicon Valley mythos would have us believe.

## LARRY PAGE AND SERGEY BRIN: GOOGLE'S DARPA ROOTS.

Larry Page and Sergey Brin met in 1995 at Stanford University, where both were Ph.D. students in computer science. Page, born in 1973 in Michigan, grew up in a tech-savvy family. His father was a computer science professor, and his mother taught programming. Brin, born the same year in Moscow, fled Soviet anti-Semitism with his family at age six, landing in Maryland; his parents were academics too, his father a math professor.

Their "origin story" begins with Backrub, [311]a research project analyzing the web's link structure, funded in part by Stanford and a National Science Foundation grant. By 1998, they'd turned this into Google, launching from a garage with a $100,000 check from Sun Microsystems co-founder Andy Bechtolsheim.

Some whisper about deeper ties. Posts on X and fringe reports suggest DARPA and intelligence agencies like the NSA and CIA seeded early internet projects, including Google's precursors. No hard proof exists, but Google's rapid ascent and later contracts (such as its 2010 NSA deal) fuel speculation. Their academic pedigree and timing in Silicon Valley's boom were key, though the "two guys in a garage" tale glosses over those institutional boosts.

## MARK ZUCKERBERG: FACEBOOK AND PRISM.

Mark Zuckerberg, born in 1984 in White Plains, New York, grew up in a middle-class household. His father was a dentist, his mother a psychiatrist. A coding prodigy, he built a messaging system for his Dad's office as a teen. At Harvard in 2004, he launched Facebook from his dorm, inspired by hacked student directories and fueled by a mix of his own cash and small investments from friends like Eduardo Saverin. The "self-made" label sticks, but Zuckerberg's path (elite prep schools, Harvard, and a safety net to drop out) hardly screams rags-to-riches. Many people say the CIA tagged him at Harvard like so many others.

Facebook's explosive growth came from opening it beyond colleges in 2006, but early lawsuits (like the Winklevoss twins' claim that he stole their idea) hint at a less solitary-genius tale. Meta's later ties to government data-sharing programs, revealed in leaks such as PRISM, raise questions about whether its origins were as organic as advertised. Privilege and timing, not just talent, built the empire.

## LARRY ELLISON: ORACLE'S CIA CONNECTION.

Larry Ellison, born in 1944 in New York City, had a rocky start. Raised by his aunt and uncle in Chicago after his single mother gave him up, Ellison dropped out of two colleges but honed coding skills at odd jobs. In 1977, he co-founded Software Development Laboratories (SDL) with $2,000, mostly his own savings. Renamed Oracle, its first big client was the CIA for a database project codenamed "Oracle,"[312] a link Ellison proudly touts[313]. Oracle's ongoing government contracts keep the theory alive. Ellison's no bootstraps hero. His breakthrough came from aligning with Cold War tech needs. Oracle's dominance in enterprise software owes much to that early federal lifeline, raising questions about how much of Silicon Valley's rise traces back to Washington.

## ELON MUSK: THE DARPA TECHNOLOGY HANDOFF.

In 1973, there was a paper titled "Toward direct brain-computer communication".[314] A direct quote from this paper: "Can these observable electrical brain signals be put to work as carriers of information in man-computer communication or for the purpose of controlling such external apparatus as prosthetic devices or spaceships?" Spaceships? You don't say.

Today, we would call this NeuraLink, an Elon Musk company. Did DARPA hand this perfected technology over to Musk to release publicly as his "invention"? I think so, along with these other "inventions."

Electric and Hybrid Vehicle Technologies (EHV), DARPA-funded program, 1992.[315] That's the basis of Tesla Motors.

Starlink? Could that be the DARPA Blackjack Program?[316] "DARPA's Blackjack program aims to develop and demonstrate the critical elements for a global high-speed network in low Earth orbit (LEO) that provides the Department of Defense with highly connected, resilient, and persistent coverage." 38 See the pattern?

In 1972, the Los Alamos National Laboratories patented a nuclear tunnel boring machine, claiming it could reach depths of eighteen-plus miles. It uses molten lithium to melt through rock, leaving behind a tunnel with a glass-like finish[317]. It has been said that Clark Engineering built a lot of dumbs

From 1993: "This report, 'An Excavation Strategy for the ESF at Yucca Mountain,' has been prepared at the request of the Nuclear Waste Technical Review Board. It represents a preliminary evaluation of the condition and suitability of a Robbins 18.6-foot Tunnel Boring Machine for the ESF program. The Defense Nuclear Agency currently owns this TBM and is being stored underground in an active state on the Nevada Test Site"[318].

In 2018, DARPA announced its latest contest, called the Subterranean or "SubT" Challenge.[319] Contest participants were to develop systems that could help humans map, traverse, and search underground locations that would otherwise be too difficult or dangerous to enter or explore. To me, following the patterns here, it sounds like they are just going to roll out the old tech and make it public via another Elon Musk company, the Boring Company.

Musk tried to introduce an above-ground MagLev train into a vacuum tunnel, reaching Mach 2. Well, there have been many reports by whistleblowers over the last thirty years of this technology underground being used secretly to connect military bases and corporate contractor science labs since the 1960s.

Basically, all of Musk's companies are MIC fronts, but they are not the only ones.

## THE PATTERN REVEALED.

Were these moguls geniuses, beneficiaries, or both? The truth, as always, is murkier than the legend.

Here's what we can see: the same pattern repeats across generations. Howard Hughes in the 1940s to 1960s. The internet pioneers in the 1990s. The social media and space tech entrepreneurs of the 2000s to 2020s. Each generation has its chosen front men, charismatic, brilliant, well-connected individuals who serve as the public face of controlled technology release.

The 30-year rule holds. The technologies we marvel at today were operational in classified programs decades ago. The individuals who bring them to market aren't always the inventors. They're the distributors, carefully selected and positioned to shepherd revolutionary technologies from black budget programs into the commercial sphere.

Why this method? Control. By channeling breakthrough technologies through specific individuals and companies with deep government ties, the intelligence community maintains oversight, ensures favorable contracts, and can revoke access or destroy careers if cooperation falters.

Look at what happened to Hughes when he started becoming too independent, too erratic. He ended up a recluse, possibly drugged, definitely controlled. Look at what happens to tech CEOs who don't play ball. Their companies face antitrust actions, their personal lives get exposed, and their boards force them out.

The message is clear: play the game, distribute the technology as directed, maintain the narrative, and you'll become one of the richest, most powerful people on the planet. Step out of line, and everything can vanish.

Elon Musk isn't the new Howard Hughes by accident.[320] He's the new Howard Hughes by design. The same system that elevated Hughes used him and is now doing the same thing with Musk. The technologies are more advanced, the stakes are higher, but the playbook remains the same.

Are Musk's "eccentricities" connected to his possible MK Ultra mind control? It's a thought.[321] I feel sorry for him, in a way, if that is true, and we, the public, are meant to believe it's all the product of individual genius, garage startups, and the free market at work. Just follow the money, trace the technologies, examine the connections, and a different picture emerges. One where the military-industrial complex seeds innovation through chosen individuals, maintaining control while appearing to champion entrepreneurship.

That's the real 30-year rule, not just that technology is suppressed, but that its release is orchestrated through carefully selected front companies and individuals who have the pedigree, the connections, and the willingness to serve as conduits for controlled disclosure, and by the by, electric cars go back to the 1890s, so are they really high-tech?

There's no doubt about Musk's intelligence. The real question is whether others, experienced in this arena for generations, are using his talents much as they did with Hughes, elevating him to legendary status before turning him into a recluse and, ultimately, a warning.

If that's true for Musk, Bezos, and the other tech titans we've examined, what does it mean for the technologies still in the pipeline? What revolutionary capabilities are being prepared for release through the next generation of charismatic frontmen? Will the tech help humanity or further enslave us?

The 30-year rule suggests we won't know for another three decades, unless someone breaks the pattern, whistleblowers come forward, or the truth becomes impossible to suppress.

That's the fight, and that's why understanding these connections matters. Because every time we accept the mythology, every time we believe the garage-startup story without questioning the deeper patterns, we give away our power to demand transparency, accountability, and real disclosure.

The technologies exist. The capabilities are real, and the question isn't "if" they'll be released to the public. It's "how," "when," and "through whom."

Understanding that those answers are chosen, orchestrated, and controlled changes everything. It means we can demand faster releases, greater transparency, greater accountability, and refuse to wait another 30 years for the next generation of breakthroughs. We are empowered to see through the mythology of the lone genius entrepreneur and recognize the deeper structure: the military-industrial complex's technology suppression and controlled-release system that has been operating for at least 80 years.

From Hughes to Musk, from atomic secrets to brain-computer interfaces, from aviation advances to Mars colonization, the pattern holds.

Recognizing the pattern of technological control through frontmen is one thing. Understanding how that control is maintained through information warfare is another. The military-industrial complex doesn't just select charismatic individuals to distribute suppressed technologies; they deploy sophisticated counterintelligence operations to ensure the public never recognizes what's happening. This is where someone like my friend John Warner IV becomes essential to understanding the full picture.

## JOHN WARNER IV: INSIDER PERSPECTIVE.

John W. Warner IV comes from the old American aristocracy. His father, U.S. Senator John W. Warner III, was a WW2 USN and later Marine veteran, Secretary of the Navy, and Chairman of the Armed Services Committee. His mother, Catherine Mellon, was a banking heiress, the daughter of Paul Mellon, who worked in OSS (precursor to the CIA) and had access to the highest levels of intelligence. His cousin is none other than Christopher K. Mellon. I was introduced to John by my good friend Jean-Luc. We became fast friends and spent a few days on John's farm in Virginia. We speak often and have relied on our friendship and our mutual interests & obsessions with The Phenomenon to keep each other grounded.

John toured most USN bases worldwide with his Dad. Debriefed his Grandfather, Paul, on WW2's secret UFO technology over lethal Hawthorn Martinis. He grew up at tables where history was made. Where classified information flowed freely in his Dad's offices, doors closed. Where the real decision-makers operated behind the democratic theater, he wandered the halls of the Pentagon from 1968 72—absorbed everything. Made it to the Kremlin in 1990 on Codel Dole as his Dad's Russian military historian at age 28. Attended the Bolshoi Ballet. Drank vodka with Premier Gorbachev.

John's not speculating about power structures. He knows them intimately and has witnessed firsthand how deception operates at the governmental, corporate, banking, and intelligence levels. The man understands compartmentalization, "need-to-know," "CIA limited hangouts," and psychological operations—unacknowledged Special Access Programs. Black budgets, the really black ones, and when he turned his full attention to the UFO phenomenon and started investigating what his family connections revealed about the topic, especially from his Dad, his cousin Chris, and Grandfather Paul, he recognized the same patterns, deception, compartmentalization, and psychological manipulation. He could tell when his father was lying, but this was something deeper, more sophisticated, and longer running. It might not just be human intelligence agencies deceiving the public. It could be something else, like NIH deceiving human intelligence agencies. It is all layers within layers, plans within plans, and deceptions wrapped in deceptions.

John, Jean-Luc, and I have spent hours discussing this. Breaking down the mechanisms, identifying the patterns, and trying to understand what's real versus what's theater. After a long while, one gets a knack for this.

The conclusion we keep reaching is that almost everything in UFO disclosure is tightly controlled. Almost every "whistleblower" is managed. Every narrative serves an agenda for both human and star beings.

John has his own way of processing The Phenomenon, through creative fiction and rigorous critical analysis. His second novel, Lion, Tiger, Bear, explores themes of contact and deception through narrative, allowing him to examine these experiences at a safe remove while still engaging with the deeper questions using philosophy, Theosophy, and ancient wisdom: the Hermetica, The Law of One, and The Vedic Texts.

John's real contribution isn't fiction; it's his unflinching analysis of how deception operates within the UFO disclosure movement itself. Coming from his unique insider perspective, he recognizes the same intelligence community tactics being deployed by both human agencies and by something else, the same compartmentalization, psychological operations, and the same limited hangouts, the same old bullshit.

What makes John's insights particularly valuable is that he's not theorizing from the outside. He's seen how power actually works at the highest levels. He understands that disclosure isn't happening through official channels as the disclosure community hopes it would. Instead, it's being carefully managed, controlled, and manipulated to serve agendas most people don't even recognize.

In our many conversations, John, Jean-Luc, and I keep reaching the same uncomfortable conclusion: almost everything in UFO disclosure is managed from above.

This doesn't mean that anything is real at all. It means we need to be far more discerning about what's presented as "truth." After all, didn't Smoking Man in the X-Files series famously say, "There is NO truth!"? I wonder about that…

John's critical eye helps cut through the noise. When Grant Cameron interviews Chris Bledsoe about classified documents suggesting DNA transmits signals into space, John asks, Where did this information come from? Who declassified it? Why is it being released now through these specific channels and people? What agenda does this narrative serve? Who ultimately benefits?

These aren't cynical questions; they're necessary ones. Because the pattern is clear, whenever the disclosure community starts asking harder questions about crash retrievals, recovered bodies, missing people, and suppressed technologies, suddenly new metaphysical information drops. Fascinating information that connects to ancient teachings, which validates consciousness research, but that also conveniently redirects attention away from the harder questions about government secrecy and technological suppression. My, my…how suspiciously convenient.

Is the information false? Maybe not entirely; it could be a partial truth embedded in a larger deception, genuine research misinterpreted, or intelligence operations testing how the community responds to spiritual narratives.

The point is one cannot know for sure, and that uncertainty, that inability to verify, to trace sources, separate truth from manipulation, that's the deception working its magic.

John's contribution isn't providing hard answers. It's modeling the kind of critical thinking required to navigate a field where deception is the norm rather than the exception, where trust must be earned through consistency and transparency, not demanded through elite credentials or insider status.

His perspective forces uncomfortable questions: Why would non-human intelligence deceive? What purpose does it serve?

Several possibilities emerge when we consider why non-human intelligence systematically deceives humanity. They might be testing us, observing how humans respond to different narratives, and measuring our belief systems, interpretative frameworks, and capacity for discernment under conditions of radical uncertainty. The deception could be protective, operating on the principle that they can't reveal themselves fully because we're genuinely not ready for the truth, making deception a form of mercy where they give us partial truths we can handle rather than full revelation that would psychologically break us in half or collapse civilization. It could be exploitation, where they're harvesting something from us like consciousness itself, emotional energy, or genetic material, and deception facilitates that harvest by keeping us compliant and unaware of what's being taken. There's the possibility of entertainment or scientific fascination, where we're interested in them, and watching humans try to understand non-human intelligence is amusing in the same way humans watch ants in a farm, with deception adding complexity to make the game more engaging. Or most disturbingly, it could be predation, where they're fundamentally hostile and deception functions as a hunting strategy designed to keep prey confused, divided, ignorant, and unable to mount an effective collective response to what's actually happening.

Which is true? Maybe all of them. Different groups with different agendas, or the same group using different approaches for different individuals.

The deception makes it impossible to know for certain, and recognizing that impossibility, that fundamental uncertainty is the first step toward genuine discernment.

Discernment is key in all aspects when dealing with The Phenomenon.

## LAYERS OF COUNTERINTELLIGENCE.

John Warner IV understands counterintelligence operations intimately and how they work, why they're necessary (from an institutional perspective), how they've been applied to the UFO topic since at least 1947, and probably far before.

The Robertson Panel in 1952: assembled physicists, scientists, and official experts. Their recommendation: study in secret, ridicule publicly, destroy the credibility of anyone investigating seriously. Seventy years later, we're still living under that paradigm. Like many others, I think the Panel was wholly corrupt, and it's more complex than simple suppression. Because suppression creates martyr dynamics. It makes people more curious and validates conspiracy thinking.

So, the new modern approach layers deception, something like this:

**Layer 1:** Denial. Nothing's happening. UFOs aren't real. Witnesses are mistaken or lying.

**Layer 2:** Limited acknowledgment. Okay, something's happening. We don't know what—probably misidentified conventional phenomena.

**Layer 3:** Partial disclosure. Fine, it's real. Some things are unexplained. We're investigating it; give us time and money.

**Layer 4:** Controlled narrative. Here's the story we want you to believe. Extraterrestrial visitors are no threat. We're managing it. Trust us, but maybe the UAPs are a military threat.

**Layer 5:** Confusion. Actually, multiple interpretations are possible. Could be ETs, interdimensional, ultraterrestrials, time travelers, or consciousness manifestations. Endless debate. No consensus.

**Layer 6:** Spiritual bypass. Focus on metaphysical implications. Love and light. We're all one. Don't worry about government secrecy, technological suppression, or the many abductions. Meditate instead. Everything is going to be hunky-dory.

Each layer serves a specific purpose, capturing a different demographic and preventing coherent resistance to actual secrecy.

The Phenomenon itself (whatever it actually is) seems to cooperate with this layering. Shows different faces to different witnesses. Provides contradictory information. Creates experiences that defy a single interpretation.

RELIGIOUS FRAMEWORK MANIPULATION.

One consistent deception pattern is that The Phenomenon uses religious frameworks to manipulate believers.

Catholics see Virgin Mary's everywhere. Protestants see angels. Hindus see the gods from their pantheon. Indigenous peoples see spirits from their traditions. New Agers see ascended masters.

Warner once told me about a friend from his high school days, a guy who ended up with a well-paying job as a dedicated Jesuit, traveling around the globe searching for signs of the Virgin Mary. At the time, Warner and the others just thought he was joking, but as it turned out, he was serious. Sadly, he's since passed away, so we will never know the extent of his mission. Warner mentioned that this friend genuinely believed in UFOs and used to say, "Angels and demons are everywhere."

Same phenomenon with different cultural packaging.

Jacques Vallée documented this extensively. Fatima "miracle" in 1917 (70,000 witnesses saw a spinning disc descend from the sky). Church calls it the Virgin Mary, and UFO researchers call it a craft. Both interpretations might be wrong. The Phenomenon might be deliberately ambiguous, triggering religious interpretation while being something else entirely.

Why? Control. Religious systems emphasize obedience, faith, and trust in authority. When The Phenomenon appears to be divine, people no longer question; they begin to accept and comply.

John Warner points out that the Vatican knows all. Their ancient archives contain centuries of contact reports. They understand The Phenomenon isn't simply "divine." However, they frame it that way for public consumption because it serves institutional control.

The same goes for other religious authorities. Islamic scholars, Russian Orthodox bishops, Jewish Kabbalah, hierarchies, Hindu priests, they all know of contact, all frame it within their traditional theological systems, use it to reinforce their authority over humanity, and The Phenomenon cooperates. It appears that each religion expects, provides "miracles" and "signs" that validate our existing beliefs. And in doing so, it keeps humanity divided by reinforcing incompatible theological frameworks. That's sophisticated deception, not just lying. It is adaptive manipulation based on the target's existing belief systems. Understanding these deception patterns is essential, but ultimately, they don't change the fundamental reality of what it means to live as someone who has experienced contact firsthand.

What should we take from this? Now that you see it, what are you going to do about it?

Warner's analysis reveals a crucial aspect of the pattern we've been examining. The technological suppression through leads isn't just about controlling hardware. It's about controlling perception, belief, and ultimately human consciousness itself. The same deception techniques that keep the public from recognizing UFO reality also keep them from recognizing that their supposed technological saviors are actually conduits for a control system that's been operating for generations, if not a millennium.

# CHAPTER 12

## REVERSE ENGINEERING THE IMPOSSIBLE

### THE 1940S CRASH WAVE AND REVERSE ENGINEERING.

Chuck Wade has evidence to support seven cases of crashed UFOs in the American Southwest between 1945 and 1948. Per Wade, the first UFO crash was at San Antonio, New Mexico, in August 1945. This craft was 25 to 30 feet long and "avocado-shaped."[322]

The second UFO crash happened the night of July 1 to 2, 1947, on the Plains of San Augustin, New Mexico, and this craft was 32 feet in diameter. The third UFO crash is being studied by MUFON investigators Chuck Zukowski and Debbie Ziegelmeyer. They are calling this site the Alternative Site, southwest of Roswell. It is theorized that this crash occurred on the night of July 4, 1947, and that the object may have been a 25-foot oval-shaped craft.[323]

The fourth UFO crash occurred at the Haut/Corso site north of Roswell the night of July 4, 1947. I contend that this crash changed the course of history, as it is now the infamous crash most of the world is familiar with. The Corona Debris Field, located 75 miles northwest of Roswell and 30 miles southeast of Corona, New Mexico, is the fifth UFO site, and we now know the craft was 100 feet in diameter and scattered truckloads of debris at the Corona Debris Field.[324]

The sixth UFO crash site is what they call the Jim Ragsdale site, located 53 miles west of Roswell in the foothills of the Capitan Mountains, with a craft 20 feet in diameter. The seventh and final site is in Hart Canyon, about 9 miles north of Aztec, New Mexico, where a 100-foot-diameter craft landed completely intact on March 25, 1948.[325]

Art Campbell and Wade conducted thorough investigations at these locations, uncovering physical evidence, including materials with unusual compositions. The samples from Saint Augustine exhibited unique isotopic characteristics, confirmed by independent laboratory analyses. In fact, over 15 labs across the United States participated in research spanning more than 10 years. All results have been recorded and released in the book "Finding the UFO Crash at San Augustin: Isotopic Metal Analysis Not of This World."[326]

## PHILIP CORSO AND REVERSE ENGINEERING CLAIMS.

Philip J. Corso was possibly the most famous figure associated with these allegations. In his book The Day After Roswell[327], a retired U.S. Army lieutenant colonel claimed to have been involved in the alleged reverse engineering of technologies recovered from a UFO crash near Roswell, New Mexico, in 1947. Corso alleges he was responsible for seeding various alien technologies, such as night vision, lasers, and fiber optics, to private contractors for reverse-engineering and development.

The book was edited by his co-author, William J. Birnes, and much of his information was removed. Corso is listed as the primary author, but some researchers have questioned the extent of his direct involvement in the writing and editing, given his age and health at the time of publication.

A manuscript or first draft titled "Dawn of a New Age"[328] is the unpublished manuscript written by Corso and is presented as the original, unedited notes and account of his alleged involvement with the study and reverse-engineering of extraterrestrial technology recovered from the famous 1947 Roswell UFO incident.

Dawn of a New Age contains Corso's handwritten notes and accounts, unedited and unchanged from his published book. Corso's son, Philip Corso Jr., claims his father was highly dissatisfied with how The Day After Roswell turned out and felt it did not accurately represent his experiences.

In Dawn of a New Age, Corso provides several names for alleged top-secret U.S. government programs related to the retrieval, study, and reverse-engineering of extraterrestrial technology from UFO crashes and incidents. These names did not make it into The Day After Roswell, and none of these claims have been backed up with FOIA documents or corroborating witness reports. Still, I find it important to highlight some of the more important and interesting items and their codenames in case future evidence reveals them to be valid.

**Project Rainbow:** According to Corso, Project Rainbow was a highly classified program tasked with collecting and analyzing all materials, debris, and technology recovered from UFO crash sites, particularly the alleged incident in Roswell, New Mexico, in 1947. Corso claims that Rainbow was headquartered at Fort Riley, Kansas, and operated under the oversight of the U.S. Army's Research and Development division.

Paul Mellon was a cavalry officer at Fort Riley in 1940-41, just saying.

**Cylinder Seal:** Corso refers to Cylinder Seal as a sub-program or offshoot of Project Rainbow, specifically focused on investigating and understanding the propulsion systems and energy sources used by the alleged extraterrestrial spacecraft. He claims that the Cylinder Seal was based at Sandia National Laboratories in New Mexico.

**Project Redlight:** Described as a compartmentalized program responsible for studying and analyzing alleged alien biological entities and their physiology. Corso claims that Redlight was primarily focused on understanding the genetic makeup and biological processes of any recovered extraterrestrial beings.

**Majic Omega:** While not providing extensive details, Corso references Majic Omega as a high-level oversight and control group tasked with managing and coordinating all government programs and operations related to the UFO phenomenon and recovered alien technology.

It's important to note that Corso's claims, including the existence and details of these alleged programs, remain highly controversial and unsubstantiated by credible evidence. After years of FOIA requests and researchers spending countless hours, these program names have yet to be corroborated.

However, I often ask myself, why would a man with as distinguished a verifiable career and record as Corso make such bold claims at the end of his life? What did he have to gain by the negative attention that his public release of decades-old, classified information brought, and did that ultimately lead to his demise?

## OTHER WHISTLEBLOWERS AND INSIDERS.

Corso is not alone in his whistleblowing about back-engineering UFOs. There have been testimonials from Boyd Bushman (2014), Thomas Castello (2020), and Bob Lazar (1989), all of whom attest to having studied recovered extraterrestrial craft and their remains at secure military R&D sites.

Ben Rich of Lockheed Skunk Works alluded to deep, classified projects advancing space technology and propulsion breakthroughs for decades in remarks at UCLA in 1993. Insiders allege Skunk Works developed Mach 5 or more stealth reconnaissance aircraft under projects like Aurora by the late 1980s, while civilian planes flew far slower.

Bob Lazar went public in 1989 with his story about reverse-engineering alien spacecraft at Area 51. Lazar recently released an autobiography, in which he explained that during his time at Area 51, his phone was tapped. This was all part of the contract he signed. They did this to ensure that none of the employees were covertly supplying secrets to foreign governments and the like.

Apparently, by tapping Bob's phone, they found out that his wife was cheating on him, so they decided not to tell Bob this but told him that he was going to be off the program for a little while without any explanation. Immediately, Bob thought they were going to kill him or harm him because of the abruptness of his being put off the project. Making an effort to save his life, he went to the local Las Vegas news station, KLAS, and started talking to the now-famous reporter George Knapp.[329] They blasted his news story all over the United States, and it went international. Thus, Bob Lazar is now infamous for leaking Area 51, which nobody knew about at the time, and was only admitted during the Obama administration, and for the reverse-engineering of UFOs not of this world.

Could all these advanced technologies be derivatives of UFO crash retrievals? Have all the leaps in technology and advancements in the past 75 years come from reverse-engineering of craft not of this Earth? I think all the evidence points in that direction. If not, it's one hell of a story that the U.S. intelligence agencies have cooked up to create disinformation and cover for advanced aerospace research, technology, and developments that seem so far from current advancements that they appear to be from out of this world.

Where We Are Now

The 30-year rule we've established suggests that technologies publicly acknowledged between 2023 and 2025 were operational in classified programs by the 1990s at the latest. What runs in black-budget programs right now won't be publicly known until the 2050s, unless disclosure accelerates dramatically beyond the current pace.

The acceleration is currently happening daily at a much faster rate. New UFO videos are being released constantly, and the Pentagon is officially admitting UAPs are a real phenomenon.[330] Whistleblowers are coming forward despite threats and ridicule. The disclosure movement is gaining serious momentum in Congress, online, and in legacy media.

Here's what's absolutely bizarre about all this disclosure happening in real time: almost nobody seems to give a shit, seriously.

A December 2025 Psychology Today article titled "Why Is No One Talking About the Aliens?" nailed this paradox perfectly. Dr. Jennice Vilhauer, Director of Emory University's Adult Outpatient Psychotherapy Program, wrote: "Something very significant has been happening in plain sight, and almost no one seems to be noticing."[331]

Think about that for a second. We've had televised congressional hearings. Multiple major network news segments. A documentary called "The Age of Disclosure" features on-the-record testimony from dozens of current and former high-level U.S. government, military, and intelligence officials. These aren't random conspiracy theorists on YouTube or the Ancient Aliens, but people with impeccable credentials describing "large numbers of sightings of unexplained aircraft, recovered crash materials they say are not consistent with known human technology, and the remains of non-human biologics."

All of these points point to the same conclusion. That mankind is not alone in the universe.

Vilhauer asks the obvious question: "If this were any other topic with implications this big, it would dominate conversations. It would be debated at dinner tables and dissected and argued endlessly by pundits and influencers online. Instead, people seem to be oddly quiet about it altogether."

She's absolutely right. If we discovered a new continent, if aliens sent us a radio signal, if scientists proved parallel universes exist, it would be THE story consuming every news cycle, every social media feed, every conversation at work and home. But actual evidence of non-human intelligence in the form of physical craft and biological remains? Crickets.

The collective silence is almost more interesting than the revelations themselves. From a psychological standpoint, the lack of reaction reveals something profound about how humans process information that threatens our fundamental worldview.

## WHY WE CAN'T HANDLE THE TRUTH

Vilhauer breaks down <u>exactly</u> why disclosure isn't landing the way it should, and it's not because people are stupid or uninformed. It's because of how our brains protect us from existential disruption.

**<u>Cognitive Dissonance:</u>** When new information conflicts with deeply held beliefs about humanity's uniqueness, the limits of technology, or the transparency of institutions, it doesn't just challenge facts; it also challenges the very beliefs themselves. It destabilizes the entire mental framework that helps people feel oriented and safe. The mind resolves this uncomfortable tension not by updating old beliefs but by disengaging from the information altogether. Ignoring the topic can serve as a way to regulate emotions and maintain psychological stability.

**<u>Cognitive Overload:</u>** We're already living in a constant state of mental saturation with political conflict, climate anxiety, rapid technological change, and worries over the cost of living.

Our brains are working overtime processing threats and novel circumstances. When new, emotionally charged information feels abstract and lacks clear instructions for action, it gets deprioritized. The brain is biased toward what feels immediately relevant and solvable. Existential questions without obvious personal consequences are easy to postpone indefinitely.

**Social Stigma:** For decades, curiosity about UFOs or non-human intelligence was culturally dismissed as unserious or fringe. Even as the conversation has shifted into formal government settings, those associations still linger powerfully. Many people may feel curious privately but simultaneously think, "I don't want to sound foolish, gullible, or extreme." This is normative social influence, the tendency to align beliefs and behaviors with what feels socially acceptable. Until the idea of non-human intelligence becomes more widely discussed without ridicule, silence is a way to protect one's reputation and social belonging, regardless of what people believe privately.

**Intolerance of Ambiguity:** The information being disclosed doesn't come with neat conclusions or clear next steps. It raises profound questions without resolving them. For many people, ambiguity is deeply uncomfortable. The mind prefers coherent narratives, even flawed ones, over unresolved complexity. When answers are incomplete, people often default to avoidance rather than sustained engagement. It's not just what is being suggested that's hard to face; it's the lack of closure about what to do with it.

**Existential Self-Protection:** If humanity is not alone, it challenges long-held assumptions about our meaning, what control and power we have, and our identity as the dominant species. These questions touch religion, mortality, and humanity's place in the universe. For many people, that level of existential disruption is too much to integrate all at once. Avoidance becomes a form of self-protection against psychological overwhelm.

Vilhauer's conclusion is a very sound rationalization that I find might be helpful to us all.

---

**"What looks like indifference may actually reflect a complex psychological response. History suggests that paradigm-shifting ideas are rarely absorbed in real time. They are resisted, minimized, and slowly normalized only after the psyche has had time to adapt."**

---

In other words, we often resist new ideas not because we don't understand them, but because accepting them requires fundamentally changing who we think we are and what we believe about reality. That's terrifying work that most people aren't ready to do.

## WHY NOW?

So, given all these psychological barriers to accepting disclosure, why is it happening now after 75 years of denial? I believe there are several real possibilities worth considering. This could be forced disclosure, where The Phenomenon becomes undeniable through increasing sightings and encounters, forcing governments to acknowledge what they can no longer suppress. Or it could be controlled narrative management by intelligence agencies managing inevitable revelation, maintaining control over the story while appearing to disclose.

Maybe it's a geopolitical shift in which multiple nations are independently developing similar capabilities, rendering secrecy pointless when Russia, China, and others have their own programs. Also consider the possibility of a technological singularity approaching, with AI advancing so rapidly that human control becomes impossible, forcing transparency before systems become completely unmanageable. There might even be a cosmic timetable in which whatever intelligence is behind The Phenomenon has a schedule we're not privy to, and now is simply the appointed time for humanity to know the truth.

Probably it's a combination of multiple factors converging simultaneously, making suppression completely unsustainable. Forcing transition from total secrecy to gradual managed transparency, but even in this disclosure process, expect the 30-year rule to continue holding. What is being acknowledged now is decades-old technology. What's actually operational now in classified programs won't be known for decades more. The most advanced capabilities may never be publicly known under any circumstances.

Unless something fundamentally breaks the pattern, whistleblowers might risk absolutely everything, including their lives. The Phenomenon could force full disclosure through undeniable mass sightings. Humanity might collectively demand transparency and refuse to accept partial truths and managed narratives. Maybe the U.S. Government and the MIC will put on a public military expo displaying antigravity craft and new physics weapons openly. An ET press conference broadcast worldwide?

Understanding the 30-year rule means understanding the massive gap between actual human capability and acknowledged human knowledge. Between what we can already do and what we're told is currently possible, and the future we could have right now, and the past we're deliberately kept in.

Closing that gap requires real disclosure. Actual disclosure. Not managed revelation drip-fed over decades, but full transparency about technologies held in classified programs, reverse-engineering programs that have been operational since the 1940s, deals potentially made with non-human intelligence, and capabilities we have but aren't using publicly because releasing them threatens existing power structures and economic systems.

Real disclosure means not only acknowledging UFOs, but also revealing what decades of research have uncovered, what has been developed from it, current capabilities, and the reasons for secrecy. The 30-year rule ends when we collectively demand it ends, and we refuse to wait for another generation to pass—demanding the truth, capabilities, and worldwide transformation now.

Not 30 years from now. Right here, Right Now.

# CHAPTER 13

## THE DNA HARVEST

*What you are has been hidden, and those secrets are to die for.*

---

**"THERE IS A SLIGHT DANGER THAT IF WE WERE SUCCESSFUL, IT WOULD DISAPPEAR. SUCKED UP INTO SOME PROGRAM SOMEWHERE, AND SUPER SOLDIERS WOULD BE MADE. SO, IF SOMEDAY I DISAPPEAR AND ALL THIS RESEARCH DISAPPEARS, AT LEAST SOMEBODY ELSE WILL KNOW WHAT WENT ON."[332] —DR. DEAN RADIN**

---

I never intended to write a chapter about DNA. A few years ago, the idea would have seemed far outside my lane, and now I suspect that The Phenomenon itself decided for me. Keep with me, it will make sense very soon. I had to do some extensive research, and what I found is surprising. From the earliest modern abduction accounts, Betty and Barney Hill in 1961[333], Travis Walton in 1975[334], Whitley Strieber in the 1980s[335], genetic harvesting appears again and again: sperm and egg extractions, tissue sampling, fetal implantation, and removal. Whether one accepts these reports literally or not, the pattern is unmistakable. Something, or someone, appears obsessed with human reproductive biology.

When I began connecting those dots publicly on what was then #UFOtwitter, the reaction was immediate and ferocious. Overnight, I found myself in a digital war zone of believers, skeptics, researchers, influencers, intelligence operatives, foreign actors, elected officials, and outright trolls. Some became my closest allies. Others made it clear they would prefer I disappear, but before we get to that story, we need to understand what makes this topic so explosive. We need to start with the molecule itself.

THE BLUEPRINT OF LIFE

Deoxyribonucleic acid—DNA—and its single-stranded messenger, ribonucleic acid (RNA), form the instruction set for nearly all life on Earth. DNA resides in the nucleus of every cell as a double helix composed of four bases: adenine, thymine, guanine, and cytosine. Only about 2 percent of the human genome codes for proteins; the remaining 98 percent, once dismissed as "junk," is now known to regulate gene expression, orchestrate chromatin architecture, and perform functions we are only beginning to comprehend. Environmental signals, electromagnetic fields, and even focused intention can switch these non-coding regions on or off through epigenetic mechanisms.

Retroviruses add another layer of intrigue. These pathogens reverse-transcribe their RNA into DNA and insert it into the host genome, where they can remain dormant for decades before reactivating. HIV is the most infamous example, but the principle has fueled speculation about "UFO-retroviruses" ever since a 1991 letter from Gene Huff to Stanton Friedman hinted at something far more sinister than a simple infection. Declassified Majestic-12 documents speak of "new strains of a retrovirus not totally understood" recovered from crash sites in New Mexico and positioned as potential bioweapons.[336]

Cutting-edge tools now allow direct manipulation of epigenetic states; bioelectronic implants deliver precise electrical pulses; optogenetics uses light; and magnetogenetics exploits magnetic fields. Transcranial magnetic stimulation already treats depression by altering brain activity; the military's Total Exposure Health initiative maps how stressors flip microRNA switches in soldiers.

As Colonel Kirk Phillips, U.S. Air Force bioenvironmental engineering chief, put it in 2017, "You can be programmed, and you can be un-programmed."[337]

This is the terrain where consciousness meets genetics, where the physical blueprint intersects with something far stranger. It's here that a small group of elite researchers began quietly collecting samples from people who report experiences that shouldn't be possible.

## ECHOES IN THE HELIX

Luis Elizondo, a University of Miami graduate with a degree in microbiology and immunology, wasn't just the alleged former director of AATIP. He was a scientist who'd studied life at its smallest scales. On The Joe Rogan Experience in October 2019, Elizondo explored an idea that stopped me cold: UAPs might represent a form of intelligence that transcends conventional technology, possibly linked to biological or consciousness-based systems.

"If you're dealing with a civilization that's millions of years ahead of us," he said, "they're not going to leave behind stone tablets or metal ships. They might be using biology itself as a technology, something that can adapt and evolve."[338]

If an intelligence wanted proof of itself to endure a hundred thousand years, what would it use? Not ruins, those erode. Maybe something alive, he suggested, something stitched into biology itself. It was the kind of hypothesis his training could back up, spotting anomalies in cells or DNA that scream "not from here."

That's when To The Stars Academy started haunting my thoughts. Elizondo wasn't the only person with a biological background working with TTSA. In fact, there were many more.

So, I started digging.

## THE COLLECTORS AND THE BIOLOGICAL NETWORK

Against this backdrop, a pattern emerged that couldn't be ignored.

The names recur: Dr. Garry Nolan (Stanford)[339], Dr. Christopher "Kit" Green (formerly CIA, Wayne State University)[340], Dr. Colm Kelleher (Bigelow Aerospace Advanced Space Studies)[341], and others. Funding traces back repeatedly to billionaire Robert Bigelow.[342]

The researchers' backgrounds only deepen the questions. Nolan's Stanford lab pioneered rapid retroviral production systems. Green, a forensic neuroradiologist and polyglot, spent decades at the CIA studying anomalous cognition and directed-energy effects. Kelleher, a biochemist, managed Bigelow's Skinwalker Ranch investigations[343] and holds patents on antiviral compounds. All three have held security clearances and defense contracts.

What makes this network especially important is that the government is already aware that these encounters result in tangible physical harm.

In April 2022, *The Sun* obtained over 1,500 pages of documents from the Defense Intelligence Agency through a Freedom of Information Act request. Among them was a report titled "Anomalous Acute and Subacute Field Effects on Human and Biological Tissues," dated March 11, 2010, prepared for the DIA as part of the Advanced Aerospace Weapon System Applications Program. The report investigated injuries to "human observers by anomalous advanced aerospace systems" and concluded that such objects "may be a threat to United States interests."[344]

The findings were shocking. Humans had been injured from "exposures to anomalous vehicles, especially airborne, and when in proximity." The injuries were often related to electromagnetic radiation and linked to "energy-related propulsion systems." The documented effects included radiation burns, brain damage, nerve damage, heart palpitations, and headaches. The report noted forty-two cases from medical files and three hundred similar "unpublished" cases where humans sustained injuries after encounters with anomalous craft.[345] The report's conclusion is basically "disclosure."

---

**"Sufficient incidents/accidents have been accurately reported, and medical data acquired, as to support a hypothesis that some advanced systems are already deployed, and opaque to full US understandings."[346]**

---

The report didn't stop at documenting injuries. It argued this medical data could be used to "reverse engineer" propulsion systems from unknown provenance." In other words, they were studying wounded experiencers not just to treat them, but to understand the technology that harmed them and figure out a way to create that same technology ourselves.

The report also featured what it called a "useful database" of biological effects compiled by the Mutual UFO Network, listing impacts from 1873 to 1994. These included apparent abduction, paralysis, eye injuries, electrical shocks, and even "unaccounted for pregnancy." The report included "fly-by ratings" and "close encounter ratings," with CE4 designating encounters resulting in **permanent psychological injuries or death.**[347]

Buried in the document was this admission.

---

**"Classified information exists that is highly pertinent to the subject of this study, and only a small part of the classified literature has been released."**[348]

---

Green's work was central to this program. In 2010, he was commissioned by AAWSAP, the secret $22 million defense initiative for which Bigelow won the contract, to write a classified paper on injuries sustained by military personnel following encounters with anomalous craft. His paper, "Clinical Medical Acute & Subacute Field Effects on Human Dermal & Neurological Tissues," was one of thirty-eight Defense Intelligence Reference Documents produced by the program. Green described himself as "the go-to physician in the Department of Defense for unexplained morbidity and mortality."[349]

His patient population read like a roster of America's most security-cleared individuals. It includes Special Forces operatives, intelligence community members, aerospace industry employees, military officers, and base security personnel. These weren't fringe experiencers making claims on internet forums but professionals with careers and clearances who reported injuries they couldn't explain and that their doctors couldn't diagnose.

Injuries usually happened during night military missions at secure sites for reconnaissance or guard duty, often involving airborne objects that emitted light, beams, or orbs. Green took on patients only after they'd accumulated thick physician case files and their doctors had exhausted conventional explanations. His assessment was clinical, "My patients were physically injured by something. They have signs on their body."[350]

Green also reported that one in ten of his patients died within seven years of their first UFO encounter.[351] The Phenomenon is not all love and light; it appears. Those are not good odds, so if you see a craft on the ground, keep your distance. I have been personally told, and others have said this publicly as well, that blue-colored orbs are responsible for the injuries in the majority of cases. If you see a blue orb, think twice before getting anywhere near it. I would run away.

Luis Elizondo, the former alleged AATIP director who went public in 2017, offered context when asked about these injuries. He compared the effects to getting too close to an aircraft engine. "If I'm in the cockpit or in the aircraft, there's no real threat," Elizondo explained. "But if I stand behind the engine when the engine is firing up, chances are I'm going to get burned, I'm going to lose my hearing. There are medical consequences." The question he asked was whether the harm was deliberate or simply a byproduct of the technology. "We think right now, preliminarily speaking, it's probably just a consequence of the advanced technology."[352]

Elizondo was explicit that these weren't random civilian sightings. "These are military eyewitnesses, in some cases, fighter pilots or security personnel who have come up close and personal with a UFO."[353]

The case of John Burroughs crystallizes the pattern. In 2015, the Department of Veterans Affairs granted disability compensation to the USAF veteran for injuries sustained during the 1980 Rendlesham Forest incident in England. This wasn't some vague acknowledgment. Some say it was a stunning moment of government admission, buried beneath layers of classification. Green himself confirmed publicly that Burroughs's medical records were among only a handful in his entire intelligence career that were formally classified. Why? Because embedded within those records were connections to special access programs, sensitive technologies, and electromagnetic field studies so compartmented that even Green, who is a lifelong intelligence insider, was initially denied access.[354]

During Burroughs's surgery, a military doctor reportedly called the hospital with exact instructions on how to repair his heart injury, suggesting the military has documented protocols for UAP-related electromagnetic effects. Green concluded that Burroughs's injuries were caused by broadband non ionizing electromagnetic radiation, the kind associated with classified directed-energy technologies and the more exotic components of UAP encounters documented by AATIP and AAWSAP.[355]

So, the government knows these encounters cause physical harm. They've documented it, studied it, and even paid disability compensation for it. Yet disclosure remains controlled, research remains classified, and experiencers remain in the dark about what's being done with their medical data and DNA.

The intelligence community, or its contracted representatives, is collecting DNA from experiencers. Not hypothetically or in theory. Actually, physically, right now, nobody's telling experiencers what they're doing with it.

## THE TO THE STARS ACADEMY OF ARTS AND SCIENCES NETWORK

To understand how this DNA collection effort connects to broader disclosure initiatives, we need to examine To The Stars Academy of Arts and Sciences (TTSA). Founded by Tom DeLonge in 2017, TTSA assembled a group of individuals with diverse and impressive backgrounds who would never interact under normal circumstances. DeLonge, who quit his hugely successful band (Blink 182) and dedicated his life to UFO disclosure, brought together a team that reads like a who's who of the intelligence, defense, and aerospace communities[356].

Looking at the TTSA board of advisors, a pattern emerges. One that is more closely tied to a biological control system happening right under our noses than little grey men visiting us from distant planets.

The TTSA founding board members and key personnel include:

**<u>Tom DeLonge:</u>** Founder, musician, and self-described catalyst for modern UFO disclosure. DeLonge is a Freemason, raised to the sublime degree of Master Mason at Widow's Son Lodge No. 17, Prince Hall Affiliation, Kansas City. He has openly used Masonic symbols in his Angels & Airwaves artwork and admitted his Masonic affiliation on Coast to Coast AM with George Knapp in the early 2000s. I also personally confirmed that this is indeed true. Did DeLonge leverage his celebrity status and Masonic connections to gain unprecedented access to high-ranking military and intelligence officials? I think that the answer is a resounding yes.

**<u>Luis Elizondo:</u>** Alleged Former Director of the Advanced Aerospace Threat Identification Program (AATIP), a career intelligence officer with roles across U.S. defense and intelligence agencies. Here's what most people miss: Elizondo is a University of Miami graduate with a degree in microbiology and immunology. He wasn't just running a UFO program; he was a scientist who'd studied life at its smallest scales. Elizondo led Pentagon investigations into Unidentified Aerial Threats and became the public face of the modern disclosure movement. While some have questioned the official documentation of his role in AATIP, colleagues who worked with him have publicly supported his claims. Elizondo left TTSA but continues advocacy work for UAP transparency. Personally, I believe that he is playing the role of disclosure advocate, and his background in counter-intel and counterinsurgency was an inroad. A direct quote from Lue,

---

**"I'm not a UFO guy, I'm not a ufologist, never have been, never will be, I'm a counter espionage and counter terrorism guy, that's what I do, counterintelligence, counter insurgencies, and it just so happens that in 2008 I was asked to apply those same skill sets into the UFO community."**[357]

---

**<u>Christopher Mellon</u>**[358]: Former Deputy Assistant Secretary of Defense for Intelligence under two presidential administrations and former Staff Director of the Senate Intelligence Committee. Mellon is part of the Mellon banking dynasty[359], one of America's wealthiest families. The Mellons built their fortune through banking (founding T. Mellon & Sons Bank in 1869, which became BNY Mellon), oil (Gulf Oil), aluminum (Alcoa), steel, and coal. Andrew Mellon served as U.S. Treasury Secretary from 1921 to 1932 and founded the National Gallery of Art. Christopher Mellon has publicly admitted to helping release the three famous UAP videos—FLIR, GIMBAL, and GOFAST—that The New York Times published in December 2017, kickstarting the current, 2017-present USGOV disclosure movement. Many consider Mellon the driving force behind recent UAP legislation and transparency efforts, but who is behind him up the National Security State food chain? He left TTSA but remains actively involved in UAP advocacy, writing op-eds, and working behind the scenes in Washington. He is also John W. Warner IV's third cousin, and they are at bitter loggerheads over disclosure narratives. Mellon worked with Senator John Warner on the Select Intelligence Committee, and "possibly the classified Majic (MJ-12) Committee," said John IV to me.

**Steve Justice**[360]: Former Director of Advanced Systems Development at Lockheed Martin's Skunk Works, where he spent 31 years leading classified aerospace programs. Lockheed Martin has long been rumored to possess crashed UFOs and to have been actively reverse-engineering them since the 1940s. Justice directed TTSA's Aerospace Division, which aimed to develop revolutionary propulsion technologies. He left TTSA in 2020 and joined Virgin Galactic as Senior Vice President. Justice has since removed all mention of TTSA from his LinkedIn profile.

**Dr. Harold "Hal" Puthoff:** [361]Co-founder and Vice President of Science and Technology. Puthoff is an experimental physicist who has advised the U.S. government for decades. His work includes: NSA service in the early 1960s focusing on advanced computing and optics; directing the CIA/DIA-funded remote viewing research at SRI (Stanford Research Institute) from 1972 to 1985 as part of the Stargate Project; advising the Department of Defense on UAP investigations through AATIP from 2007 to 2012; and ongoing consulting roles with NASA, DoD, and intelligence agencies on cutting-edge technology and "psi (psionic) research." Puthoff's long history in classified programs and anomalous cognition research makes him a central figure in the intersection of consciousness studies and UFO phenomena.

**Jim Semivan:**[362] Co-founder and Vice President of Operations. Semivan is a retired CIA Senior Intelligence Service member and current U.S. government national security consultant. His decades-long CIA career and continued security clearances position him as a bridge between the classified world and public disclosure efforts. Semivan has also publicly discussed his own high-strangeness experiences, including apparent abduction phenomena involving himself and his wife.

**<u>Dr. Garry Nolan, a Stanford immunologist and geneticist, was</u>** enlisted by TTSA as a scientific expert. Nolan earned his B.S. from Cornell and his Ph.D. in genetics from Stanford. He is the Rachford and Carlota A. Harris Professor in the Department of Microbiology and Immunology at Stanford University School of Medicine. He co-developed the 293T-based rapid retroviral production system and the cloning of the NF-$\varkappa$B p65/RelA DNA regulatory factor. DNA and immunology. Needless to say, Nolan is very proficient and interested in DNA, and by the way, he doesn't like me very much!

His involvement with TTSA is notable, particularly in the context of the organization's early work on UAP research and the analysis of the Atacama skeleton, which he detailed in a 2018 statement on the TTS website. This statement highlighted his excitement about joining the team to study phenomena ignored by mainstream science, suggesting a significant role at that time. Nolan's 2018 analysis of the six-inch Atacama skeleton revealed a human fetus with severe genetic mutations, discrediting earlier claims of extraterrestrial origin,[363] and the controversy surrounding this work raises deeper questions.

**<u>Dr. Steven Greer</u>**[364], a prominent ufologist and founder of the Disclosure Project and Center for the Study of Extraterrestrial Intelligence (CSETI), has made controversial claims about the Atacama skeleton and the scientific analysis conducted by Nolan.

Greer's documentary "Unacknowledged" is well worth a watch.

The Atacama skeleton is a six-inch mummified humanoid discovered in Chile's Atacama Desert in 2003 and was featured in Greer's 2013 documentary Sirius, where he initially speculated it might be extraterrestrial. Nolan, as a Stanford immunologist, analyzed its DNA and concluded it was a human fetus with rare genetic mutations, a finding published in Genome Research in 2018.

Greer's subsequent criticisms suggest misconduct, including allegations of financial influence from the Department of Defense. In a letter dated May 14, 2018, addressed to various academic and institutional figures, including Stanford's Ann M. Arvin, Greer wrote:

"It has also come to my attention that Nolan received a $3.2 million Department of Defense Teal Award approximately one month after I provided the DNA samples to him in October 2012."

This statement appears on the Sirius Disclosure website under the section "Steven M. Greer, MD – Letter to Stanford University," published on May 25, 2018. Greer identifies a link between the timing of the DoD/CIA award and the DNA samples, suggesting that Nolan may have been financially incentivized to falsify the results. He further states, "The lack of controls, the methods used, and so forth were so 'blatantly incompetent' that their only conclusion is that the study was corrupted from the beginning to obtain a pre-determined conclusion."[365]

Despite Steven Greer's allegations of the $3.2 million DoD/CIA bribe to alter the Atacama skeleton's DNA results, Nolan has not publicly responded, instead letting his peer-reviewed 2018 Genome Research study speak. In that study, he noted, "This was an unusual specimen with some fairly extraordinary claims… it would be an example of how to use modern science to answer the question 'what is it?'"

Nolan has been very public about his rationale for wanting to be part of the insider knowledge surrounding The Phenomenon. In an interview with Stanford Magazine in 2023, Nolan frames his Atacama work as a curiosity-driven project that serendipitously connected him to UAP research, not a government-orchestrated cover-up. He noted, "When I agreed to be in the movie, I was like, 'OK, this is going to bring me to the attention of people who might really know what's going on, and maybe people will contact me"[366]

Seems like he got what he wanted; he is now one of the main vectors for disclosure via the U.S. military-industrial complex. Nolan has continued to appear in public discussions about UAPs, often alongside figures like Luis Elizondo and others formerly associated with TTS, including interviews on Tucker Carlson Tonight in August 2022 and at the SALT iConnections conference in May 2023.[367] These, along with countless podcasts, put Nolan right in the middle of the DoD/MIC planned controlled (false?) "disclosure."

However, records indicate that Nolan resigned from his official position with TTS on August 31, 2018. This departure is documented on the Exopaedia website, which notes that he was initially listed as a consultant but stepped away from that role. Along with Elizondo, Nolan has left the TTSA.[368] The dissociation has me wondering whether they left only because the rumor was that the money they were promised ran out, or whether their DoD/CIA handlers wanted them to distance themselves from DeLonge? Regardless, TTSA, now TTS, having dropped "Arts and Science" from the name, is fitting, I would say.

**Norman Kahn:** Member of TTSA's advisory board and a Johns Hopkins biology Ph.D. who'd tracked bio-weapons for the CIA. Kahn is a Senior Fellow at the Council on Strategic Risks[369], where he supports CSR's work on biological threats, and currently serves as Principal and President of Counter-Bio LLC, providing consulting services on national security issues, with particular emphasis on weapons of mass destruction and biological weapons.

His career at the Central Intelligence Agency spanned over thirty-one years, including multiple assignments in the Directorate of Intelligence (currently the Directorate of Analysis) and the Directorate of Science and Technology. In his last assignment, he created and directed the Intelligence Community's Counter-Biological Weapons Program, shifting the IC's resource allocation against the biological weapons threat and greatly expanding the scope of bioweapons collection and analysis across the IC and the broader U.S. government.

Dr. Kahn holds a bachelor's degree in biology from the City College of New York and a Ph.D. in Oceanography from the University of Rhode Island. Oceanography? Can't figure that one out, but maybe the movie The Abyss is based on something that really happened?

This is his LinkedIn profile: "Ground-breaking former Central Intelligence Agency Senior Executive with extensive program management and budget experience. Created, developed, and directed the Intelligence Community's premier biological weapons intelligence activity. Acknowledged strategic thinker and subject matter expert, sought after Government-wide for guidance on biological weapons issues. Reputation for cross-Community collaboration, risk-taking, innovation, and results. Top Secret/SCI clearance with current BI and Full Scope Polygraph."[370]

Seems like old Norm has his finger on the pulse of bioweapons.

**<u>Dr. Colm Kelleher:</u>** Another former advisory board member of To the Stars Academy. Kelleher is a biochemist with a Ph.D. in cell and molecular biology from Trinity College Dublin, whose expertise in biochemistry provides a significant link across his diverse research endeavors.[371]

He has a history of collaborating with Hal Puthoff and Robert Bigelow at the National Institute for Discovery Science (NIDS)[372], a privately funded organization founded by Bigelow to investigate fringe science and paranormal topics, including ufology, which later transitioned into Bigelow Aerospace Advanced Space Studies (BAASS) to continue this work, which was significantly centered around investigations at Skinwalker Ranch in Utah.

Kelleher also served as a program manager for the Advanced Aerospace Weapon System Applications Program (AAWSAP)[373], a government-funded UAP study, which Lue Elizondo says he was also part of. Colm authored the book Brain Trust: The Hidden Connection Between Mad Cow and Misdiagnosed Alzheimer's Disease (2004), which explores the public health risks posed by prion diseases and links them to cattle mutilations.[374] Interestingly, he also held the 2008 patent EP2137172A1, which focuses on phenothiazine derivatives for antiviral treatments. This patent was withdrawn in 2009 with no further explanation.[375]

His tenure with TTSA ended with his resignation from the advisory board in October 2019, as noted in SEC filings. Another advisor exists with more questions than answers.

In his book Brain Trust, Kelleher hypothesizes that cattle mutilations might be linked to a covert sampling program to monitor prion spread in livestock. He writes:

"Are the cattle mutilations discovered in the last 30 years part of a covert, illegal sampling program designed to learn how far the deadly prions have spread throughout the nation's livestock and beef products?"

In a 2006 interview with The Daily Grail, he noted: "Pattern A from multiple lines of evidence produced our hypothesis that it was a sampling operation. By the way, the sampling operation could just as easily be focused on other infectious entities apart from prions, for example, foot and mouth disease virus or any other agent that might create panic in the cattle industry if it became widely known."[376]

This suggests that mutilations might involve monitoring biological threats, potentially including extraterrestrial biological entities (as per David Grusch's 2023 testimony). The phenothiazine derivatives described in Kelleher's patent, with their antiviral and possible anti-prion effects, could, in theory, be applied to studying such biologics if UAPs involve non-human entities. I want to say that all of this is speculative on my part, and, aside from what I presented here, there is no evidence of any known UAP-related biological samples. This all seems to me like there may be a covert biological war taking place on Earth between humans and non-human intelligence, and it is directly associated with biologics.

I really like LinkedIn for hearing it from the horses' mouths, and this is right from Colm, "Experienced program manager in biotechnology and aerospace with successful management of DoD contracts, commercial biotech programs, aerospace ECLSS programs on tight deadlines and under budget." While Colm was at Prosetta Biosciences before working for Bigelow, he was "managing Department of Defense Contract (USAMRIID) antiviral drug discovery" and "Led teams in developing small molecule hits through iterative structure activity relationships (SAR) and live virus testing in cells and animals through collaborations with government biodefense labs (USAMRIID)." He also "managed outsourced medicinal chemistry projects in the United States and in other countries."

Colm is a very interesting connection here to biologics. He has also been a high-level, long-term employee of Robert Bigelow.

**Adele Gilpin:** Bucknell biology B.A., Johns Hopkins epidemiology Ph.D., plus a law degree. She'd led NIH trials and worked on DoD trauma research since 2007. If UAPs left biological traces, like health quirks in witnesses, her stats could prove it wasn't chance. She founded GilpinPhillips BIOMED, offering services in medical device, pharmaceutical, and biologic regulations; scientific misconduct and IRB issues; and clinical research design. Adele Gilpin's professional footprint extends beyond regulatory oversight into the realm of applied neuroscience through GilpinPhillips BIOMED, LLC's involvement in advanced clinical research. One notable study listed on ClinicalTrials.gov[377] investigates non-invasive neuromodulation techniques for optimizing brain performance, a concept that resonates with the emerging convergence of consciousness, genetics, and technology. The parent company, Wave Neuro[378], positions itself at the cutting edge of personalized brain health, leveraging EEG-based mapping and transcranial magnetic stimulation[379] to "reset" neural oscillations. While marketed as wellness and cognitive enhancement, these methods echo into classified research trajectories in bioelectronic control systems[380] and neuroplasticity manipulation, areas historically linked to defense initiatives. Gilpin's dual expertise in epidemiology and law provides a discreet framework for legitimizing such interventions under the banner of clinical science. If disclosure involves technologies that blur the line between biology and consciousness, then partnerships like these may represent the infrastructure for integrating those breakthroughs into mainstream medicine quietly, methodically, and without triggering public alarm.

The word "biologics" is very notable here, and I think it is a key to understanding UFOs.

The FDA defines biologics as, "Biological products include a wide range of products such as vaccines, blood and blood components, allergenics, somatic cells, gene therapy, tissues, and recombinant therapeutic proteins."[381]

David Grusch, a former Air Force intelligence officer and UAP whistleblower, testified before the U.S. House Subcommittee on National Security on July 26, 2023, claiming the U.S. government was concealing a program to retrieve and reverse-engineer unidentified flying objects. During this testimony, he used the term "biologics" in a striking context.

His exact quote: "I was informed, in the course of my official duties, of a multi-decade UAP crash retrieval and reverse engineering program… I spoke with those officials who had direct knowledge of non-human biologics that were recovered from these crash sites."[382]

David Grusch's use of "biologics" in his 2023 testimony refers to alleged non-human biological materials from UAP crash sites, a stark contrast to the FDA's definition of biologics as therapeutic products. Adele Gilpin's company, Gilpin BIOMED, with its focus on biologics regulation, scientific misconduct, and clinical research design, could theoretically support research into such materials, especially given her past consultancy with TTS. She is still listed on the board of advisors. While no direct evidence links Gilpin to Grusch's claims, her expertise aligns with the regulatory and ethical challenges of studying unconventional biologics, offering a plausible correlation.

These people must have a common core that drives them, and it looks like it's more related to biology, DNA, and virology than to chasing flying saucers full of little grey aliens.

The pattern becomes clear: TTSA assembled individuals from intelligence (Elizondo, Semivan, Kahn), intelligence and defense policy (Mellon), classified aerospace (Justice, Puthoff), cutting-edge genetics (Nolan), biochemistry and virology (Kelleher), and epidemiology/biologics regulation (Gilpin). These are not people who would normally collaborate. As I previously noted, the only other place you see such diverse backgrounds working together is in a Masonic Lodge, where the local janitor sits next to a congressman, and all are equal.

In 2022, TTSA rebranded as simply "To The Stars" and shuttered everything except its entertainment division. Mellon, Elizondo, and Justice had all left the company. Rumors suggest that Donald Trump's 2016 election victory threw the disclosure project into a tailspin. Hillary Clinton and John Podesta were reportedly positioned to be the White House team that would disclose UFO reality to the public. When Trump won, funding that was supposed to flow into TTSA allegedly dried up, forcing key personnel to leave to make a living. Mellon and some military generals and admirals publicly came out against Trump during the 2024 election. Bitterly so.

What remains is the network. The connections. The pattern of intelligence, defense, aerospace, and genetic research all converging on the same questions: What are these things? Where do they come from? What do they want, and most importantly for this chapter, what makes experiencers different at the genetic level?

TTSA may have failed as a business venture, but it succeeded in establishing a public-private partnership model for UFO research that continues to this day. The same individuals who were on TTSA's board continue their work through other channels, still collecting data, analyzing samples, and pursuing the same questions about consciousness, genetics, and non-human intelligence.

## DNA AS A FRACTAL ANTENNA

I stumbled on Nick Cook's Reality Antennas: "The Deep Clues in DNA That Link Us to Unlimited Potential" post. Cook is a former aerospace journalist and the author of The Hunt for Zero Point, an investigative report and history that exposes classified government projects to build gravity-defying aircraft with an uncanny resemblance to flying saucers.[383]

Nick is also an honorable mention recipient of the BICS 2021 Essay Contest.[384] The contest challenged entrants to submit essays that made the case for the survival of human consciousness beyond a reasonable doubt. Dr. Jeffrey Long[385] was a runner-up in the same contest. It seems that Robert Bigelow has had his hands and his millions of dollars in all things paranormal, from UFOs to Skinwalker Ranch to this. I'm seeing a pattern: it all starts with lights in the sky and UFOs, then you land in consciousness and life-after-death research, and Bigelow is currently spending more money than anyone else (publicly) on all of this.

In the Reality Antennas post, Cook hypothesizes that DNA is a fractal antenna capable of more than science can explain, and that we, as humans, have even begun to understand. He writes:

"The pioneering work of the late Dr Martin Blank, an expert in cellular bioelectromagnetics, who made a case for the fact that living DNA acted as a 'fractal antenna' that plugged us directly into our environment – as evidence, he cited the damage our DNA suffers from constant bombardment by very low-intensity non-ionizing radiation which is common to all wireless technology and powerline transmission and not just damage to human DNA, but across all species throughout the biome."[386]

Dr. Blank's paper on this topic, co-authored by Reba Goodman in 2011, can be viewed at the U.S. National Library of Medicine.

Cook continues, "The question of damage to our DNA couldn't be more important, but so too is the issue of how our DNA might act as a 'transceiver', a device able to transmit as well as receive energy; or as we are beginning to view it in The Light, as information (the flipside of energy). Because how do we derive all the bits of data that give us our view of the world (aka reality)? A 'fractal antenna' is a single antenna that can operate across a wide frequency range. Cell phones use such devices. Different parts of the DNA chain, we learn, are conductive and non-conductive, allowing it to act like a binary switch, a digital encoding/decoding system. Overall, DNA begins to resemble a device that's not only capable of receiving information but also of storing and transmitting it. The fractal antennas within our DNA look a bit like kaleidoscope imagery but seem to act a lot like computer chips. What the heck is DNA receiving all this information for? Might it, he asks, be a mechanism via which we receive consciousness information from the 'information field'? The discovery of apparent nanoscale 'transmit/receive modules' in our DNA raises a lot more questions than it answers."

Grant Cameron's interview with Chris Bledsoe, the famous experiencer and author of UFOs of God[387]. Chris was talking about classified documents he had been shown, suggesting that human DNA emits a signal into space at a wavelength of 156 megahertz, which is supposedly detectable on radar by the US military. He says the document said that the human skeleton acts as an antenna, DNA as a transmitter, and hair as the receptor[388]. I have not been able to locate this document, so it's just speculation and rumor, but it's an interesting side note to be aware of.

What if our DNA is built to receive, and something's been tweaking the signal?

All of this fits too nicely. Elizondo's microbiology could theorize a biomarker; Nolan's genetics research into experiencer DNA could find it and weaponize it; Puthoff's physics could explain the transmission; Kahn and Kelleher could trace its roots; and Gilpin could chart its spread and lobby for its legal use. TTSA wasn't just chasing lights; they were probing us.

Those old texts, Egyptian, Libyan, and Abrahamic, kept mentioning yeast, something I learned during my conversations with Seth Peribsen. I also learned that doing protocols to basically knock the dust off of your antenna by taking a few over-the-counter natural supplements, you are then able to interact with non-human intelligence more effectively. What if it's an antenna, a living switch flipped by an intelligence eons ago, and that antenna is DNA? Are we returning to something bigger, or are we being neutered? Is our DNA being edited to meet a different mold, pun intended, that NHI wants us to fill?

Whistleblower David Grusch's words gnawed at me, "biologics," not just crashed ships. What if UAPs aren't visitors but architects, and the proof's in our cells, in our DNA? Maybe it's something biological, coded into us, waiting to be heard. Maybe the sky's not the limit. Maybe it's our DNA.

Konstantin Meyl's scalar-wave theory provides a potential physical mechanism for how this all works, DNA as a longitudinal-wave antenna, with introns serving as resonance chambers for information transfer beyond light speed. If consciousness can influence genetic expression and specific genetic profiles predispose consciousness to expanded perception, the boundary between mind and matter dissolves.[389]

Our chakras are said to emit torsion fields, and that DNA has a unique frequency for each person and thing. It's been said that Deep State folks can track us this way via space-based telemetry.

This isn't fringe speculation. The basic principle that DNA responds to electromagnetic fields is established science. Blank and Goodman (2011) demonstrated that DNA acts as a fractal antenna in electromagnetic fields, capable of receiving and transmitting information across a wide range of frequencies.

If external fields can influence DNA, and if certain genetic configurations make individuals more receptive to anomalous information, then we're not just talking about passive genetic traits. We're talking about active receivers, living antennas tuned to frequencies most people can't consciously detect.

## THE CADUCEUS AND THE DOUBLE HELIX

An important symbol is the caduceus, which is a staff entwined by two serpents, sometimes with wings and a sphere on top. The caduceus originated with the Babylonians around 3500 BC as a symbol of the god Ningishzida, who served as a mediator between humans and deities such as Ishtar.[390] In Greek mythology, it became associated with Hermes (Mercurius Trimegistus), the messenger god, and with the Egyptian god Thoth. It represented his power to bring sleep or wakefulness and to make peace between quarreling parties and served as his symbolic staff of authority.

The similar-looking but distinct Rod of Asclepius[391] features just one serpent and is the proper symbol of the medical profession, representing Asclepius, the Greek god of healing. However, the caduceus is often mistakenly used in place of the Rod of Asclepius by modern physicians. After the Renaissance, the caduceus also came to be associated with commerce and trade, appearing on merchant family crests and seals.

There is still much to discover about DNA, RNA, and the complex mechanisms that govern gene expression and regulation. As our knowledge grows, we may unravel more mysteries, unlock new potential for understanding and treating various diseases, and gain deeper insights into the fundamental nature of life itself.

## ANDREW'S STORY

That's what Andrew Radziewicz revealed, and it's what set off the firestorm that would eventually engulf me.

Andrew is a third-generation New York City firefighter who became a high-strangeness magnet. He has psychic abilities he can't turn off, contact experiences since childhood, and a UFO encounter in 1999 while serving in the Coast Guard with twenty other witnesses. After meeting Dr. Steven Greer and learning the CE5/HIC (Human-Initiated Contact) protocol in 2011, Andrew began training with psychic medium Robert Hansen on Long Island. Hansen told him straight out, "You have the gift."

Andrew's abilities developed rapidly. He began doing readings for fellow firefighters, helping families connect with deceased loved ones, and making peaceful contact with UFOs using consciousness protocols, and the contact wouldn't stop. It was constant, overwhelming, affecting his work, his family life, his sanity.

Then came the New York Post article in 2016. A reporter, Andrew, had never spoken or published a piece about him without warning, outing him publicly as a psychic firefighter who communicates with extraterrestrials. The article went through multiple editorial channels at the Post, got placed in Page Six, and suddenly Andrew's private experiences became public knowledge.[392]

That's when Mary Rodwell, who is an Australian researcher specializing in experiencer children, told him something that changed everything. "You need to find a geneticist," she said. "I think there's something different with your DNA."[393]

Andrew didn't know any geneticists. He was a firefighter sitting on a beach in Australia, trying to figure out what to do with abilities that kept intensifying. So, he took a shot through social media. He'd heard of Dr. Garry Nolan through Diana Pasulka's research. He reached out cold, sending photos and videos of his contact experiences. "I don't know what to make of this. I don't know why it's happening."

Nolan responded. They Skyped. "You're not crazy. I've heard this before," Nolan told him. "How did you fake those videos?"

"I didn't," Andrew said. "You can get them tested wherever you want." That's when the questions from Nolan started. "Has anyone in your family experienced this?"

Andrew asked his brother, who confirmed there had been several sightings together. Curious, Andrew then questioned his mother, not expecting much of a response. To his surprise, she recounted an incident from 1973 or 1974: in broad daylight, while sitting on the steps of his grandmother's house with her sister and brother, they saw a black disc glide overhead. They quickly jumped into a Jeep and followed the object along train tracks to an electrical substation in Floral Park, where they watched it silently hover above the power station before it suddenly disappeared.

His mother stayed silent, never confiding beyond the family due to the intense stigma. In the 1970s, coming forward meant being called "crazy Uncle Betty."

The pattern was there, running through his family. His grandmother's, his great-grandmother's stories, which Andrew had never heard, started surfacing. This wasn't just him; it was generational.

Nolan saw it too. "I'd like to look at your DNA," he said. "I think there's a link in your family."

Then came the request that would later become controversial: "Is it okay if I share your experiences with Kit Green, Colm Kelleher, Jacques Vallée, and Hal Puthoff?"

Andrew just wanted answers, trusting these credentialed scientists to do the right thing and give him feedback on what made him different.

Here's what Andrew learned about the division of labor: Gary Nolan collects DNA. Kit Green focuses on brain scans,[394] particularly from experiencers who've had health effects or defects from their encounters. They need a funder because the government isn't officially funding this research. That funder is Robert Bigelow, simple as that.[395]

Here's what Andrew didn't get: results, transparency, or any answers about what they found in his DNA or what they're doing with it now.

---

**"IF YOU ASK JOHN BURROUGHS OR OTHER EXPERIENCERS WHO'VE GONE THROUGH THIS," ANDREW TOLD ME, "THEY SAY THE SAME THING. 'GARRY NOLAN ASKED FOR MY DNA,' OR 'KIT GREEN DID,' AND NO ONE WILL TELL US WHAT THEY'RE DOING WITH OUR DNA."**

---

## THE CLIP THAT CHANGED EVERYTHING

In January 2023, I posted a sixty-second clip from James Iandoli's Engaging the Phenomenon podcast. James, the guy who'd nudged me into starting my own podcast, UFOs on the Level, had a knack for drawing out the wild stuff, and Andrew delivered. He dropped a bombshell about experiencer DNA and how heavyweights like Dr. Garry Nolan and Dr. Kit Green were collecting it, aiming to craft a drug that could flip the switch on UFO and psychic encounters.

Andrew stated plainly:

---

**"DR. KIT GREEN AND DR. GARRY NOLAN ARE EXPERIMENTING WITH MAKING A DRUG BASED OFF OF EXPERIENCER DNA TO TURN ON AND OFF PSYCHIC ABILITIES."**

---

I'd been knee-deep in this rabbit hole myself, thanks to Diana Pasulka's American Cosmic, where "James" (later revealed as Nolan) mused about the same thing.[396] John Burroughs' Rendlesham saga[397] backed it up, health wrecked by a close encounter; he claimed Kit Green saved him but demanded his DNA in return. No answers, just silence when all of the experiencers asked what was being done with their DNA.

When Andrew laid it out, it clicked every box I'd been ticking in my research. So, I snagged the clip, posted it to X, and watched it explode. Tom DeLonge even retweeted it, and the post's views went stratospheric. The clip rocketed past 100,000 views in the first few days.

Then the hounds came, and the counterattack began.

The backlash was swift and brutal. Twitter/X lit up with attacks from trolls, skeptics, even folks I'd known and trusted, demanding I yank the post. Within hours, Nolan messaged me directly: "Take it down, Jon. It's not true." I was tying my kid's shoes, getting her out the door to school, and from the time he sent me the DM (Direct Message), it was only 20 minutes before I replied. Bam, he blocked me, and I could no longer respond or interact with him. After that, my podcast and posts were shadow-banned as well. My reach collapsed to near zero, channel views tanking from thousands to zilch, tweets vanishing into the void. Online "Friends" urged me to delete the post. Skeptics called me reckless, and even some allies distanced themselves. I thanked Nolan for the clarification via a tweet and asked Andrew for his side.

Silence followed, except for the escalating demands that I remove the clip. I refused.

All for sharing Andrew's words, not mine. The words were not mine; they were Andrew's, spoken on a public platform. If they were false, the correction should come from the source, not the messenger. Instead, the pressure intensified.

It wasn't just a personal slap; it was a neon sign screaming they'd hit a nerve. Andrew has been vocal about this since 2017, and Nolan even personally told him about the "antenna" in experiencer brains, tied to junk DNA that might not be junk at all. So why the meltdown now?

I got pissed, doubled down, and dropped a massive thread on X with every scrap of evidence, Burroughs, Pasulka, firsthand accounts of DNA grabs, some maybe against people's will. So, I dug deeper. I laid everything out in a fifty-three-part Twitter thread titled "OK #ufotwitter lets start this MEGATHREAD with facts and RECEIPTS!" What emerged was a web of connections too consistent to dismiss. John Warner IV told me to repost it monthly, and I do, because the truth doesn't hide in silence.

Diana Pasulka's 2019 book American Cosmic introduced a pseudonymous scientist, "James," who was racing to develop "a medicine, an antidote" that would allow humans to interface with The Phenomenon on our terms. Readers quickly identified James as Garry Nolan. In the book, James collects DNA and MRI scans from experiencers. He speaks of creating a pharmacological key to turn anomalous cognition on or off.

John Burroughs, who was involved in the Rendlesham Forest incident, has repeatedly described the same pattern. In interviews with Linda Moulton Howe and others, Burroughs says Nolan, Green, and Kelleher all requested his DNA. When he refused, tissue from a later surgery was taken anyway under a Department of Defense contract.

In a 2022 interview, Nolan speculated openly with the caveat of "if... maybe... wouldn't it be fun to think about" about a drug that could modulate interaction with The Phenomenon. Critics seized on the hypothetical framing. Yet the pattern of DNA collection, brain imaging, and Bigelow funding is not hypothetical. It is documented across multiple independent experiencers.

The gatekeepers can shadowban, block, and demand silence, but the pattern has become impossible to hide.

## WHAT THEY'RE DOING WITH OUR DNA

Andrew asked the simple question that everyone should be asking: What are they doing with experiencer DNA once they collect it?

Nolan and Green won't say. Not fully, but the evidence suggests they're trying to understand the mechanisms of consciousness at the genetic level and maybe recreate them.

Think about what this means.

Some experiencers have special abilities. Telepathy, precognition, healing, manifestation, capacities mainstream science denies, but the military and intelligence communities know are real. Remote viewing programs proved this. Psychic espionage worked, and consciousness measurably affects reality.

If genetic markers really do line up with these abilities, and DNA variations can predict who develops them, things get unsettling fast. Because now you're not waiting for experiencers to appear. You're screening for them. Entire populations could be scanned for genetic profiles suggesting latent abilities, with promising individuals quietly pulled into classified programs before they ever know what they're capable of. Psychic potential cherry-picked before it even switches on.

Once the genes are identified, the next step is obvious. You don't just find ability, you enhance it. Pharmaceutical triggers. Neurological amplifiers. On-demand activation. Suddenly, you're not talking about natural experiencers anymore, but engineered ones. Super-soldiers. Super-spies. Analysts whose abilities can be powered up like a system.

And if you can turn those abilities on, you can turn them off. The same mechanisms that amplify can suppress. That's where control enters the picture. Only approved individuals have access, while everyone else is chemically or genetically locked out. Consciousness itself becomes classified technology, clearance required.

From there, the line gets darker. You don't wait for experiencers at random. You manufacture them—clone optimal genetic profiles. Use gene-editing tools like CRISPR and whatever comes after it to introduce these markers into selected candidates—no chance involved. You build psychics to spec.

And that may not even be the most important part. Because if experiencers are genetically different *because* The Phenomenon deliberately altered them, then those differences become a roadmap. You're no longer just studying people. You're studying the way The Phenomenon modifies biology and how it interfaces with consciousness. At that point, reverse-engineering their technology isn't about recovered craft anymore. It's about decoding the genetic engineering of humanity itself. Andrew thinks they're developing drugs— pharmaceutical interventions based on experiential genetics that could activate or deactivate anomalous experiences. Turn psychic abilities on or off like a switch.

Sound crazy? We already have drugs affecting consciousness dramatically, like psychedelics, dissociatives, and entheogens. Why not drugs targeting specific receptors correlated with psychic phenomena?

Andrew handed his DNA to Nolan years ago, seeking validation, only to be stonewalled about what they did with it. Same story with Burroughs. Kit Green's brain scans and Nolan's gene hunts, funded by Robert Bigelow's deep pockets, hinted at a trillion-dollar prize, a drug or tech to juice up psychic soldiers or AI war machines. Imagine Special Ops with no comms, just telepathy, or Terminator bots with ET-tuned consciousness, unstoppable, no rations needed.

Some say black ops SEAL Teams have had these psionic abilities for many years. Genetic enhancements, too.

Andrew's thoughts on junk DNA and how tones and meditation might turn it on naturally, no pills required. He'd felt it himself at times, the hairs standing up, a tone in his skull, and boom, craft outside his Melbourne home, no CE5/HIC (Human Initiated Contact) needed. If they can harvest that from our genes, amplify it with frequencies blasted from satellites, they could awaken or sedate whole populations. That's when the claws come out, and weaponization talk makes people cranky, Andrew said, and I felt it firsthand.

These events are current and are impacting individuals within our communities. Many are stepping forward, regardless of potential ridicule, professional repercussions, or personal challenges, demonstrating that the pursuit of truth is valued above personal comfort.

## DEAN RADIN'S TRANSPARENT PATH.

Meanwhile, Dr. Dean Radin at the Institute of Noetic Sciences has taken a different, more transparent approach. For decades, he has subjected psi phenomena to rigorous laboratory controls, including Ganzfeld telepathy, presentiment, and observer effects on quantum systems, and has found persistent, replicable anomalies. "If psychic phenomena are real," Radin writes, "then they're part of nature, and as such they're subject to scientific scrutiny."[398]

In 2021, Radin's team screened more than 3,000 individuals for psychic ability and family history, then sequenced the exomes of 13 high-scoring "psychics" and 10 controls. A single nucleotide variation emerged in a non-coding region adjacent to the TNRC18 gene on chromosome 7. Every psychic carried the GG allele; seven of nine controls carried the GA allele. The paper concludes cautiously that the conservative interpretation is random sampling error, yet "when the results are considered in relation to other lines of evidence, the results are more provocative".[399] [398]

Radin estimates the GG variant may confer latent psi capacity to roughly 60 percent of the population. Historical persecution, such as the witch trials and the Inquisition, could explain its absence in the remaining 40 percent. The inheritance pattern is autosomal dominant; each carrier parent has a 50% chance of passing the trait to each child. "Every culture in the world has folklore about families where people seem to be psychic," Radin notes. "That in turn suggests that there are genetics involved."

Radin's genetic work has practical implications beyond identification. In his research profile, he has noted that discovering such a biological marker "would inform environmental or pharmacologic means of enhancing or suppressing this ability". This aligns with emerging technologies for modulating consciousness.

Radin has collaborated with Cognigenics, a biotech firm he co-founded to pioneer non-invasive genetic medicine for the brain using intranasal RNAi to silence disease-driving genes and restore neural balance in psychiatric and neurodegenerative disorders. Their lead candidate, COG-301, is a siRNA therapeutic delivered intranasally via lipid conjugates to downregulate the 5-HT2A serotonin receptor in brain regions linked to anxiety and psychosis. In preclinical models, similar shRNA neuromodulators, such as COG-201, have shown improved memory, reduced anxiety, and no off-target effects.[400]

In a 2024 lecture titled "Consciousness, Psi, and the Future of Human Potential," Radin connected this directly to his psi genetics research. He explained screening psychic families for inherited talents, then sequencing DNA to compare cases and controls: "We thought, well, maybe there's psychic talent, and we did find a difference between the psychics and the non-psychics".[401]

This led to co-founding Cognigenics: "As a result of that... I co-founded a biotech company where we wanted to see could we use modern genetic engineering methods like CRISPR... to modulate genes, gene expression in the brain uh to enhance cognition."

The delivery method? Intranasal spray, bypassing the blood-brain barrier:

---

**"WE ULTIMATELY WANT TO GO TO UH CREATING WHAT AMOUNTS TO A COCKTAIL AND WE DO THIS INTRANASALLY. SO INTRANASAL DELIVERY GOES INTO..THE BLOOD-BRAIN BARRIER INTO THE BRAIN. WHICH WOULD MAKE YOU A TEMPORARY OR PERMANENT DEPENDING ON KIND OF EDIT YOU USE. SUPER PSYCHIC. WE THINK WE CAN DO THAT"**

---

Read that again.

He said, "Think! Think!? You know they can do this, and they've been doing it already if he is saying this publicly.

Currently, the company focuses on Alzheimer's and mild cognitive impairment for funding purposes, with a compound that shows over 100% improvement in memory tasks in mice and rats. "You would take this as a [nasal spray] you'd sniff it... it is literally downregulating certain receptors in the brain that are associated with...loss of memory".

Yet Radin voiced stark concerns about the dual-use potential.

"**THERE IS A SLIGHT DANGER THAT IF WE WERE SUCCESSFUL, IT WOULD DISAPPEAR... SUCKED UP INTO SOME PROGRAM SOMEWHERE AND SUPER SOLDIERS WOULD BE MADE... SO IF SOMEDAY I DISAPPEAR AND ALL THIS RESEARCH DISAPPEARS AT LEAST SOMEBODY ELSE WILL KNOW WHAT WENT ON.**"

This chilling caveat underscores the ethical tightrope of turning genetic psi markers into a deployable tool, a validation, perhaps, of the very gatekeeping I encountered. The difference is that Radin is publishing his work, speaking openly about it, and warning about the dangers. He's not secretly collecting DNA and refusing to share the results.

It sounds like he fears both his life and his research.

Bigelow's transition from researching UFO phenomena to investigating life-after-death experiences is evidenced by his support of the BICS essays, such as Dr. Jeffrey Long's, which suggest a connection between these subjects. Long's surveys on near-death experiences indicate that individuals often report increased psychic sensitivity following such events, including encounters with ghosts and UFOs. According to Andrew, near-death experiences or practices like CE5/HIC (Human-Initiated Contact) may serve as mechanisms for facilitating these encounters, with the appearance of craft serving as potential evidence of access to new states of awareness.

Yet the field's a mess: UFO aficionados, Deep State researchers, ghost hunters, and Bigfoot chasers don't talk to one another; they point fingers and dismiss other people's opinions. We're cogs in the same wheel, missing the machine part wholesale. Congress gets it, though. Andrew dropped a bombshell on me: multiple members have had close encounters, some up close and personal, and that has been driving the classified briefings post-Grusch. They're haunted by the unknown, demanding answers. Beware of the divide-

and-conquer strategy used by the UFO gatekeepers, and remember: sometimes it's self-inflicted.

## WHY DNA MATTERS FOR DISCLOSURE?

Understanding experiencer genetics changes everything about disclosure. Because it means:

This isn't random. The Phenomenon is selecting specific individuals based on genetic profiles. Contact isn't arbitrary, it's targeted. Some bloodlines are more involved than others. Some families are tracked across generations. The pattern suggests intention, planning, and long-term programs.

We're part of something larger. Not just witnesses or the victims of curiosity or abduction. Active participants, willing or not, in genetic programs serving purposes we don't fully comprehend. Our DNA is involved. Our children's DNA. Our lineages extend backwards and forwards in time.

The government knows. Nolan and Green are collecting data for someone. Military and intelligence agencies have studied experiencer genetics for decades, finding correlations between contact and genetic markers, and confirming that experiencers' claims are credible.

Unlike purely subjective experiences, genetic markers are measurable. Falsifiable. Scientific. You can't dismiss genetic evidence as hallucination or delusion. This makes experiencer testimony scientifically valid in ways previously impossible.

If experiencers are genetically distinct because ancient genetic manipulation created us (remember the royals?), then the entire human origins narrative collapses. It threatens the paradigm. We're not purely natural evolution. We were designed. Engineered. Modified repeatedly across millennia. That changes everything about human self-understanding.

Whatever programs created genetic variations in the first place haven't stopped. It's continuing. Modern abductions, hybrid programs, and genetic sampling is ongoing. We're not studying ancient history; we're part of an active program happening now.

This is the reason DNA is significant. It also explains why Andrew's decision to speak up is important, and why it matters that those who have had experiences are seeking answers about the use of their genetic data.

Because if we're the experiment, if humanity, or at least certain lineages, represents a long-running genetic program managed by non-human intelligence, then we deserve to know. We deserve access to the data collected about us, an understanding of who we are, who we're becoming, and the purposes we serve.

## LIVING AS A GENETIC EXPERIMENT

Some UFO experiencers have said that ETs have told them we are "genetic royalty." They said we have a 12-strand DNA sequence on purpose, which is extremely rare or even unique in our universe. That's why so many star nations of both polarities have paid so much interest to us. "Divine order" Twelve is a sacred number on Earth and in our universe: 12 months, 12 hours, 12-year Buddhist animal cycle, 12 apostles, 12 Zodiacs, etc.

What does it mean to know you're genetically distinct? That your DNA marks you as part of a program you didn't consent to? That contact running in your family isn't chance but design?

For Andrew, it means accepting he's different. Not better, just different. His psychic abilities aren't imagination, and the contact experiences aren't delusions. His genetics confirm what his experiences taught: that he's part of something larger, stranger, more complex than mainstream science acknowledges.

For other experiencers, it means validation. Years of being told you're crazy, imagining things, seeking attention, and being undermined by genetic evidence. You're not making it up. Something is different, measurably, scientifically, and undeniably, but it also means uncertainty. Because we don't know what the genetic markers mean. We don't know which programs we're part of, whether genetic distinctions are an advantage or a vulnerability, who controls this information, and what they're doing with it, or whether we can opt out. If genetics predispose you toward contact, if markers attract The Phenomenon's attention, if bloodlines are tracked, can you escape? Can you protect your children? Or once marked, always marked?

These aren't comfortable questions, but they're necessary. Because pretending we're not part of genetic programs doesn't make those programs stop. It just keeps us ignorant while they continue.

Better to know, to understand what we are, even if the answers are disturbing and demand transparency about what's being done with our DNA. We need to know what's being discovered, what the implications are, and to face the truth, however strange, then live comfortably in lies.

## WE ARE THE EVIDENCE

Robert Bigelow's fortune has underwritten much of this frontier, UFO crash-retrieval programs, Skinwalker Ranch, consciousness-survival contests, and DNA collection from experiencers. The same network that quietly collects samples also funds the search for consciousness beyond the brain.

The gatekeepers can block me, hoard DNA, and drip-feed disclosure, but the tide's turning and the pattern is now too large to conceal.

Your DNA carries more than personal ancestry. It carries a deeper record of a species being modified, monitored, and guided by intelligence we're only beginning to acknowledge. If you're an experiencer, your genetics are likely to show it through markers that suggest your brain processes reality differently, variations that indicate enhanced consciousness, and differences that make you more compatible with whatever The Phenomenon is. None of that is a defect or an abnormality. It's design, ancient and ongoing, and a purpose-driven creation of human subpopulations capable of roles in a larger drama unfolding across timescales we don't comprehend.

We are the evidence: our DNA and our experiences together prove that The Phenomenon isn't just visiting; it's involved. Intimately. Fundamentally. Across millennia, that evidence can't be suppressed forever because we exist. We're here. We're talking. We're comparing notes. We're discovering patterns and demanding answers.

The gatekeepers collected our DNA, and now we want to know what they found, what it means, or what we are becoming.

Asking is not too much. It's a basic right to understand what you are genetically, which programs you're part of, and what purposes your DNA serves. Disclosure isn't just about UFOs in the sky. It's about DNA in our cells and genetic programs running through humanity, about understanding ourselves not as isolated individuals or random evolution but as designed beings serving purposes larger than we've been told. This is the disclosure that matters, the truth that changes everything, and precisely what they're trying to control by collecting our DNA and not sharing results. The control is breaking down. There are now too many experiencers, genetic profiles, and patterns emerging, and too much evidence accumulating.

DNA is no longer merely a chemical script. It has become a battleground for healing, for weaponization, for profit, and perhaps for the future of human evolution itself.

Unraveling its secrets may finally illuminate what the lights in our skies have been trying, for decades, to tell us about who and what we really are.

Until then, keep asking questions, demanding transparency, sharing experiences, and comparing notes.

Because you're not imagining it, you're not crazy. You're genetically marked for involvement in something humanity is only beginning to remember, and that makes you crucial. Not a victim or a curiosity, but a key player in disclosure happening from the ground up, cell by cell, gene by gene, experiencer by experiencer.

Your DNA knows even if your conscious mind doesn't. Trust it. Trust yourself. Trust the process.

We are the experiment, and we're also the experimenters waking up. Recognizing what we are and reclaiming agency over our genetic futures.

That's the revolution, the disclosure, and it changes everything.

My theory during the early days of COVID was that forcing the vaccine on the entire population could have been a preemptive measure. This is all theory, not based on any verifiable evidence, but follow me on this one. China is well known for hacking sensitive military and Military Industrial Complex documents and information. What if the UFO crashes near Roswell in the late 1940s and 1950s, together with non-human intelligences, brought an entirely new type of retrovirus? After years of study, the US identified it and kept it in a file for further study of its potential for weaponization, as we always do. Well, what if China hacked one of our labs and got the recipe? They have no idea what it is or where it came from, and decided to make it in a lab in Wuhan. The lab tech has no idea what he is doing and infects himself and the entire world with an Alien Retrovirus, which only a handful of scientists know to be an Alien Retrovirus.

The world implodes, but we have a vaccine, and we had it fast. We already had it because we had COVID in our back pocket as a weapon. Oops?

Seems legitimate if you ask me.

Or maybe all of that is true, but it was for a more helpful purpose. Maybe we went about releasing the virus and thus making the worldwide vaccine a requirement because the powers that be know something is imminent. They know that non-human intelligence will be interacting with humans, and this would be a way to inoculate us against their germs, like a reverse World War scenario.

Maybe the COVID vaccine is helping the forthcoming UFO battle for Earth, or maybe it all goes back to who can make the most money from the military-industrial complex.

# CHAPTER 14

## THE WHITE LADY

Contact, Consciousness, and Transformation

I've shared researchers' findings, scientists' data, and whistleblowers' testimonies. I've walked you through technology conspiracies and DNA harvesting, through ancient mystery schools and modern cover-ups—theory after theory, fact after fact, connection after connection with actual receipts.

I have something that in many ways is more difficult to share now.

But before I share the experiences of all the other brave souls who've gone public with their encounter and before I present their protocols, deceptions, unified theories, and their transformations, I have to tell you what happened to me.

I'm not just researching this as an outside observer taking notes from a safe distance. The phenomenon touched me directly, and I need you to know that before we go any further.

### THE WHITE LADY

I wish I'd written down the exact date, moon phase, or even the time. All those details that make researchers nod and say, "interesting." But I didn't. When it happens, you're not thinking about documentation. You're just there, present in the moment, and overwhelmed. Trying to process what your eyes are seeing, your body is feeling, and what's happening to you.

What I do remember from this experience is that it was in my backyard. The thing that stood out most was that she came from the northeast, and there's a sycamore tree there with big, white bark. She came from that direction, across my backyard, to where I was standing.

Before this happened, I'd gone through a transformation, you could say. I'd completed the Rosicrucian grades, the whole initiatory process. I had multiple experiences with orbs, even with my family present. I'd been in groups that did CE5 protocols, brought down orbs, and filmed them with night-vision cameras. Real physical stuff. Not imagination or meditation visions. Actual objects in the sky responding to consciousness.

But more than that, I'd gone through something internal. I'd stopped being afraid, and that's huge. I used to joke, before I started the podcast, that I was scared a white van was going to come down the road, and the men in black were going to grab me if I talked too openly about UFOs and all of this. Like if you say too much, they'll shut you up. That fear was real for me and others because it had been reported to have happened in the past. Then, at some point, I just let it all go, and the stigma disappeared. I no longer felt like I had to hide my experiences anymore, be scared of them, or give a damn what people thought. I talked openly about seeing ghosts as a kid, about all the weird stuff that happened, about orbs, about everything. And I think that's when it happened, when I became that open. That's fearless. Maybe that's what opened the door. I guess I might never know.

It wasn't during some tragedy or a low point in my life that so many others have cited as the source of their interaction with The Phenomenon. I had a family, a job, a great life, and was deeply into the podcast, talking to amazing people, researching like crazy. Jean-Luc and I were having these incredible conversations, connecting dots. Life was good. I was just ready, I guess. Open to whatever came next. I'd accepted that if something were going to happen, it would happen. And I wasn't afraid anymore.

Then SHE APPEARED.

She came to me out of the northeast, bathed in White a pure white light, but feminine. Unmistakably feminine. Not in a sexual way, in an essential way. A presence of power wrapped in grace. Ancient and immediate all at once.

Behind her stood two dark figures. Cloaked in hoods that were either black or dark, dark blue, I couldn't tell for certain. They radiated a strong masculine energy that made me perceive them as being sentinels, guardians, or even enforcers. They hung back, but their presence was heavy and very intimidating. This wasn't a gentle invitation. This was serious.

She held out a sword, palms up, offering it to me.

That's the moment everything crystallized. The sword. The offer. The weight of what it meant.

And then the vision hit me.

## THE VISION, MILLENNIA IN SECONDS

Have you ever seen those super-rapid-cut scenes in movies where they try to cram 3000 years into 30 seconds? That's the only way I can describe it. They jammed a millennium of experience into my head in an instant.

Bloody battles in foreign lands. Desert heat. Sand and stone. Death. So much death. Destruction that I was responsible for, partially responsible for, at least. Again and again, across lifetimes, but with different physical bodies, repeating the same pattern. Take the sword, go to the hot place, fight for her, destroy, cleanse, repeat.

The message was clear: you must fight for me again.

This was not a request; it was a reminder. Like we'd made a deal a long time ago, and it was time to honor it. You agreed to this. You've always done this. It's time again. Take the sword. Go to the desert. Do what needs to be done.

For the greater good, right? Always for the greater good. The cosmic excuse for violence wrapped in righteousness.

NO. NOT THIS TIME.

I said no. I'm not doing it.

I don't know if I said it out loud or just thought it so hard that it didn't matter. The message was clear either way.

I'm not doing it again!

The two dark figures stepped closer towards me. The intimidation ramped up with their silent pressure. I received the impression from both of them as, "we don't want to do this, but we will if we must." It was a strong reluctance mixed with duty or obligation, and they weren't happy about it either, but orders are orders nonetheless.

I held my ground.

I have a family. I'm not doing it. I'm just not going to do it.

That was the line I drew right there. I'd done this before, I could feel it in my bones, but not this time. Not again. I'd come into this life with a family, responsibilities, and a choice. And I was choosing them, choosing peace, and choosing to break the cycle.

The energy shifted. Something passed between the two figures, something like neither of us wants to do this. Reluctant enforcers who would follow through if they had to, but were hoping I'd make it easy.

I didn't make it easy. I'm not doing it. Forget it.

And then that was it. Done. They withdrew. Not defeated, not victorious. A stalemate. Your move is registered. We're done here.

## THE AFTERMATH, NO REGRETS, NO VICTORY

Here's the weird part: I didn't feel bad about it. No regret or sense that I'd failed some cosmic test. But I also didn't feel like I'd won either. No triumph or sense of dodging a bullet, it was just very neutral. Like I'd made a choice and that was that. The universe accepted it and moved on.

I felt free. Like I'd asserted sovereignty over my own existence in a way I never had before. Not over some institution, military, or government. It felt like this was a victory over myself, in the face of something ancient and powerful that was asking me to give that up again. I said no to a goddess, and the sky didn't fall.

Nothing negative followed this interaction. Things got better, actually. More positive and the synchronicities, oh man, the synchronicities started to escalate. That's when I started meeting other people who'd had similar experiences. Other people who'd seen the White Lady, too.

# I'M NOT ALONE, THE GLOBAL PATTERN

Through some synchronicity, and I mean real synchronicity, universe-connecting-dots-I-hadn't-asked-it-to-connect synchronicity, I started meeting other experiencers. People who wouldn't normally cross my path. These people come from diverse backgrounds, various countries, and distinct spiritual traditions. Nevertheless, each reported having seen the entity that I refer to as the White Lady.

Jean-Luc Infini and I connected after my experience. After we became friends, I learned that he'd had his own encounter: different context and details, but the same essence of the white feminine presence. As always, the experience was profound and life-changing. He got it immediately when I told him.

Chris Bledsoe. You most likely know his story if you're in this community: the Lady, white orbs, and his transformative experiences on the Cape Fear River. When I heard about his encounters, the parallels were undeniable. Different manifestation, same presence. He has described this in countless podcasts and in his book, "UFO of God."

Filmmaker Richard Stanley was making a BBC documentary about Otto Rahn and the Holy Grail. He had an encounter with the White Lady at Montségur, a Cathar fortress in France, which is also the site of the final massacre of the Cathars by the Roman Catholic church. He heard her feet crunching across the stones of the castle. She stared right at him. Then disappeared through a wall. That experience made him quit his career as a filmmaker. He moved to Montségur, became a guide, pledged his sword to her every full moon. The man completely reoriented his entire life around one encounter.

And there are others. People I've met through this work who've had experiences they won't discuss publicly. They'll share privately and carefully with others who've been there. But not on a podcast or in a book. For them, it's too personal, powerful, and easy to misunderstand or ridicule.

I respect that. I get it. It took me a long time to share this publicly. I'm only doing it now because I think other people need to hear it and to know they're not crazy, alone, or just making it up in their heads.

Here's the thing I keep coming back to. This wasn't the first time I saw her. You might remember this from the opening chapter, but I'm coming back to it on purpose.

When I was about ten years old, I was standing at the bottom of the stairs in the dark. There was a woman at the top. All white. Glowing, like a one-piece white gown, luminous in a way that didn't make sense given how dark the hallway was. My first thought was that it was my mom, which tells you how real it looked. I reached over and flipped the light switch. She vanished, and I knew, the way a ten-year-old knows things they can't explain, that what I'd just seen was not my mother or anyone else, for that matter, that I knew as a human.

I didn't connect those two experiences for a long time. Decades, actually. A glowing white feminine presence at the top of the stairs when I was a kid, and a glowing white feminine presence crossing my backyard forty-some years later, offering me a sword. It appeared that they both had the same energy and quality of light. I had the same unmistakable sense that whatever was standing there was aware of me specifically and had something to communicate.

What happened right after that childhood sighting is something I've told people as a funny story for years, and it is funny, but I'm starting to wonder if there's something else in it, too. The winter Olympics were on television. I was totally into the bobsled team. So, I grabbed a cardboard box, dragged it to the top of those same stairs, stapled a makeshift sled, sat down on it, and decided I was going to be on the US bobsled team. I launched myself down the staircase on a piece of corrugated cardboard at full speed and broke my arm at the bottom.

Now, obviously, I broke my arm because I was a dumb kid who rode a cardboard box straight down a flight of stairs, directly into a wall. I'm not saying the White Lady pushed me. But I've thought about the sequence. I saw her, standing right there at the top of those stairs, and then I went right back to that same spot, over and over, sledding down them as if she'd never been there. Like I was daring something. Like a ten-year-old version of what I did forty years later in my backyard, standing my ground, refusing to be moved. Maybe the stubbornness runs deeper than I thought, and it's been the consistent variable this whole time.

Or maybe I was just a kid who watched too much Olympics coverage and had no fear of consequences. That's probably also very much true.

## THE GODDESS ACROSS CULTURES

Once I started researching, I found the pattern everywhere. The White Lady isn't unique to Western esoteric traditions or modern UFO experiencers. She's global, ancient, and showing up across time and culture with a consistency that's hard to explain away.

The White Buffalo Calf Woman is a Native American traditional story. She came down and taught the people. With her, she brought the sacred pipe and sacred knowledge. The experience transformed how the Lakota people understood their relationship to the divine and to each other. Different name, same energy. White. Feminine. Teaching. Transforming.

I learned of the Occitan Tradition from Amanda Mariamne, who'd studied it extensively in southern France. In the Cathar regions, they say: first you meet the Black Madonna, then you meet the White Lady. It is akin to a progression or spiritual journey. The Black Madonna, dark, womb-like, transformative, comes first. She breaks you down, shows you death and rebirth, and teaches you about cycles. Then, if you're ready, the White Lady appears. Light. Ascension. Calling you to service.

Amanda herself had the Black Madonna experience years before she ever encountered material about the White Lady. She described being shown reincarnation cycles, the womb of existence, and how light interacts with darkness at the level of divine principle. It brought no karma or punishment. The lesson she was taught was that we choose to incarnate through desire and will. It changed her life. Three years later, she started researching the White Lady tradition, and the recognition hit her: that's the pattern. Black Madonna first, then White Lady.

Throughout history, there have been multiple accounts of Marian Apparitions. This entails the Virgin Mary appearing to children, peasants, and everyday people. Fatima. Lourdes. Guadalupe. Medjugorje. Always the same, a white or glowing light, feminine, delivering messages, appearing and changing lives. The Catholic Church has its own interpretation of these events. Still, the experiencers describe something entirely different, an experience similar to mine, as well as those of Richard Stanley and Chris Bledsoe.

The Cathars and Templars both venerated the divine feminine in ways that got them branded heretics and slaughtered for it. The Cathars called their spiritual leaders Perfecti, male or female; it didn't matter. They believed in direct gnosis, direct experience of the divine with no priestly middleman required. The Templars found something in the Holy Land that fundamentally changed them. Something feminine. Whether it was Mary Magdalene's teachings, the Black Madonna icons they brought back, or direct contact with the same presence I encountered in a backyard in Maumee, Ohio, I can't say. But something got into them, and the Church noticed, eventually coming for both orders with everything it had to destroy them.

She is not bound by our religious categories or our modern skepticism. She shows up anyway, in every era, in every culture, whenever the conditions are right, and someone is open enough to receive her. A force older than the institutions that have tried to suppress her memory. A consciousness with her own timeline and her own purposes, and she has never once waited for official permission to pursue them.

## THE QUESTIONS I CAN'T ANSWER

Was it real? Completely, undeniably real, more vivid and present than most of my waking life, physical in a way that dreams and imagination are not.

The harder question isn't whether it happened. It's what kind of experience we're actually talking about. Physical? Interdimensional? Consciousness-based? I was in my backyard, fully awake, and I experienced it. But would my neighbor have seen her if they'd stepped outside at that moment? Honestly, I have no idea. It felt both grounded and completely beyond the physical at the same time, which I realize is an unsatisfying answer. It's the only honest one I've got.

The sword, the intimidation when I refused, the eventual withdrawal, that whole sequence has the shape of a test. Like they were checking whether I'd break the pattern this time, or if I had the will to refuse, when I held my ground, I could only feel them accepting it, maybe? It's hard to know the difference from inside the experience.

What if saying yes had led somewhere dark? The impression being given to me was that the greater good is how it's always sold, lifetime after lifetime, and I've been a weapon for causes I never fully understood. That vision of centuries of destruction, I genuinely can't tell you whether that was memory or some warning, and maybe that was the whole point. More than anything else, it felt like an ancient commitment I'd made and forgotten. The sense that I'd agreed to this long ago, that I'd served as warrior or knight or instrument across many incarnations, and this was just supposed to be another round. Take the sword, fight, repeat. But this time, I had a family, a life I actually wanted, and, for once, the answer was NO.

My reason for refusing was straightforward: family. Yet my decision runs deeper than that. I'm tired of repeating the same cycle. Exhausted by destruction dressed up as righteousness, fed up with being a tool for forces I can't fully grasp, no matter how ancient or powerful they are. I wanted peace and to choose my kids' laughter over some cosmic obligation I never consciously signed up for. Looking at it that way, the decision wasn't even close.

Did I make the right call? I honestly don't know. Maybe I failed something important, or I broke free from something that was using me. Maybe both are simultaneously true. What I'm certain of is that the choice was mine. Not predetermined, coerced, or written into some script, I was acting out. Mine. That matters more to me than whether it was correct.

Will she return? Since that encounter, there have been no similar experiences or adverse consequences. However, there has also been no definitive closure either. Instead, there has been a notable silence, as if the outcome of my decision is being observed to assess how I proceed with this chapter of my life, now that I have elected to engage fully with it.

# WHY I'M TELLING YOU THIS

Other experiencers need to hear that they're not alone. If you've seen the White Lady, or something like her, you're not crazy, and you're not making it up. You're part of a pattern that stretches further back than any of us can trace. Others have been there; you are not the first and won't be the last.

The goddess tradition is real and active right now, today, in the 21st century. Not ancient history or metaphorically, because as we see, she's interacting with people in the present tense, and my guess is she always has been. Whether the lights in the sky and the White Lady are part of the same Phenomenon, or she's one interface between human awareness and something vast we lack language for, I can't say with certainty. One thing I am sure of is that dismissing any of it as folklore is a mistake.

For the first time that I am aware of, we now know that saying no is an option, and I want that on the record. You don't have to accept every offer, every calling, every cosmic obligation just because it arrives wrapped in beauty and ancient authority. Even if it feels divine, well, especially if it feels divine, trust your gut. I said no to a goddess, and the universe didn't end. I believe that my life got better, more authentic, more mine.

Sovereignty matters even with higher beings, maybe especially so. If something is truly benevolent and genuinely aligned with human wellbeing, it will respect your free will and accept your refusal. The fact that the White Lady and her sentinels withdrew when I held my ground tells me something meaningful about the nature of that encounter. Either they respected my choice, or they didn't have the authority to override it. Either way, real power existed in that moment on my side of the exchange. So does yours.

The phenomenon is not just nuts-and-bolts craft or reverse-engineered technology. It is in one aspect, but it's also consciousness meeting consciousness. Entities that seem to recognize you across lifetimes and present choices whose consequences reach further than you can see, physical and metaphysical bleeding into each other, ancient and immediate at the same time.

That encounter changed everything for me. I am not researching this from the outside. I'm in it, have always been in it, and whatever I discover or share or conclude from here forward, none of it is academic. It's personal. This book is about understanding what happened to me as much as it's about understanding what's happening to all of us.

## WHAT I KNOW NOW

What she actually was, I can't tell you. Goddess, alien, interdimensional being, projection of my own higher consciousness, archetypal force that appears differently across cultures but draws from a single source. All of the above. None of the above. I've stopped pretending research alone will work that out.

Whether refusing the sword was the right call, that's equally unresolvable. Maybe I failed something important, or I broke free from something that was using me. Maybe I'll understand it in twenty years, or maybe the question stays open until the end. I've made my peace with not knowing.

What remains is what I do know, and it's enough to keep moving.

The Phenomenon is personal. Not just lights in the sky or DNA samples or reverse-engineered craft. It knows you, recognizes you across time, shows up in your backyard, and offers you a sword and waits to see what you do with that moment. That is not an abstraction. That is contact.

Free will is real and worth defending. Even when facing something that radiates power and beauty and ancient authority, the right to say no belongs to you. Don't surrender it to anyone or anything, human, alien, or goddess.

This pattern runs deeper than any single tradition can contain or explain. Cathar mystics and Lakota prophets, medieval knights and modern experiencers, ancient goddess veneration and contemporary UFO contact, all connected by something I can feel but can't fully name. The thread is real. I've felt it in my hands.

Once this happened, I started looking for others who had this experience and connecting with them. It's more like we found each other in some strange way. Along the way, share your story carefully, but share it, because we need each other's accounts to make sense of our own. The community of experiencers stretches further than you know, and you are not an outlier in it.

Always remember that this lifetime is yours. Whatever cosmic obligations might exist, whatever ancient patterns might be pulling at you, this family, these choices, this moment belong to you. Protect them. The universe can wait.

Now let me share other voices, other experiencers, other perspectives, because my story is one thread in a much larger tapestry, and honestly, some of the other threads are more remarkable than mine.

Their voices matter as much as mine—maybe more. The Phenomenon is vast, and no single encounter captures it, so we need the full range of what people have seen, felt, and been changed by.

So here they are. The ones who've been there and come back to tell us what they saw, what they learned, what they chose, and how it changed them. Listen carefully. Their stories might resonate with yours or challenge everything you think you know. Either way, they're telling the truth as they lived it, and that matters more than any theory or framework we might try to build around it.

The Phenomenon speaks through experience, contact, and transformation. These are the voices of those who've heard its call.

# CHAPTER 15

## EXPERIENCER VOICES

After sharing my White Lady experience and putting myself out there in ways that still make me uncomfortable, I need to be clear about something: We all think we are special, but I am not special. I'm not chosen, uniquely gifted, spiritually advanced, or cosmically important.

I'm just one more person who experienced something that shouldn't be possible according to our official narratives. One more experiencer in a global community of millions who've seen, felt, and have been changed by things that mainstream society refuses to acknowledge. That community crosses all boundaries we humans create: every race, culture, economic class, and religion across every continent.

The Phenomenon doesn't discriminate. Humans do.

Which is why Patricia Avant's work matters so much. Why her film "Black People Do See UFOs" hit me like a revelation when I first watched it, and why her courage to confront stigma head-on opened doors that needed opening.

Because stigma doesn't just keep people silent, it creates hierarchy. It determines whose experiences get taken seriously and whose get dismissed. It shapes which voices enter the discourse and which remain marginalized in UFO communities. Still, despite our claims of open-mindedness, despite our shared experiences with ridicule and suppression, we've replicated the same racial dynamics that poison broader society.

We need to own that and do better, and Patricia's work shows us how.

### THE COMEDIAN'S JOKE

There's a comedian's bit that went viral. I won't name him, but the setup is classic: "Black people don't see UFOs."

The punchline builds on historical trauma: "We're not getting on any ship where we don't know the length of the trip or where we're going." Audience laughs. Because it's funny, dark humor rooted in real horror, the Middle Passage, slavery, the trauma that shapes Black consciousness in America, even generations later, but it also reinforces a lie. A pervasive cultural narrative that says Black people don't have these experiences, don't participate in UFO culture, don't see or care about The Phenomenon.

Patricia titled her film to directly combat that lie. "Black People Do See UFOs." Present tense, active voice as a statement of fact.

Not "some Black people" or "Black people occasionally" or "Black people claim to."

Black people do see UFOs. Period. End of discussion, and the evidence backs her up. But first, she had to overcome the compounded stigma, the double layer of not being believed that comes from being both an experiencer and a Black woman in America.[402]

## PATRICIA'S FOOTAGE

When I first watched Patricia's film, I stopped everything and sat there, transfixed. Because what she captured on film multiple times and consistently, with ordinary camera equipment from her backyard, defies easy explanation.

Objects that sometimes appear as stars, but when you zoom in, they're not stars. They change and morph. They display structure that shouldn't be there.

One sequence shows what appears to be a bright point of light. Standard UFO fare, and could be anything, could be nothing. Then Patricia zooms in. The object starts "performing," as she describes it. Dancing. Pulsating through every color in the spectrum. Red to pink to orange to white. Extending what appears to be a protrusion, something reaching out from the main body.

She slowed the film's playback, and as she examined it frame by frame, a structure emerged. Geometric patterns emerged, accompanied by formations that seemed nearly biological, reminiscent of watching a flower bloom or an organism progressing through stages of development.

There's a moment in clip 16 of her collection that still sends chills down my spine. The object suddenly goes dark—Patricia assumes it has disappeared, but she keeps recording. Later, when she reviews the footage in slow motion with the brightness increased, she notices something is still present, and another shape begins to emerge from it, as if it's emerging from an opening and moving across the object's surface.

"It's like it's giving birth," Patricia says when we discussed it. "I don't know what else to call it." I don't either. If it is a technology, it appears organic and changes shape like a living creature. What object that looks like a star acts for the camera, shifts colors, grows appendages, or opens portals? I am at a loss.

She's got dozens of these clips, and they are not one-off anomalies. Consistent phenomena appear night after night in her backyard. Close enough that she can film them with consumer-grade equipment and responsive enough that they seem aware they're being watched.

## WHY ISN'T EVERYONE SEEING THIS?

Patricia asked the same question I asked after my orb experience. "I couldn't imagine anybody else saw this stuff with me."

She sent footage to NASA and got bounced around, eventually connected to someone who looked at it and said, "These are great," but then "I don't know if I'm the right person." It was then passed to Rhonda Shaw, a Black woman working at NASA. Patricia specifically sought her out, shocked that there were Black people at NASA at all.

Rhonda asked Patricia several questions. Where are you? What time? What direction? Then emailed her back and told her, "Don't break my camera and don't zoom out that far."

That was it. No follow-up. No analysis. No explanation.

The message was received. We see what you're filming, and we're not talking about it publicly.

Because that's how it works: official channels acknowledge privately, deny publicly, suppress systematically, and Patricia (like so many experiencers) is left wondering, "Am I crazy?" Is this real? Why is this happening to me?

I know that she's not crazy. Her footage is real, and it's not just happening to her; it's happening across communities, countries, and the world. To people of every background who look up, who pay attention, who remain open to experiencing something beyond the approved narrative.

*The Phenomenon is democratic. Our response to it isn't.*

## THE STIGMA WITHIN THE STIGMA

Being a UFO experiencer carries stigma. We've all felt it. The eye rolls. The nervous laughter. The subtle distancing when you mention you've seen something unusual. Even close friends and family struggle to take you seriously.

Now add race, gender, and living in a community where discussing UFOs might seem like escapism when you're dealing with systemic racism, economic inequality, police violence, and even daily struggles just to stay alive.

Patricia described it, "There's stigma inside stigma inside stigma."

She explained to me that there are multiple layers of stigma faced by UFO experiencers. The first is the pervasive belief that UFOs simply aren't real, so anyone who claims to have seen one must be crazy, lying, or mistaken. Even if someone accepts that UFOs might exist, another stigma emerges, skepticism about why these phenomena would appear to a particular person, leading to questions about their motives: are they seeking attention, trying to make money, or hoping to build a cult following? For Black people, an additional barrier exists, as cultural stereotypes suggest that UFO sightings are not part of their lived reality, dismissing such experiences as exclusive to white suburban communities or as New Age or hippie fantasies. On top of all this, Black women face the harshest disbelief; they are often not believed about their experiences in the workplace, with medical professionals, or during encounters with police, and the idea of adding alien contact to that list only heightens the skepticism and marginalization they endure.

Each layer makes it harder to come forward, documenting experiences riskier, and building community within your own demographic nearly impossible. What is painful is that UFO communities are largely white, even though The Phenomenon impacts everyone; these groups often mirror societal biases and not always through explicit racism, but in terms of who receives attention, whose research is supported, and whose experiences are acknowledged.

These words will forever live rent-free in my mind and are direct quotes from Patricia during our podcast.

---

### "WHO GIVES A FUCK ABOUT A UFO?"

### "IF THEY CAN'T COME DOWN HERE AND FUCKIN' TAKE US OUT OF THIS SITUATION THEN WHY DO I CARE IF THEY ARE UP THERE, APPARENTLY, THEY DON'T CARE"

---

When mainstream UFO conferences feature panel after panel of white male researchers. When books about UFO experiences focus almost exclusively on white experiencers. When the face of "serious" UFO investigation is white and male and credentialed in ways that exclude people who don't have academic pedigrees or military backgrounds.

The message is clear: your experiences might be real, but you're not the right messenger.

Patricia pushed back. Made the film. Put "Black" right in the title and forced the conversation and the response? Mostly positive. People were grateful when someone finally said it. She had black experiencers reaching out privately to share their own encounters, feeling less alone.

However, it also brought out the internet trolls and skeptics. Some people claimed it's a floating seat cushion. One guy on Twitter/X insists you can't get that kind of footage with that camera, therefore it's fake.

Standard experiencer harassment. Except amplified by racial undertones. The assumption that she's grifting, exaggerating, seeking attention. The refusal to engage with the evidence on its merits because that's easier than confronting what the evidence suggests: that The Phenomenon is real, ongoing, affecting people across all demographics, and that our institutions are lying about it.

## WHAT'S THE PURPOSE?

Patricia asks the question that haunts every experiencer, Why am I seeing this?

Not "what is it," though that matters, but why her? Why now, and why does it keep coming back? Why does it perform, change, and reveal structures when she films it?

Is it intentional? Are they, whoever they are, whatever they are, showing themselves deliberately? Choosing specific witnesses? Allowing documentation, or is it random? Wrong place, right time? Patricia happens to look up when most people don't. Does she have the right camera, persistence, and the right openness, or is it a case of synchronicity at work?

I don't know, but I suspect there's selection happening. Not random or purely intentional, but something in between.

Many experiencers exhibit comparable characteristics, such as openness, curiosity, engagement in spiritual practices or meditation, a capacity to critically evaluate official narratives, and an ability to accept paradox without requiring immediate resolution.

Patricia embodies all of this. She's an artist, a writer, "late blooming" as she describes herself. She is spiritually attuned, fascinated by ancient texts, and convinced that "the purpose of life is to find your way back."

Back to what? Unity. Source. God. The cosmic intelligence that mystery schools teach about, the mystics experience, that consciousness research is beginning to validate.

She's developing exactly the capacities mystery schools cultivate, and The Phenomenon responds.

Not because she's special, but because she's available. Present and pay attention, and do not dismiss experiences that don't fit materialist frameworks. When she films what appears in the sky before her, studies it, and shares it despite stigma and harassment, she's doing something critical. She's documenting, providing evidence, and building the case that this is real, it's ongoing, and it affects everyone. She is modeling courage by showing other Black experiencers (showing all experiencers from marginalized communities) that coming forward is possible. That your story matters and your evidence counts.

That you are not alone.

## THE BROADER MESSAGE

Patricia's film isn't just about Black African American experiences with UFOs. It's about recognizing that The Phenomenon is universal. Still, our response to it is shaped by culture, bias, and by power structures that determine whose reality gets validated and whose does not.

This is not a series of separate failures. It is one system showing up in different places. The same apparatus that buries UFO evidence decides which voices are legitimate and which can be ignored. It walls off consciousness research, protects racial hierarchies, and seals inconvenient knowledge behind institutional gates.

Control works by managing credibility and by deciding whose experiences count and whose never quite qualify.

So, when African American experiencers are sidelined, when Indigenous contact traditions are treated as myth, when women's reports are brushed aside, the pattern is familiar gatekeeping through credentials, class, and cultural permission. The same logic that keeps disclosure locked behind classification, that hides manuscripts in Vatican archives, that makes vanished skeletons disappear into storage rooms no one is allowed to enter.

And when we accept those rules, when we narrow the field to seem reasonable or respectable, we become part of the system. We make it smaller. Safer. Easier to manage.

We do their work for them.

Patricia's film says, No more.

Black folks do see UFOs. Indigenous people do see UFOs. Women do see UFOs. Poor people, incarcerated people, disabled people, queer people, immigrants, refugees, everyone sees UFOs. Some experience NHI or extraterrestrial contact. Some families report generations of contact.

Because The Phenomenon doesn't respect our hierarchies, it appears to consciousness, to awareness, to whoever is present and open, regardless of demographic categories, and once we recognize that. Once we truly embrace the diversity of experiencers, once we platform marginalized voices and validate their evidence with the same seriousness we give credentialed white male researchers, then disclosure becomes inevitable.

Because you can't suppress millions of voices or dismiss consistent testimony across every demographic, you can't maintain the cover-up when the experiencer community itself refuses to replicate suppression dynamics.

That's why Patricia's work matters beyond her specific footage. It's a challenge. A line in the sand. An insistence that all experiencers deserve respect, all evidence deserves examination, all voices deserve amplification, and it's a reminder that The Phenomenon has always been democratic. We're the ones who made it hierarchical, and we're the ones who need to change.

So, when I share my White Lady experience and add my voice to this chorus, I'm standing in a tradition that includes Patricia and countless other marginalized experiencers who came forward despite compounded stigma.

I'm honoring their courage and learning from their example. Recognizing that my relative privilege: white, male, educated, I realize platform and personal connections come with responsibility.

Responsibility to amplify voices that face barriers, I don't. To platform experiences from communities I'm not part of and to recognize that my story isn't more valid just because I tick certain demographic boxes.

The Phenomenon doesn't care about those boxes. Neither should we.

So, here's what I'm asking of you. When you hear an experiencer's story, check your assumptions. When someone from a marginalized community shares evidence, examine it on its merits before dismissing it. When you build UFO communities and conferences and research projects, look at who's included and who's excluded and recognize that full disclosure requires full inclusivity. That understanding The Phenomenon requires hearing from everyone it affects. That breakthrough will come not from waiting for government admission but from building experiential solidarity across all boundaries.

Patricia's doing that work. So are many others. Are we ready to support them, learn from them, and follow their lead?

Because if we're serious about disclosure, if we want the truth about UFOs and consciousness and non-human intelligence, we need to start by telling the truth about ourselves. About whom we listen to, who we believe, and who we're willing to stand with.

Black people do see UFOs; they've been seeing them all along. Just like everyone else, we just haven't been listening, and it's past time to change that.

So, you've accepted that The Phenomenon is real. You've overcome the stigma enough to investigate seriously. You've heard experiencer testimony, examined evidence, maybe even had your own sighting.

Now what?

Do you wait passively, hoping something happens to you, relying on random chance, on being in the right place at the right time, or do you treat contact as something that happens to you rather than something you can initiate? Or do you take agency and recognize that consciousness itself might be the interface and learn protocols for human-initiated contact?

That's CE5/HIC (Human Initiated Contact)—close Encounters of the Fifth Kind. The fifth category in the classification system starts with distant sightings and progresses to direct contact: CE1 is a distant sighting, CE2 involves physical effects such as burns, radiation, or electromagnetic interference, CE3 involves entities observed, CE4 involves abduction or direct interaction, and CE5/HIC involves human-initiated contact.

Dr. Steven Greer popularized the term, developed formal protocols, and trained thousands of people worldwide. While Greer's protocols become controversial with accusations of cult behavior, charging significant money for events, and claims that seem too grandiose to verify, the core insight remains valid.

Consciousness can initiate contact. Meditation and intention can bring them in. The Phenomenon responds to awareness, to invitation, and to focused human consciousness, and practitioners across demographics, methodologies, and philosophical frameworks are independently confirming this. It works. Not every time. Not predictably just consistently enough that dismissing it as a coincidence or delusion becomes untenable.

But beware who you summon. Are they benevolent or regressive? Can we tell? Is CE5 reckless? Are we primitive Pacific Islanders calling for imperialistic Captain Cook and the all-powerful British Navy? Will they conquer us by way of subterfuge, religious indoctrination, and infiltration over time? It's a myth that all "star nations" and "Visitors" are benevolent, since, by all accounts, we live in a Yin-Yang duality universe.

Let's take the risk for now.

Let me introduce you to three people doing this work with different approaches, but the same fundamental recognition that consciousness is the key.

D. Baron Bolton goes by Buddy. Also "Alien Protocols." Or "Psychic X." Each name captures a different facet of his work: consciousness exploration, contact protocols, and psychic development.

Buddy's a modern enigma. Experiencer since childhood. Trained in remote viewing, healing, and psychokinesis. He has studied with people connected to official programs, the ones that aren't supposed to exist but clearly do. He's worked with Dr. Kit Green, and he understands that consciousness isn't limited by space or time, that psi abilities are real and can be developed, that The Phenomenon responds to specific states of awareness, and that he teaches it. For free. Won't accept payment. He will accept donations to keep himself alive; he's not monetizing consciousness development or contact protocols. He's sharing because that's what the work requires: service, not profit.

When we talked, Buddy explained his approach, "You put out the intention with love and respect."[403]

That's it. That's the core protocol. Not complicated visualization exercises or specific mantras or ritual procedures. Just intention, love, respect, and nothingness meditation. Getting to that state where thinking stops, ego quiets, where you're just present awareness without agenda or expectation. That's where contact happens, the frequency they meet you on.

The AATIP briefing deck is one of the most revealing artifacts from the Pentagon's UFO program. Leaked after AATIP's existence was confirmed in 2017, it sparked debate about what the government knows and what it plans to do with that knowledge. The slides go beyond propulsion and physics. They dive into human performance, cognitive enhancement, biological manipulation, psychotronic weapons, and unique cognitive human interface experiences.

Slide 9 is the bombshell. It suggests UAPs don't just defy physics, they interact with consciousness. "Instantaneous sensor disassembly" implies they respond to observation itself. Fear brings fear. Openness brings contact.

That's the protocol. No rituals, no mantras. Just intention, love, respect, and nothingness meditation. Drop the ego. Become pure awareness. That's the frequency they meet you on. Not guaranteed, but possible. Probably, if you practice.[404]

Bolton also emphasizes the genetic component. His mother had stunning psychic abilities, and he couldn't get away with anything. She could predict events with annoying accuracy. Buddy posits that the capacity passes through the maternal line, concentrating over generations of intuitive women who protect families, read situations, and sense danger. Remember, the Divine Feminine is the principle of creation, intuition, receptivity, and interconnected life, the intelligence that births, nurtures, feels, and integrates, balancing force with flow and power with wisdom rather than domination.

Not everyone has a strong genetic predisposition, but almost everyone can develop these capacities to some degree. It's like athletic ability; some people are naturally gifted. Everyone can improve with training, and training is what Buddy offers. Remote-viewing techniques, meditation practices, and even healing modalities. Understanding how consciousness interacts with physical reality, how intention affects outcomes, and how Gestalt relationships work between observer and observed.

He calls it "consciousness-naut" work. Exploring inner space, the way astronauts explore outer space. Mapping the terrain of awareness, discovering capacities most people never develop, learning to navigate non-ordinary states safely and effectively, and the UFO phenomenon? That's where inner and outer space meet, where consciousness exploration leads to contact with non-human intelligence. Where developing psi abilities opens doors to interaction.

Bolton's living proof that this works. He doesn't need to convince skeptics. Bolton's not building a following, selling books, or creating a brand. He's just doing the work, helping others learn, documenting what's possible when you approach The Phenomenon correctly. "Correctly" means with humility, with love, with respect for positive-polarity NHI minds that vastly exceed ours in capability and wisdom. We can respect regressive NHI just like we can "respect" the technology, military prowess, and engineering capability of Nazi Germany, just not their racist, warlike, conquering genocidal ideology, for example.

My approach differs from Bolton's in context but not in principle. Where Buddy works solo or in small, informal groups, most people integrate CE5/HIC (Human-Initiated Contact) into group settings.

I hosted a CE5/HIC (Human-Initiated Contact) event with 10 brothers, Freemasons, and Rosicrucians at an off-grid cottage in Wilkesburg, Ohio, powered solely by solar and wind. No light pollution. Just fellowship, nature, and intention to make contact.

Two nights. Different protocols each night. All documented.

Night one: We used meditation assisted by binaural beats, specific frequency patterns that help induce altered states. I played it all night. Deep-focus music designed to entrain brainwaves to theta and delta frequencies, where consciousness becomes most fluid and receptive.

We meditated together. Then skywatcheed and things appeared.

Brilliant orange-red lights moved steadily, seeming purposeful. We ruled out satellites after examining flight records, orbital paths, and aircraft listings; none matched the coordinates. These objects shifted direction and appeared to respond when we noticed them.

Everyone present, including trained observers such as ex-military personnel and pilots, witnessed these events. We shared the night vision camera, filmed together, and all agreed that what we saw was truly unexplained.

Night two got weirder. It was cloudy at the start. We did a guided CE5/HIC (Human-Initiated Contact) meditation, 30 minutes of focused intention, visualization of contact, and opening ourselves to communication. Post-meditation, a clear circle appeared directly above our location. Just that one spot. Everywhere else remained overcast, and the orbs came again, visible through my SiOnyx color night vision camera.

Meditation came before any visible appearance. Focused intention was linked to manifestation, and consciousness set the stage for contact.

This outcome was not by chance. A group of ten individuals meditated together with a clear purpose, creating energetic harmony and opening themselves as a collective. In response, The Phenomenon made itself known, clearly, measurably, and on multiple occasions.

The Masonic context matters, not because Freemasonry has special contact privileges, but because Masonic lodges are designed as spaces for consciousness work. The ritual, symbols, and the degrees train awareness, expand perception, and develop capacities that remain dormant in most people. Ancient Zep Tepi Egyptian priests were said to have done the same in their highly decorated, frequency-generating temples (each temple may have had a different frequency), as did the later pharaonic-age priest caste.

Rosicrucianism explicitly teaches these techniques. Meditation. Visualization. Energy work. Chants. Singing. Understanding how consciousness interfaces with subtle realities. Preparing initiates for experiences that official culture denies exist.

So, when Freemasons and Rosicrucians do CE5/HIC (Human-Initiated Contact), we're not just meditating; we're activating capacities developed through initiatory practice. We're using frameworks preserved in mystery schools specifically for engaging non-ordinary realities and it works. Consistently. Across different groups, different locations, and different protocols. The specific method matters less than the underlying principle; focused consciousness creates the conditions for contact.

This is reproducible. Anyone can do it. You don't need Masonic degrees or Rosicrucian training—those help, but they're not requirements. The Phenomenon doesn't care about credentials. It responds to consciousness, to openness, to invitation.

What matters: sincerity, respect, patience, practice.

**Jaime Paul Lamb** approaches CE5/HIC (Human-Initiated Contact) through a different framework: not modern UFO protocols but ancient magical tradition. Hermetic arts. Neoplatonic cosmology. Planetary magic.

When I first talked to Jaime about UFOs, he said he wasn't "a gray alien guy." Not interested in spaceships, cattle mutilations, or physical craft narratives. Then I mentioned "off-world intelligence," and his mind lit up.

Because Jaime constantly works with off-world intelligence. Not as a UFO contact but as a magical practice rooted in Western esoteric tradition. He invokes planetary demons, not "demons" in the Hollywood sense but in the classical sense. "Planetary familiars." Intelligences associated with celestial spheres.

In cosmological frameworks, Earth is regarded as a terrestrial sphere located within the sublunar realm, encompassing elements, physical matter, and incarnate existence. Beyond this realm lie the seven planetary spheres: the Moon, Mercury, Venus, the Sun, Mars, Jupiter, and Saturn. Each of these spheres is considered to possess a unique form of consciousness and an associated intelligence. Access to these spheres is traditionally believed to be achievable through specific practices.

Jaime's a practicing classical "magician." He uses astrology, tarot, and ritual protocols to contact planetary intelligences. He receives information, guidance, and sometimes direct experience of these entities.

Is that different from CE5/HIC (Human Initiated Contact)? Only in terminology. The practice is identical: meditation, focused intention, and opening awareness to non-human intelligence. The cosmology differs, ancient geocentric model versus modern extraterrestrial framework, but The Phenomenon might be the same.405

For millennia, mystery schools have understood and instructed protocols for establishing contact with non-human intelligences. Although they did not use modern terminology for UFOs, these traditions offered frameworks and techniques for engaging entities beyond the physical human realm. Terms such as planetary spirits, angels, demons, and gods were used interchangeably, reflecting a shared recognition that non-human intelligences exist and can be accessed through consciousness.

What if CE5/HIC (Human Initiated Contact) isn't discovering something new but rediscovering something old, and Greer's controversial protocols are a modern repackaging of mystery school practices that have worked for centuries?

That's Jaime's perspective, and it makes sense. Because when you strip away cultural frameworks, UFOs versus planetary demons, versus angels, the core practice remains. Enter an altered state, focus intention, open awareness, and wait receptively for a response.

At times, nothing happens. Other instances bring only subtle impressions. There are also occasions when direct contact occurs with visual, auditory, telepathic, and experiential experiences.

Maybe they're the same across frameworks. Perhaps "planetary demon," "angel," and "extraterrestrial" all describe the same phenomenon from different cultural perspectives. Maybe mystery schools were contacting beings we now call aliens, or better yet, "star beings." Could modern experiencers be engaging multi-polarity entities the ancients called "gods"

The Phenomenon doesn't change, only our interpretation does, and Jaime's work reminds us that this isn't new. Humans have been making contact for millennia. The protocols exist. The knowledge was preserved. We just forgot (or were made to forget by the elite powers-that-be) that these practices work.

## MY EXPERIENCES.

I've done CE5/HIC multiple times. With other brothers from various lodges and esoteric orders. Solo and in groups. Using different protocols and no protocol (just intention and openness), things happen. Not every time or dramatically, just consistently enough that I can't dismiss it as a coincidence.

The orb experience with my family was spontaneous and happened after years of openness, meditation practice, and personal consciousness development. I'd prepared the ground even if I hadn't formally done CE5/HIC that day.

The sessions with my Brothers, those were intentional. We'd meditate, sometimes for hours, using binaural beats or silence. Guided visualization or just presence and lights would appear. Objects that shouldn't behave that way. Movements that defied conventional explanation.

Multiple witnesses. Video documentation. Night vision confirmation. All the evidence skeptics demand, except they don't accept it when you provide it. Because acknowledging the evidence means confronting implications they're not ready to face, they're not ready to face them. However, for those of us doing the work the evidence is overwhelming. This is real. It's reproducible, it works.

Not like flipping a switch or a guaranteed event every session, but consistent enough that probability becomes certainty. This isn't random chance or delusion. It is contact, and the more you practice, the stronger the connection becomes. The Phenomenon learns you, you learn The Phenomenon, and a relationship develops. Not friendship exactly, these aren't human relationships. It's more about rapport or mutual recognition in these ongoing interactions.

That's what Kevin calls "secret superhero" work from the earlier chapter. You're not broadcasting this, starting a cult, or monetizing contact. You are quietly developing the practice, making contact, learning what's possible, and the knowledge spreads from person to person. Teacher to student. Experiencer to experiencer. The way mystery schools transmitted knowledge was through direct experience, not through books, lectures, or theories.

You can read about CE5/HIC, study protocols, and watch videos of other people's experiences. Still, until you do it yourself, you meditate, focus your intention, open your awareness, and wait for a response, you don't know. You're operating on belief or skepticism, not on experience, and experience changes everything.

## THE COMMON THREAD.

Different approaches, frameworks, and cultural contexts deliver the same core recognition. Consciousness is the interface.

Not technology or random chance, and not by passively waiting for them to decide to show up. Consciousness, human awareness, focused, opened, and extended beyond normal parameters, creates conditions for contact.

Why is this? Several possibilities emerge when you think deeply about the mechanism. They might be monitoring consciousness itself, able to perceive when humans enter specific states of awareness, detecting when we meditate deeply or reach that state of nothingness where ego dissolves, pure presence emerges, and when we radiate love and openness, creating a signal they can perceive like a beacon cutting through dimensional static. Or it could be quantum entanglement operating at the consciousness level, where focusing intention toward them creates actual entanglement across space-time so that information transfers instantaneously, and they know we're calling, giving them the choice of whether to respond. Another possibility is that they're fundamentally multidimensional, existing in realms we don't normally perceive with our limited sensory apparatus, and meditation alters our perceptual frequency enough that we shift into states where their dimension overlaps ours, making contact possible not because they come to us but because we meet them halfway in that liminal space between worlds. Or perhaps most radically, maybe there's no "they" as separate entities at all, maybe consciousness is fundamental rather than emergent from matter, and what we call UFOs and entities or contact experiences is consciousness recognizing itself, exploring its own infinite nature, playing at the boundaries between subject and object in a cosmic game of self-discovery.

I don't know which explanation is correct. Probably some combination, and it's more complex than any single framework captures.

It works consistently and reproducibly for me and others, regardless of practitioner, methodology, or culture. This consistency is crucial for disclosure, understanding The Phenomenon, and human evolution.

We're not powerless or waiting for them to decide. We can initiate, develop, and learn. Protocols are in place, effective for all, and the information is accessible. It isn't hidden, rarely taught, or recognized by mainstream institutions and official culture.

However, it is real and probably spreading. As more people practice, document, and share experiences, the paradigm shifts. From passive witness to active participant. From victim of abduction to initiator of contact. From fear to curiosity to a relationship.

CE5/HIC matters because it proves agency and shows consciousness as a primary force. Contact is a choice, not something that happens passively. As more people embrace these abilities and consciousness exploration becomes routine, disclosure will naturally follow.

Because you can suppress government documents. You can classify videos and sensor data, harass witnesses, and discredit researchers.

You can't suppress direct experience, classify consciousness, or prevent people from meditating, focusing their intention, and making contact themselves.

The gatekeepers could be losing control. Not because they're choosing to release information, but because information is becoming irrelevant. People are having experiences directly, learning for themselves, and bypassing official channels entirely.

That's the revolution and the disclosure that matters. Not congressional hearings or military admissions. Individual humans discover that they have the capacity for contact, develop that capacity, and share protocols with others. (in my humble opinion).

Person to person. Experiencer to experiencer. The way mystery schools are always taught and as that spreads, as the community grows, as more people confirm these capacities exist, the old paradigm of secrecy and control won't work well. Official denial becomes untenable. Materialist science becomes obsolete, and it's happening slowly now. Control systems based on limiting human potential collapse.

That's why CE5/HIC matters. Not just as a method for seeing lights in the sky. As a tool for consciousness evolution and proof that we're more than we've been told. It's a pathway to reclaiming agency in relationships with intelligences beyond the human, and once you know that and experience it directly, everything changes.

The question isn't whether UFOs are real. It is. Are you ready to make contact yourself? Are you prepared for what that might reveal, and are you willing to do the work?

Because The Phenomenon is waiting. Has always been waiting for consciousness to reach the frequency where contact becomes natural, easy, and ongoing. Where the barrier between human and non-human intelligence dissolves, and we remember what we have forgotten. That we're not alone, we never were, and connection requires only awareness, intention, and openness. For me and many others I know, the protocols are available, the practices work, and the invitation stands.

What happens next is up to you.

# CHAPTER 16

## LIVING WITH THE MYSTERY

### DECEPTIONS - THE PHENOMENON LIES

After talking about Patricia's courage and CE5/HIC potential for contact, I need to introduce an uncomfortable truth: The Phenomenon deceives as a matter of practice.

It lies to experiencers, presents false narratives, and creates elaborate scenarios that seem real until they collapse under scrutiny. It uses our beliefs, expectations, and cultural frameworks against us. Showing us what we want to see or are prepared to accept. Anything that will keep us confused and divided.

This isn't speculation; it's been documented across decades of serious research. Jacques Vallée built his career on recognizing this pattern. John Keel saw it and tried to warn people as well. Every honest investigator eventually confronts it; The Phenomenon is not straightforward. It is a trickster, a deceiver, and a shapeshifter.

Ignoring this reality and pretending that all contact is benevolent, that all entities are helpful, and that every message is the truth leads to confusion and exploitation.

We need to examine the known deceptions and try to understand what we're dealing with.

### LIVING AS AN EXPERIENCER–INTEGRATION AND HOPE

I started chapter fourteen with my White Lady experience. The encounter that drove me to the choice I made or didn't make, one that I live with every day. The sword I refused and the oath I wouldn't take. The part of me that stayed behind when I chose this life, family, and incarnation, and now, after walking you through all this collective wisdom, I need to bring it back to what this actually means.

What does it mean to live as an experiencer? To carry this knowledge and to function in a world that denies what you've experienced? To integrate encounters that don't fit consensus reality and remain sane, grounded, and effective while knowing things most people dismiss as fantasy?

That's the real work, and what this closing section is about. No more evidence, theory, or analysis. How does one cope with this? How can you live with these truths and hold onto hope, knowing the extent of the deception, secrecy, and the suffering they cause?

## THE ISOLATION OF KNOWING

Being an experiencer is isolating. Even with a growing community, more acceptance and disclosure accelerating, it's still fundamentally lonely, even though there are millions of us.

Because you can't fully explain to someone who is understandably ignorant, asleep, and hasn't experienced it themselves. Words and frameworks fail, and it's just not in their reality. The experience transcends language, defies conceptual understanding, and operates at levels where communication breaks down.

You try. You describe the light, the presence, the communication that wasn't words but was clear. You explain the missing time, the physical effects, the before-and-after difference in how you perceive reality. You share the downloads, synchronicities, and the ongoing sense of being watched, guided, and tested. The whole story of our hidden history, the whole Shebang, and people smile, nod, say supportive things, or perhaps ridicule you. You see it in their eyes; they don't really believe you. Or they believe you experienced something but doubt your interpretation. They may be uncomfortable and want to change the subject. They say, "I believe that _you_ believe your story." Wow, how childishly denigrating, how shallow-minded.

Even close friends and family. The people who love you and want to support you can't fully understand you in this way because they haven't been there or felt what you've felt. They haven't had their comfortable reality dissolved and reconstituted differently. They have not yet awakened and may never in this lifetime.

As Warner often says, "They have just polished their shiny hardwood floor of reality, and here you come along with an axe. Some folks will get violently defensive if you start swinging it."

So, you stop sharing. Not completely, then you find select people, other experiencers, and researchers who understand. Those kindred spirits floating around here, there, everywhere, blue collar workmen, brave soldiers and sailors, frostbitten Tibetan monks, nonconformist scientists, keen-minded homemakers, penniless artists, tired nurses, overworked and underpaid teachers, zillionaire blue-blood racing drivers, common everyday small-town students, stalwart firefighters, cops, humble Hindu gurus, etc. with most of your life and your relationships, you keep this part separate. Hidden. Protected, and that isolation hurts. Not dramatically or acutely but constantly. High-grade loneliness comes from knowing something profoundly fundamental about reality that most people don't know, understand, and won't accept.

Here's what I've learned: insufferable isolation is also a gift. Because it forces you inward, it makes you develop a relationship with the experience itself rather than seeking external validation. It builds capacity for solitude, independent knowing, and trusting your own perception even when consensus reality disagrees. In philosophy, it's known as "The Dark Night of the Soul," and it changes you at the DNA level.

You become self-validating. Not in a narcissistic sense because you remain open to being wrong, updating your beliefs, and always learning from others. In a fundamental sense, you know what you experienced and understand the bigger picture. That knowing doesn't depend on others believing you, and it can't be taken away by ridicule, dismissal, or institutional denial.

True power is gained through isolation and facing reality outside of consensus, building the ability to stand alone when needed. Psychologist Carl Jung recognized and taught this principle.

It's lonely, but it's also liberating, and it's preparation for what's coming as disclosure accelerates, more people experience contact, and the paradigm shifts. Those who've learned to hold this knowledge in isolation become teachers, guides, and anchors for others entering similar territory.

## INTEGRATION—NOT BELIEVING BUT KNOWING

There's a difference between believing something and knowing it. Belief requires faith, can be shaken by doubt, and depends on external confirmation. Knowing is direct, unshakeable, and self-evident.

Experiencers know. That's what makes us different. Not that we're more spiritual, evolved, or specially chosen. Just that we've had direct contact with something beyond normal human experience, and once you know, you can't unknow it. However, knowing doesn't mean understanding. I know my White Lady experience was real. I don't fully understand what it meant. I know the lights I've seen aren't conventional aircraft. I don't know what it is or where it's from. They could be one of our advanced crafts or something not built by human hands. I know consciousness extends beyond the physical body. I don't know how or why or what that implies about death, reality, or human potential.

Knowing and understanding are different, and the integration is the process of closing that gap. Not by forcing conclusions but by living with the questions and letting the experiences settle by observing how it changes you personally over time.

For me, integration has been a gradual process, marked by years of processing, examining, and trying to understand what I experienced and what it asks of me.

Initially, I tried to fit it into existing frameworks like mystery school teachings, hermetic philosophy, or gnostic Christianity. Each provided a partial understanding, and each fell short of capturing the full experience.

Then I tried to research it away. Read everything. Listened to every podcast. I talked to every researcher and tried to contextualize my experience within the broader phenomenon, to understand it through accumulated knowledge.

That helped, but only partially. Because my experience isn't anyone else's, the frameworks others provide are tools for personal discernment, not answers. The research illuminates patterns but doesn't resolve personal meaning.

Eventually, slowly, and painfully, I recognized that the integration isn't about understanding. It's about accepting and living with mystery alongside probable facts. It is about functioning effectively despite not having all the answers and letting the experience work on me rather than trying to force it into comprehension.

With that acceptance and willingness to not know, remain in uncertainty, and to trust the process even when confused, that's when real integration began.

The anxiety decreased, and my obsessive searching relaxed. The need for external validation faded, and I started just living with it and carrying the knowledge with me while letting it inform my choices without dominating my life.

That's integration. It's not a resolution or complete understanding. It is just accepting that this happened, and it changed you.

Because the experience, however confusing or isolating, also gave me gifts. It expanded my awareness and deepened my compassion. It revealed beauty in existence that most people never perceive and connected me to something vast, ancient, intelligent, cosmic, and mysterious.

Those gifts remain even when understanding eludes you. They're not contingent on figuring everything out. They're just there and part of you now. Ultimately, they are integrated within you whether you understand them or not.

## HOPE IN THE MIDST OF DARKNESS

Recognizing how much of reality is hidden from us and how much we've been lied to, how systematically humanity has been controlled by elites, institutions, religions, monarchies, and perhaps regressive star nations, that's heavy. That's dark as hell, and can lead to despair, rage, and giving up. Please don't ever give up. I've felt all of that as well. Anger at institutions maintaining secrecy. Grief for the suffering that the overarching secrecy causes—despair about whether anything will ever truly change, and yet changes are happening.

Here's what keeps me going and where hope comes from, even in the midst of bottomless darkness.

The Phenomenon as a whole continues unabated, regardless of human attempts to control it. Whatever it is, it's not waiting for government permission to exist. It keeps appearing, contacting people, and it's operating on its own timeline. Human institutions can suppress knowledge, suppress people, but they can't suppress The Phenomenon itself.

More people are waking up. My older friends have seen this happening since the consciousness-expanding 1960s, maybe even since the Renaissance, when Leonardo da Vinci famously wrote: "I awoke, only to find the rest of the world asleep." Every day, more experiencers come forward, and new researchers begin serious investigations. More people are rejecting official narratives and are seeking the truth directly. The global awakening is happening slowly, unevenly, and unmistakably. I'm not alone in these assertions, oh no.

People like Scott Wolter, Graham Hancock, Greer, John W. Warner IV, and more are on the same journey.

Digital technology makes suppression harder, and global communication makes isolation almost impossible. The old gatekeeping methods don't work as they once did in this modern era.

Consciousness is primary, and whatever The Phenomenon is, it responds to awareness, intention, and to consciousness development in humans. That means power isn't solely centralized in institutions or technologies. It's within our capacity to develop, awaken, and expand beyond the current limitations.

Direct experience cannot be stopped. Gatekeepers can try to restrict information or intimidate witnesses, but they cannot prevent contact or personal transformation through meditation and connection to consciousness.

Change is accelerating rapidly. Look at UFO discourse just twenty years ago versus now. Currently, we have Congressional hearings, Pentagon acknowledgments, and mainstream media coverage. Military pilots and whistleblowers are coming forward to testify before Congress. It's happening faster than institutions like the MIC, IC, and Congress can manage. In ways they can't fully control. With disclosure comes "New physics", weapons, and, more alarmingly, a new arms race to reverse engineer UFO/consciousness technology in secret. Ask yourself, where did the MIC corporations get their fancy new tech from? Why are the advancement and rollout of whiz-bang tech and A.I. so…darn…fast? Are they worried that another country will reveal it before the US can?

Remember, we're not alone in this; there are millions of experiencers worldwide. Thousands of serious researchers now speak openly, along with hundreds of credible witnesses and a growing network of people who know, have experienced, and refuse to accept "official narratives." We're building a community that began way back in 1952 with the Aerial Phenomena Research Organization (APRO). We are sharing knowledge, supporting each other, and are now faster, stronger, and better informed than ever before.

The truth has momentum. Once a certain threshold is crossed and enough people know, the paradigm shifts and becomes irreversible. We might be at or near that threshold right now. The tipping point is where disclosure becomes inevitable, not because traditional conservative institutions grant it, but because collective consciousness and the public demand it.

That's hope. Not naive optimism or denial of how bad things are, but recognition that despite everything, secrecy, suppression, and deception, the truth is emerging. Slowly, messily, persistently, and we are all part of that emergence. Every experiencer who speaks up. Every researcher and insider who investigates seriously. Every person who questions official narratives and seeks understanding directly. Every conversation is like the ones in this chapter—every connection made between people who know.

We're the mechanism for disclosure, not waiting for institutions or dependent on official permission, and just sharing, investigating, experiencing, learning, and growing together.

That's powerful and hopeful, and what keeps me going when the darkness feels overwhelming.

## CLOSING THE CIRCLE—BACK TO THE WHITE LADY

I told you about refusing the sword. About choosing this life, this family, and this incarnation over whatever the White Lady offered. About the part of me that stayed behind. The warrior I was or could have been.

I live with that choice every day. Not with regret, as I stand by the decision. With awareness of the cost and the path not taken. Of the version of myself that exists elsewhere, or even else when, serving in ways I chose not to serve here, and I wonder, was it really my choice? Or was the choice itself part of the plan? Was refusing the sword exactly what was needed? Was staying in this life, body, and this limited awareness precisely the point?

If the choice existed at all, it may not have been about escaping the world but entering it under constraint. A (Soul choice)[406], in this framing, isn't the ego selecting outcomes, more of consciousness consenting to forget itself long enough to experience consequence and learn from it in some way. (The Higher Self)[407] isn't issuing commands from above; it's the wider intelligence that understands the strategy behind limitation, why refusing the sword matters, and remaining in the body matters. Why acting from partial awareness generates the pressure necessary for remembrance. From that perspective, the plan was never to avoid the trap, but to understand it from the inside, because only then does choice regain meaning. Two ways of looking at that experience are completely different.

I don't know which it is, but I understand the paradox because I made a choice. The choice was predetermined, and both are true in some sense, and they exist simultaneously. The warrior who fights in the desert and the man who writes this book, both me, neither me, something beyond the binary choice.

That's what living as an experiencer means—holding paradox. Existing in multiple realities simultaneously, knowing things that don't fit together, that shouldn't all be true, yet somehow are. Bilocation, Tri-location, time not being linear in a way that makes all things possible.

The White Lady was real. She offered something; I refused, and I think that refusal connected us. Bound us and made me part of something I'm still not ready to understand, yet fully, maybe that's okay. Fully understanding isn't the point. Maybe the point is to live with the questions and carry the mystery within me. Functioning as a bridge between the interdimensional, metaphysical worlds, most people don't know or believe exist.

I think there is some way that's what we all are, those of us who've had these experiences. We are bridges and connectors, people who've touched something beyond normal human awareness, brought it back, and are changed by it, carrying it forward into consensus reality.

We are the evidence. Not government press conferences or Pentagon reports. Us. Our experiences and testimonies. Our willingness to speak the truth even when ridiculed, to maintain knowing even when isolated, and to integrate the impossible into daily life.

That's the work and the calling. We are not special or chosen. Just experienced and therefore responsible for sharing what we can. Support others going through it and build bridges between worlds, paradigms. Between the knowing and not-knowing.

The White Lady knew what she was asking, and she knew I'd refuse because both were necessary—the asking and the refusing. The sword was offered, and the sword was declined. The warrior who serves by not serving, who fights by choosing family, who fulfills prophecy by denying it.

I'm living it. Day by day. Word by word. Connection by connection. Writing this book, sharing these stories, and creating space for others to recognize their own experiences and to find a community to integrate the impossibility.

That's enough because it's what I chose. What we all choose, each experiencer in our own way. To live with the knowledge and to carry the burden. To find hope in the midst of darkness and trust that it matters somehow, even when we can't see the full plan.

The sword is still there. I feel it sometimes. The weight I'm not carrying. The battles I'm not fighting. The warrior I'm not being in that way, but maybe I'm being a warrior differently. Through words and connections, and refusing to be silent even when it's easier to stay quiet. Through building community even when isolated and maintaining hope even when darkness feels overwhelming.

Is that my service and what I chose when I refused the sword? To fight here, now, in this way, with consciousness rather than steel, truth rather than force? With integration rather than separation?

Maybe that's what all experiencers are doing, each in our own way, fighting battles that don't look like battles. Serving purposes we don't fully understand. Fulfilling roles, we never consciously chose but somehow knew we would.

Welcome to the fellowship of experiencers, the gift, and the burden, to knowing what most people don't, to carrying what most people couldn't, to living in multiple realities simultaneously.

It's isolating, confusing, and overwhelming, but it's also our damn day job, our dutiful calling, our responsibility. Humanity is our client.

The White Lady watches. The Phenomenon continues. The mystery deepens, and yet all of us experiencers, seekers, mystics, all of us bridges between worlds, we carry on. Day by day. Experience by experience. Until the paradigm shifts and the truth can no longer be suppressed. Until humanity awakens to a reality that's been here all along.

Waiting for consciousness to be ready to perceive it. For hearts brave enough to accept it and for minds flexible enough to integrate it.

That time is coming, it's already here, and each one of us is the evidence. We're the proof and the bridge.

But here's something I didn't fully grasp until I had my experience, and I started researching these connections for this book.

## A GLOBAL PHENOMENON - THE WHITE LADY ACROSS CULTURES

I'm not alone. Not even close. The radiant feminine presence I encountered, the one who offered me the sword and asked me to fight for her again in the desert, isn't unique to me. She's appearing globally, across cultures, continents, and even time.

Different names, different contexts, but with the same core encounter, a luminous woman in white, bringing prophetic messages about humanity's future. Here are only a few of those cases.

## FÁTIMA, PORTUGAL – 1917

Three shepherd children, Lúcia, Francisco, and Jacinta, were tending their family's sheep near the village of Fátima when she appeared. They described her as a woman dressed entirely in white, more brilliant than the sun, shedding rays of light clearer and stronger than crystal filled with sparkling water. The Lady appeared to them six times between May and October 1917, always on the thirteenth day of the month. Each time, she delivered messages about prayer, penance, and humanity's future. She also warned of coming wars, the spread of Communism, and called for devotion to prevent a global catastrophe. On October 13, 1917, approximately seventy thousand people gathered at Fátima to witness what the children said would be a final sign. What happened next became known as the Miracle of the Sun. Witnesses reported seeing the sun dance, spin, and plunge toward Earth, casting multicolored lights across the crowd. Even skeptics in attendance, including journalists, documented the event. The Catholic Church officially recognized these apparitions as worthy of belief in 1930. They take time to review the event and have strict criteria for officially recognizing it.[408] In 2017, Pope Francis canonized Francisco and Jacinta Marto as saints. Throughout their lives, the children's testimony never wavered, even under interrogation and imprisonment by authorities who tried to force them to recant. Sound familiar? A radiant woman in white. Prophetic warnings. Messages about humanity's choices. A call to remember something we've forgotten.

One more detail worth noting is that October 13, 1917, was the date of the Miracle of the Sun and the Lady's final appearance at Fátima, and it falls exactly 610 years to the day after Friday, October 13, 1307. That was the date King Philip IV of France ordered the simultaneous arrest of the Knights Templar across his kingdom, beginning their brutal persecution and eventual dissolution.

The Templars, who answered to no authority but the Pope himself, were accused of heresy, tortured into false confessions, and systematically destroyed. Their crime? Philip wanted their wealth, and the charges included worshipping feminine divine principles, the very energies the institutional Church had spent centuries suppressing.

Six centuries and a decade later, on the same date, a radiant woman in white appears to shepherd children, bypasses all ecclesiastical authority, delivers prophetic warnings, and manifests a miracle witnessed by seventy thousand people. The Church eventually validates the apparitions, but only after the people have already received the message directly.

Coincidence? Maybe, however, I don't believe in coincidences.

Could it be that the Divine Feminine operates on timelines we're only beginning to recognize? She appears when she chooses, to whom she chooses, on dates that echo through history. The Templars were crushed for allegedly honoring her. Six hundred ten years later, she returns on the anniversary of their persecution, speaking directly to children, demonstrating that no institution can control when or how she manifests.

I don't know what that synchronicity means, but I notice it, and in a book about patterns, suppression, and the return of feminine consciousness, it feels very significant.

## CHRIS BLEDSOE - NORTH CAROLINA, 2007-PRESENT

Fast forward ninety years to North Carolina. Bledsoe, a deeply religious family man and successful contractor, found himself in crisis. He was suffering from financial collapse from the 2007 recession, as well as a debilitating illness. As he was standing by the Cape Fear River, he cried out to God for help. What happened next changed his life forever. Bledsoe experienced four hours of missing time during which he encountered luminous orbs and non-human entities. When he returned, his illness was cured, but the encounters didn't stop. Five years later, in 2012, she appeared to him, a radiant feminine figure he calls "The Lady." Bledsoe describes her as a glowing, divine presence who radiates benevolence and comfort. She delivers messages about love, humanity's future, and the balance between good and evil forces. She warns of deceptive narratives about alien threats being used to manipulate public perception. The Vatican sent representatives to investigate. Former CIA officer Jim Semivan publicly confirmed Bledsoe's credibility after years of investigation. NASA scientists visited his property. The orbs continue to appear, witnessed by multiple people, documented on video and photographs. Chris Bledsoe's Lady isn't Catholic iconography, but she's the same archetype, radiance, and prophetic messaging. Same call to awakening along with prophecy and much more.[387]

## WHITE BUFFALO CALF WOMAN - LAKOTA TRADITION

Going back even further, centuries, perhaps millennia, is a remarkably similar story of two young Lakota scouts hunting during a time of famine when they saw something approaching across the prairie. A woman dressed in white buckskin, floating above the ground. She identified herself as wakȟáŋ, holy, possessing supernatural powers. One scout approached her with lustful intent and was instantly reduced to bones. The other, who recognized her sacred nature, was told to return to his people and prepare for her arrival. White Buffalo Calf Woman spent four days with the Lakota people. She brought them the Sacred Pipe and taught them the Seven Sacred Rites, ceremonies for maintaining balance with Mother Earth and Wakȟáŋ Tȟáŋka, the Great Spirit. She instructed them that as long as they performed these ceremonies, they would remain caretakers and guardians of sacred land. Before leaving, she promised to return. She told them there would be four ages, and she would look back upon them once each age. At the end of the four ages, she would return. As she walked away, she rolled on the ground four times, transforming from a beautiful woman into a black buffalo, then red, then yellow, and finally white before disappearing into the clouds. After her departure, great herds of buffalo surrounded the camp, and food became plentiful.[409]

Three different cultures, time periods, and contexts, and this is what they share. The reports of a common radiance and the same color. All three figures appear in white or radiant, brilliant light. Fátima's Lady was described as more brilliant than the sun. Bledsoe's Lady is a luminous being of light. White Buffalo Calf Woman wore white buckskin and transformed into a white buffalo. The color isn't incidental because it represents purity, wisdom, and spiritual enlightenment. These beings don't just wear white, they radiate it. They are light made manifest, and also all share a prophetic message with the witnesses. Each appearance centers on humanity's behavior and our collective future. Fátima called for prayer for world peace and warned of coming wars. White Buffalo Calf Woman brought sacred laws for living in balance with creation. Bledsoe's Lady shares messages about a coming shift in human consciousness and warns against deceptive narratives. These aren't random encounters; they're interventions or course corrections with warnings and opportunities. In comparative mythology, these manifestations represent what scholars call the Divine Feminine, a cosmic force of creation, wisdom, and transformation that resurfaces throughout human history in different cultural forms. She's Sophia in Gnostic tradition. Isis in Egyptian mythology. The Queen of Heaven in multiple cultures, even Hathor. The same intelligence wears different masks appropriate to different people and their cultural connotations. If you notice, in each encounter, the feminine presence wields absolute spiritual authority. She isn't subordinate to masculine divine figures; she is the primary messenger. She chooses when to appear and to whom and delivers prophecies and teaches, along with sacred rituals. She demonstrates power that transcends normal reality, bringing about "miracles" and healing. These encounters fundamentally change those who experience them. The Fátima children devoted their lives to her message. Chris Bledsoe's entire existence reoriented around his ongoing contact, and the Lakota people received their most sacred ceremonies and practices. My own life trajectory shifted after refusing the sword. You don't have casual encounters with this presence; you are marked, changed, and then set on a different path.

I didn't initially understand my White Lady encounter in this broader context. I thought it was personal, unique, and specific to my journey. In fact, initially I suspected that the IC was attempting to influence me via (psychotronic) weaponry, and that still might be the case. Psychotronic weapons are devices designed to manipulate human consciousness, behavior, or physiology through electromagnetic, acoustic, or other forms of directed energy, targeting the nervous system and psychological processes of individuals or populations.[410] We can't attribute that to Fatima or The White Buffalo Calf Woman, since the technology didn't exist yet, but for Bledsoe and me, it's still a legitimate possibility. After my encounter, I thought that maybe I was special, chosen, or different. I wasn't. Or rather, we all are. The phenomenon doesn't respect our cultural boundaries or religious categories. The White Lady appears to Portuguese Catholic children, North Carolina Protestant contractors, Native American scouts, and Middle Eastern experiencers with equal authority. She doesn't ask permission from institutional religion or wait for official channels. She shows up, delivers her message, and changes lives. This suggests something profound about the nature of contact. It isn't random, and it follows patterns we're only beginning to recognize. The Divine Feminine is this radiant, powerful, prophetic presence who has been engaging with humanity for as long as we've been recording our experiences. She appears during times of crisis or transition, when individuals and cultures face crucial choices. She brings warnings and wisdom, ceremonies and teachings, challenges, and opportunities. She asks us to remember what we've forgotten and to reconnect with sacred principles. She wants us to understand our role as guardians of creation rather than dominators of nature, and crucially, she appears to ordinary people. Shepherd children. Struggling contractors. Young hunters. Not kings or priests or powerful institutions. Regular humans who are willing or maybe even genetically or physically able to receive the message and are brave enough to share it despite ridicule and persecution. That's the real pattern. The Lady doesn't work through official channels. She bypasses them entirely and shows up directly. Delivering the message to those who will listen and empowering those the system has marginalized. Sound familiar? It should be because that's exactly how UFO contact works, too. It happens to farmers, truck drivers, housewives, and children. It bypasses official disclosure and circumvents government control. It goes straight to the people. The White Lady encounters and UFO experiences might be more connected than we realize. Different aspects of the same phenomenon. Different frequencies of the same intelligence. Using different modalities of the same ongoing contact between human and non-human consciousness. When I refused the sword, when I chose this life over whatever she offered, I thought I was making an individual decision about my personal path. Still, maybe I was participating in something much larger. A pattern that includes those Portuguese children and Chris Bledsoe and countless Lakota medicine people and experiencers around the world, whom we'll never hear about, and we may never. Maybe we're all part of the same story, but just different chapters and verses. It is the same essential narrative of contact between humanity and something vastly more intelligent, more ancient, and powerful than our limited frameworks can comprehend. Maybe the Divine Feminine, the White Lady, however she appears, is one primary interface through which that contact occurs. She is not the only interface, although a significant one. A frequency of the phenomenon that has been consistent across cultures and centuries. That's both humbling and empowering. Humbling because my experience isn't unique or special and empowering because it connects me to a global community of experiencers across time. I'm not alone in this. None of us is. The White Lady is real. She appears globally and brings transformation. The IC is fully aware that she's still active, engaging with humanity, and still delivering messages we desperately need to hear. Are we listening? The IC is for sure. Bledsoe has been inundated with IC since his story became public. Jim Semivan is a strong supporter and now a friend of Bledsoe. As a reminder, he is also a founding member of To The Stars. What does that tell you? It's been said that the IC is very interested in the people who have experienced the White Lady, mainly because she is not talking to them, and they want to know why that is and what she wants. They don't want to know whether she's real; they know she is, or they wouldn't be spending their time and resources investigating the experiencers and The Phenomenon.

Think about that for a moment.

The most powerful intelligence apparatus in human history, with every surveillance tool and technological advantage imaginable, can't make contact with her. Still, she appears to shepherd children, struggling contractors, indigenous scouts, and ordinary people who possess something the intelligence apparatus doesn't have and can't weaponize.

What is it?

What's the frequency she operates on that bypasses all their technology, all their protocols, and all their institutional power? I suspect it is the frequency of love.

# CHAPTER 17

## REUNITED IN REALMS BEYOND

A Mountain of Evidence for Consciousness After Death.

The gatekeepers can harvest your DNA, map your brain, and try to weaponize your consciousness. But there's one thing that they cannot control, suppress, or classify, and that is what happens when consciousness separates from the body entirely.

The evidence for that separation, for survival beyond death, is not hidden in classified files or locked behind security clearances. It's available to anyone willing to look.

When Dr. Jeffrey Long joined me for a conversation about near-death experiences (NDEs), UFOs, and consciousness, we immediately found ourselves exploring the boundaries of reality. Dr. Long's journey began with a simple but profound question: "I wanted to know if NDEs were real by directly asking the NDErs themselves, and the answer is resounding yes as a result of my research." His work, published in medical journals and listed in the National Library of Medicine, has helped establish the credibility of NDEs with scientists and the medical community.

### A UNIVERSAL HUMAN EXPERIENCE

One of the most striking aspects of Dr. Long's research is the consistency of near-death experiences across all boundaries, cultural, religious, and geographical. This is not a Western phenomenon or a Christian fantasy, and it's not a product of cultural conditioning. It is truly universal.

Dr. Long reflected on this universality: "It makes no difference whether you're a Muslim in Egypt or a Hindu in India, a Christian in the United States, or an atheist anywhere, wherever on the planet you have your near-death experience, and whatever your prior belief was, the content of that near-death experience will be strikingly similar. So, they're absolutely not substantially modified by pre-existing beliefs. I mean, it's literally an experience that could unify the world, and it's a common thread of what we experience across all boundaries and beliefs."

Think about what that means in a world fragmented by religion, politics, nationality, and ideology. NDEs present evidence of something that transcends all those divisions. The Muslim, the Hindu, the Christian, the atheist, they all report the same core elements. Out-of-body consciousness. A tunnel of light. Overwhelming love. Deceased relatives. A life review. A boundary they cannot cross, then they return.[411]

This consistency is precisely what makes NDEs scientifically compelling. When you study thousands of cases across all demographics and find the same patterns emerging again and again, that's not cultural conditioning, that's evidence of something real.

Note: You can ask any combat veteran, firefighter, rescue worker, fighter pilot, racing driver, or mountain climber about their unique NDE experiences. Most will say that when they retire, they can think much faster, have far better awareness, and, most importantly, absolutely control their fear.

## THE CHALLENGE OF GOING PUBLIC

Dr. Long shared the challenges of researching NDEs, especially early on: "For about the first eight to ten years that I did my NDE research, if you went to that website, I was Dr. Jeff, that was it, there was no way I could be identified. So, I literally worked anonymously." He understood that in the medical community, publicly advocating for consciousness survival could be career suicide. Better to collect the data quietly, build the evidence, establish the credibility, and only then reveal your identity, but after his book Evidence of the Afterlife was published [385]"All of a sudden, it was on the NBC Today Show, then on Oprah, and then eight days later it became a New York Times bestseller... I had to really come out, and then we had to change the website—well, it's no longer Dr. Jeff, it's now Jeffrey Long MD."

This mirrors the pattern we've seen throughout this book. Researchers investigating consciousness, UFOs, and anomalous phenomena face enormous pressure to stay silent, remain anonymous, and stay within what society deems as acceptable boundaries.

The gatekeepers enforce this silence through ridicule (a very powerful tool), shame, career consequences, and social ostracism, but eventually, when the evidence becomes overwhelming and the public interest undeniable, some researchers choose to step forward publicly.

## LOVE AS THE DOMINANT FORCE

One of the most compelling aspects of NDEs, according to Dr. Long, is the consistent message of love and unity. "Remarkably consistently, people come back from a near-death experience with the understanding that love is the dominant force in the universe. In the afterlife, we're love—who we are, all that we are, everything that we are." He added, "That Oneness, that connection and unity of everything, took me a long time with near death experiences to go, 'Well, I don't see that in my earthly life, I don't understand that, and that doesn't make any sense.' but it was only after I saw that a few—geez, we're probably up to hundreds, probably over a thousand near death experiences saying that—so again, it's real scientifically, and it's consistently observed."

This observation is crucial. Dr. Long, trained as a physician and radiation oncologist, approached NDEs with scientific skepticism. He didn't want to believe; he wanted to know, and what thousands of cases told him, over and over, was that consciousness experiences itself as fundamentally connected, unified, and rooted in love.

In our earthly experience, we feel separate. We experience conflict, division, and fear, building walls between nations, religions, and individuals, but near-death experiencers consistently report that this separation is an illusion.

At the deepest level, he and I believe that all our consciousnesses are one.

If this is true, and the evidence suggests it is, then what are we to make of the DNA harvesting, the consciousness weaponization, the control systems we've explored in previous chapters? Perhaps they represent attempts to manipulate a reality that is fundamentally beyond manipulation. Both involve consciousness operating outside normal parameters, communication that bypasses language.

Or can reality truly be manipulated? If we consider the perspectives shared by various sources within the Secret Space Program (SSP) narrative and others, we're forced to ask uncomfortable questions. Could the soul itself, understood as a unique quantum field energy matrix, be harvested, contained, or even reused in advanced cyborgs or clones through what some call fifth-density spiritual science? Are our souls commodities to be traded? When Vatican missionaries swept through pagan regions like the UK and South America between the 1200s and 1600s, were they genuinely spreading faith or harvesting souls and creating new forms of servitude? Does the advent of technologies like the Musk Neuralink chip offer a clue to this deeper reality?

Can we truly know what the ultimate truth is? Given the increasingly public testimonies regarding the use and misuse of super-advanced off-world technology in Unacknowledged Special Access Programs (USAPs) as referenced even in congressional hearings, we should question the boundaries of what is possible rather than accept firm assertions.[412] [413]

If cloning is now a reality, why not consider the possibility of "soul transfer"? Could emotions like love be resources that off-world or human engineers attempt to manipulate? What about hate, envy, greed, or lust for power? Is it possible that anything and anyone can be re-engineered or manipulated, including our deepest feelings?

Consider this: "If someone says, 'I'm your older sister, I love you, so do as I say, now, or I'll tell Dad, and he'll whip you!'— does love itself become a tool for manipulation in our everyday lives?" Where do we draw the line between genuine emotion and the use of emotion as leverage? Much of this issue is very dark and sinister. A 50-50 light/dark balance is needed.

## UFOS AND NON-PHYSICAL CONSCIOUSNESS

We explored the intersection of UFOs and consciousness. Dr. Long observed, "Near death experiences are exclusively via consciousness interacting with a non-physical phenomenon...

That's exactly why there's that overlap with UFOs, which so often are described as an interaction with non-physical communication or at least communication that's radically different from our usual earthly everyday communication."

This connection between NDEs and UFO experiences keeps surfacing. The parallels run deep. Consciousness operating outside normal parameters, communication that bypasses language, experiencers profoundly changed and are dismissed by mainstream authorities, yet carry an overwhelming subjective reality for those who experience them.

I reflected on my own experiences, sharing, "My Dad, when he was younger, saw a UFO with multiple people and completely believed. Then I saw another one again. So, my entire life, I grew up thinking it's real, there's no reason to doubt my father, he's not going to lie to me that these UFOs are genuine. I've had my own experiences with multiple people and by myself, and it's like, well, as you said, once you have that experience, there's no going back. Same thing with near-death experience, from everything that I've read from you and all your research, it profoundly changes your life, and those two things are completely connected with The Phenomenon and consciousness."

Dr. Long added, "Now that we know unequivocally from near-death experiences that there's consciousness existing apart from the body—often that early element called an out-of-body experience—unequivocally, right? That is a real consciousness that we all have, that is a part of our physical self that can separate when we're in a life-threatening crisis."

This statement deserves emphasis. We know unequivocally that consciousness can exist apart from the body. This is not speculation or wishful thinking but documented across thousands of cases where people accurately report events they witnessed while clinically dead, brains showing no activity, hearts stopped. They saw things, heard conversations, and moved through physical space, all while their bodies lay unconscious.

If consciousness can separate from the body during a crisis, what does that tell us about the nature of consciousness itself? What does it mean for the DNA-consciousness connection explored in the previous chapter? Perhaps DNA serves as an antenna or interface for consciousness in physical reality, but consciousness itself exists independently.

## THE BIGELOW CONNECTION: FOLLOWING THE MONEY

Throughout this book, we've seen one name appear again and again: Robert Bigelow. The billionaire funded UFO investigations, Skinwalker Ranch research, paid for DNA collection from experiencers, brain scans, and consciousness studies. In Chapter 13, we noted that Bigelow's money flows to researchers such as Garry Nolan, Kit Green, and Colm Kelleher, who collect biological samples from people who report high-strangeness encounters.

Bigelow didn't stop with UFOs and DNA. He also funded the largest prize in history for scientific evidence of consciousness survival. Dr. Long described his experience with the Bigelow Institute for Consciousness Studies contest, "In 2021, a billionaire by the name of Bigelow put a huge amount of prize money into a contest for the best scientific evidence of survival of consciousness... I just submitted my essay—25,000 words too, I mean, geez, that's about half a book... One day, I'm sitting here going through my email, hum dum dum, and I see in the subject line, 'You won $50,000.' So, like everybody else, when you see a subject line like that, you take the mouse right, and I started bringing it over to delete, and then I said, 'Wait a minute,' and I just started reading the first few words. I went, 'Wait, what?' and I didn't believe it. So, thank God—how would you like to delete a $50,000 prize?"

Why would controversial Bigelow, a man obsessed with UFOs and alien technology, pour millions into consciousness-survival research? Because he understands what the intelligence community understands, consciousness is the key to everything. If consciousness survives death, can separate from the body and interact with non-physical realities, then controlling it, enhancing it, and weaponizing it becomes the ultimate strategic priority. The same network collecting experiencer DNA (Chapter 13) is also funding consciousness-survival research. They're studying both ends, how consciousness interfaces with biology while embodied, and where consciousness goes when separated from biology. This is not a coincidence but a systematic investigation of consciousness as a phenomenon that transcends mere biology.

## SEEING THE FUTURE: FREE WILL AND PREDETERMINED EVENTS

We also touched on the role of free will and the idea that the future is not fixed. Dr. Long explained, "I've analyzed 834 near-death experiences when I asked directly, 'Did you become aware of future events?'... Around 20% of people said yes... The exception to that is fairly consistent. In near-death experiences, during their NDE, they become aware of future children... when they get that information, they later find that's exactly what happens, they have exactly that number of children, exactly that many males and females."

This raises fascinating questions about the nature of time and consciousness. If consciousness can perceive future events during an NDE, and if those events later unfold exactly as perceived, what does that tell us about the relationship between consciousness and time? Is the future already determined? Or does consciousness, when freed from the constraints of the physical brain, operate in a realm where past, present, and future exist simultaneously?

Remember the quantum physics concepts from earlier chapters, the idea that observation collapses probability into reality, and that consciousness may play an active role in manifesting physical outcomes. NDEs suggest that consciousness, when not bound by a physical body, may perceive time itself differently, not as a linear sequence of past-present-future, as something more like a spherical landscape that can be viewed from above.

## ENCOUNTERS WITH NON-HUMAN ENTITIES.

Our conversation included stories of encounters with non-human entities. Dr. Long said, "There are basically two different ways to go after that question. One: beings encountered in that earthly, if you will, heavenly realm—these are almost always very kind, benevolent beings, extremely wise, loving, they feel an overwhelming sense of love and compassion from those other conscious entities in the afterlife realm... In the afterlife realm, it seems to be that type of positivity."

He continued, "We have exactly two people who had very detailed encounters with what—non-earthly alien physical life—and I'm fascinated by one of them, Sandy T., who was talking with me at that conference. She talked about the first place she visited, a world entirely water... She encountered intelligent life interacting there, encountered other life—again, none of these beings that she encountered anywhere near anthropomorphic."

This detail is extraordinary. During her near-death experience, Sandy T. visited what she described as another world, not the typical "heavenly realm" with deceased relatives, but an alien environment with non-human intelligent life. An ocean world with beings that were not humanoid in any way. She experienced this not as a dream or hallucination. It was with the vivid, hyper-real clarity that characterizes NDEs.

What are we to make of this? An astral projection perchance? If consciousness can travel to other physical or non-physical realms during an NDE and encounter extraterrestrial forms of intelligence, then perhaps UFO experiencers who report being taken aboard craft or visiting other worlds are describing real events, just accessed through consciousness rather than physical transportation. Perhaps the "abduction" experience and the "near-death" experience are two sides of the same phenomenon, consciousness operating beyond the physical body, interacting with realities we don't yet understand.

## THE CENTRAL MESSAGE: YOU WILL SURVIVE.

At the very heart of our discussion, Dr. Long offered what I believe is the centerpiece of his research and a messaging statement that encapsulates the hope and wonder at the core of these experiences:

---

**"EVERY SINGLE PERSON IS GOING TO HAVE THEIR CONSCIOUSNESS SURVIVE THEIR BODILY DEATH, WILL BE REUNITED WITH THEIR DECEASED LOVED ONES, AND BE IN A REALM THAT IS WAY, WAY BETTER IN EVERY WAY THAN OUR PHYSICAL EARTHLY LIFE. SO THAT'S KIND OF EXCITING TO BE AWARE OF THAT BASED ON A MOUNTAIN OF EVIDENCE."**

---

Read that again. Every single person, not just the religious or the spiritually advanced or those with the right DNA markers or the right brain scans. <u>Everyone.</u>

You will survive. Your consciousness will continue. You will reunite with those you love, and the realm you enter will exceed anything you've experienced in physical life.

This is the message the gatekeepers cannot suppress (from now on, in my opinion). They can classify documents, ridicule researchers, harvest DNA, and build consciousness-weaponizing technologies. However, they cannot prevent what happens to each of us when we die, cannot stop the continuation of consciousness, and can't keep us from returning to the realm of love and unity that is our true home. (Well, that's my hope anyway).

This conversation was a journey through personal stories, scientific research, and philosophical reflection. It's clear that NDEs and UFO encounters are more than just anomalies; they are windows into the deeper mysteries of consciousness, love, and the universe itself.

So, let's connect all the dots. We've explored how technology is controlled and released through charismatic front people

(Chapter 11). We've seen how DNA is collected from experiencers to weaponize or enhance consciousness abilities potentially (Chapter 13). We've learned that consciousness itself can operate independently of the body, that it survives death, that it's fundamentally rooted in love and unity rather than separation and fear.

What does this mean? Essentially, the systems of control we've been discussing are all attempts to influence forces that ultimately lie beyond their reach. Furthermore, if those in power truly had the wisdom or technology to control these elements, the evidence suggests they do not do it effectively. While these entities may attempt to control consciousness, a phenomenon that is, by its nature, infinite, they find themselves facing an impossible task. They're also trying to weaponize love, but, by definition, love resists such manipulation. Moreover, attempts to keep secrets about our true nature are ultimately futile, as the experience of death itself unveils the reality of who we are to each person in time.

This suggests that the greatest secret may be that we are not truly fighting for our consciousness, our souls, or even for disclosure of hidden truths; these things are inherently ours. No amount of gatekeeping can prevent you from discovering your essential nature at the moment of death. Similarly, no degree of DNA collection can strip away your intrinsic identity, and secrecy cannot forever hide the fundamental truth that consciousness is primary, love is real, and we are all deeply interconnected.

According to thousands of carefully documented cases analyzed by scientists like Dr. Jeffrey Long, many individuals who have experienced near-death experiences consistently report profound encounters with unconditional love, a sense of unity, and the continuation of consciousness beyond physical death. These cases, collected and studied over the years, provide compelling evidence that consciousness is not confined to the body and that love and connection are universal truths, not merely subjective feelings. This body of scientific analysis strengthens the argument that our true nature and connectedness are not only philosophically meaningful but also observable phenomena.

# CHAPTER 18

## THE HEART OF CONTACT

After covering technology, suppression, deception, and genetic programs, it's important to address a core issue: love. Not sentimentality or romance, but the deeper connection experiencers describe as central to contact, more impactful than technology or entities.

This is what truly changes people with a sense of being known and accepted. Love is often overlooked amid the focus on technology or secrecy, yet it is undeniable and shapes how they see the world. This chapter goes in a bit of a different direction than what we have been discussing, but I feel it is vitally important.

### THE MASCULINE AND FEMININE BALANCE

Duann Kier channels "The Consortium," a loose group of beings from other star systems and dimensions who assist humanity's awakening. She didn't choose this, a Christian fundamentalist with a theology degree who had to leave organized religion because her psychic gifts wouldn't stop manifesting.

The Consortium's primary message is that you're awakening to your divinity while still in physical form. Bringing heaven to earth. "As above, so below," not a metaphor, a literal description of consciousness evolution happening now.

The messages are about the return of the Divine Feminine, but she's clear, this isn't about women versus men. It's about integrating qualities that got separated, suppressed, and imbalanced across millennia of patriarchal control.

Divine Feminine is receptivity, intuition, nurturing, and emotional intelligence. It's cyclical rather than linear, being rather than doing, trusting the process rather than controlling the outcomes, direct knowing through feeling rather than intellectual analysis. Believing is seeing, not the other way round. These qualities are labeled weak, inferior, and untrustworthy. Particularly when they manifested in women, but also when they appeared in men. "Real men" don't cry. Don't show vulnerability. Don't trust intuition or prioritize emotional connection. That's the invisible wound generations of humans taught to suppress half of what makes us whole.

Divine Masculine isn't toxic masculinity. Its strength in service and protection of the vulnerable, directed will toward worthy goals, courage in the face of danger, and action aligned with wisdom. Warrior consciousness that fights for rather than against. Balanced masculine is intentional, clear, decisive, and protective, strong enough to be gentle, powerful enough to surrender, and confident enough to be vulnerable. But what happens when masculine operates without the feminine balance? You get domination. Control. Hierarchy. Violence. Power over, rather than power with others. The systems we've explored throughout this book, suppression, classification, gatekeeping, and control, could all be manifestations of unbalanced masculine energy. If you look at some ancient Egyptian predynastic statues, the queen and king are arm in arm, equal.

When the feminine operates without the masculine balance, it creates a lack of boundaries. Enabling dysfunction, passive victimhood, and the inability to protect oneself or others. Receptivity without discernment.

We need both, integrated and operating together. In individuals, regardless of biological sex, in relationships, in communities, and in modern civilization.

Contact experiences often catalyze this integration. Something about encountering non-human intelligence, consciousness expansion, and recognizing a larger reality is that it breaks down rigid gender programming. It helps men access emotional depth, intuition, and vulnerability, and helps women claim power, voice, and agency, moving everyone toward becoming more whole.

The Divine Feminine returns not to replace the masculine but to dance with it, and their union births a new humanity. Conscious. Balanced. Integrated. Capable of handling what's coming.

The Divine Feminine isn't just returning as an abstract principle or channeled teaching. She's been appearing directly, physically, globally, delivering the same message across cultures and centuries.

From my research, here's what I believe is the most important ability, the one the White Lady recognizes and the intelligence community fundamentally lacks: empathy.

Not sympathy, feeling sorry for someone, nor compassion, recognizing someone's suffering and wanting to help. Empathy, feeling what they feel, experiencing their interior state directly, understanding from the inside rather than outside.

This isn't a weakness, I believe it's a superpower.

Because empathy makes manipulation impossible, you can't deceive someone who feels your actual intentions or maintain lies to someone who perceives your emotional truth directly. Nor can you control populations that empathically sense when narratives are false.

That's why it's been systematically suppressed. Why "sensitive" became an insult and "emotional" meant unreliable. It's why generations of humans, particularly men, were taught that feeling deeply made you weak, vulnerable, and unsuited for power or leadership.

Empathy represents a genuine form of power, rooted in connection rather than control, and resistant to corruption.

Experiencers often develop heightened empathy post-contact. Some report that it is overwhelming initially. Like feeling others' pain, joy, their confusion, or fear. All of it hits at once without filters, but with practice, grounding, and learning boundaries, empathy becomes a tool for understanding, healing, connecting, serving, and more.

You feel when someone needs help before they ask, or you sense when someone's lying before they reveal the truth. You know when to push and when to support. You can navigate relationships with a precision that is impossible through intellectual analysis alone.

That's not a gift for everyone, not even initially for those who have it; it's a burden or a curse. But if it is developed, refined, and wielded consciously? It's how you change the world. One connection at a time. One real moment of being truly seen and truly seeing. A bridge between hearts where division existed before.

The Phenomenon operates empathically. That's why contact feels so intimate. Why do experiencers report feeling as if they know them completely, and that communication happens mind-to-mind, heart-to-heart, beyond words? They're empathic naturally. We're potentially empathic, and contact accelerates that potential into actuality for humans.

As more humans develop empathy (as the return of the Divine Feminine makes this capacity valued rather than ridiculed), disclosure becomes easier.

Because empathic humanity can handle truth, can feel into complexity without needing simple answers, and can hold paradox. Allowing us to connect with non-human intelligence without fear dissolving into hostility.

Empathy is disclosure. Real disclosure. Not information transfer, simply connection. Recognition. Feeling into the truth of what's happening and responding from wholeness rather than fear.

## LOVE IN PRACTICE

This all sounds beautiful theoretically, but how do you live it? How do you embody love and empathy in a world that often rewards neither?

It begins with yourself, because you can't give what you don't have or love others if you hate yourself, making self-compassion not selfish but a prerequisite. Treat yourself with the same kindness you'd show a dear friend, forgiving your mistakes, honoring your journey, and accepting your imperfections as part of the path rather than obstacles to overcome. From that foundation of self-acceptance, you can feel fully, without suppression or spiritual bypassing, recognizing that grief, anger, fear, and joy are all valid, all provide information, and all are part of being human. When you feel them fully and let them move through you rather than getting stuck, emotions become wisdom instead of problems. Express that authenticity openly by telling people you love them without waiting or assuming they know, saying it, meaning it, making it specific because "I love you more than the stars in the sky, never forget that" means infinitely more than generic "love you," and that vulnerability creates connection while connections heal isolation. Listen deeply to others, truly listen, because most people aren't really heard when we're just waiting for our turn to talk or planning responses while they speak, so give the rare gift of real listening by setting aside your agenda and feeling into what they're actually communicating through words and the feelings underneath, witnessing them fully in what becomes love in action. Serve without agenda by helping because it feels right, not because you'll get something back; hold space for others' growth without needing credit; support causes that matter even when invisible; and embody service as love by responding to need rather than seeking validation.

At the same time, maintain boundaries fiercely because love doesn't mean letting people harm you, accepting dysfunction, or sacrificing yourself on the altar of others' needs and understanding that boundaries are love too, protecting your capacity to serve sustainably by saying no when yes would deplete you, and removing yourself from toxic situations, since healthy boundaries enable healthy love. Try to see the divine in everyone, including people who hurt you and systems that oppress you, not to accept harm but to recognize that underneath everyone is consciousness exploring itself, everyone is struggling and deserves compassion even when requiring consequences, knowing that seeing divinity doesn't erase accountability but adds essential context.

Choose love over fear repeatedly, daily, moment by moment, recognizing that fear will offer a sense of apparent safety. In contrast, love requires courage, choosing love anyway, not recklessly but wisely and consistently, moving toward connection rather than isolation, openness rather than defensiveness, trust rather than suspicion.

Forgive yourself first and then others, not because they deserve it but because you deserve freedom from carrying resentment, understanding that forgiveness isn't forgetting or excusing or necessarily reconciling but releasing, letting go, freeing energy bound up in anger so it can flow toward creativity, toward joy, toward whatever comes next in your evolution. Celebrating without waiting until problems are solved or goals achieved or conditions are perfect, celebrating now the small moments, the ordinary beauty, your existence, others' existence, life itself, because it's weird and sometimes difficult, but ultimately a magnificent experiment in consciousness having experiences worth celebrating simply for happening at all.

Connect with people, animals, nature, with art, music, whatever makes you feel part of something larger, because if isolation is death, then connection is life, so choose connection even when it's scary or awkward, even when messy, especially then when it matters most.

This isn't naive or ignoring darkness, but practicing light even while acknowledging it. Both exist and are real, but both matter, and you get to choose which you feed. Which you amplify and embody.

I feel as if we should choose love over and over again until it becomes the default. It becomes who you are, and after that, you can't imagine choosing anything else.

This is the work and path that leads to growth and transforms the world through love. Like everything else, it will take patience and practice, and the results will be worth the struggle.

## THE WHITE LADY'S GIFT

I once chose family over a cosmic obligational decision, and that still leaves me with questions. What stood out most was the unconditional acceptance I received, no punishment or disappointment, just my choice being honored without judgment.

True love means respecting someone's free will, even when it doesn't align with our preferences. It's not about getting what you want but supporting others in their own choices, regardless of personal beliefs or desires.

This depth of acceptance, offered even by "The Phenomenon," honors our sovereignty and validates our paths. Experiencing such love inspires us to treat others with the same respect, encouraging transformation. Ultimately, disclosure isn't just about understanding UFOs; it's about recognizing the unconditional love at the foundation of everything we're now remembering.

We've covered so much in this book. Hidden histories and suppressed technologies. Consciousness abilities and genetic programs. Deceptions and hope. Control systems and awakening, but underneath it all is Love. The force that drives disclosure. The experience that changes experiencers permanently.

You are loved. Completely. Unconditionally. By intelligence vast beyond comprehension, and that love is inviting you to remember your own nature, capacity, and connection to everything.

Not because you're special but because you exist. In my opinion, existence itself is love manifesting. You are love exploring itself. All of this whole strange journey through UFOs and consciousness and awakening, it's love recognizing itself. Playing, growing, and ever evolving.

Trust that. Even when evidence seems lacking, and the world feels dark, even when isolation feels crushing. Trust that underneath everything is love. Supporting you and guiding you. It's waiting patiently for you to remember what you've always been.

Then live from that remembrance. Embody it, share it, and let it guide choices, inform relationships, and shape how you move through this world.

Because that's the real work, not the government admitting UFOs exist, but you remembering love exists. Choosing to be that love in action, but consistently, courageously, and most of all authentically.

The heart knows. You need to trust it, follow it, and let it lead you home.

# CHAPTER 19

## LIVING AWAKE

It's a heavy journey, with some dark truths and uncomfortable realities. Systems of control and suppression operate across every level of human society, possibly across time itself.

So now what?

How do you live with this knowledge and function in a world that denies what you now know? Then attempt to integrate impossible truths into your life while staying sane, grounded, and effective?

How do you stay awake without being overwhelmed?

Better yet, how can you sleep at night? No more evidence or theory, just practical wisdom for living awake in a sleeping world and maintaining hope in the face of darkness, and taking action when systems seem immovable.

### INTEGRATION IS ONGOING

There are two main truths, for lack of a better term, that I find helpful to illuminate for you here. The first truth about living awake is that it's not a destination. It's a process. You don't "figure it out" and then relax into knowing. You keep discovering, adjusting, and integrating new information that challenges previous understanding.

I'm still integrating my various experiences years later and don't fully understand what happened or what they meant. Still processing how those encounters changed me, marked me, set me on the path I'm walking now.

You'll be the same with your experiences, research, and your awakening. This doesn't end because it just evolves, deepens, and complexifies. Each answer generates new questions, and each breakthrough reveals new mysteries.

That's not failure; it's how consciousness expansion works. You don't arrive at the final truth, only spiral upward through successive approximations, each level revealing more than the previous while maintaining humility about what is still unknown.

Living awake means embracing that uncertainty, holding paradox, and keeping functioning in society despite not having a complete picture. You must continue making decisions with partial information and acting from the best understanding while staying open to being wrong.

That's uncomfortable because humans want certainty, clear answers, and to know we're right, we've figured it all out.

Certainty isn't possible with this material. The Phenomenon appears to demand ongoing uncertainty. It consistently shows us that our knowledge is incomplete. The only way to lessen that anxiety is to accept the uncertainty. You stop seeking closure and start appreciating the process of exploration.

Peace comes not from knowing everything. It comes from accepting you never will.

## BALANCE IS ESSENTIAL

The second truth is you can't live entirely in the "woo" of The Phenomenon. While some researchers focus on "nuts and bolts" (physical craft and radar data), "woo" covers the parts that don't fit into standard science. You can't spend all your time researching UFOs, practicing CE5/HIC, discussing consciousness, and exploring phenomena. You'll lose grounding and effectiveness, and possibly the connection to people who haven't had these experiences. That is why balance is needed.

Start with physical health through exercise, nutrition, sleep, and basic maintenance, because consciousness exploration is no excuse for neglecting the body, and you need to ground yourself in physical reality even as you explore non-physical dimensions. Maintain relationships with people who don't know or care about UFOs, hidden history, or The Phenomenon. Those who keep you human, normal, and anchored, who remind you that most people's concerns, like family, work, and daily life, matter even if they seem trivial from an awakened perspective. Hold down a job, contribute economically, and maintain stability, because financial independence is freedom. At the same time, poverty is a trap, and you shouldn't sacrifice material security for spiritual exploration when you can do it all. Practice normalcy by watching stupid movies, engaging in mundane activities, letting your mind rest from heavy material, and understanding you're not abandoning truth by taking breaks from it. Cultivate humor by laughing, especially at the sheer absurdity of our situation, where consciousness awakening meets discussions of star beings harvesting DNA and ancient Atlantean mystery schools, embracing the bizarre rather than taking yourself too seriously, because I certainly don't. Engage in service by helping others, not just other experiencers but regular people with regular problems. Do some volunteering, practice kindness, and make the world slightly better in immediate, tangible ways that counteract the tendency toward isolation and grandiosity that consciousness work can foster.

Balance doesn't mean compromising truth. It means integrating truth into functional life and being awake while staying sane. Knowing things most people don't, while staying connected to people who don't want to know.

That's the art and the skill. That's what separates genuine integration from getting lost in "woo-woo."

## COMMUNITY MATTERS

You're not alone. That's crucial. It feels like it sometimes, especially when first awakening, when nobody around you understands, when you can't share experiences without being dismissed or ridiculed, but you're not alone. There are millions of experiencers globally. Thousands of researchers. Hundreds of serious investigators. A growing network of people who know, who've experienced, who refuse to accept official narratives.

Seek out others, make connections, and build relationships, not just online (though online searching is useful), but also in person when you can. Look for CE5 or HIC groups, smaller gatherings, conferences, or any place where like-minded people come together.

Community provides validation through awakened others who've had similar experiences, understand without needing extensive explanation, and believe you because they've been there themselves. It offers support when integration is hard, when experiences are overwhelming, when isolation feels crushing, because community holds you, reminds you you're not crazy, helps you process what seems impossible to process alone. Community builds collective knowledge that exceeds individual understanding, where what you've learned complements others' knowledge, so that together you build a more complete picture than anyone could construct in isolation. It sharpens discernment through multiple perspectives that prevent getting locked into single interpretations, challenging your assumptions, testing your theories, and keeping you intellectually honest when it's easiest to drift into comfortable certainty. Community enables action because change requires collective effort, and while individual awakening matters deeply, structural transformation needs movements, networks, coordinated action that isolated individuals cannot achieve. And perhaps most importantly, community creates joy through finding your people, sharing experiences, laughing about absurdity together, which is a gift you shouldn't underestimate on this journey with others who genuinely get it.

Be selective. Not every community is healthy. Some become cults. Some reinforce delusions. Some are infiltrated by grifters, by intelligence operatives, by people with agendas not aligned with truth.

Discernment in choosing community matters as much as individual discernment. Look for: Intellectual humility (admitting uncertainty), Ethical grounding (service over ego), Critical thinking (questioning everything, including themselves), Emotional health (not desperate, not grandiose, not paranoid), Practical results (actual lives being lived, not just theory.

Find those communities. Build them if they don't exist. You'll need them. We all do.

Living awake isn't passive. It isn't just knowing things. It requires action. Appropriate action given your circumstances, abilities, resources, but action nonetheless!

Knowing demands a response, and once you understand the suppression, you can't unknow it. You recognize control systems and can't pretend they don't exist, and after you've experienced contact, you can't go back to consensus reality.

Support other experiencers by believing them when they come forward, or at least not dismissing them, offering resources, sharing what you've learned, helping them feel less alone in what becomes genuine service that genuinely matters. Develop whatever abilities you have, whether intuition, healing, manifestation, or enhanced perception, through dedicated practice, not to impress people but to become a more effective human, since consciousness evolution serves everyone when wielded ethically. Politely and factually question official narratives when evidence contradicts them, encouraging critical thinking without alienating others. Vote with your attention by supporting researchers doing real work, ignoring grifters monetizing The Phenomenon, amplifying voices demonstrating integrity while marginalizing those spreading disinformation, because your attention is currency and you should spend it wisely. Create through art, writing, music, film, or however you express yourself, sharing perspectives through creative work that reaches people logical arguments can't reach, since consciousness awakening happens through multiple channels, and you should use yours. Protect yourself by not sacrificing your career, family, or stability for disclosure activism because martyrdom serves nobody. Be strategic and choose your battles, operating within your capacity to sustain. Stay ethical by not exploiting this knowledge, not manipulating people, not starting cults, not claiming authority you don't have, because power corrupts and consciousness power especially corrupts, making humility and service orientation essential when there's already too much corruption out there. Most of all, keep living by not letting awakening consume everything in your life, because you're still human with a body, needs, relationships, and responsibilities that deserve honoring since awakening enhances life rather than replacing it.

These actions look different to everyone. Kevin Fuller is practicing Martinism quietly. Patricia making her film. Warner investigating from his insider position. Friends online researching and sharing. I am writing this book.

Whatever your action is, do it. Don't wait for permission, until you know everything, or until the conditions are perfect. Start now, with what you have. Where you are now.

Because action is how paradigms shift. Not through dramatic revelations or official announcements. Through countless individuals taking small steps. Sharing experiences. Building communities. Refusing to pretend they don't know.

That's disclosure. Real disclosure. From the ground up. Person by person. Action by action.

I won't lie, this material is heavy-duty stuff. Control systems are real, suppression is systematic, and deception is pervasive, while power structures violently resist change. Progress is slow, and suffering continues, good for the soul, I reckon.

Some days feel hopeless, like nothing changes. The gatekeepers are too powerful, secrets too deep, momentum too strong toward continued suppression and control.

I feel that pain. Often. Especially after researching Nazi occultism, elite networks, or DNA harvesting programs. The darkness can be overwhelming, but here's what keeps me going.

Truth has momentum, and once knowledge escapes, it spreads. The Internet changed the whole game, making it impossible to control information access as it had been previously. Every disclosure and testimony, every leaked document, builds pressure until the dam breaks. Consciousness is evolving, not as a belief but as an observable fact. More people are awakening, experiencing contact, developing abilities, and questioning narratives, and collective consciousness is rising despite suppression efforts. The younger generation is different, in my opinion. Gatekeepers are losing ground with every whistleblower, leaked document, and congressional hearing, playing defense now and controlling damage rather than maintaining secrecy. Even slow, managed progress is still progress. The Phenomenon continues relentlessly, not waiting for disclosure, appearing, and contacting people, pushing toward revelation whether the gatekeepers approve or not. We're not alone in this fight because we have each other, with communities growing, networks strengthening, and collective wisdom accumulating into something that feels less like scattered individuals and more like a movement.

This is evolution, not just social change; it is species evolution. Consciousness expansion is happening biologically, culturally, and spiritually right in front of us. We're part of humanity, becoming something more. That's bigger than disclosure. That's transformation.

It's already happening. Look around. Fifteen years ago, few were discussing UFOs seriously. Now we have Congressional hearings, Pentagon acknowledgment, mainstream media coverage. Ten years from now? I can't imagine how much further we'll be.

So yes, darkness is real. So is awakening and hope. Suppression is real. Control is real. Progress often hides behind discomfort, and every major leap forward starts with a moment that feels unsettling.

Not naive hope or ignoring problems. Grounded hope based on observable trends toward transparency, toward consciousness evolution, toward humanity remembering what it forgot.

That hope sustains me. It should sustain us collectively as we navigate the transition from the old to the new paradigm.

You've reached the end of this book, but not the end of the journey. The journey continues, for you, me, and for all of us, awakening to reality stranger and more magnificent than we were taught.

I don't have any answers. Never claimed to. I have experiences, research, connections, insights, and massive uncertainty about what it all means, but I know this: You're not crazy. Your experiences are real. Your knowing is valid, and your intuition is trustworthy. Your DNA marks you for involvement in something older and larger than you realize.

You're waking up. That's uncomfortable and disorienting. That's also exactly what's needed. Individual by individual. Experience by experience. Awakening is spreading through human consciousness like dawn spreading across the planet.

You're part of that dawn. Not special, but you're one among millions, and essential. Because the paradigm shifts when enough people refuse to stay asleep. When enough people trust their experiences over the authority's lies and reclaim the power they were told they don't have.

That's you. Whether you feel ready or not.

You are the disclosure. Your experience, knowing, and refusal to pretend, along with the willingness to live awake despite the cost, make you special.

So, here's my invitation: keep going. Keep questioning, experiencing, developing, sharing, and building community. Above all, keep supporting discernment and holding hope despite the darkness. Live awake and stay grounded, take action, support others, and above everything else, trust yourself. I still don't know what the White Lady was. I still don't know what the sword meant or what I gave up by refusing it. That question has followed me through every chapter of this book, through every conversation on the podcast, through every rabbit hole I've crawled into at two in the morning when I should have been sleeping. I have a feeling the answer won't fit on the pages I have left. That story isn't finished. Neither is mine.

If you want to keep going with me, find me on UFOs on the Level. That's where the conversation continues, where the research goes deeper, and where the next pieces of this are taking shape. The community that's forming around this work is the realest thing I've built, and there's room for you in it.

What comes next will go further than this book did. I can promise you that much.

For now, though, this is where I leave you.

Live awake. That's enough. That's everything.

That's disclosure.

So Mote It Be.

# GLOSSARY

**160th SOAR (Special Operations Aviation Regiment)-**U.S. Army elite helicopter unit nicknamed "Night Stalkers"; operates classified stealth aircraft, including the MH-X stealth Black Hawk used in Operation Neptune Spear; trains at classified locations, including Area 51 and China Lake Naval Weapons Station.

**AATIP-**Advanced Aerospace Threat Identification Program; a DoD-linked effort often referenced in modern UAP reporting.

**AAWSAP-**Advanced Aerospace Weapon System Applications Program; a U.S. DoD-funded initiative associated with anomalous studies.

**Altered State / Altered State of Consciousness-**Non-ordinary awareness states (trance, meditation, hypnagogic) linked to anomalous perception and contact.

**Air America-**CIA proprietary airline and front company (1959-1976); conducted covert operations throughout Southeast Asia during the Vietnam War; operated the Quiet One stealth helicopters for classified missions into North Vietnam; beholden to CIA, State Department, and Pentagon.

**Angels-**Non-physical intelligences conceptualized as benevolent messengers in esoteric traditions.

**Archons-**Metaphysical rulers of the material world in Gnostic tradition, associated with cosmic authority, control, and the obstruction of spiritual knowledge.

**AQM-34 Firebee-**Ryan Aeronautical target drone (1951-) converted to reconnaissance platform; basis for Model 147 Lightning Bug series; flew over 3,435 combat missions during Vietnam War; small size and fiberglass construction gave minimal radar cross-section; first large-scale operational UAV deployment in military history.

**ARPANET-**Early DoD-funded computer network, precursor to the Internet.

**Block Universe-**A four-dimensional spacetime model where past, present, and future co-exist as a unified structure.

**CE4-**Close Encounters of the Fourth Kind. In the Hynek/MUFON classification system, CE4 designates encounters resulting in "permanent psychological injuries or death." Distinguished from CE1-CE3 (sighting, physical evidence, contact) and CE5 (human-initiated contact).

**CE5 / HIC-**Close Encounters of the Fifth Kind; human-initiated contact protocols.

**CFR-**Council on Foreign Relations; influential U.S. foreign policy think tank.

**Channeling-Communication** with non-physical entities or intelligence

**CIA**-Central Intelligence Agency (U.S.).

**Consciousness**-Subjective awareness and functional interface for anomalous interaction. The state of being awake, aware of one's surroundings, and capable of subjective experience, including feelings, thoughts, and sensations.

**DARPA / ARPA**-Defense Advanced Research Projects Agency; key in tech suppression and pipeline.

**DC-130 Hercules**-Modified C-130 cargo aircraft serving as "mother ship" for drone launches; carried up to four BQM-34 Firebee target drones or two Ryan Model 147 reconnaissance drones under wings; included launch control officers and airborne technicians; critical component of Vietnam War UAV operations.

**Demons**-Historically, viewed as chaotic or malevolent non-physical intelligences; sometimes reframed as NHIs.

**DIA**-Defense Intelligence Agency

**DIRD-Defense Intelligence Reference Documents**. Classified research papers produced under the AAWSAP/AATIP programs. Thirty-eight DIRDs were commissioned, covering topics from advanced propulsion to biological effects of UAP encounters. Dr. Kit Green's paper on field effects on human tissue was one such document.

**Djinn**-(or jinn/jinni) are supernatural, often invisible beings from Arabian mythology and Islamic theology, created from "smokeless fire". They possess free will, can be good or evil, and have immense powers like shape-shifting, teleportation, and, in folklore, granting wishes. They live in parallel worlds, often appearing as animals or humans.

**DNA**-Genetic material referenced in alleged harvesting and hybridization programs.

**Divine Feminine**- an ancient, universal archetype representing intuitive, nurturing, creative, and receptive energy that exists within all individuals, regardless of gender. It acts as a spiritual, compassionate counter-balance to the analytical, action-oriented divine masculine, promoting inner healing, wisdom, and emotional connection

**DUMBs**-Deep Underground Military Bases, alleged covert facilities for exotic tech.

**Egregore (or Egregor)**-is a concept in Western esotericism for a non-physical, psychic entity or "thoughtform" created and sustained by the collective thoughts, emotions, and intentions of a distinct group of people, developing a semi-autonomous existence that influences its members and culture, like a group's shared beliefs or a corporate identity. Essentially, it's a powerful, shared idea given life by a collective mind, from national spirits to brand personas, strengthening group identity and purpose.

**EC-121R ("Batcat")**-Modified Lockheed Warning Star aircraft used in Operation Igloo White; relayed sensor data from ground-based acoustic and seismic sensors along the Ho Chi Minh Trail to computer centers in Thailand; operated 1968-1973; later partially replaced by QU-22B drones due to vulnerability.

**Entanglement**-Quantum phenomenon where particles share linked states beyond classical physics.

**Esotericism**- hidden, specialized, or secret knowledge intended only for a small group of initiated or enlightened individuals, rather than the general public

**EVP**-Electronic Voice Phenomenon; anomalous audio signals.

**Experiencer** - Preferred term for individuals with direct UFO/contact experiences

**FOIA**-Freedom of Information Act; a mechanism for declassifying UFO-related documents.

**Freemasonry**- the world's oldest and largest non-religious fraternal organization, dedicated to character development, morality, and charity among its members

**Gnosis**-Direct experiential spiritual insight is central to mystical traditions. Esoteric knowledge of spiritual truth, which the ancient Gnostics considered essential for salvation.

**Hermeticism**-Esoteric tradition emphasizing cosmology, mentalism, and the unity of macrocosm and microcosm.

**Hermetic Order of the Golden Dawn**- A secret society from the Western esoteric tradition, heavily influenced by Rosicrucianism and inspired by Freemasonry, primarily focused on the study and practice of occult Hermeticism and metaphysics in the late 19th and early 20th centuries. Known as a magical order, the Hermetic Order of the Golden Dawn was active in Great Britain and concentrated on theurgy and spiritual growth. Many modern ideas of ritual and magic central to contemporary traditions like Wicca and Thelema were inspired by the Golden Dawn, which became one of the most influential forces in 20th-century Western occultism.

**High Strangeness** – a high concentration of bizarre, absurd, or highly unusual elements in a paranormal or UFO report, where events defy conventional explanation. Coined by Dr. J. Allen Hynek, it describes encounters that seem surreal, often blending physical evidence with inexplicable, "magical," or synchronistic, non-linear occurrences.

**Ho Chi Minh Trail**-A complex network of roads, paths, and waterways extending over 12,000 miles through eastern Laos and Cambodia; North Vietnam's primary supply route to support Viet Cong operations in South Vietnam; target of Operation Igloo White electronic surveillance system; transported tens of thousands of personnel and hundreds of thousands of tons of materiel annually.

**Hughes 500P ("Quiet One")**-Classified stealth helicopter developed by Hughes Tool Company for CIA; modified OH-6A with five-bladed main rotor, four-bladed tail rotor, and extensive sound-dampening modifications; conducted successful covert missions into North Vietnam in December 1972 to place wiretaps; technology not publicly revealed until 2008 (36 years after operational use); considered the quietest helicopter ever built.

**IC (Intelligence Community)**-Collective term for U.S. intelligence agencies involved in secrecy and disclosure.

**Initiatic**— refers to the introductory, transformative process of bringing a new member into a specialized group or mystery.

**ISC (Infiltration Surveillance Center)-**Nerve center of Operation Igloo White located at Nakhon Phanom Royal Thai Air Force Base, Thailand (1968-1973); processed sensor data from Ho Chi Minh Trail using advanced computers; analyzed acoustic, seismic, and chemical sensor signals to direct immediate airstrikes against North Vietnamese supply convoys; pioneering example of automated battlefield intelligence.

**JPL**-Jet Propulsion Laboratory; NASA-affiliated research center tied to aerospace and occult history.

**KJV**-King James Version of the Bible; cited in esoteric and UFO interpretive frameworks.

**Knights Templar**- a wealthy and powerful medieval Catholic military order founded around 1118 to protect Christian pilgrims in the Holy Land. Recognized by their white mantles with a red cross, these "warrior monks" combined religious vows with military service, becoming key fighters in the Crusades and developing an advanced early banking system before their sudden, dramatic fall in 1307.

**Limited hangout**-Intelligence propaganda technique where partial truth is revealed to prevent discovery of the whole truth; admits to lesser secrets to protect greater ones while appearing transparent.

**Lockheed**-Aerospace company linked to advanced technology and alleged reverse-engineering programs.

**LUCIFER / LUCI**-Vatican-linked infrared telescope at Mount Graham.

**MIC**-Military-Industrial Complex; recurring theme in tech suppression.

**MKUltra**- was an illegal, clandestine CIA program (1953–1973) focused on behavioral modification, interrogation, and mind control using drugs like LSD on unwitting subjects. It involved unethical human experiments at over 80 institutions, including universities and prisons, and was later exposed as a major abuse of power.

**MUFON**-Mutual UFO Network; civilian UFO investigation group.

**Mystery Schools**-Ancient initiatory systems teaching esoteric knowledge.

**NASA**- National Aeronautics and Space Administration, a United States government agency established in 1958 responsible for civilian space exploration, aeronautics research, and space technology. It focuses on studying Earth, the solar system, and the universe to innovate for humanity.

**NDE**-Near-Death Experience is a profound, subjective, and often spiritual experience reported by people who have come close to death or were temporarily declared clinically dead.

**Neutrinos**- a fundamental subatomic particle with no electric charge, an incredibly tiny mass, and a "left-handed" spin, allowing it to pass through ordinary matter almost entirely unimpeded

**NICAP**-National Investigations Committee on Aerial Phenomena, a historic civilian UFO research group.

**NHI**-Non-Human Intelligence; includes extraterrestrial, interdimensional, and non-physical entities.

**Non-Ionizing electromagnetic radiation**-Electromagnetic radiation that lacks sufficient energy to ionize atoms. Includes radio waves, microwaves, and some UV. Pentagon reports concluded UAP-related injuries were caused by "broadband non-ionizing electromagnetic radiation" associated with advanced propulsion systems.

**Non-Local Awareness**-Perception beyond physical senses or spatial limits; key in remote viewing.

**NRO**-National Reconnaissance Office; U.S. agency managing satellite intelligence and linked to UAP monitoring.

**OH-6A ("Loach")**-Hughes light observation helicopter; nickname derived from LOH (Light Observation Helicopter); basis for CIA's Quiet One stealth modifications; extensively used in Vietnam War; compact design made it ideal for covert operations and sound-dampening modifications.

**NSA**- National Security Agency, a U.S. intelligence organization focusing on signals intelligence and cybersecurity. In dating and slang contexts, it means "No Strings Attached," indicating casual, non-committal physical relationships. The agency is often jokingly referred to as "No Such Agency" due to its historical secrecy.

**Operation Paperclip**-Post-WWII program relocating German scientists to U.S. research.

**Operation Neptune Spear**- a U.S. Navy SEAL raid that killed Osama bin Laden on May 2, 2011, in Abbottabad, Pakistan; exposed the existence of stealth Black Hawk helicopter when one crashed and had to be destroyed; also known as Operation Geronimo; utilized classified MH-X stealth helicopters developed decades earlier but never publicly acknowledged; demonstrated ongoing 30-year rule for advanced military technology.

**Operation Igloo White**-Covert U.S. electronic warfare operation (1968-1973) deploying thousands of automated sensors along Ho Chi Minh Trail to detect and facilitate airstrikes on North Vietnamese supply convoys; also known as "Electronic Battlefield"; integrated air-dropped sensors, airborne relay aircraft, and computer processing; pioneered modern networked sensor warfare; demonstrated early large-scale UAV deployment; cost approximately $1 billion annually.

**OSS**-Office of Strategic Services; WWII-era precursor to the CIA.

**OTO (Ordo Templi Orientis)** is an international fraternal and religious organization founded in the early 20th century, centered on the Law of Thelema ("Do what thou wilt") as proclaimed by Aleister Crowley.

**PBC**-Public Benefit Corporation; corporate structure adopted by TTSA.

**Planetary Spirits**-Esoteric concept of intelligences linked to celestial bodies.

**PSI**-Umbrella term for anomalous phenomena like telepathy and psychokinesis, parapsychological or psychic faculties or phenomena.

**PTSD**-Post-Traumatic Stress Disorder; a condition referenced in relation to the experience of trauma.

**Psychotronic weaponry-**Devices designed to manipulate human consciousness, behavior, or physiology through electromagnetic, acoustic, or other forms of directed energy, targeting the nervous system and psychological processes of individuals or populations.

**Retrocausality**-Concept of effects influencing causes backward in time; tied to quantum and consciousness theories.

**Remote Viewing (RV, CRV / ERV)** Structured protocols for perceiving distant or hidden targets using non-local awareness.

**Robertson Panel**-1953 CIA-led committee assessing U.S. handling of UFO reports.

**Rosicrucianism**-Mystical tradition linked to esoteric orders. a member of a secretive 17th- and 18th-century society devoted to the study of metaphysical, mystical, and alchemical lore. An anonymous pamphlet of 1614 about a mythical 15th-century knight called Christian Rosenkreuz is said to have launched the movement.

**RPV (Remotely Piloted Vehicle)-**1960s-1970s term for aircraft flown entirely by remote control; predecessor to modern UAV designation; used for Vietnam War-era drones like Ryan Firebee; distinguished from autonomous UAVs by requirement for constant remote guidance; loss of signal would result in drone continuing last command until fuel exhaustion.

**Ryan Model 147 Lightning Bug**-Reconnaissance drone series based on the Firebee (1962–). Flew 3,435 missions in Vietnam: 1,016 deployed, 578 lost. Featured 23 variants for different intel roles, including high- and low-altitude tasks and combat decoy. One unit completed 68 missions before being downed. Introduced autonomous navigation and programmed flight paths.

**SRICF (Societas Rosicruciana in Civitatibus Foederatis)**-Rosicrucian research society; the author is a member.

**SECDEF**-Secretary of Defense; appears in the disclosure context and in the UAPTF establishment.

**Skinwalker Ranch**-Utah site of anomalous phenomena studied under DIA programs.

**Synchronicity**-Meaningful coincidence concept by Carl Jung.

**Theosophy**-Modern esoteric movement synthesizing metaphysics and spiritual evolution.

**TTS / TTSA**-To The Stars Academy of Arts and Sciences; disclosure-focused organization founded by Tom DeLonge.

**Tulpa**-Tibetan concept of thought-form manifesting as an independent entity.

**UAV (Unmanned Aerial Vehicle)-**Aircraft capable of controlled, sustained flight without human pilot aboard; distinguished from cruise missiles by being designed for recovery and reuse; includes both autonomous (self-navigating) and remotely piloted variants; first large-scale military deployment was Vietnam War (1962-1973) with Ryan Model 147 Lightning Bug; precursor to modern combat drones like MQ-1 Predator and MQ-9 Reaper.

**UAP**-Unidentified Anomalous Phenomena; modern term replacing UFO.

**UAPTF**-Unidentified Aerial Phenomena Task Force; DoD entity established in 2020.

**UAT**-Unidentified Aerial Threats; term used in defense contexts for potential hostile anomalous objects.

**UFO**-Legacy term for unidentified flying objects.

**Ufology-**the study of unidentified flying objects and related anomalous phenomena through historical, investigative, and analytical methods.

**Ufologist-**an individual who investigates and analyzes UFO reports, evidence, and related phenomena.

**USAF / USN**-U.S. Air Force and U.S. Navy; key military branches in UAP investigations.

**USAP**-Unacknowledged Special Access Program; extreme secrecy classification for reverse-engineering projects.

**USO**-Unidentified Submersible Object; anomalous craft observed underwater.

**USSR**-Former Soviet Union; referenced in Cold War UFO secrecy context.

**VATT**-Vatican Advanced Technology Telescope; an observatory linked to esoteric and astronomical research.

**Vril**- All-encompassing "vital energy" or life force introduced in Edward Bulwer-Lytton's 1871 novel The Coming Race, utilized by a subterranean superhuman race (the Vril-ya) to heal, destroy, and control their environment. It represents an advanced, mysterious power source often associated with telepathy, telekinesis, and advanced technology.

**Vinh wiretap-**CIA covert mission (Dec 6-7, 1972) used a Quiet One helicopter to install a wiretap on North Vietnamese lines near Vinh, flying undetected past anti-aircraft defenses. The intercept yielded valuable intelligence for Henry Kissinger during the Paris Peace Talks and operated from December 1972 to May 1973. The operation remained classified for decades.

**White Lady**— A cross-cultural apparition of a female divinity typically characterized by white attire and blinding light. Examples include the Virgin Mary (Fátima), the White Buffalo Calf Woman (Lakota), and "The Lady" (Bledsoe). These figures are historically viewed as "messengers of the shift," appearing at pivotal moments in human history to restore spiritual balance or deliver warnings.

**Woo (or "woo-woo")**— A shorthand used to describe the unconventional, mystical, or paranormal elements of the UFO phenomenon

# END NOTES

1 C. Woodyard, *Haunted Ohio*, vols. 1-7 (Kestrel Publications, 1991-2008).

2 Central Intelligence Agency, "Report of the Scientific Panel on Unidentified Flying Objects (Robertson Panel)," 1953, https://www.cia.gov/readingroom/docs/CIA-RDP81R00560R000100010001-0.pdf

3 F. S. Saunders and J. E. Harkins, *The Cultural Cold War: The CIA and the World of Arts and Letters* (The New Press, 1968).

4 C. Chabris and D. Simons, *The Invisible Gorilla: And Other Ways Our Intuitions Deceive Us* (Crown, 2010).

5 M. Kloor, "The Pentagon's UFO Videos: A Skeptical Perspective," *Issues in Science and Technology*, May 28, 2021, https://issues.org/pentagon-ufo-videos-skeptical-perspective/

6 U.S. Department of Defense, "DOD Establishes Unidentified Aerial Phenomena Task Force," press release, August 14, 2020, https://www.defense.gov/News/Releases/Release/Article/2314065/dod-establishes-unidentified-aerial-phenomena-task-force/

7 Senate Intelligence Committee, *Senate Report 116-233, Intelligence Authorization Act for Fiscal Year 2021*, 2020, https://www.congress.gov/congressional-report/116th-congress/senate-report/233

8 Joseph P. Farrell, *McCarthy, Monmouth, and the Deep State* (Lulu, 2019).

9 D. E. Keyhoe, *The Flying Saucers Are Real* (Fawcett, 1950).

10 J. A. Hynek, *The UFO Experience: A Scientific Inquiry* (Ballantine Books, 1972).

11 J. Vallée, *Passport to Magonia: From Folklore to Flying Saucers* (Regnery, 1969).

12 Friedman, S. (2008). *Flying Saucers and Science*. New Page Books.

13 S. M. Greer, *Disclosure: Military and Government Witnesses Reveal the Greatest Secrets in Modern History* (Crossing Point, 2001).

14 G S. Greer, *Sirius*, documentary (Sirius Disclosure, 2013).

15 Tom DeLonge, "Tom DeLonge Shares UFO Revelations," interview by George Knapp, *Coast to Coast AM*, March 27, 2016, radio broadcast.

16 E. Mitchell, *The Way of the Explorer* (New Page Books, 2004).

17 Space Systems Command, "NRO Successfully Launches NROL-77," accessed January 2026, https://www.ssc.spaceforce.mil/Newsroom/Article/4357732/nro-successfully-launches-nrol-77-mission-through-national-security-space-launc

18 WikiLeaks, "Tom DeLonge Emails to John Podesta," 2016, https://search.wikileaks.org/?query=tom+delonge

19 T. DeLonge and A. J. Hartley, *Sekret Machines: Chasing Shadows* (To The Stars Media, 2016).

20 H. Cooper, L. Kean, and R. Blumenthal, "Glowing Auras and 'Black Money': The Pentagon's Mysterious U.F.O. Program," *The New York Times*, December 16, 2017, https://www.nytimes.com/2017/12/16/us/politics/pentagon-program-ufo-harry-reid.html

21 Cooper, H., Kean, L., & Blumenthal, R. (2017, December 16). Glowing auras and 'Black Money': The Pentagon's mysterious U.F.O. program. *The New York Times*. Retrieved from https://www.nytimes.com/2017/12/16/us/politics/pentagon-program-ufo-harry-reid.html

22 H. E. Puthoff, US5845220A: Communication Method and Apparatus with Signals Comprising Scalar and Vector Potentials without Electromagnetic Fields, U.S. Patent and Trademark Office, 1998; Puthoff, US11777198 & US10992035: Communications System, U.S. Patent and Trademark Office, 2021.

23 C. Kelleher and G. Knapp, *Hunt for the Skinwalker: Science Confronts the Unexplained at a Remote Ranch in Utah* (Paraview Pocket Books, 2005).

24 F. Shapiro, *Eye Movement Desensitization and Reprocessing: Basic Principles, Protocols, and Procedures*, 2nd ed. (Guilford Press, 2001).

25 American Psychological Association, *Clinical Practice Guideline for the Treatment of Posttraumatic Stress Disorder (PTSD)*, 2017.

26 Central Intelligence Agency, "Robertson Panel Report," 1953.

27 Albert Einstein, "On the Electrodynamics of Moving Bodies," *Annalen der Physik* 17, no. 10 (1905): 891–921

28 Cornelis W. Rietdijk, "A Rigorous Proof of Determinism Derived from the Special Theory of Relativity," *Philosophy of Science* 33, no. 4 (1966): 341–344; Hilary Putnam, "Time and Physical Geometry," *The Journal of Philosophy* 64, no. 8 (1967): 240–247.

29 Y.-H. Kim et al., "Delayed 'Choice' Quantum Eraser," *Physical Review Letters* 84, no. 1 (2000): 1–5, https://doi.org/10.1103/PhysRevLett.84.1

30 John A. Wheeler, "The 'Past' and the 'Delayed-Choice' Double-Slit Experiment," in *Mathematical Foundations of Quantum Theory*, ed. A. R. Marlow (New York: Academic Press, 1978), 9–48.

31 Hugh Everett III, "'Relative State' Formulation of Quantum Mechanics," *Reviews of Modern Physics* 29, no. 3 (1957): 454–462.

32 J. Ellis McTaggart, "The Unreality of Time," *Mind* 17, no. 68 (1908): 457–474.

33 Alexandra David-Néel, *Magic and Mystery in Tibet* (1929; repr., New York: Penguin Books, 1971).

34 Éliphas Lévi, *The Great Secret, or Occultism Unveiled* (1860; modern editions vary).

35 Nafeez Mosaddeq Ahmed, *The War on Truth: 9/11, Disinformation and the Anatomy of Terrorism* (Northampton, MA: Olive Branch Press, 2005); David Ray Griffin, *The New Pearl Harbor: Disturbing Questions about the Bush Administration and 9/11* (Northampton, MA: Olive Branch Press, 2004).

36 Daniel McKenzie, *Conspiracy Theory in America* (Austin: University of Texas Press, 2013).

37 *Jeane Dixon Papers: A Register of Her Papers in the Library of Congress*

(Washington, DC: Library of Congress, 2021), hdl.loc.gov

38 William Bengston, *The Energy Cure: Unraveling the Mystery of Hands-On Healing* (Boulder, CO: Sounds True, 2010).

39 William F. Bengston and David Krinsley, "The Effect of the 'Laying On of Hands' on Transplanted Breast Cancer in Mice," *Journal of Scientific Exploration* 14, no. 3 (2000): 353–364.

40 William F. Bengston, Margaret Moga, Marc J. Cavanna, and David S. Akman, "Delayed Onset of Tumor Growth in Rats After Inoculation with Tumor Cells and Treatment with 'Laying on of Hands,'" *Journal of the Society for Integrative Oncology* 1, no. 1 (Winter 2003): 7–13

41 "Children's Christmas Parade to Feature Tex Hoppus as Grand Marshal," *Ridgecrest Daily Independent*, December 3, 2021, https://www.ridgecrestca.com/news/childrens-christmas-parade-to-feature-tex-hoppus-as-grand-marshal/article_5e2a5a1a-56be-11ec-a018-dbf995e6b79a.html

42 Rotary Club of Ridgecrest, "George 'Tex' Hoppus: Speaker Profile," accessed January 2026, https://portal.clubrunner.ca/2828/speakers/daaed6a7-12ee-45a1-b766-7376e24649b1.

43 *Arming the Fleet: The Naval Ordnance Test Station at China Lake, California, and the Evolution of Weapons Systems* (Washington, DC: Naval History & Heritage Command, 2013), https://govbooktalk.gpo.gov/2013/11/07/arming-the-fleet-the-compelling-story-of-a-secret-navy-base-in-the-desert/.

44 Thomas A. Bass, "China Lake's Stealthy Cloud Seeders," *Popular Science* 243, no. 5 (November 1993): 56

45 Richard Sauder, *Underground Bases and Tunnels: What Is the Government Trying to Hide?* (Kempton, IL: Adventures Unlimited Press, 1995), https://archive.org/stream/pdfy-mT6Wq_1G5ULLS7F7/Underground+Bases+And+Tunnels+%5BWhat+Is+The+Government+Trying+To+Hide%5D_djvu.txt.

46 U.S. Patent 3,693,731, "Melt-Down Drilling Apparatus," filed September 22, 1970, and issued September 26, 1972

47 J. W. Neudecker, "Subterrene Tunneling Machine Systems: A Preliminary Study," Los Alamos Scientific Laboratory Report LA-

5354-MS, September 1973,
https://www.osti.gov/servlets/purl/4444905.

48 Matthew Bogdanos, "The Casualties of War: The Truth about the Iraq Museum," *American Journal of Archaeology* 109, no. 3 (July 2005): 477–526.

49 Douglas Porch, "The Other Gulf War: British Intervention in Iraq, 1941," *Joint Force Quarterly* (DTIC), 2004, https://apps.dtic.mil/sti/tr/pdf/ADA524596.pdf

50 "Anglo-Iraqi War," Wikipedia, last modified January 2026, https://en.wikipedia.org/wiki/Anglo-Iraqi_War

51 Matthew Bogdanos, "The Casualties of War: The Truth about the Iraq Museum," *American Journal of Archaeology* 109, no. 3 (July 2005): 477–526.

52 Robert M. Poole, "Looting Iraq," *Smithsonian Magazine*, February 2008, https://www.smithsonianmag.com/arts-culture/looting-iraq-16813540/

53 *Archaeology Magazine*, "Conversations: Building Trust in Iraq," January/February 2004, https://archive.archaeology.org/0401/etc/conversations.html

54 CNN, "Q&A Interview With Ashton Hawkins, Giuseppe Proietti," May 16, 2003, transcript excerpt featuring Col. Matthew Bogdanos, https://transcripts.cnn.com/show/i_qaa/date/2003-05-16/segment/01

55 Matthew Bogdanos, "The Casualties of War: The Truth about the Iraq Museum," *American Journal of Archaeology* 109, no. 3 (July 2005): 477–526.

56 Assyrian International News Agency, "Iraq Returns 27,000 Antiquities to National Museum," March 12, 2025, http://www.aina.org/news/20250312105617.htm

57 IraqiNews.com, "27,000 Artifacts Returned to Iraqi National Museum," March 12, 2025, https://www.iraqinews.com/iraq/27000-artifacts-returned-to-iraqi-national-museum/

58 Adel Fakhir, "Twenty Years after the US Invasion, Where Are Iraq's Antiquities?" *Al Jazeera*, April 7, 2023, https://www.aljazeera.com/features/2023/4/7/20-years-after-the-us-invasion-where-are-iraqs-antiquities

59 S. Vitali, J. B. Glattfelder, and S. Battiston, "The Network of Global Corporate Control," *PLoS ONE* 6, no. 10 (2011): e25995, https://doi.org/10.1371/journal.pone.0025995https://doi.org/10.1371/journal.pone.0025995

60 *The Daily Bulletin* (Honolulu), "A Pre-Historic City," May 22, 1884, 4, https://chroniclingamerica.loc.gov/lccn/sn82016412/1884-05-22/ed-1/seq-4/

61 "Giant Human Skeletons," Wikipedia, last modified January 2026,
    https://en.wikipedia.org/wiki/Giant_human_skeletons

62 The Archaeologist, "The Mysterious Elongated Skulls of Paracas: A
    Glimpse into Ancient Practices," accessed January 2026,
    https://www.thearchaeologist.org/blog/the-mysterious-elongated-
    skulls-of-paracas-a-glimpse-into-ancient-practices

63 German Archaeological Institute, *Tepe Telegrams—Publications Overview*
    (2015–2024), https://www.dainst.blog/the-tepe-
    telegrams/publications/

64 Oliver Dietrich et al., "Establishing a Radiocarbon Sequence for
    Göbekli Tepe. State of Research and New Data," *Neo-Lithics* 1/2013,
    https://www.academia.edu/41312549/

65 Robert M. Schoch, "The Great Sphinx," personal research site, accessed
    January 2026, https://www.robertschoch.com/sphinx.html

66 Jean-Pierre Protzen and Stella Nair, "On Reconstructing Tiwanaku
    Architecture," *Latin American Antiquity*, JSTOR,
    https://www.jstor.org/stable/991648

67 "Osireion," Wikipedia, last modified January 2026,
    https://en.wikipedia.org/wiki/Osireion

68 History Skills, "The Unexplained Osireion," accessed January 2026,
    https://www.historyskills.com/classroom/ancient-history/osireion/

69 "Yonaguni Monument," Wikipedia, last modified January 2026,
    https://en.wikipedia.org/wiki/Yonaguni_Monument

70 "Marine Archaeology in the Gulf of Khambhat," Wikipedia, last
    modified January 2026,
    https://en.wikipedia.org/wiki/Marine_archaeology_in_the_Gulf_of
    _Khambhat

71 Eirik Sinclair, "Atlantis and Pre-Flood Civilizations," *UFOs on the Level*,
    accessed January 2026.

72 E. J. Andrews and Eirik Sinclair, *Voyage of the Thundergods: The Civilization
    of Atlantis Revealed* (PPC Preservation Society, 2015), Kindle edition.

73 Kevin Fuller, "Mystery Schools and Modern Consciousness: Martinism
    and the UFO Phenomenon," *UFOs on the Level*, accessed January
    2026.

74 John Gilbert, *Not as Above, Not as Below: How We Got the Emerald Tablet
    Wrong* (Rose Circle Books), accessed January 11, 2026,
    https://rosecirclebooks.com/not-as-above-not-as-below-by-john-
    gilbert/

75 Walter Burkert, *Ancient Mystery Cults* (Cambridge, MA: Harvard
    University Press, 1987).

76 Tim Wallace-Murphy, *What Islam Did For Us* (London: Watkins, 2006).

77 Tim Wallace-Murphy, *The Templar Legacy* (New York: HarperCollins,
    1998).

78 Malcolm Barber, *The New Knighthood* (Cambridge: Cambridge University Press, 1994).

79 Karen L. King, *What Is Gnosticism?* (Cambridge: Harvard University Press, 2005).

80 Alan Butler and Stephen Dafoe, *The Knights Templar* (London: Watkins, 2006).

81 Helen Nicholson, *The Crusades* (Westport: Greenwood Press, 2004).

82 Jonathan Riley-Smith, *The Crusades: A History* (New Haven: Yale University Press, 2005).

83 Arkon Daraul, *A History of Secret Societies* (New York: Citadel Press, 1961).

84 Hugh J. Schonfield, "Where Did Baphomet Originate?" *Adept Initiates*, accessed January 2026.

85 Gershom Scholem, *Kabbalah* (New York: Penguin, 1974).

86 William M. Schniedewind, *How the Bible Became a Book* (Cambridge: Cambridge University Press, 2004).

87 Ean Begg, *The Cult of the Black Virgin* (Grand Rapids: William B. Eerdmans, 2006).

88 Titus Burckhardt, *Sacred Art in East and West* (Bloomington: World Wisdom, 2001).

89 Seyyed Hossein Nasr, *Sufi Essays* (Chicago: ABC International Group, 1999).

90 Henry Corbin, *History of Islamic Philosophy* (London: Kegan Paul, 1993).

91 Ian Richard Netton, *Muslim Neoplatonists: An Introduction to the Thought of the Brethren of Purity* (London: Routledge, 1982).

92 Mark Sedgwick, *Western Sufism* (Oxford: Oxford University Press, 2016).

93 David Stevenson, *The Origins of Freemasonry* (Cambridge: Cambridge University Press, 1988).

94 Robert Lomas, *The Invisible College* (London: Transworld, 2002).

95 Wouter J. Hanegraaff, *Esotericism and the Academy* (Cambridge: Cambridge University Press, 2012).

96 Joseph Campbell, *The Power of Myth*, with Bill Moyers (New York: Doubleday, 1988).

97 Marvin W. Meyer, *The Gospel of Thomas: The Hidden Sayings of Jesus* (San Francisco: HarperSanFrancisco, 1992).

98 Mircea Eliade, *The Forge and the Crucible: The Origins and Structure of Alchemy* (Chicago: University of Chicago Press, 1978).

99 W. Kirk MacNulty, *Freemasonry: A Journey Through Ritual and Symbol* (London: Thames & Hudson, 1991).

100 Jalal al-Din Rumi, *The Essential Rumi*, translated by Coleman Barks (San Francisco: HarperOne, 1995).

101 Malcolm Barber, *The Trial of the Templars* (Cambridge: Cambridge University Press, 2006).

102 Alain Demurger, *The Last Templar* (London: Profile Books, 2009).

103 Stephen Howarth, *The Knights Templar* (New York: Barnes & Noble, 1982).

104 Barbara Frale, *The Templars: The Secret History Revealed* (New York: Arcade, 2009).

105 John L. Allen Jr., *Pope Benedict XVI* (London: Bloomsbury, 2005).

106 CIA Reading Room overview; *Wikipedia* ("Stargate Project").

107 Russell Targ and Harold Puthoff, "Information Transmission Under Conditions of Sensory Shielding," *Nature* 251 (1974): 602–607.

108 Paul H. Smith, *Reading the Enemy's Mind* (New York: Tom Doherty/Forge, 2005).

109 George V. Coyne, "The Vatican Observatory: A Historical Overview," Vatican Observatory Publications, 2008.challenge Church teachingAfter the Funes 2008 interview paraphraseJosé Gabriel Funes, "L'ex

110 George V. Coyne, "The Vatican Observatory: A Historical Overview." *Vatican Observatory Publications*, 2008.

111 John Pollard, *The Vatican and the Roman Curia* (Oxford: Oxford University Press, 2014).

112 José Gabriel Funes, "L'extraterrestre è mio fratello," interview by Francesco M. Valiante, *L'Osservatore Romano*, May 14, 2008.

113 Associated Press. "Catholic Church Reports Revenue Losses Amid Pandemic, Including $100 Million Hit to Vatican Finances." July 2020.

114 Associated Press (July 2020); *The Guardian* (July 2020); CBS News (Aug 2020).

115 *The Guardian*, "Catholic Church Lobbied for Taxpayer Funds, Got $1.4bn," July 2020.

116 CBS News. "Catholic dioceses got billions in COVID aid." August 2020.

117 Templarportugal.com; Wikipedia; Military History Fandom, "Order of Christ (Portugal)," accessed January 2026.

118 Wikipedia; Cambridge.org, "Robert the Bruce and Excommunication," accessed January 2026.

119 World History Encyclopedia, "Etchmiadzin Cathedral," June 8, 2018, https://www.worldhistory.org/Etchmiadzin_Cathedral/; Wikipedia, "Etchmiadzin Cathedral," accessed January 2026; Wikipedia, "Archbasilica of Saint John Lateran," accessed January 2026; Medievalists.net, "Archaeological Project Reveals New Insights on World's First Cathedral," accessed January 2026.

120 *National Catholic Reporter*, "Pope Renames Vatican Secret Archives amid Image Concerns," October 2019.

121 James M. Robinson, ed., *The Nag Hammadi Library* (San Francisco: HarperCollins, 1988).

122 Diego de Landa, *Relación de las Cosas de Yucatán* (1566).

123 José Gabriel Funes, "L'extraterrestre è mio fratello," *L'Osservatore Romano*, May 2008.

124 Sandra Zimdars-Swartz, *Encountering Mary: From La Salette to Medjugorje* (Princeton: Princeton University Press, 1991).

125 John De Marchi, *The True Story of Fátima* (Vatican International Publications, 1952).

126 Congregation for the Doctrine of the Faith, "The Message of Fatima," Vatican, June 26, 2000.

127 Jacques Vallée, *Passport to Magonia: From Folklore to Flying Saucers* (Chicago: Henry Regnery, 1969).

128 Jacques Vallée, *The Invisible College* (New York: Dutton, 1975).

129 David Stannard, *American Holocaust: Columbus and the Conquest of the New World* (New York: Oxford University Press, 1992).

130 John Thornton, *Africa and Africans in the Making of the Atlantic World, 1400–1800* (Cambridge University Press, 1998).

131 Michael D. Coe, *Breaking the Maya Code* (London: Thames & Hudson, 1992).

132 Samuel Noah Kramer, *History Begins at Sumer* (Philadelphia: University of Pennsylvania Press, 1981).

133 Erik Hornung, *The Ancient Egyptian Books of the Afterlife* (Ithaca: Cornell University Press, 1999).

134 Zainab Bahrani, Jeremy Larsen, and Richard Zettler, *Catastrophe!: The Looting and Destruction of Iraq's Past* (Chicago: The Oriental Institute, 2008).

135 *The Guardian*, "Iraq's Ancient Treasures Lost in Looting," April 13, 2003.

136 Danielle Mattioli, "The Vatican Secret Archives: Access, Control, and Historical Sensitivity," *Journal of Ecclesiastical History* 67, no. 3 (2016).

137 Elaine Pagels, *The Gnostic Gospels* (New York: Random House, 1979).

138 Louis Dupré and James A. Wiseman, *Light from Light: An Anthology of Christian Mysticism* (New York: Paulist Press, 2001).

139 Bernard McGinn, *The Presence of God: A History of Western Christian Mysticism*, multiple vols. (New York: Crossroad Publishing).

140 Nicholas Goodrick-Clarke, *The Occult Roots of Nazism: Secret Aryan Cults and Their Influence on Nazi Ideology* (New York: New York University Press, 1992).

141 Stephan Anthes, "Ariosophy and the Occult Foundations of the Third Reich," *Journal of Esoteric Studies* 12, no. 2 (2015): 44–61.

142 Joscelyn Godwin, *Arktos: The Polar Myth in Science, Symbolism, and Nazi Survival* (Kempton, IL: Adventures Unlimited Press, 1996).

143 Edward Bulwer-Lytton, *The Coming Race* (London: Bernard Quaritch, 1871).

144 Heather Pringle, *The Master Plan: Himmler's Scholars and the Holocaust* (New York: Hyperion, 2006).

145 Isrun Engelhardt, ed., *The Ernst Schäfer Tibet Expedition 1938–1939: Scientific Results and Ideological Context* (Leiden: Brill, 2015).

146 Michael Moynihan and Stephen E. Flowers, *The Secret King: The Myth and Reality of Nazi Occultism* (Los Angeles: Feral House, 2007).

147 Joseph P. Farrell, *Reich of the Black Sun: Nazi Secret Weapons and the Cold War Allied Legend* (Kempton, IL: Adventures Unlimited Press, 2004).

148 Karl Hüser, *Wewelsburg 1933–1945: Cult and Terror Center of the SS* (Paderborn: Bonifatius, 1998).

149 Jim Marrs, *The Rise of the Fourth Reich: The Secret Societies That Threaten to Take Over America* (New York: William Morrow, 2008).

150 Joseph P. Farrell, *The Philosopher's Stone: Alchemy and the Secret Research Behind the Nazi Atomic Program* (Kempton, IL: Adventures Unlimited Press, 2009).

151 Joseph P. Farrell, *Nazi International: The Nazis' Postwar Plan to Control the Worlds of Science, Finance, Space, and Conflic*

152 Kevin McClure, "Flying Saucers: A Modern Myth of Things Seen in the Sky," *Fortean Studies* 4 (1998): 112–145.

153 Michael J. Neufeld, *Von Braun: Dreamer of Space, Engineer of War* (New York: Knopf, 2007).

154 Mark Walker, *Nazi Science: Myth, Truth, and the German Atomic Bomb* (New York: Plenum Press, 1995).

155 Dean Reuter, Colm Lowery, and Keith Chester, *The Hidden Nazi: The Untold Story of America's Deal with the Devil* (Washington, DC: Regnery History, 2019).

156 Council on Foreign Relations, "FAQs," accessed January 2026, https://www.cfr.org/about/faqs

157 The Trilateral Commission, "About Us," accessed January 2026, https://www.trilateral.org/about/

158 *Standard Oil Co. of New Jersey v. United States*, 221 U.S. 1 (1911). https://supreme.justia.com/cases/federal/us/221/1/.

159 The Rothschild Archive. "Rothschild and Gold." https://www.rothschildarchive.org/business/n_m_rothschild_and_ sons_london/rothschild_and_gold.

160 Federal Reserve History. "The Meeting at Jekyll Island." https://www.federalreservehistory.org/essays/jekyll-island-conference.

161 Edwin Black, "The Horrifying American Roots of Nazi Eugenics," History News Network, 2003.

162 Wikipedia, "Kaiser Wilhelm Institute of Anthropology, Human Heredity, and Eugenics," accessed January 2026, https://en.wikipedia.org/wiki/Kaiser_Wilhelm_Institute_of_Anthropology,_Human_Heredity,_and_Eugenics

163 Encyclopedia Britannica, "Skull and Bones," accessed January 2026, https://www.britannica.com/topic/Skull-and-Bones-Yale

164 Wikipedia, "Cremation of Care," accessed January 2026, https://en.wikipedia.org/wiki/Cremation_of_Care

165 Encyclopedia Britannica, "The Bohemian Club," accessed January 2026, https://www.britannica.com/topic/The-Bohemian-Club

166 Wikipedia, "Le Cercle," accessed January 2026, https://en.wikipedia.org/wiki/Le_Cercle

167 Encyclopedia Britannica, "F-117," accessed January 2026, https://www.britannica.com/technology/F-117

168 DARPA, "HAVE BLUE and the Origin of Stealth Technology," February 1, 1977, accessed January 2026, https://www.darpa.mil/node/2080

169 National Museum of the United States Air Force, "Lockheed F-117A Nighthawk," accessed January 2026, https://www.nationalmuseum.af.mil/Visit/Museum-Exhibits/Fact-Sheets/Display/Article/198056/lockheed-f-117a-nighthawk/

170 White House (Office of the Press Secretary), "Statement by the President Regarding the United States' Decision to Stop Degrading Global Positioning System Accuracy," May 1, 2000, https://clintonwhitehouse4.archives.gov/WH/EOP/OSTP/html/0053_2.html

171 GPS.gov (archival), "Selective Availability (FAQs)," accessed January 2026, https://archive.gps.gov/systems/gps/modernization/sa/faq/

172 GPS.gov, "Selective Availability," accessed January 2026, https://www.gps.gov/selective-availability

173 DARPA, "DARPA Vignettes: ARPANET," accessed January 2026, https://www.darpa.mil/sites/default/files/attachment/2025-01/darpa-vignette-arpanet.pdf

174 IEEE History Center, "Milestones: Birthplace of the Internet, 1969," accessed January 2026, https://ethw.org/Milestones:Birthplace_of_the_Internet,_1969

175 CERN. "A Short History of the Web." Accessed January 2026. https://home.cern/science/computing/birth-web/short-history-web.

176 World Wide Web Foundation. "History of the Web." Accessed January 2026. https://webfoundation.org/about/vision/history-of-the-web/.

177 Wikipedia, "AN/PVS-4," accessed January 2026, https://en.wikipedia.org/wiki/AN/PVS-4

178 Defense Technical Information Center (DTIC), *Use of Night Vision Devices by U.S. Army Units in Vietnam*, final report, November 30, 1966, AD0377920, https://apps.dtic.mil/sti/citations/AD0377920

179 Smithsonian Magazine, "Seeing in the Dark: The History of Night Vision," May 19, 2017, https://www.smithsonianmag.com/innovation/seeing-dark-history-night-vision-180963357/

180 SRI International, "Artificial Intelligence: CALO," accessed January 2026, https://www.sri.com/hoi/artificial-intelligence-calo/

181 Annie Jacobsen, *The Pentagon's Brain: An Uncensored History of DARPA, America's Top-Secret Military Research Agency* (New York: Little, Brown and Company, 2015).

182 Public Law 114-90, *U.S. Commercial Space Launch Competitiveness Act (SPACE Act of 2015), Title IV—Space Resource Exploration and Utilization*, November 25, 2015, https://www.congress.gov/114/plaws/publ90/PLAW-114publ90.pdf

183 Defense Advanced Research Projects Agency. "About DARPA." Accessed January 2026. https://www.darpa.mil/About/.

184 Defense Advanced Research Projects Agency. "The Sputnik Surprise." October 4, 1957. https://www.darpa.mil/node/2113.

185 Malik, Tariq. "U.S. Spy Satellite Agency Gives NASA 2 Space Telescopes." *Space.com*. June 4, 2012. https://www.space.com/16000-spy-satellites-space-telescopes-nasa.html.

186 Jason Davis, "NRO Gives NASA Two Hand-Me-Down Telescopes," Planetary Society, June 7, 2012, https://www.planetary.org/articles/nasa-gets-two-hand-me-down

187 Mark Memmott, "Reports: Secret Stealth Black Hawk Helicopters Used in Bin Laden Raid," NPR, May 5, 2011, https://www.northcountrypublicradio.org/news/npr/136017082/reports-secret-stealth-black-hawk-helicopters-used-in-bin-laden-raid.

188 Rob Verger, "The Stealth Helicopters Used in the 2011 Raid on Osama bin Laden," *Popular Science*, June 23, 2021, https://www.popsci.com/story/technology/osama-bin-laden-raid-anniversary-stealth-helicopters/

189 Cutting Dynamics, "The Mystery of the Stealth Black Hawk Helicopter," accessed January 2026, https://www.cuttingdynamics.com/news/the-mystery-of-the-stealth-black-hawk-helicopter/

190 The Mystery of the Stealth Black Hawk Helicopter," Cutting Dynamics, accessed February 2, 2026, https://cuttingdynamics.com/2022/05/13/stealth-black-hawk-mystery/. O'Neil's quote also appears in multiple sources documenting Operation Neptune Spear, including: Tyler Rogoway, "This Is The First Photo Ever Of A Stealthy Black Hawk Helicopter," The Drive, November 27, 2020, https://www.twz.com/35342/this-is-the-first-image-ever-of-a-stealthy-black-hawk-helicopter.

191 Ibid. The stealth Black Hawk program was reportedly exhumed after the successful bin Laden raid, with variants used in Syria during operations to rescue American hostages and target ISIS leadership. See also: David Cenciotti, "Five years ago today the raid that exposed the Stealth Black Hawk helicopter," The Aviationist, May 2, 2016, https://theaviationist.com/2016/05/02/five-years-ago-today-the-raid-that-exposed-the-stealth-black-hawk-helicopter/.

192 David Cenciotti, "What About A 'Stealth Little Bird'?" The Aviationist, May 25, 2021, https://theaviationist.com/2011/05/25/a-stealth-little-bird/. Originally based on James R. Chiles, "Air America's Black Helicopter," Air & Space Magazine, November 16, 2013, https://www.smithsonianmag.com/air-space-magazine/air-americas-black-helicopter-24960500/.

193 Chiles, "Air America's Black Helicopter." The Hughes Tool Company received a $200,000 contract from ARPA in 1968 to develop noise-reduction technologies for the OH-6A helicopter. See also: "Vinh wiretap," Wikipedia, accessed February 2, 2026, https://en.wikipedia.org/wiki/The_Vinh_wiretap

194 Chiles, "Air America's Black Helicopter." PS-44 was a secret CIA base in southwest Laos where cameras were discouraged and photographing the Quiet One was strictly forbidden. Crews were warned about the risk of discussing operations even in bars and brothels throughout Southeast Asia.

195 Joseph Trevithick, "The CIA Built a Special Helicopter to Sneak Into North Vietnam," Trench Art (Medium), May 3, 2015, https://medium.com/war-is-boring/the-cia-built-a-special-helicopter-to-sneak-into-north-vietnam-b1bb0ea35a7b. Henry Kissinger later stated the intelligence from the Vinh wiretap was "excellent," though he claimed he "never questioned where it came from."

196 "Operation Igloo White," Wikipedia, accessed February 2, 2026, https://en.wikipedia.org/wiki/Operation_Igloo_White. The operation was conducted from late January 1968 until February 1973 by the 553rd Reconnaissance Wing and VO-67, a specialized U.S. Navy unit.

197 "Ryan Model 147," Wikipedia, accessed February 2, 2026, https://en.wikipedia.org/wiki/Ryan_Model_147. The Ryan Model 147 Lightning Bug was developed from the earlier Ryan Firebee

target drone series, with the first reconnaissance variant (Model 147A "Fire Fly") contracted on February 2, 1962.

198 "History of unmanned aerial vehicles," Wikipedia, accessed February 2, 2026, https://en.wikipedia.org/wiki/History_of_unmanned_aerial_vehicles. The 350th Strategic Reconnaissance Squadron, 100th Strategic Reconnaissance Wing operated Ryan Firebees launched from modified DC-130A Hercules transport aircraft. See also: Ryan Aeronautical Firebee Drones II, War History, December 14, 2024, https://warhistory.org/@msw/article/ryan-aeronautical-firebee-drones-ii.

199 Eugene Nielsen, "Operation Igloo White: The Electronic War in Vietnam," Spotter Up, September 20, 2025, https://spotterup.com/operation-igloo-white-the-electronic-war-in-vietnam/. The Infiltration Surveillance Center at Nakhon Phanom Royal Thai Air Force Base was the nerve center where computers processed sensor data for targeting.

200 "Igloo White: the Automated Battlefield," The Future of Things, March 31, 2022, https://thefutureofthings.com/3902-igloo-white-the-automated-battlefield/. Different sensor types included acoustic, seismic, magnetic, and chemical "sniffer" sensors designed to detect ammonia from human urine.

201 John T. Correll, "Igloo White," Air & Space Forces Magazine, May 30, 2008, https://www.airandspaceforces.com/article/1104igloo/. The North Vietnamese drove animals up the trail and hung buckets of urine in trees to trigger false sensor readings.

202 Matt Novak, "How the Vietnam War Brought High-Tech Border Surveillance to America," Paleofuture (Gizmodo), September 24, 2015, https://gizmodo.com/how-the-vietnam-war-brought-high-tech-border-surveillan-1694647526. Operation Igloo White laid the foundation for modern electronic warfare, sensor networks, and unmanned surveillance systems used in contemporary conflicts.

203 Margaret Kane, "Compaq Acquires Zip2," ZDNet, February 15, 1999, https://www.zdnet.com/article/compaq-acquires-zip2/

204 SEC Press Release, "eBay to Acquire PayPal," July 8, 2002, https://www.sec.gov/Archives/edgar/data/1103415/00009120570 2026650/a2084015zex-99_1.htm

205 Geni.com. "Joshua Norman Haldeman." Accessed January 2026. https://www.geni.com.

206 A. John Clement, *The Kalahari and Its Lost City* (London: Longmans, 1967), https://archive.org/details/kalahariitslostc0000ajoh

207 National Post, "The First Chiropractor Was a Canadian Who Claimed He Received a Message from a Ghost," February 6, 2018, https://nationalpost.com/health/the-first-chiropractor-was-a-canadian-who-claimed-he-received-a-message-from-a-ghost

208 Wikipedia. *"Maye Musk."* Accessed January 2026.
   https://en.wikipedia.org/wiki/Maye_Musk.

209 Informit, "Chiropractic History: D.D. Palmer and Spiritualism," 2009,
   https://search.informit.org/doi/pdf/10.3316/informit.9006935296
   20786

210 J. Archer, "Elon Musk's Anti-Semitic, Apartheid-Loving Grandfather,"
   *The Atlantic*, September 21, 2023,
   https://www.theatlantic.com/technology/archive/2023/09/joshua-
   haldeman-elon-musk-grandfather-apartheid-antisemitism/675396/

211 W. S. Rehm, "Who Was Who in Chiropractic: A Necrology," in *Who's
   Who in Chiropractic International: History–Education*, 2nd ed. (Littleton,
   CO: Who's Who in Chiropractic International Pub. Co., 1980), 322–
   323.

212 Rehm, Bill. "The Lost City of the Kalahari: A South African Legend
   Revisited." *South African Archaeological Bulletin* 35, no. 132 (1980):
   322–325.

213 Goldie, Fay. *Lost City of the Kalahari*. Cape Town: A. A. Balkema, 1963.

214 Clement, A. J. *The Kalahari and Its Lost City*. London: Longmans, 1967.

215 Bill Rehm, "The Lost City of the Kalahari: A South African Legend
   Revisited," *South African Archaeological Bulletin* 35, no. 132 (1980):
   322–325.

216 AntiquarianAuctions.com, "Goldie & Haldeman: Lost City of the
   Kalahari (1963)," accessed January 2026,
   https://antiquarianauctions.com/lots/lost-city-of-the-kalahari-
   includes-elon-musk-s-grandfather-s-own-account-of-his-search-for-
   the-lost-city

217 J. N. Haldeman, "Lost City of the Kalahari," *South African Archaeological
   Bulletin* 13, no. 49 (March 1958): 39,
   https://doi.org/10.2307/3887604

218 G. A. Farini, *Through the Kalahari Desert* (London: Sampson Low,
   Marston, Searle & Rivington, 1886).

219 Nathan Bomey, "Elon Musk on Twitter: 'Accelerating Starship
   Development to Build the Martian Technocracy,'" *USA TODAY*,
   June 24, 2019,
   https://www.usatoday.com/story/tech/2019/06/24/elon-musk-
   twitter-accelerating-starship-development-mars/1545195001/

220 Ira Basen, "In Science We Trust," CBC longform, accessed January
   2026, https://newsinteractives.cbc.ca/longform/technocracy-
   incorporated-elon-musk/

221 Encyclopedia Britannica, "Howard Hughes: Later Years," accessed
   January 2026, https://www.britannica.com/biography/Howard-
   Hughes/Later-years

222 Wikipedia, "Hughes Aircraft Company," accessed January 2026,
   https://en.wikipedia.org/wiki/Hughes_Aircraft_Company

223 UNLV Special Collections. *"Hearings of the U.S. Senate Special Committee… (1947)."* https://special.library.unlv.edu/node/56805.

224 PBS. *"Las Vegas: Howard Hughes."* n.d. Accessed January 2026. https://www.pbs.org/wgbh/americanexperience/features/lasvegas-hughes/.

225 CIA. *"The Exposing of Project AZORIAN."* https://www.cia.gov/stories/story/the-exposing-of-project-azorian/.

226 UNLV Special Collections, "Hearings of the U.S. Senate Special Committee (1947)," accessed January 2026, https://special.library.unlv.edu/node/56805

227 Wikipedia, "Operation Matador (1975)," accessed January 2026, https://en.wikipedia.org/wiki/Operation_Matador_(1975

228 Central Intelligence Agency, "The Exposing of Project AZORIAN," March 17, 2020, https://www.cia.gov/stories/story/the-exposing-of-project-azorian/

229 Jessica Bursztynsky, "What to Know About Jared Birchall, Elon Musk's Right-Hand Man," *Fast Company*, April 18, 2025, https://www.fastcompany.com/91319028/what-to-know-about-jared-birchall-elon-musks-right-hand-man

230 *TIME* Magazine, "The Nation: The Keepers of the King," December 13, 1976, https://time.com/archive/6852298/the-nation-the-keepers-of-the-king/

231 Anson Shupe, "Mormonism and the FBI," in *The FBI and Religion: Faith and National Security Before and After 9/11*, ed. Sylvester A. Johnson and Steven Weitzman (Oakland: University of California Press, 2017), 113–34.

232 John Heinerman and Anson Shupe, *The Mormon Corporate Empire* (Boston: Beacon Press, 1985), 157.

233 Shupe, "Mormonism and the FBI," 113–34.

234 Tracy Walder and Jessica Anya Blau, *The Unexpected Spy: From the CIA to the FBI, My Secret Life Taking Down Some of the World's Most Notorious Terrorists* (New York: St. Martin's Press, 2020).

235 Ibid., Shupe, "Mormonism and the FBI," 113–34.

236 Michael McPheters, *Agent Bishop: True Stories from an FBI Agent Moonlighting as a Mormon Bishop* (Springville, UT: CFI, 2009).

237 Amy B. Zegart, *Spies, Lies, and Algorithms: The History and Future of American Intelligence* (Princeton: Princeton University Press, 2022), 78–82.

238 Zegart, *Spies, Lies, and Algorithms*, 78–82.

239 "CIA Application Process," Central Intelligence Agency, accessed January 30, 2026, https://www.cia.gov/careers/how-we-hire/.

240 "A Portrait of Mormons in the U.S.," Pew Research Center, July 24, 2009, https://www.pewresearch.org/religion/2009/07/24/a-portrait-of-mormons-in-the-us/.

241 Dallin H. Oaks, "Following the Pioneers," *Ensign*, November 1997, 72–75.

242 BYU Honor Code Office, "BYU Honor Code," Brigham Young University, accessed January 30, 2026, https://reu.byu.edu/honorcode.

243 The Church of Jesus Christ of Latter-day Saints, "Why Mormons Don't Drink Alcohol, Tea, and Coffee," Pacific Area Newsroom, accessed January 30, 2026, https://pacific.churchofjesuschrist.org/why-mormons-dont-drink-alcohol-tea-and-coffee.

244 BYU Interviews (@byuinterviews), "Rather have a sip of alcohol or on a Live a puppy," Instagram reel, January 13, 2026, https://www.instagram.com/reel/DTeAV9rkphF/.

245 Emma Carillo, "BYU students unsure of TikToker's motive for on-campus interviews," *The Daily Universe*, January 20, 2023, https://universe.byu.edu/2023/01/20/byu-students-question-tiktokers-motive-for-on-campus-interviews/.

246 Robert Carpenter (@robert_carpenter), "Break the Word of Wisdom or take a puppy's life? Here's what they said...," YouTube Shorts, May 7, 2025, https://m.youtube.com/shorts/.

247 Kelsey Dallas, "Why Does the FBI Have So Many Latter-day Saint Agents?" *Deseret News*, February 18, 2021, https://www.deseret.com/faith/2021/2/18/22287039/why-are-there-so-many-mormon-members-church-jesus-christ-latter-day-saints-fbi-agents-mia-maids.

248 Shupe, "Mormonism and the FBI," 122–23.

249 Melissa Sanford, "Mormon Culture Helps BYU Grads Qualify for Intelligence Careers," *The Daily Universe*, December 6, 2019, https://universe.byu.edu/2019/12/06/mormon-culture-helps-byu-grads-qualify-for-intelligence-careers/.

250 Shupe, "Mormonism and the FBI," 117.

251 Sanford, "Mormon Culture Helps BYU Grads."

252 James Bamford, "The NSA Is Building the Country's Biggest Spy Center (Watch What You Say)," *Wired*, March 15, 2012, https://www.wired.com/2012/03/ff-nsadatacenter/.

253 Ashton Marra, "How Utah Landed the NSA's Massive Data Center," *The Salt Lake Tribune*, June 7, 2013.

254 Judson Berger, "Utah's NSA Data Center Fed by Tri-State Electrical Grid," *Fox News*, October 23, 2013.

255 Tom Gjelten, "NSA's Utah Data Center Will Store a 'Haystack' of Data," NPR, June 10, 2013,

https://www.npr.org/2013/06/10/190384784/nsas-utah-data-center-will-store-a-haystack-of-data.

256 University of Utah Continuing Education, "Data Center Technologies Certificate," accessed January 30, 2026.

257 "Hatch: NSA Data Center a Boon for Utah," *Deseret News*, June 6, 2013.

258 Robert Gehrke, "How Utah Landed the NSA Data Center," *The Salt Lake Tribune*, June 7, 2013.

259 Michael W. Homer, *Joseph's Temples: The Dynamic Relationship between Freemasonry and Mormonism* (Salt Lake City: University of Utah Press, 2014).

260 "Nauvoo Lodge Minutes, 15–16 Mar 1842 (Featured version)," Joseph Smith Papers, accessed January 2026, https://www.josephsmithpapers.org/paper-summary/minutes-15-16-march-1842/1

261 The Church of Jesus Christ of Latter-day Saints, "Masonry," Church history topic, accessed January 2026, https://www.churchofjesuschrist.org/study/history/topics/masonry

262 David J. Buerger, "The Development of the Mormon Temple Endowment Ceremony," *Dialogue: A Journal of Mormon Thought* 34, no. 1–2 (2001): 75–122.

263 The Church of Jesus Christ of Latter-day Saints, "Temple Endowment," Church history topic, accessed January 2026.

264 National Archives (Prologue Blog), "The 1824 Presidential Election and the 'Corrupt Bargain,'" October 22, 2020, https://prologue.blogs.archives.gov/2020/10/22/the-1824-presidential-election-and-the-corrupt-bargain/

265 National Archives, "Monroe Doctrine (1823)," Milestone Documents, accessed January 2026, https://www.archives.gov/milestone-documents/monroe-doctrine

266 Paul E. Johnson, *A Shopkeeper's Millennium: Society and Revivals in Rochester, New York, 1815–1837* (New York: Hill & Wang, 1978/2004).

267 Whitney R. Cross, *The Burned-Over District* (Ithaca: Cornell University Press, 1950).

268 USHistory.org, "Religious Revival," Second Great Awakening overview, accessed January 2026, https://www.ushistory.org/us/26a.asp

269 Library of Congress, "Today in History—October 26: The Erie Canal," accessed January 2026, https://www.loc.gov/item/today-in-history/october-26

270 Religious Studies Center (BYU), "From Plymouth Rock to Palmyra," accessed January 2026, https://rsc.byu.edu/1820/plymouth-rock-palmyra

271 Stuart Campbell et al., "The Mirror, the Magus and More: Reflections on John Dee's Obsidian Mirror," *Antiquity* 95, no. 384 (2021): e8, https://doi.org/10.15184/aqy.2021.132

272 Livia Gershon, "Obsidian 'Spirit Mirror' Used by Elizabeth I's Court Astrologer Has Aztec Origins," *Smithsonian Magazine*, October 7, 2021, https://www.smithsonianmag.com/smart-news/magic-mirror-used-by-queen-elizabeth-is-court-astrologer-has-aztec-origins-180978830/

273 Wikipedia, "Enochian," last modified January 2026, https://en.wikipedia.org/wiki/Enochian

274 Donald C. Laycock, *The Complete Enochian Dictionary: A Dictionary of the Angelic Language as Revealed to Dr. John Dee and Edward Kelley* (San Francisco: WeiserBooks, 2001).

275 FAIR Latter-day Saints, "Book of Mormon/Translation/Urim and Thummim," FAIR, accessed January 2026, https://www.fairlatterdaysaints.org/answers/Book_of_Mormon/Translation/Urim_and_Thummim

276 Jeremy Corbell and George Knapp, *Weaponized* podcast episodes (parts 1–3), YouTube, 2025.

277 Lon Milo DuQuette, *Enochian Vision Magick: A Practical Guide to the Magick of Dr. John Dee and Edward Kelley* (Newburyport, MA: Weiser Books, 2019).

278 Nick Madrid, "Decoding Immaculate Constellation: An Intelligence Framework Hidden in Plain Sight," Medium, June 23, 2025.

279 Kenneth W. Godfrey, "Freemasonry in Nauvoo," *Encyclopedia of Mormonism*, 1992, https://eom.byu.edu/index.php/Freemasonry_in_Nauvoo

280 The Church of Jesus Christ of Latter-day Saints, *The Pearl of Great Price: Joseph Smith—History* 1:27–65, accessed January 2026, https://www.churchofjesuschrist.org/study/scriptures/pgp/js-h?lang=eng.

281 Royal Skousen, "Worthy of Another Look: John Gilbert's 1892 Account of the 1830 Printing of the Book of Mormon," *Journal of Book of Mormon Studies* 21, no. 2 (2012): 58–72, https://scholarsarchive.byu.edu/jbms/vol21/iss2/6/

282 Kent P. Jackson, "Joseph Smith's Cooperstown Bible: The Historical Context of the Bible Used in the Joseph Smith Translation," *BYU Studies* 40, no. 1 (2001): 41–70, https://scholarsarchive.byu.edu/byusq/vol40/iss1/3/

283 Alex D. Smith, Christian K. Heimburger, and Christopher James Blythe, eds., *The Joseph Smith Papers: Documents, Volume 9—December 1841 to April 1842* (Salt Lake City: Church Historian's Press, 2019).

284 The Church of Jesus Christ of Latter-day Saints, "Changes to the Book of Mormon," Church History Topics, accessed January 2026, https://www.churchofjesuschrist.org/study/history/topics/changes -to-the-book-of-mormon

285 Kevin Christensen, "Truth and Method: Reflections on Dan Vogel's Approach to the Book of Mormon," *FARMS Review* 16, no. 1 (2004): 287–354, https://scholarsarchive.byu.edu/msr/vol16/iss1/15/.

286 The Church of Jesus Christ of Latter-day Saints, "Moses," *Pearl of Great Price*, accessed January 2026, https://www.churchofjesuschrist.org/study/scriptures/pgp/moses

287 R. Grant Athay, "Worlds without Number: The Astronomy of Enoch, Abraham, and Moses," *BYU Studies Quarterly* 8, no. 3 (1968): 225–269, https://scripturecentral.org/archive/periodicals/journal-article/worlds-without-number-astronomy-enoch-abraham-and-moses

288 The Church of Jesus Christ of Latter-day Saints, "Frequently Asked Questions About the Temple Garment," accessed January 2026, https://www.churchofjesuschrist.org/temples/temple-garment-faq

289 Wikipedia, "Killing of Joseph Smith," accessed January 2026, https://en.wikipedia.org/wiki/Killing_of_Joseph_Smith

290 Joseph Smith Papers, "Timeline of Joseph Smith's Life," chart, PDF, accessed January 2026, https://www.josephsmithpapers.org/bc-jsp/content/jsp/library/pdf/chart1.pdf

291 FAIR Latter-day Saints, "Mormonism and Freemasonry—Joseph Smith's Involvement," accessed January 2026, https://www.fairlatterdaysaints.org/answers/Mormonism_and_Free masonry/Joseph_Smith%27s_involvement

292 U.S. National Park Service, "The 1847 Trek," Mormon Pioneer National Historic Trail, accessed January 2026, https://www.nps.gov/mopi/learn/historyculture/the-1847-trek.htm

293 History Channel, "Brandon Fugal—Owner of Skinwalker Ranch," cast page for *The Secret of Skinwalker Ranch*, accessed January 2026, https://www.history.com/shows/the-secret-of-skinwalker-ranch/cast/brandon-fugal

294 Wikipedia, "Brandon Fugal," accessed January 2026, https://en.wikipedia.org/wiki/Brandon_Fugal

295 Church Newsroom, "2024 Statistical Report of The Church of Jesus Christ of Latter-day Saints," April 5, 2025, https://newsroom.churchofjesuschrist.org/article/2024-statistical-report

296 Church Newsroom, "2023 Statistical Report of The Church of Jesus Christ," April 6, 2024, https://newsroom.churchofjesuschrist.org/article/2023-statistical-report-church-jesus-christ

297 Lee Davidson, "Who Has a Bigger Supermajority … Latter-day Saints," *The Salt Lake Tribune,* January 21, 2019, https://www.sltrib.com/news/politics/2019/01/21/who-has-bigger/

298 Lee Davidson, "With Utah Legislature's Mormon Supermajority, Is It Representative of the People?" Salt Lake Tribune, December 12, 2016, https://archive.sltrib.com/article.php?id=4663941&itype=CMSID.

299 Wikipedia, "Finances of the Church of Jesus Christ of Latter-day Saints," accessed January 2026, https://en.wikipedia.org/wiki/Finances_of_the_Church_of_Jesus_Christ_of_Latter-day_Saints

300 Christie Porter, "SEC Fines LDS Church for Hiding $32 Billion in Assets," *Salt Lake Magazine,* February 22, 2023, https://saltlakemagazine.com/sec-fines-lds-church/

301 The Church of Jesus Christ of Latter-day Saints, *General Handbook: Serving in The Church of Jesus Christ of Latter-day Saints,* current online edition, accessed January 2026, https://www.churchofjesuschrist.org/study/manual/general-handbook.

302 Brad Stone, *The Everything Store: Jeff Bezos and the Age of Amazon* (New York: Little, Brown and Company, 2013).

303 U.S. Department of Defense, "History of DARPA," Defense Advanced Research Projects Agency, accessed January 2026, https://www.darpa.mil/about-us/timeline.

304 John Greenewald Jr., "Lawrence Preston Gise FBI File Destroyed," X (formerly Twitter), January 15, 2024, https://x.com/blackvaultcom

305 U.S. Atomic Energy Commission, *Annual Report, 1964,* National Archives Catalog, accessed January 2026, https://catalog.archives.gov/

306 Janet Abbate, Inventing the Internet, Inside Technology series (Cambridge, MA: MIT Press, 1999).

307 Patrick Webb, "DARPA and Big Tech Speculation," *Leading Report,* January 2024, https://leadingreport.com/darpa-big-tech.

308 Amazon Web Services, "AWS and U.S. Intelligence Community Partnership," AWS Public Sector Blog, accessed January 2026, https://aws.amazon.com/government-education/

309 DARPA, "Information Processing Techniques Office History," accessed January 2026, https://www.darpa.mil/

310 DARPA, "LifeLog Program Overview," archived document, 2004, FOIA Release, https://www.darpa.mil/

311 Katie Hafner and Matthew Lyon, *Where Wizards Stay Up Late: The Origins of the Internet* (New York: Simon & Schuster, 1996).

312 U.S. Central Intelligence Agency, "Oracle Database Project," FOIA Release, 1977, CIA Reading Room.

313 Matthew Symonds, *Softwar: An Intimate Portrait of Larry Ellison and Oracle* (New York: Simon & Schuster, 2003).

314 J. Vidal, "Toward Direct Brain-Computer Communication," *Annual Review of Biophysics and Bioengineering* 2, no. 1 (1973): 157–180.

315 U.S. Department of Defense, "Electric and Hybrid Vehicle Technologies Program," DARPA Report, 1992.

316 DARPA, "Blackjack Program Overview," accessed January 2026, https://www.darpa.mil/program/blackjack.

317 U.S. Department of Energy, "Nuclear Tunnel Boring Machine Patent," Los Alamos National Laboratory, 1972.

318 U.S. Defense Nuclear Agency, "Excavation Strategy for the ESF at Yucca Mountain," Technical Report, 1993.

319 DARPA, "Subterranean Challenge Overview," accessed January 2026, https://www.darpa.mil/program/darpa-subterranean-challenge.

320 Richard Hack, *Hughes: The Private Diaries, Memos and Letters* (Beverly Hills: New Millennium Press, 2001).

321 U.S. Central Intelligence Agency, "MKUltra Program Documents," FOIA Release, CIA Reading Room.

322 Chuck Wade, "Seven UFO Crashes & Retrievals in New Mexico," accessed January 14, 2026, https://www.yumpu.com/en/document/read/10469642/seven-ufo-crashes-retrievals-in-new-mexico-chuck-wade.

323 Mutual UFO Network (MUFON), "Roswell Alternative Site Investigation," MUFON Case Files, accessed January 2026, https://www.mufon.com/.

324 Stanton T. Friedman and Don Berliner, *Crash at Corona: The U.S. Military Retrieval and Cover-Up of a UFO* (New York: Paragon House, 1992).

325 Scott Ramsey, *The Aztec UFO Incident* (New York: New Page Books, 2012).

326 Chuck Wade, *Finding the UFO Crash at San Augustin: Isotopic Metal Analysis Not of This World* (Roswell: Roswell Connection Press, 2010).

327 Philip J. Corso and William J. Birnes, *The Day After Roswell* (New York: Pocket Books, 1997).

328 Philip J. Corso, *Dawn of a New Age* (Unpublished Manuscript, Corso Family Archives).

329 George Knapp, "Bob Lazar: Area 51 and UFOs," *KLAS-TV Investigative Report*, 1989.

330 U.S. Department of Defense, "Unidentified Aerial Phenomena Task Force Reports," FOIA Release, 2020.

331 Jennice Vilhauer, "Why Is No One Talking About the Aliens? What Psychology Reveals About Our Resistance to Uncomfortable Truths," *Psychology Today*, December 15, 2025, https://www.psychologytoday.com/us/blog/living-forward/202512/why-is-no-one-talking-about-the-aliens.

332 Dean Radin, "Consciousness, Psi, and the Future of Human Potential," YouTube, March 15, 2024, https://youtube.com/

333 John G. Fuller, *The Interrupted Journey: Two Lost Hours "Aboard a Flying Saucer"* (New York: Dial Press, 1966)

334 Travis Walton, *Fire in the Sky: The Walton Experience* (New York: Marlowe & Company, 1996).

335 Whitley Strieber, *Communion: A True Story* (New York: William Morrow, 1987).

336 Stanton T. Friedman, *Top Secret/Majic: Operation Majestic-12 and the United States Government's UFO Cover-up* (New York: Marlowe & Company, 1996).

337 U.S. Air Force, "Total Exposure Health Initiative," Bioenvironmental Engineering Briefing, 2017.

338 Joe Rogan, "Luis Elizondo on UAPs and Consciousness," *The Joe Rogan Experience*, Podcast Episode #1383, October 2019.

339 Garry Nolan, Interview by Curt Jaimungal, *Theories of Everything Podcast*, 2022.

340 Christopher Green, "Neuroimaging and Anomalous Cognition," Wayne State University Research Papers, 2004

341 Colm A. Kelleher," Archives of the Impossible, Rice University, accessed January 14, 2026, https://impossiblearchives.rice.edu/flash-talk-speakers/colm-a-kelleher.

342 Leslie Kean, *UFOs: Generals, Pilots, and Government Officials Go on the Record* (New York: Crown Publishing, 2010).

343 Colm A. Kelleher and George Knapp, *Hunt for the Skinwalker: Science Confronts the Unexplained at a Remote Ranch in Utah* (New York: Paraview Pocket Books, 2005).

344 "Anomalous Acute and Subacute Field Effects on Human and Biological Tissues," Defense Intelligence Agency report, March 11, 2010, released via Freedom of Information Act, April 2022; reported in The Sun, April 5, 2022.

345 Brandon Specktor, "UFOs Left 'Radiation Burns' and 'Unaccounted for Pregnancies,' New Pentagon Report Claims," Live Science, April 5, 2022.

346 "Anomalous Acute and Subacute Field Effects on Human and Biological Tissues," DIA report, 2010.

[347] The Sun, "UFO Encounters Left Witnesses with Radiation Burns, Brain Problems & Damaged Nerves, Claims Pentagon Docs," April 5, 2022.

[348] Ibid.

[349] Tim McMillan, "Inside the Pentagon's Secret UFO Program," Popular Mechanics, February 14, 2020.

[350] Joe Murgia, "Kit Green's Most Trusted Psychic," UFO Joe, https://www.ufojoe.net/kit-green-psychic1/.

[351] Chris Sharp, "Former CIA Officer Unveils UFOs Have Killed US Military and Cause Brain Damage," TweakTown, May 2, 2024.

[352] Luis Elizondo, interview with Tucker Carlson, Fox News, April 7, 2022.

[353] Ibid.

[354] John Burroughs, "The Injury That Should Have Changed Everything-- But Didn't," Roswell Daily Record, September 1, 2025.

[355] "69% of Scientists Too Scared to Research UFO Health Effects," UFO News, September 4, 2025.

[356] To The Stars Academy of Arts & Science, "Mission and Research Overview," accessed January 2026, https://tothestarsacademy.com/

[357] *Calling All Beings* podcast, episode #33, interview with Luis Elizondo, 2021.

[358] Christopher Mellon, "Why We Need to Take UFOs Seriously," *The Hill*, March 2018.

[359] David Cannadine, *Mellon: An American Life* (New York: Knopf, 2006).

[360] Lockheed Martin, "Advanced Systems Development Overview," Skunk Works Division, accessed January 2026, https://www.lockheedmartin.com/.

[361] Hal Puthoff, "CIA/DIA Remote Viewing Research at SRI," *Journal of Scientific Exploration* 10, no. 1 (1996): 63–76.

[362] Jim Semivan, Interview by Bryce Zabel, *Need to Know Podcast*, 2021.

[363] Garry Nolan, "Analysis of Atacama Skeleton," *Genome Research* 28, no. 4 (2018): 423–431.

[364] Steven M. Greer, *Unacknowledged: An Exposé of the World's Greatest Secret* (Charlottesville: Crossing Point, 2017).

[365] Steven M. Greer, "Letter to Stanford University," Sirius Disclosure, May 25, 2018, https://siriusdisclosure.com/.

[366] *Stanford Magazine*, "Garry Nolan on UAP Research," interview, 2023.

[367] SALT iConnections, "UAP Panel Discussion," May 2023, Conference Proceedings.

[368] Exopaedia, "TTSA Personnel Changes," accessed January 2026, https://www.exopaedia.org/

369 Council on Strategic Risks, "Senior Fellows," accessed January 2026, https://councilonstrategicrisks.org/.

370 Norman Kahn, LinkedIn Profile, accessed January 2026, https://www.linkedin.com/in/norm-kahn-9267a087/

371 Simon & Schuster, "Colm A. Kelleher: Author Page," accessed January 2026, https://www.simonandschuster.com/authors/Colm-A-Kelleher/23515040

372 National Institute for Discovery Science (NIDS), "Research Overview," archived report, 2002.

373 U.S. Defense Intelligence Agency, "Advanced Aerospace Weapon System Applications Program (AAWSAP)," FOIA Release, 2008.

374 Colm A. Kelleher, *Brain Trust: The Hidden Connection Between Mad Cow and Misdiagnosed Alzheimer's Disease* (New York: Paraview Pocket Books, 2004).

375 European Patent Office, "EP2137172A1: Phenothiazine Derivatives for Antiviral Treatments," filed 2008, withdrawn 2009.

376 The Daily Grail, "Interview with Colm Kelleher," 2006, https://www.dailygrail.com/

377 U.S. National Library of Medicine, "Study NCT02990793: Neuromodulation for Cognitive Optimization," ClinicalTrials.gov, accessed January 2026, https://clinicaltrials.gov/study/NCT02990793

378 Wave Neuro, "Research and Technology Overview," accessed January 2026, https://www.waveneuro.com/research

379 U.S. Food and Drug Administration, "Transcranial Magnetic Stimulation Devices," accessed January 2026, https://www.fda.gov/

380 Annie Jacobsen, *The Pentagon's Brain: An Uncensored History of DARPA, America's Top-Secret Military Research Agency* (New York: Little, Brown and Company, 2015).

381 U.S. Food and Drug Administration, "What Are Biological Products?" accessed January 2026, https://www.fda.gov/

382 U.S. Congress, House Oversight Committee Hearing on UAPs, Testimony of David Grusch, July 26, 2023.

383 Nick Cook, "Reality Antennas: The Deep Clues in DNA That Link Us to Unlimited Potential," *Medium*, 2021, https://medium.com/.

384 Bigelow Institute for Consciousness Studies, "2021 Essay Contest Winners," accessed January 2026, https://bigelowinstitute.org/.

385 Jeffrey Long, *Evidence of the Afterlife: The Science of Near-Death Experiences* (New York: HarperOne, 2010).

386 Martin Blank and Reba Goodman, "DNA Is a Fractal Antenna in Electromagnetic Fields," *International Journal of Radiation Biology* 87, no. 4 (2011): 409–415.

387 Chris Bledsoe, *UFO of God: The Extraordinary True Story of Chris Bledsoe* (New York: St. Martin's Press, 2023).

388 Grant Cameron, Interview with Chris Bledsoe, *Whitehouse UFO Blog*, 2020, https://www.presidentialufo.com/.

389 Konstantin Meyl, *Scalar Waves: Theory and Experiments* (Villingen-Schwenningen: INDEL Verlag, 2012).

390 Jeremy Norman, *The Caduceus and the Rod of Asclepius: Medical Symbols and Their Origins* (San Francisco: HistoryofMedicine.com, 2010).

391 U.S. National Library of Medicine, "The Rod of Asclepius and Its Use in Medicine," accessed January 2026, https://www.nlm.nih.gov/

392 New York Post, "Psychic Firefighter Claims UFO Contact," Page Six, 2016.

393 Mary Rodwell, *The New Human: Awakening to Our Cosmic Heritage* (Queensland: ACERN Publishing, 2016).

394 Christopher "Kit" Green, "Neuroimaging and Anomalous Cognition," Wayne State University Research Papers, 2004.

395 Andrew Radziewicz, "The UFO Gatekeepers (Live via UNIDENTIFIED-S4)," *UFOs on the Level*, accessed January 2026.

396 Diana Walsh Pasulka, *American Cosmic: UFOs, Religion, Technology* (New York: Oxford University Press, 2019)

397 John Burroughs, Interview by Linda Moulton Howe, *Earthfiles*, 2018

398 Dean Radin et al., "Genetic Correlates of Psi Phenomena: Exome Sequencing Study," *Journal of Scientific Exploration* 36, no. 2 (2022): 215–240.

349 Dean Radin, "Consciousness, Psi, and the Future of Human Potential," lecture, Institute of Noetic Sciences, 2024

400 Cognigenics Inc., "Pipeline Overview," accessed January 2026, https://www.cognigenics.com

401 Dean Radin, "Consciousness, Psi, and the Future of Human Potential," Lecture, Institute of Noetic Sciences, 2024

402 Patricia Avant, "Black People Do See UFOs: Breaking Down Barriers in Contact Experiences," *UFOs on the Level*, accessed January 2026.

403 Buddy Bolton, "Alien Protocols: CE5 and Consciousness Contact," *UFOs on the Level*, accessed January 2026.

404 Mindsublime. "Advanced Aerospace Threat and Identification Program (AATIP) Slide 9." *Mindsublime Blog*, January 2020. https://mindsublime.blogspot.com/2020/01/advanced-aerospace-threat-and.html?m=1.

405 Jaime Paul Lamb, "Ancient Magical Traditions and Modern Contact," *UFOs on the Level*, accessed January 2026.

406 Dolores Cannon, *Between Death and Life: Conversations with a Spirit* (Huntsville, AR: Ozark Mountain Publishing, 1993).

407 Jane Roberts, *The Seth Material* (Englewood Cliffs, NJ: Prentice-Hall, 1970).

408 John De Marchi, The Immaculate Heart: The True Story of Our Lady of Fatima (New York: Farrar, Straus and Young, 1952)

409 "White Buffalo Woman," Aktá Lakota Museum & Cultural Center, St. Joseph's Indian School, accessed January 20, 2026, https://aktalakota.stjo.org/lakota-legends/white-buffalo-woman/

410 Timothy L. Thomas, "The Mind Has No Firewall," Parameters 28, no. 1 (Spring 1998): 84-92, https://press.armywarcollege.edu/parameters/.

411 Jon Majerowski, "Dr. Jeffrey Long – Near Death Experiences, UFOs and the Consciousness Connection," *YOUFOLOGY Podcast*, YouTube video, https://youtu.be/uxZNwJUydRI

412 Wikipedia, "Special Access Program," accessed January 2026, https://en.wikipedia.org/wiki/Special_access_program

413 Defense Counterintelligence and Security Agency, "SA001: Special Access Program Overview—Student Guide," accessed January 2026, https://www.cdse.edu/Portals/124/Documents/student-guides/SA001-guide.pdf

# RESOURCES FOR YOUR JOURNEY

## NOTABLE INDIVIDUALS

**Robert Bigelow (1944–).** Billionaire aerospace entrepreneur; funded Skinwalker Ranch research; BAASS/AAWSAP contractor; founder of Bigelow Aerospace and the Bigelow Institute for Consciousness Studies. **Source:** Knapp & Kelleher, *Hunt for the Skinwalker.*

**Chris Bledsoe (1958–).** North Carolina experiencer; "The Lady" contactee; investigated by CIA, NASA, and Vatican representatives. **Source:** Bledsoe, *UFO of God.*

**Wernher von Braun (1912–1977).** Nazi rocket scientist; Operation Paperclip recruit; Saturn V chief architect; SS officer. **Source:** Neufeld, *Von Braun: Dreamer of Space, Engineer of War.*

**Boyd Bushman (1928–2014).** Lockheed Martin scientist; known for deathbed claims regarding UFO reverse-engineering. **Source:** Greenewald, *The Black Vault Files: Bushman.*

**Grant Cameron (1953–).** Canadian UFO researcher; specialist in U.S. presidential UFO involvement, consciousness phenomena, and experiencer contact research. **Source:** Cameron, *Managing Magic.*

**Thomas Castello (dates unknown).** The alleged Dulce Base whistleblower claimed knowledge of underground genetic research operations—source: Branton, *The Dulce Book.*

**Philip J. Corso (1915–1998).** U.S. Army Lt. Colonel claimed Roswell debris seeded technologies such as fiber optics and integrated circuits. **Source:** Corso, *The Day After Roswell.*

**Aleister Crowley (1875–1947).** British occultist; founder of Thelema; a major influence on Western esotericism. **Source:** Kaczynski, *Perdurabo: The Life of Aleister Crowley.*

**Kurt Debus (1908–1983).** Operation Paperclip scientist; NASA's first launch operations director; expert in high-voltage plasma physics—source: NASA, *Debus Biography.*

**Tom DeLonge (1975–).** Musician and Blink-182 co-founder; TTSA founder; Freemason (Widow's Son Lodge No. 17); major UFO disclosure advocate—source: DeLonge, *Sekret Machines.*

**Dietrich Eckart (1868–1923).** German journalist; early mentor to Adolf Hitler; influential member of the Thule Society. **Source:** Goodrick-Clarke, *The Occult Roots of Nazism.*

**Luis Elizondo (1972–).** Former AATIP director; counterintelligence officer; holds microbiology/immunology background; TTSA co-founder—source: *60 Minutes* interview (Elizondo).

**Stanton Friedman (1934–2019).** Nuclear physicist; pioneering Roswell investigator; prominent advocate of the extraterrestrial hypothesis—source: Friedman, *Crash at Corona.*

**Adele Gilpin (dates unknown).** Founder of Gilpin BIOMED; epidemiology Ph.D.; TTSA advisor; expert in biologics and regulatory pathways. **Source:** Gilpin, *Gilpin Biomed Publications*.

**Christopher "Kit" Green (1943–).** Former CIA medical officer; neurologist at Wayne State; leading researcher in anomalous cognition and experiencer brain studies—source: McCredie, *The Experience*.

**Steven Greer (1955–).** Emergency physician; founder of CSETI and the Disclosure Project; developer of CE5/HIC contact protocols—source: Greer, *Unacknowledged*.

**David Grusch (1987–).** Air Force intelligence officer; 2023 congressional UAP whistleblower; claimed access to retrieved non-human biologics—source: Kean & Blumenthal, *The Debrief Interview*.

**Rudolf Hess (1894–1987).** Deputy Führer of Nazi Germany; documented occult interests; mysterious 1941 solo flight to Scotland. **Source:** Köpf, *Hess: The Führer's Disciple*.

**Heinrich Himmler (1900–1945).** Reichsführer-SS, the architect of SS occult ideology, established Wewelsburg ritual practices—source: Longerich, *Himmler*.

**L. Ron Hubbard (1911–1986).** Scientology founder; participant in Jack Parsons' Babalon Working ritual. **Source:** Atack, *A Piece of Blue Sky*.

**J. Allen Hynek (1910–1986).** Astronomer; scientific advisor to Project Blue Book; creator of the Close Encounter classification system; founder of CUFOS—source: Hynek, *The UFO Experience*.

**Kelly Johnson (1910–1990).** The Lockheed Skunk Works director led the development of the U-2, A-12, and SR-71 reconnaissance aircraft—source: Rich & Janos, *Skunk Works*.

**Steve Justice (1955–).** Lockheed Martin Skunk Works director (31 years); head of TTSA's Aerospace Division—source: TTSA Engineering Briefings.

**Hans Kammler (1901–1945?).** SS General; Riese Project director; associated with alleged Nazi antigravity research; possibly transferred via clandestine Operation Paperclip channels. **Source:** Agoston, *Blunder!*.

**Leslie Kean (1959–).** Investigative journalist; co-author of the 2017 NYT UAP disclosure article; author of *UFOs: Generals, Pilots, and Government Officials Go on the Record*. **Source:** Kean, *UFOs: Generals, Pilots & Government Officials Go on the Record*.

**Colm Kelleher (1955–).** Biochemist; BAASS/Skinwalker Ranch researcher; antiviral patent holder; long-time Bigelow researcher. **Source:** Knapp & Kelleher, *Hunt for the Skinwalker*.

**Donald Keyhoe (1897–1988).** Marine Corps pilot; early UFO disclosure advocate; author of *The Flying Saucers Are Real*. **Source:** Keyhoe, *The Flying Saucers Are Real*.

**George Knapp (1952–).** Investigative journalist; broke the Bob Lazar story; co-author of *Hunt for the Skinwalker*. **Source:** Knapp & Kelleher, *Hunt for the Skinwalker*.

**Bob Lazar (1959–).** Claimed S-4/Area 51 employment; alleged involvement in UFO reverse-engineering; went public in 1989—

source: Corbell & Knapp, *Bob Lazar: Area 51 & Flying Saucers*.

**Jim Marrs (1943–2017).** Investigative journalist; author exploring hidden history, conspiracies, and government secrecy. **Source:** Marrs, *Rule by Secrecy*.

**Terence McKenna (1946–2000).** Ethnobotanist; philosopher; developed "stoned ape theory;" major voice in psychedelic studies—source: McKenna, *Food of the Gods*.

**Christopher Mellon (1957–).** Former Deputy Assistant Secretary of Defense for Intelligence; Mellon family; TTSA co-founder; facilitated release of Navy UAP videos. **Source:** Mellon, *Congressional Testimony on UAP*.

**Jacques de Molay (1243–1314).** Last Grand Master of the Knights Templar; executed in Paris; symbolically influential in esoteric traditions. **Source:** Barber, *The Trial of the Templars*.

**Garry Nolan (1964–).** Stanford immunologist: retroviral systems pioneer; experiencer of genetics research; analyzed the Atacama skeleton. **Source:** Nolan, *Stanford Interviews*. Doesn't like me at all.

**Jack Parsons (1914–1952).** JPL co-founder, rocket scientist, Thelemite, conducted the Babalon Working. **Source:** Pendle, *Strange Angel*.

**Harold "Hal" Puthoff (1936–).** Experimental physicist; NSA/CIA/DIA contractor; director of SRI remote-viewing program; AATIP advisor; TTSA co-founder. **Source:** Puthoff, *CIA/SRI Remote Viewing Papers*.

**Ben Rich (1925–1995). The** director of the Lockheed Skunk Works made statements on advanced aerospace technology at UCLA (1993)—source: Rich & Janos, *Skunk Works*.

**David Rockefeller (1915–2017).**Banker; Trilateral Commission co-founder; CFR chairman; influential global policy figure—source: Rockefeller, *Memoirs*.

**Viktor Schauberger (1885–1958).**Austrian natural scientist; known for implosion/vortex theories; associated postwar with alleged antigravity concepts. **Source:** Coats, *Living Energies*.

**Rudolf von Sebottendorf (1875–1945).** Founder of the Thule Society; major figure in German occult-nationalist movements—source: Goodrick-Clarke, *The Occult Roots of Nazism*.

**Jim Semivan (1955–).** Retired CIA Senior Intelligence Service officer; TTSA co-founder and VP Operations; experiencer. **Source:** TTSA Interviews with Semivan.

**John F. Stratton Jr. (dates unknown). Former DIA official; re-branded "UFO" as "UAP" within the Intelligence Community. Source: ODNI UAP Terminology Briefings.**

**Jacques Vallée (1939–).** Computer scientist; seminal ufologist; proposed the interdimensional/control-system hypothesis; author of *Passport to Magonia*. **Source:** Vallée, *Passport to Magonia*.

**John W Warner IV. (1962–).** American author and gentleman farmer known for historical fiction that blends meticulously researched military history with elements of speculative technology and international intrigue. He is the son of banking heiress Catherine Mellon and the late John W. Warner III (R-VA), who served as a

U.S. Senator, Secretary of the Navy, and Chairman of the Armed Services Committee (KBE). His maternal grandfather was philanthropist Paul Mellon (OSS, KBE). As a former professional racing driver in the Grand Am and American Le Mans Series, Warner brings a unique perspective to stories involving high-level military intelligence and geopolitical conflict. He turned to writing after a 100 MPH racing accident in 2005; his deep research into Ferdinand Porsche and WWII weaponry during his recovery inspired the Little Anton series. READ THESE BOOKS John W. Warner IV, *Little Anton: A Historical Novel Series*, Part 1-3 (New York: M60 Media LLC, 2019). *Lion, Tiger, Bear* (New York: M60 Media LLC, 2021). *Sanity Was A Luxury: An Historical Novel* (n.p.: M60 Media LLC, 2023).

## FILMS AND DOCUMENTARIES

**Avant, Patricia** (Director). *Black People Do See UFOs.* 2023. Documentary exploring racial dynamics in UFO experiences and communities, featuring experiencer testimonies and footage.

**Fox, James** (Director):

*The Phenomenon.* 2020. Comprehensive examination of the UFO phenomenon featuring government officials, military witnesses, and historical documentation.

*Moment of Contact.* 2022. Investigation of the 1996 Varginha, Brazil incident involving alleged non-human beings.

*The Program.* 2024. Documentary on government UFO programs and disclosure efforts.

**Greer, Steven M.** (Director/Producer):

*Sirius.* 2013. Explores extraterrestrial life and consciousness, featuring analysis of the Atacama humanoid specimen and Greer's CE-5 protocols.

*Unacknowledged.* 2017. Exposé on UFO secrecy featuring testimony from military and intelligence witnesses from the Disclosure Project.

*Close Encounters of the Fifth Kind: Contact Has Begun.* 2020. Focuses on the CE-5/HIC (Human Initiated Contact) protocol for making contact with non-human intelligence.

*The Lost Century: And How to Reclaim It.* 2023. Details alleged 100 years of UFO secrecy, technology suppression, and impact on human development.

*Contact: The CE-5 Experience.* 2023. Follow-up to *Close Encounters of the Fifth Kind*, demonstrating contact protocols and experiencer testimonies.

*Battle for Disclosure.* 2024. Documentary centered on ongoing UFO disclosure efforts and institutional resistance.

**Knapp, George** (Investigative Journalist):

"Bob Lazar: Area 51 and UFOs." *KLAS-TV Investigative Report.* 1989. Breaking news coverage that first brought Bob Lazar's claims about Area 51 and UFO reverse-engineering to public attention.

**Related Media:**

*Communion* (1989). Film adaptation based on Whitley Strieber's 1987 book documenting his alleged abduction experiences.

*Fire in the Sky* (1993)—a film based on Travis Walton's 1975 abduction experience and the book *The Walton Experience*.

*The Joe Rogan Experience*, Episode #1383 (October 2019). Luis Elizondo interview discussing UAPs, consciousness, and biological technology.

*Theories of Everything Podcast* (2022). Garry Nolan interview with Curt Jaimungal on experiencer genetics and UAP materials research.

*Coast to Coast AM* (February 26, 2017). Tom DeLonge and Peter Levenda interview with George Knapp discussing *Sekret Machines: Gods, Man, and War*.

*Calling All Beings Podcast*, Episode #33 (2021). Luis Elizondo interview on counterintelligence approaches to UFO phenomena.

*Need to Know Podcast* (2021). Jim Semivan interview with Bryce Zabel on the intelligence community and UAP.

**To The Stars Academy Media:**

*Unidentified: Inside America's UFO Investigation* (History Channel, 2019-2020). Documentary series produced by TTSA featuring Luis Elizondo and declassified UAP encounters from the military.

**Sekret Machines Series** (Tom DeLonge, Peter Levenda, A.J. Hartley):

Nonfiction: *Gods, Man, and War* (2016), with a foreword by Jacques Vallée

Fiction novels: *Chasing Shadows* and subsequent installments, blending narrative with documented UFO research.

## ORGANIZATIONS AND RESOURCES

ACERN (Australian Close Encounter Resource Network). Founded by Mary Rodwell. acern.com.au

CE5/HIC (Human Initiated Contact) Contact. Protocols and app for human-initiated contact. ce5film.com

FREE (Foundation for Research into Extraterrestrial Encounters). Experiencer research and support. experiencer.org

MUFON (Mutual UFO Network). Civilian UFO investigation organization. mufon.com – Allegedly infiltrated by the IC.

Project Unity. YouTube channel and research platform hosted by Jay. Covering current UAP developments.

To The Stars Academy (TTSA). Founded by Tom DeLonge. Research and entertainment organization.

## GOVERNMENT PROGRAMS AND DOCUMENTS

AATIP (Advanced Aerospace Threat Identification Program). The Pentagon UFO research program (2007-2012) was publicly acknowledged in 2017. Allegedly.

AAWSAP (Advanced Aerospace Weapon System Applications Program). Predecessor to AATIP, with a broader scope including paranormal research.

"Anomalous Acute and Subacute Field Effects on Human and Biological Tissues" (DIA, March 11, 2010). Classified AAWSAP report documenting 42 medical cases and 300 unpublished cases of UAP-related injuries. Released via FOIA April 2022.

MKUltra. CIA program (1953-1973) studying mind control, consciousness manipulation, and chemical interrogation.

Operation Paperclip. Post-WWII program (1945+) bringing Nazi scientists to the United States.

Robertson Panel. 1952 CIA-sponsored panel recommending UFO debunking and public education program.

Wilson-Davis Notes. Leaked documents discussing alleged reverse engineering programs. Discussed in congressional contexts.

## HISTORICAL EVENTS AND LOCATIONS REFERENCED

Baghdad Museum Heist (April 2003). During the looting of the Iraq National Museum, approximately 17,300 artifacts were taken.

Friday, October 13, 1307. Coordinated the arrest of the Knights Templar across France.

Fatima, Portugal (1917). "Miracle of the Sun" was witnessed by approximately 70,000 people.

Göbekli Tepe, Turkey. Ancient megalithic site (circa 9600 BCE), challenging conventional archaeology.

Roswell, New Mexico (1947). Alleged UFO crash and recovery.

Rosslyn Chapel, Scotland (1446-1484). Associated with Templar knowledge preservation and Masonic symbolism.

Wewelsburg Castle, Germany. The SS headquarters under Heinrich Himmler was used for Nazi occult practices.

## ANCIENT TEXTS AND MANUSCRIPTS

The Emerald Tablet. Hermetic text, original Arabic from the 9th century, with multiple mistranslated versions in circulation.

Epic of Gilgamesh. Sumerian/Babylonian epic mentioning the flood narrative and ancient gods.

Genesis 6:1-4. Biblical passage describing "Sons of God" and the Nephilim.

Nag Hammadi Library. Gnostic gospels discovered in 1945, buried circa 400 CE.

Dead Sea Scrolls. Ancient Jewish texts discovered 1947-1956.

Gospel of Judas. A Gnostic gospel published in 2006 that presents an alternative narrative.

## SECRET SOCIETIES AND ESOTERIC ORDERS

Bavarian Illuminati. A secret society founded in 1776 by Adam Weishaupt.

Bilderberg Group. Annual invitation-only conference of political and business elites (founded 1954).

Bohemian Grove. Private men's club in California, site of annual elite gatherings.

Council on Foreign Relations (CFR). Foreign policy think tank (founded 1921).

Freemasonry. Fraternal organization preserving esoteric knowledge, various rites, and degrees.

Golden Dawn (Hermetic Order of the). Magical order (1887-1903), members included Aleister Crowley.

Le Cercle. Secretive foreign policy and intelligence gathering group.

Rosicrucians (SRICF - Societas Rosicruciana in Civitatibus Foederatis). Masonic esoteric research society.

Skull and Bones. Yale University Secretary Society.

Thule Society. German occultist group (founded 1918) influenced Nazi ideology.

Trilateral Commission. International policy discussion group (founded 1973).

Vril Society. The German secret society focused on esoteric knowledge and advanced technology.

## NOTABLE INDIVIDUALS IN ESOTERIC HISTORY

Robert Bigelow (1944–). Billionaire aerospace entrepreneur, funded Skinwalker Ranch research, BAASS/AAWSAP contractor, Bigelow Institute for Consciousness Studies founder.

Chris Bledsoe (1958–). North Carolina experiencer, "The Lady" contactee, investigated by CIA/NASA/Vatican.

Wernher von Braun (1912–1977). Nazi rocket scientist, Operation Paperclip, NASA Saturn V designer, SS officer.

Boyd Bushman (1928–2014). Lockheed Martin scientists' deathbed testimony on UFO reverse-engineering programs.

Grant Cameron (1953–). Canadian UFO researcher, presidential UFO knowledge specialist, consciousness and contact researcher.

Thomas Castello (dates unknown). The alleged Dulce Base whistleblower claimed knowledge of an underground genetic research facility.

Philip J. Corso (1915–1998). U.S. Army Lt. Colonel claimed that Roswell debris led to the development of fiber optics and integrated circuits.

Aleister Crowley (1875–1947). British occultist, founded Thelema, influential in Western esotericism.

Kurt Debus (1908–1983). Operation Paperclip scientist, second-in-command at NASA, high voltage plasma physicist.

Tom DeLonge (1975–). Blink-182 musician, TTSA founder, Freemason (Widow's Son Lodge No. 17), UFO disclosure advocate.

Dietrich Eckart (1868–1923). German journalist, early mentor of Hitler, and a member of the Thule Society.

Luis Elizondo (1972–). Former AATIP director, counterintelligence officer, microbiology/immunology degree, TTSA co-founder.

Stanton Friedman (1934–2019). Nuclear physicist and Roswell researcher advocated the extraterrestrial hypothesis for decades.

Adele Gilpin (dates unknown). Gilpin BIOMED founder, epidemiology Ph.D., TTSA advisor, biologics regulation expert.

Christopher "Kit" Green (1943–). Former CIA, Wayne State

neurologist, anomalous cognition researcher, experiencer, and brain studies.

Steven Greer (1955–). Emergency physician, CSETI/Disclosure Project founder, CE5 protocols developer.

David Grusch (1987–). Air Force intelligence officer, 2023 congressional UAP whistleblower, claimed non-human biologics recovered.

Rudolf Hess (1894–1987). Nazi Deputy Führer, occult interests, mysterious flight to Scotland, 1941.

Heinrich Himmler (1900–1945). Reichsführer-SS established the SS as an occult order with Wewelsburg rituals.

L. Ron Hubbard (1911–1986). Scientology founder, participated in Parsons' Babalon Working ritual.

J. Allen Hynek (1910–1986). Astronomer, Project Blue Book consultant, developed the Close Encounter classification system, and was the founder of CUFOS.

Kelly Johnson (1910–1990). Lockheed Skunk Works director, advanced aerospace developments.

Steve Justice (1955–). Lockheed Martin Skunk Works director (31 years), TTSA Aerospace Division head.

Hans Kammler (1901–1945?). SS General, Riese Project director, alleged Nazi UFO/antigravity research, possibly brought to America via Operation Paperclip.

Leslie Kean (1959–). Investigative journalist, *UFOs: Generals, Pilots, and Government Officials Go on the Record*, author.

Colm Kelleher (1955–). Biochemist, BAASS/Skinwalker Ranch researcher, antiviral patent holder, Bigelow employee.

Donald Keyhoe (1897–1988). Marine Corps pilot, *author of The Flying Saucers Are Real, and* early government cover-up advocate.

George Knapp (1952–). Investigative journalist who broke the Bob Lazar story, co-author of Hunt for the Skinwalker.

Bob Lazar (1959–). Claimed Area 51 employment, alleged UFO reverse-engineering at S-4, went public in 1989.

Christopher Mellon (1957–). Former Deputy Assistant Secretary of Defense for Intelligence, Mellon banking dynasty, TTSA co-founder, and release of Navy UAP videos.

Jacques de Molay (1243–1314). The last Grand Master of the Knights Templar was burned at the stake in Paris.

Garry Nolan (1964–). Stanford immunologist, retroviral systems pioneer, and experiencer genetics researcher analyzed the Atacama skeleton.

Jack Parsons (1914–1952). JPL co-founder, rocket scientist, devoted Thelemite, performed Babalon Working.

Harold "Hal" Puthoff (1936–). Experimental physicist, NSA/CIA/DIA contractor, SRI remote viewing director, AATIP advisor, TTSA co-founder.

Ben Rich (1925–1995). Lockheed Skunk Works director made statements about extraterrestrial technology in 1993 remarks at UCLA.

David Rockefeller (1915–2017). Banker, Trilateral Commission co-founder, CFR chairman.

Viktor Schauberger (1885–1958). Operation Paperclip scientist, torsion field/antigravity researcher, natural science principles.

Rudolf von Sebottendorf (1875–1945). Founder of the Thule Society.

Jim Semivan (1955–). Retired CIA Senior Intelligence Service, TTSA co-founder, and VP Operations.

John F. Stratton Jr. (dates unknown). Former DIA official, re-branded UFO as UAP, the intelligence community.

Jacques Vallée (1939–). Computer scientist, ufologist, proposed interdimensional hypothesis, *Passport to Magonia* author.

## GENETIC AND CONSCIOUSNESS RESEARCH

Caudate-Putamen Abnormalities. Brain structure differences documented in experiencers by Dr. Nolan.

Mitochondrial DNA Variations. Maternal lineage markers are potentially associated with contact experiences.

Neural Plasticity Markers. Genetic factors affecting consciousness processing abilities.

RH Negative Blood. Blood type showing disproportionate representation in experiencer populations.

## ADDITIONAL RESOURCES

Fermilabs- Neutrino research facility. Resources at neutrinos.fnal.gov

Smithsonian Institution. Referenced regarding the collection and alleged suppression of giant skeleton evidence.

Vatican Secret Archives. Now, the "Vatican Apostolic Archives" is a restricted collection of historical documents.

# ABOUT THE AUTHOR

**JON MAJEROWSKI** is a husband, father, CISSP-certified information security professional, Freemason, and experiencer based in Maumee, Ohio. He hosts the *UFOs on the Level* podcast, where he conducts in-depth conversations with researchers, experiencers, insiders, and practitioners exploring UFOs, consciousness, and unexplained phenomena.

As a member of several initiatory orders, Jon brings an insider perspective on esoteric traditions and mystery school knowledge to his investigation of the UFO phenomenon, or as he puts it, "The Phenomenon." His approach combines personal experience, decades of critical research, and a commitment to helping other experiencers feel less alone.

Jon lives with his wife and daughters, balancing family life with consciousness exploration and disclosure activism.

## Masonic Affiliations:

- Fulton Lodge Free and Accepted Masons #248

- 32° AASR – NMJ (Ancient Accepted Scottish Rite, Northern Masonic Jurisdiction)

- Zenobia Shrine – Shriners International

- Grand Council Royal & Select Masons of Ohio #68

- Grand Chapter of Royal Arch Masons, Ohio #111

- St. Omer Commandery No. 59, Knights Templar

- Michael Collins Council, U.D., Knight Masons

- Key to the Sea – Allied Masonic Degrees (AMD)

- Michael Collins Council, U.D., Knight Masons

- Key to the Sea – Allied Masonic Degrees (AMD)

- Societas Rosicruciana in Civitatibus Foederatis (SRICF), Ohio James E. Olmstead College – Grade VII, Adeptus Exemptus

**Connect with Jon: Twitter/X:** jonmajerowski

**Podcast:** *UFOs on the Level*          **Website:** contactandcontrol.com

# INDEX